Non-Formal Education

CERC Studies in Comparative Education

1. Mark Bray & W.O. Lee (eds.) (2001): *Education and Political Transition: Themes and Experiences in East Asia.* Second edition. ISBN 962-8093-84-3. 228pp. HK$200/US$32.

2. Mark Bray & W.O. Lee (eds.) (1997): *Education and Political Transition: Implications of Hong Kong's Change of Sovereignty.* ISBN 962-8093-90-8. 169pp. [Out of print]

3. Philip G. Altbach (1998): *Comparative Higher Education: Knowledge, the University, and Development.* ISBN 962-8093-88-6. 312pp. HK$180/US$30.

4. Zhang Weiyuan (1998): *Young People and Careers: A Comparative Study of Careers Guidance in Hong Kong, Shanghai and Edinburgh.* ISBN 962-8093-89-4. 160pp. HK$180/ US$30.

5. Harold Noah & Max A. Eckstein (1998): *Doing Comparative Education: Three Decades of Collaboration.* ISBN 962-8093-87-8. 356pp. HK$250/US$38.

6. T. Neville Postlethwaite (1999): *International Studies of Educational Achievement: Methodological Issues.* ISBN 962-8093-86-X. 86pp. HK$100/US$20.

7. Mark Bray & Ramsey Koo (eds.) (2004): *Education and Society in Hong Kong and Macao: Comparative Perspectives on Continuity and Change.* Second edition. ISBN 962-8093-34-7. 323pp. HK$200/US$32.

8. Thomas Clayton (2000): *Education and the Politics of Language: Hegemony and Pragmatism in Cambodia, 1979-1989.* ISBN 962-8093-83-5. 243pp. HK$200/US$32.

9. Gu Mingyuan (2001): *Education in China and Abroad: Perspectives from a Lifetime in Comparative Education.* ISBN 962-8093-70-3. 252pp. HK$200/US$32.

10. William K. Cummings, Maria Teresa Tatto & John Hawkins (eds.) (2001): *Values Education for Dynamic Societies: Individualism or Collectivism.* ISBN 962-8093-71-1. 312pp. HK$200/US$32.

11. Ruth Hayhoe & Julia Pan (eds.) (2001): *Knowledge Across Cultures: A Contribution to Dialogue Among Civilizations.* ISBN 962-8093-73-8. 391pp. HK$250/US$38.

12. Robert A. LeVine (2003): *Childhood Socialization: Comparative Studies of Parenting, Learning and Educational Change.* ISBN 962-8093-61-4. 299pp. HK$200/US$32.

13. Mok Ka-Ho (ed.) (2003): *Centralization and Decentralization: Educational Reforms and Changing Governance in Chinese Societies.* ISBN 962-8093-58-4. 230pp. HK$200/ US$32.

14. W.O. Lee, David L. Grossman, Kerry J. Kennedy & Gregory P. Fairbrother (eds.) (2004): *Citizenship Education in Asia and the Pacific: Concepts and Issues.* ISBN 962-8093-59-2. 313pp. HK$200/ US$32.

15. Alan Rogers (2004): *Non-Formal Education: Flexible Schooling or Participatory Education?* ISBN 962-8093-30-4. 306pp. HK$200/ US$32.

Order through bookstores or from:

Comparative Education Research Centre
Faculty of Education, The University of Hong Kong, Pokfulam Road, Hong Kong, China.
Fax: (852) 2517 4737; E-mail: cerc@hkusub.hku.hk; Website: www.hku.hk/cerc

The list prices above are applicable for order from CERC, and include sea mail postage; add US$5 per copy for air mail.

No.7 in the series and Nos. 13-15 are co-published by Kluwer Academic Publishers and the Comparative Education Research Centre of the University of Hong Kong. Kluwer Academic Publishers publishes hardback versions.

CERC Studies in Comparative Education 15

Non-Formal Education

Flexible Schooling or Participatory Education?

Alan Rogers

Comparative Education Research Centre
The University of Hong Kong
Kluwer Academic Publishers

First published 2004
Comparative Education Research Centre
The University of Hong Kong
Pokfulam Road, Hong Kong, China

© Alan Rogers

ISBN 962 8093 30 4

In this book, I have created a story. And I have chosen the language in which to clothe it. It is my own story. I do not expect you to agree with this story, but I hope that you will be able to understand it through the language I have chosen. And I hope that at the least it will challenge you to create your own story.
Roger Allen: Beyond My Pen, 2001

Contents

List of Abbreviations

The following are the abbreviations which have been used most commonly in the text. The world of development and especially the world of the non-governmental organisations use abbreviations and acronyms extensively. Many are so well known that they have become words in their own rights and their initial meaning is sometimes lost (e.g. UNESCO, UNICEF, USAID etc); these have been omitted to ensure the list does not become too long. Others are so common as to be worthy of omission (e.g. EFA for Education for All or NGO for non-governmental organisation).

Abbreviations which have been used once with explanation or in one section only and which are explained in that section have also on the whole been omitted.

Abbreviations used in the references have also been omitted since these are explained in the bibliography (e.g. Coun Eur for Council of Europe).

Abbreviations within quotations have been given as originally written. Abbreviations which have themselves become the name of a programme (e.g. MOBRAL in Brazil, TOSTAN in Senegal or PROPEL in India) have also been omitted.

ABET	Adult Basic Education and Training
ACAPES	an NFE programme of primary schools in Senegal
ACCESS	Appropriate Cost-Effective Centres for Education within the School System (Action Aid programme in many countries)
ACCU	Asian Cultural Centre for UNESCO, Tokyo
ADB	Asian Development Bank
ADEA	Association for the Development of Education in Africa
AID	abbreviation for USAID adopted in USA
ANFE	Adult Non-formal Education
ANTEP	Association of Non-Traditional Education Programmes (the Philippines)
AUPEP	Adult Upper Primary Education Programme (Namibia)
BHN	Basic Human Needs
BLCC	Bunyad Literacy Community Council (Pakistan)
BNFE	Bureau of Non-formal Education (the Philippines)
BRAC	Bangladesh Rural Advancement Council (usually known as BRAC)
BUNYAD	NGO in Pakistan
CAMPE	Campaign for Popular Education, umbrella NGO in Bangladesh
CBO	Community Based Organisation
CEDEFOP	European Centre for the Development of Vocational Training, based in Thessaloniki, Greece

CERID	Centre for Educational Research, Innovation and Development, Tribhuvan University, Nepal
CESO	Centre for the Study of Education in Developing Countries, The Hague, Netherlands
CIDA	Canadian International Development Agency
CIE	Center for International Education, University of Massachusetts, Amherst, Massachusetts, USA
COL	Commonwealth of Learning, based in Vancouver, Canada
CONFINEA	International Conference on the Education of Adults, sponsored by UIE
COPE	Complementary Opportunities for Primary Education, programme in Uganda
DECS	Department of Education, Culture and Sports (the Philippines)
DNFE	Department or Directorate of NFE (various countries)
DFID	Department for International Development (UK)
EMIS	Educational Management Information Service
EU	European Union
FAO	Food and Agricultural Organisation of the United Nations
FE	further education
GAT	General Agreement on (Tariffs and) Trade
GSS	an NGO in Bangladesh
HRD	Human Resource Development
ICED	International Center for Educational Development (USA)
ICT	information and communications technologies
IDRC	International Development Research Centre (Canada)
IEC	International Extension College, Cambridge, UK
IIEP	UNESCO International Institute for Educational Planning, Paris
IIZ-DVV	German aid agency for adult education
ILO	International Labour Organisation
IRD	Integrated Rural Development
ISCED	International Standard Classification for Educational Data
MIS	Management Information Service
MOBRAL	a literacy programme in Brazil
MSU	Michigan State University, USA
NAMCOL	Namibia College of Open Learning
NFAE	Non-formal Adult Education
NFBE	Non-formal Basic Education
NFE A and E	Non-formal Accreditation and Equivalency Programme in the Philippines
NFPE	Non-formal Primary Education
NGO	non-governmental organisation
ODA	Overseas Development Administration (UK aid agency until replaced in 1997 by DFID)
PAR	participatory action research

PEER	Programme for Education for Emergencies and Reconstruction (UNESCO supported programme)
pers comm	personal communication
PRA	participatory rapid or rural appraisal
PROAP	Principal Regional Office for Asia and the Pacific (UNESCO)
PROPEL	programme run by the Indian Institute for Education, Pune, India
PROTEC	programme run in South Africa
REC	Rural Education Centres (Swaziland)
SAP	Structural Adjustment Policies or Programme
SC(US)	Save the Children (USA)
SEAMEO	South East Asia Ministers of Education Organisation
SIDA	Swedish International Development Agency
TOSTAN	an educational programme run in Senegal
UBE	Universal Basic Education
UIE	UNESCO Institute of Education, Hamburg, Germany
UNAM	University of Namibia
UPE	Universal Primary Education
VET	vocational education and training

Series Editor's Foreword

The Comparative Education Research Centre (CERC) at the University of Hong Kong is proud and privileged to present this book in its series CERC Studies in Comparative Education. Alan Rogers is a distinguished figure in the field of non-formal education, and brings to this volume more than three decades of experience. The book is a masterly account, which will be seen as a milestone in the literature. It is based on the one hand on an exhaustive review of the literature, and on the other hand on extensive practical experience in all parts of the world. It is a truly comparative work, which fits admirably into the series

Much of the thrust of Rogers' work is an analysis not only of the significance of non-formal education but also of the reasons for changing fashions in the development community. Confronting a major question at the outset, Rogers ask why the terminology of non-formal education, which was so much in vogue in the 1970s and 1980s, practically disappeared from the mainstream discourse in the 1990s and initial years of the present century. Much of the book is therefore about paradigms in the domain of development studies, and about the ways that fashions may gloss over substance.

Rogers begins the book by noting that the language of non-formal education is now back on the agenda, not only in less developed countries but also in industrialised nations. He adds that there is a new feel about the term – a very different tone from that of the 1970s and 1980s. Now, he suggests, the language sounds unsure of itself; and in some settings it is influenced by the discourse of lifelong learning. Rogers proceeds to analyse why the terminology faded away in the 1990s, and why it is being revived and in what form. The book contains fascinating analyse of discourse patterns in a wide array of contexts, together with analyses of practice on the ground in diverse settings.

In some respects, this book is historical. It shows changing tides and the evolution of ideas at local and global levels through detailed analysis of a huge literature. At the same time, the book is visionary. It sees beyond the changing fashions to desirable futures for education in a broad range of settings. Rogers is greatly to be applauded for this work, which CERC is delighted to publish in partnership with Kluwer Academic Publishers.

Mark Bray
Chair Professor of Comparative Education
Dean, Faculty of Education
The University of Hong Kong

1

Introduction

The Assembly recognises that formal educational systems alone cannot respond to the challenges of modern society and therefore welcomes its reinforcement by non-formal educational practices.

The Assembly recommends that governments and appropriate authorities of member states recognise non-formal education as a de facto partner in the lifelong process and make it accessible for all.

This is not the statement of some international agency dealing with so-called 'Third World countries' but of the Parliamentary Assembly of the European Council; the date is not the 1970s or 1980s but December 1999 (Coun Eur 1999).

Non-formal Education (NFE) is back on the agenda on a world-wide scale, in both 'Western' and 'developing' societies.[1] In one of the most authoritative and comprehensive statements to date on lifelong learning, NFE occurs time and again (Aspin et al. 2001: 79, 117, 202, 208, 221 etc.). Speaking of lifelong education, one author states explicitly "this can become a matrix with formal and non-formal education" (Duke 2001: 510). Jarvis (2001b: 21) uses the term as meaning "any form of systematic learning conducted outside of a formal organisation". Courses on Nonformal Education have been introduced in the last few years in several universities in both the West and developing countries. The UNESCO Institute of Education recently ran an international seminar on 'Nonformal education: stock-taking and prospects' as well as regional meetings such as 'Non-formal Education in Morocco' (UIE 2001); and UNESCO issued a report on *Literacy and Nonformal Education in the E9 Countries* (UNESCO 2001b). In 1996, the Association for the Development of Education in Africa (ADEA) launched a major programme in non-formal education in

---

[1] I use the term 'developing countries' to indicate those countries which the UNDP has identified as low in human development indicators and which are in receipt of aid from the richer (mostly former imperialist) states – countries which collectively are often identified by such terms as 'South' or 'Third World'. I use the term 'the West' to refer to those richer countries which offer aid to developing countries and which hold themselves up as models of modern society. I hope that the reader will accept this usage on the grounds that there are no terms which are free from disadvantages and misunderstandings. The discourse involved is discussed below pp.13-17.

at least 15 countries of sub-Saharan Africa, and many of these countries have established co-ordinating 'working groups on non-formal education' (ADEA-WG). Throughout the world, the practice of what is called non-formal education is increasing and widening in scope, often with donor support. For example in 2001 the World Bank ran an international 'Distance Learning Seminar: use of outsourcing in the implementation of Literacy and Non-Formal Basic Education Programs', the report of which opened with the words: "Increasing number of countries are preparing with partial finance from the World Bank non-formal basic education projects..." (World Bank 2001: 1), and in May 2003, the Bank was advised to extend its assistance to adult and non-formal education (World Bank 2003). In 2001, a conference was held in London under the title 'Non-formal Education in Post-Conflict Sierra Leone' (Musa 2001). The Africa Educational Trust states in its 2001 report, "AET supports non-formal literacy and vocational training programmes" (AET 2001).

The language of non-formal education then has been taken up again by policy-makers and practitioners, not only in the developing world but also among more economically advanced nations. But there is a new feel about this use of the term Non-formal Education, a very different tone from that of the 1970s and 1980s when the concept and language first emerged. The language sounds unsure of itself; and, influenced by the discourse of lifelong learning, it often uses the term 'non-formal learning' rather than non-formal education. However, the area of discussion is exactly the same. For example, a report on vocational education, *Making Learning Visible: the identification, assessment and recognition of non-formal learning in Europe,* defines non-formal learning (carefully distinguished from accidental/informal learning as well as from formal learning) as "semi-structured", consisting of *"planned and explicit* approaches to learning introduced into work organisations and elsewhere, not recognised within the formal education and training system ... In Germany and Austria, the issue of non-formal learning is a new and unresolved one. Five years ago, it was hardly discussed. Today, a debate on the role of non-formal learning is gradually evolving" (Bjornavold 2000: 11, 56, 204, my italics). In 2000 the Commission of the European Union issued a Memorandum on Lifelong Learning and followed this up with a Communication 'Making a European Area of Lifelong Learning a Reality'. Both are founded on a comprehensive approach to all kinds of "purposeful learning activity, formal, ... nonformal ... and informal ..." (EU Memo 2000: 8; EU Comm. 2001). Since they both speak of non-formal learning as being "provided" and talk of "nonformal settings for learning", it is clear that the Commission is referring to what earlier writers called 'non-formal education'. And the policy is being implemented: the ALICE Project (2000) refers explicitly to NFE.

But the meaning of the term 'non-formal education' is much more opaque than it was twenty or thirty years ago. The 'great debate' on NFE, started in 1968 when Philip Coombs included a chapter entitled 'Non-Formal Education: to catch up, keep up and get ahead' in his seminal book *The World Educational Crisis: a systems approach,* dominated most educational discussions in the 1970s and early 1980s. This publi-cation initiated a massive outburst of interest in NFE: "a debate has been raging about the role of nonformal education" (Ahmed 1982: 138). The description 'Non-formal Education' became for a time an imprimatur, and programmes bearing this title attracted substantial funding. Academic departments were founded on its currency, and their publications flooded from the presses. Most of the debate took place in the North America (there was rather less in Western Europe) and most of the programmes so labelled were located in developing countries (again, there was much less in the West). Research centres in NFE were established, many Ministries created Departments, Divisions or Directorates of NFE, and most educational evaluation reports contained sections devoted to NFE programmes. For nearly twenty years, the distinction between 'formal' and 'non-formal' education was the guiding light of educational planning, funding and evaluation in developing countries. It is possible that no other educational programme or ideology (not even 'popular education') had received such intensive discussion and such widespread support.

However, currently it is often not clear whether the term as used refers to learning programmes for adults or for children. Today's NFE in many contexts means alternative forms of primary schooling for out-of-school children – the street children of Nairobi, the girls excluded from schools in Pakistan, the drop-outs of Botswana – rather than less formal learning programmes for adults. Flexible modes of providing schooling for young people is now what many governments look to non-formal education to fulfil, especially in the light of growing populations, the escalating costs of education combined with more limited funding, the search for partnerships with civil society, and new educational targets set internationally. In some countries, the Departments or Directorates of Non-Formal Education set up in the 1970s to provide literacy training and basic education for adults are being pressed to meet the educational and training needs of young people. This is in part the result of global pressures on education. The Education for All (EFA) Programme launched in 1990 with a commitment to equalise the educational needs of young people and adults has come to concentrate on education for young student-learners, and pressure groups such as the Global Campaign for Education have led to an increased focus on primary education. 'Non-formal education' often means 'alternative primary or basic schooling for out-of-school youth'.

The language of NFE then is today a force in many educational policy statements, but the clarity behind the idea seems to have been lost. A once powerful concept has lost its way. This book seeks to examine this phenomenon. It raises the question why NFE had such great popularity and power for a short period, why it died and why it is being revived and in what form. It queries whether the language of NFE should be abandoned, whether its abolition would leave something of a vacuum, or whether anything of value would be lost, thrown out with the changed discourse. It asks whether there is or can be any unified concept underlying the wide range of programmes labelled 'non-formal education' today.

The structure of the book

This study of non-formal education, past and present, falls into four sections. Since "the genesis of social practices and discourses is ... of crucial importance for an understanding of them" (Cooke & Kothari 2001: 169, 172), a 'genealogy' of NFE is needed. The first part thus explores the cultural and educational contexts from which the debate arose and from which NFE took the shape it did. The second section describes the debate about NFE which took place in the 1970s and 1980s and the issues which arise from it. The third section looks at a wide range of programmes which today call themselves 'non-formal education', to try to assess what the term 'non-formal' has come to mean in the field. The final section addresses the disparity between the theory of NFE and the practice of NFE and seeks to discover if there is some unifying principle or whether the term should be abandoned as unmeaningful or unhelpful – whether the concept has any value as a tool of analysis and/or as a tool of planning. It proposes a possible new paradigm by which NFE today can be assessed.

For some people today, the term 'non-formal education' is passé. In a 1999 survey of changing international aid to education (King & Buchert 1999), the phrase is carefully eschewed in a way which would have been unthinkable twenty years previously. The main discourses around education talk about basic, continuing, recurrent or lifelong education or learning. USAID (2001) in its review of basic education in eleven countries of sub-Saharan Africa uses the language of decentralisation instead of NFE. The sound of the words 'non-formal education' echoes uncomfortably through some of the corridors of academic discussion and educational policy-making today, although others continue to use them for lack of a better alternative.

Indeed, in some parts of the world, the term 'non-formal education' is decidedly unpopular. I remember a senior figure in the Namibian Ministry responsible for Basic Education saying, "We don't use the term 'non-formal' here. It smacks of 'non-white'". Such a comment reveals the assumption that the term 'formal' in educational discussions carries with it positive connotations, and that therefore 'non-formal' implies a more negative image. But there are others who feel exactly the reverse; that the concepts which lie behind the word 'formal' in education are the enemy, and that 'non-formal' is the celebration of liberation, throwing off the shackles of formality which have for so long prevented education from being education. They would argue that 'non-formal' is not just everything that is left over after the formal system has been created and resourced. Rather – precisely because it is non-formal – it is the freedom from everything that is not within a very restricted (and restrictive) set of walls. These people would see 'non-formal' as much closer to 'non-violent' with its connotations of revolution than to 'non-white' with its images of oppression.

Nevertheless, a concept which was born within the world of development assistance has now become relevant within a wider arena, in particular in Western contexts. Among the many characteristics of the discourse of lifelong learning are two features which relate directly to our discussions. First, the discourse of lifelong learning renders the distinctions between the traditional divisions of education (primary, secondary and tertiary/higher) less important, it "presupposes an integrated, holistic and seamless approach to the whole of education" (Aspin et al. 2001: xliii). The concept implies the essential unity of learning in different areas and at different stages of life (Bjornavold 2000). Secondly, lifelong learning sets out to identify the wide range of learning opportunities throughout life, especially those outside the existing spheres of school and college – opportunities in the workplace, in voluntary movements, in religious activities, in the commercial world etc.. It is in the course of this reshaping of the educational landscape – first unifying and then sub-dividing the world of planned learning opportunities – that the use of the term 'non-formal' has been revived within the lifelong learning discourse by agencies such as OECD and the European Union. NFE today then springs from a different root from the 1970s. The reintegration of the whole field of education brought about by the discourse of lifelong learning has at the same time led to a search for terminology which covers "alternative educational programmes", especially for marginalised, excluded and/or subordinated populations.

Why this book was written

It is this changing landscape that has caused me to write this book. It comes out of the interaction between two kinds of activities in which I have been engaged over the last thirty or so years. On the one hand, since 1985 I have been helping international post-graduate students to learn about non-formal education, a subject which they seem to appreciate highly and regard as important for their own understanding of the theory and practice of education. In the course of this teaching, I discovered that there is no textbook on NFE for students apart from the seminal works of Coombs and Ahmed in the 1970s.[2] Several reports by the IIEP contain significant material but these are usually dated, short and closely context-dependent, so that the broader concepts have not been addressed. The series of studies which Michigan State University at East Lansing and the Center for International Education at the University of Massachusetts, Amherst (USA) produced in the 1970s and 1980s have ceased. The subject still ranks among the topics to be included in international encyclopaedias of education, but these articles primarily restate old orthodoxies. An occasional paper in an academic journal or seminar report has also appeared. But there has been nothing substantial to disperse the conceptual fog. I have therefore been pressed by a number of colleagues, staff and students to write something to fill what both they and I see as a real gap. This book is intended as a contribution to the literature on adult, non-formal, lifelong education. It has arisen directly from my teaching and has been written in large part for students, although I hope that others will also find it useful.

---

[2] I regret that information about the first full study of NFE to appear since the 1970s, D. Poizat, *L'éducation nonformelle* published by L'Harmattan, collection Education comparée, 2003, reached me too late to be used in the preparation of this book.

More importantly, this book springs from my concern with programmes of non-formal education in developing countries. Since the early 1970s, I have been privileged to work in many different NFE activities – developing project proposals, training facilitators, creating teaching-learning materials, conducting evaluations and research. Most of this work has been in south Asia but it has extended to Africa with something of a toehold in Latin America. What I discovered here is the gap between the theories of NFE which the agencies employed and the practice of NFE. It seems to me that most NFE programmes today are in danger from two things – either they lack a clear conceptual framework, or they live with a major distance between what they claim to do in the name of NFE and what they in fact do in the field.

Theory and practice

In this analysis, I have been heavily influenced by the arguments of Argyris and Schon (1976; see also Long & Long 1992). They pointed out the difference between what they call 'espoused theory' and 'theory in use'. Espoused theory is what we *say* we are doing, often with complete faith in our ability to fulfil these aims and ambitions. Theory in use is what in fact underpins the actions which we take, what we actually *do*. There is frequently a considerable gap between these two theories. We may say that our programmes are built on a particular ideal – for example, liberation and justice, or participation, or that we aim at certain specific outcomes – at greater equality, greater inclusiveness, empowerment of the participants, for example. Yet our activities may reveal that in fact we are often trying to defend the *status quo*, the dominance of educationalists, for example, and that we are frightened of the true liberation of those who participate in our programmes and even more of those who do not. What we do may on occasions contradict what we say or even what we believe we are doing.

This is particularly true in the case of NFE. The use of the term 'non-formal' in educational contexts has become increasingly unfocused. Some agencies apply the term to programmes which others would not call 'non-formal', and they may find it hard to describe exactly what they mean by the term. The cause of this gap seems to me to be the vacuum which exists in reconceptualising NFE more than 25 years after the basic work had been completed on defining the term and developing educational programmes based on the implications of those definitions. For the discourses which surround NFE have changed substantially over the intervening period, and despite the amount of ink spilt over the meaning and implications of the term, there is no source to which those who are responsible for the development and/or implementation of programmes in the field can turn to help them to clarify their own minds.

A discussion which seeks to unravel the various strands of the tapestry which has been and now is non-formal education will thus be of value – to students who have no textbook; to planners, administrators and policy makers who create programmes which they call non-formal, not quite sure whether what they mean by 'non-formal' is what others would recognise as being 'non-formal'; to practitioners who try to develop on the ground approaches which they believe will fit their own understanding of 'non-formal' education; to evaluators and researchers as they assess programmes against some kind of criteria of non-formality; and to all of us working in educational and training programmes, to see whether, when we promote what is called 'nonformal education', we are in fact implementing clearly identified educational principles.

Policy and practice: I believe that it is important for us to do this. For the effectiveness of all that we do depends on the clarity with which we hold the logic frame of our chosen task. We will achieve more if we are clear about what it is that we are trying to do and the context within which we are working. Commitment alone will not be enough, if we are vague about our aims and strategies. It is arguable that if we provide educational programmes which we call 'non-formal', we shall diminish our effectiveness to the extent that we are unclear about what we mean by the term.

This book then is offered as a contribution not just to academic analysis but to the clarification of policy and practice in the field of non-formal education. It is in part concerned with different and frequently clashing discourses, with discourses created within one socio-cultural context and transferred into another. But it is also concerned with the practice of NFE, with the creation of policies and the implementation of non-formal programmes in the field.

A non-formal book?

And here we run into a problem – how a book dealing with non-formal education can itself be 'non-formal'. Without turning the book into an interactive training manual or study guide as in distance learning programmes, it is not easy to develop true interaction between myself (the author) and the reader/user. My hope is that everyone who picks up this book will not just read it but will use it in their own way – picking and choosing, approaching the sections in any order according to their immediate interests and concerns. It can of course be read straight through in the order in which it is set out – an order that has arisen from several years of teaching the subject. But it may not meet your needs at the moment, in which case I hope you find the index adequate for your purpose.

Defining non-formal education

There is however one area of interactivity which may be suggested at the start. Everyone reading this will have some idea of what they mean by 'non-formal education'. It might be best to begin with that idea, however vague it may be. I normally ask the participants in my courses to set down in writing what they believe NFE is, so as to focus their mind before we start. I suggest that there are at least two ways in which this can be done:

a) they can choose two or three *examples of educational or training programmes* which they know well and which they would say (at least to themselves) are 'non-formal'. They can then draw from these case studies what appear to be the essential characteristics, the common principles of NFE;

b)   or secondly they may wish to start by drawing up their own *definition of non-formality in education* and see if they can find some programmes which fit that definition, which display the essential characteristics and principles of NFE.

This is not as easy as it looks, but you will probably find it worth a try, despite the time you will need to spend on it.

Such an exercise reveals that there is a great deal of uncertainty about the meaning of non-formal education, both in theory and practice. So let me admit right from the start that this book does not aim at increasing certainty by passing on my own views to the readers/users (although my own views will be expressed, sometimes quite strongly). Rather, it is meant to raise many questions, to challenge you to explore for yourself some of the literature on NFE and associated subjects, to evaluate some of the programmes which you know which may or may not call themselves non-formal – to help you to clear your own mind, to come to your own conclusions about what NFE means in your own context. To adapt the manifesto of another recent book on education, this book is intended to be "a series of explorations with critical intent", without attempting to "force one synthesis":

> We do not believe it desirable to do this at the moment... We are more concerned to keep educational theory alive and well. We are prepared to live with the uncertainties, equivocations, and live controversies which necessarily characterize any healthy discipline. We do not believe that the practice of education can be well served in the long run by the intellectual inertia of anti-theoreticism. It strikes us as ... ironic... that we should find ourselves invited ... to stop thinking imaginatively and innovatively about education – to stop thinking about the very institution whose job it is to sustain and reproduce a thinking society. (Blake et al. 1998: 19)

The aim of this book is to encourage all of us to think more deeply about what we mean when we term any programme 'non-formal', either in policy documents or in the field.

The collection of material for this book has taken many years, particularly during a number of visits to different countries. I am grateful to the many persons who suffered my interviews or who sent me material relating to their programmes. While at the University of Reading, I enjoyed many discussions with staff and especially students under the watchful eye of Keith Watson. Various colleagues such as Anna Robinson-Pant, Brian Street and Diana Coben contributed to make this book richer. I was fortunate to spend six months at the Center for International Education at the University of Massachusetts, an early centre of innovation in NFE, and although the staff I hoped to work with were not present during this stay, the kindnesses I received, the interaction with the students, and the resources available enabled me to get most of the framework of the book completed. The writing has taken longer than I planned because of the pressure of other activities, mainly at the University of Nottingham. I must thank all of these for their help, especially the students in the seminar group at Amherst who challenged every statement I made and refused to answer for me the questions I posed. But the faults remain mine.

Part I

The Context

... certain ideas burst upon the intellectual landscape with tremendous force. They resolve so many fundamental questions at once that they seem to promise that they will resolve all fundamental problems, clarify all obscure issues. (Geertz 1993)

In this first Part, I argue that the concept of NFE arose during a time of two major sets of changes.

The first were occurring **within the field of development**:

a)   a move away from an elitist modernisation-and-growth approach to development to one based on mass integrated rural development and social change; and

b)   a move away from a deficit (needs-based) paradigm of development to a paradigm based on disadvantage, an understanding that development consisted as much of changing the structures of society as of providing inputs.

The second set of changes (closely related to these changes in development approaches) were taking place in regard to new analyses of **education in developing countries**, with calls for and programmes of reform to enable education to achieve developmental goals more effectively.

It is out of this context that the discourse of non-formal education was created. This section examines first the developmental changes and secondly the educational reform agenda at that time.

2

The Development Context:
The Call for Reorientation

In the early 1970s, international development agencies announced a concerted effort to address the plight of the 'poorest of the poor' in less developed countries. These agencies chose the term nonformal education to refer to local-level programs for the adult poor. (LaBelle & Ward 1994: 4141)

The debate about non-formal education debate arose at the end of the 1960s and persisted during the 1970s within the context of discussions on education in developing countries. There was very little discussion at that time about NFE per se in relation to more industrialised societies. It is important to appreciate this context of development, including the changes which have taken place in the understandings, and to a lesser extent in the practice, of development over the intervening years for any understanding of what NFE meant at the time.

DEVELOPMENT AS DISCOURSE

'Development', in the sense of "the idea that deliberate action can be undertaken to change society in chosen directions considered desirable" (Youngman 2000: 240), has been operating on a global scale since the late 1940s. Recent examinations have suggested that the field of activity known as 'development' is in fact a construct of Western aid agencies; what can be seen as members of a well-funded aid industry created the concept of development (Mitchell 1991). They defined the societies which they termed as 'under-developed', they formed 'the Third World' (Crush 1995; Escobar 1995; see King & Buchert 1999: 183-184) through a dichotomy of 'them' and 'us', of 'modern' and 'traditional' (Leach & Little 1999: 295-296), implicitly setting such countries in juxtaposition with what was seen as a typified Western way of life (Cooke & Kothari 2001: 12, 170). More recently they have divided this 'Third World' into two categories, distinguishing the so-called 'highly indebted poor countries' (HIPC) from the rest.

This is not of course the language of the 'developing societies' themselves, although in their desire for aid assistance, they have often come to use and sometimes

13

even internalise the discourses of the West. And the discourses which the Western agencies (both government and NGO) have employed have helped to create the activities they approve of and engage in, including non-formal education (Robinson-Pant 2001). We therefore need to look at the discourses within the development field at this time in order to understand non-formal education (de Beer 1993: 343-363).

Discourses and Development

Discourse is not of course the same as language.

> A discourse is a collection of statements (involving knowledge or validity claims) generated at a variety of times and places, in both speech and writing, ... which hangs together according to certain principles as a unitary collection of statements. A great variety of discourses can be generated within any one language. And moreover, a single discourse can include statements in a variety of different languages. (Think of scientific discourse). (Blake et al. 1998: 14)

But a discourse is more than this. "A 'discourse' is not just a set of words, it is a set of rules about what you can and cannot say and about what" (Apthorpe & Gasper 1996: 4).[1] "Discourse not only includes language, but also what is represented through language" (Grillo & Stirrat 1997: 13). Discourses are "power-knowledge configurations, systems of ideas and practices that form the objects of which they speak. Discourses are not about objects but rather constitute them 'and in the practice of doing so conceal their own invention' " (Hall 1999: 134 citing Foucault 1972: 49).

One of the most detailed analyses of discourse has come from the writings of James Gee.

> A Discourse is composed of ways of talking, listening, reading, writing, acting, interacting, believing, valuing, and using tools and objects, in particular settings and at specific times, so as to display or to recognize a particular social identity... The Discourse creates social positions (or perspectives) from which people are 'invited' ...to speak, listen, act, read and write, think, feel, believe and value in certain characteristic, historically recognizable ways, in combination with their own individual style and creativity.
>
> There are innumerable Discourses in modern societies: different sorts of street gangs, elementary schools and classrooms, academic disciplines, police, birdwatchers, ethnic groups, genders... and so on. Each is composed of some set of related social practices and social identities (or 'positions'). Each Discourse contracts complex relations

---

[1] I owe this and other references to Dr Anna Robinson-Pant. I am greatly indebted to her in what follows, both through her paper presented at the Uppingham Seminar 2000 and through several exchanges on this and other matters.

of complicity, tension and opposition with other Discourses...
Discourses create, produce and reproduce opportunities for people to
be and recognize certain kinds of people. (Gee 1996: 10)

Few people actively make a choice or decide to use this or that discourse. It is
more a question of identifying when a discourse (as part of communicative practices)
fits a particular situation at a point of time and with a particular set of people. For a
discourse is an act of people: "Discourses are composed of people, of objects (like
books), and of characteristic ways of talking, acting, interacting, thinking, believing,
and valuing, and sometimes characteristic ways of writing, reading, and/or inter-
preting... Discourses are out in the world, like books, maps and cities" (Gee 1992: 20).
And a discourse creates a community of people:

> ...any Discourse is defined in terms of who is and who is not a member,
> and sometimes in terms of who are 'higher' and 'lower', more 'central'
> and 'less central' members... any Discourse is ultimately defined in
> relationship to and, often, in opposition to, other Discourses in the
> society... If we define 'ideology' as beliefs about the appropriate
> distribution of social goods, such as power, prestige, status, distinction,
> or wealth, then Discourses are always and everywhere ideological. Each
> Discourse necessitates that members, at least while they are playing
> roles within the Discourse, act as if they hold particular beliefs and
> values about what counts as the 'right sort' of person, and the 'right'
> way to be in the world, and thus too, what counts as the 'wrong' sort
> and the 'wrong' way... (Gee 1992: 142; see also Gee 1999)

A discourse however not only creates new models of the world; it also
determines the range of activities which the members of the discourse community
approve of. The point of a discourse is not just to alter the way we look at the world
but to alter the world. "A discourse (e.g. of development) identifies appropriate and
legitimate ways of practising development as well as speaking and thinking about it"
(Grillo & Stirrat 1997: 13). A discourse "is not the expression of thought; it is a
practice, with conditions, rules and historical transformations. To analyze development
as a discourse is 'to show that to speak is to do something – something other than to
express what one thinks; ... to show that to add a statement to a pre-existing series of
statements is to perform a complicated and costly gesture'" (Escobar 1995: 216, citing
Foucault 1972: 209). "The discourse of development is not merely an 'ideology' that
has little to do with the 'real world'... The development discourse has crystallized in
practices that contribute to regulating the everyday goings and comings of people in
the Third World. How is its power exercised in the daily social and economic life of
countries and communities? How does it produce its effect on the way people think
and act, on how life is felt and lived?" (ibid: 104). "Discourses are ... multi-layered,
verbal and non-verbal, they are rule-bound, the rules being either manifest or latent,

they determine actions and also manifest them, they are embedded in forms of life (cultures), of which they are simultaneously co-constituent" (Wodak 1996: 17).

Because of this, a discourse contains within itself diverse and even conflicting viewpoints. An example sometimes cited is that of the discourse of criminology: "It is possible [within that discourse] both to affirm and deny a connection between crime and mental pathology. What is shared by both those who affirm and deny this are the concepts of crime and pathology and, moreover, access to research and argument both supportive and conflicting but couched in similar terms and referring to shared criteria for judgment of the evidence" (Blake et al. 1998: 14). Any discourse can in fact become a site of contest between different perspectives. And discourses change over time and under stress. The members of a discourse community are not "trapped within some coherent but unpliable metaphysical framework" (Blake et al. 1998: 14-15); they are active creators of that discourse.

Discourses of Development: The analysis of development in the light of discourse was elaborated most effectively in a collection of essays edited by Jonathan Crush (1995) and in the writings of Arturo Escobar (1995), drawing on the works in socio-linguistics of writers and philosophers such as Foucault (1972). They see development as a construct imposed on or 'sold to' developing countries by Western agencies so that the inhabitants of such countries come to define themselves in the terms of this discourse (as 'under-developed', for example).

> ...development discourse is embedded in the ethnocentric and de-structive colonial (and post-colonial) discourses designed to perpetuate colonial hierarchies rather than to change them. It has defined Third World peoples as the 'other', embodying all the negative characteristics (primitive, backward and so forth) supposedly no longer found in 'modern', Westernized societies. This representation of Third World realities has provided the rationale for development experts' belief in modernization and the superiority of the values and institutions of the North. (Parpart 1995a: 253)

> Development 'discourse', then, is more than a new way of labelling the ideologies behind the various trends in development policy...it is a 'regime of representation' that 'constructs the world' (Crush) and 'constructs the objects of development.' It is the framework which enables us to see and helps us to assign value to those things that we have seen. (Robinson Pant 2000)

Thus the definitions of 'developing countries' and of 'development' themselves created a grouping of nations and states who had nothing else in common. But at the same time, the definition created a sense of common identity among these disparate states. Discourses carry with them a set of values. Those who look at development in terms of discourse then will "deal neither with development as technical performance nor with development as class conflict, but with development as a particular cast of mind. For development is much more than a socio-economic endeavour, it is a perception which models reality" (Sachs 1992: 1).

There are of course many discourses, even within a field such as development·or education. But these tend to fall into what may be called families of discourses. For example, within the development field, there is a family of discourses based on ideologies of modernisation, "...a modernist regime of knowledge and disciplinary power" (Crush 1995: xiii).

And in one sense discourses are transferable: the language of one discourse may be used within quite different kinds of programme.[2] For example, the Freirean discourse of conscientisation and empowerment is often used to try to justify activities which are directive, with pre-set agency-determined goals and which cannot lead to liberation. Youngman points out that the language of what he calls the populist model of development "was co-opted by the aid providers" such as the World Bank (Youngman 2000: 105). This is one possible interpretation of the many programmes of so-called 'non-formal' education which display all the same characteristics as formal education.

Voice and discourse: A discourse then is an expression of power. The concept of 'voice' expresses this – for 'voice' represents those whose interests are being served through any particular discourse (Aronowitz & Giroux 1991). It is not always clear who constructs discourses, whose 'voice' is being heard. Nor are the reasons for the construction of discourses such as those surrounding development always clear: they seem to relate to issues of control, hegemony, very similar to colonial issues of order and stability.

Dominant discourses are often taken up by subaltern groups, so that the real voice is not always heard. When talking about development, they frequently speak in terms which are primarily in the interests of dominant groups. Equally, there are many cases of a changed discourse but continued practice, where existing activities remain untouched but are clothed in a different language. Argyris and Schon's concepts of espoused theory and theory in practice are especially valid here (see above p.6).

FRAMEWORKS AND DISCOURSES OF DEVELOPMENT

Since the 1950s, I would suggest, three main paradigms may be discerned in discussions about development, three frames of reference which have influenced the planning and implementation of development programmes. Each of these has its own family of discourses. We can define these as the paradigms of **deficit**, of **disadvantage** and of **difference**. All three continue today; but the dominance of the deficit construct which was challenged in the 1970s by the construct of disadvantage,

---

[2] Aid agencies often use the language of partnership to obscure their relative power relations with local bodies, as B L Hall 1986 has pointed out.

is now being challenged by the construct of difference in 'an alternative development' (Sachs 1992; Burkey 1993; Rahman 1993; see Corbridge 1995; Hettne 1995).

It may be helpful to set out these three paradigms and their associated approaches to development in diagrammatic form to help to establish what I see as their relationship, before examining each of them in more detail.

Table 2.1:
Different sets of development discourses, their interaction and
their implications for education

DEFICIT	DISADVANTAGE	DIFFERENCE
1. Approach of a) modernisation and growth (higher and elite education) b) Human Resource Development (vocational education)		
2. Approach of Basic Human Needs (mass education for both young and adults; literacy campaigns)	1. Approach of Dependency (compensatory education; popular education; NFE)	
3. Approach of Post-welfare Development a) SAP (UPE and continuing education) b) poverty eradication (livelihoods education)	2. Approach of Social Transformation; exclusion/inclusion (UBE)	1. Approach of Participatory or Alternative Development (decentralised/diversified education)

While there is some connection between these different sets of discourses and the passing of time, it may not be helpful to see one as succeeding an earlier discourse, even incrementally, for earlier discourses do not die out with the emergence of another contradictory discourse. The deficit paradigm is alive and well today, although it is multi-faceted and contested. It may instead be more helpful to see them as three strands which are woven into a plait, with one or another emerging more prominently at a particular time or in a particular context.

A study of these changing paradigms will help us to locate and account for the emergence of non-formal education and the language in which it was clothed at the time.

The Framework of Deficit

The framework of deficit or 'deprivation' is still the paramount paradigm for most development today. "Hundreds of millions of people living in the South suffer from hunger, malnutrition, and preventable disease, and are illiterate or lack education and modern skills" (*South Commission* 1990: 23). The argument is that "countries are undeveloped because of their internal characteristics, such as the lack of educated and skilled people" (Youngman 2000: 56), not from any external factors.

In this paradigm (e.g. McClelland 1961; Lerner 1958; Schumpeter 1961), the 'problem of under-development' is constructed as a deficit on the part of the 'less developed countries'. These 'backward' countries are thought to 'lack' various elements which the 'more developed' areas of the world possess and which lead to economic growth – things like capital, infrastructure, communication systems, power supplies, technical know-how etc.. 'Traditional patterns' are seen in opposition to modernity and entirely negatively. Their "traditional value systems, social structures, technology, and behaviors ... are not conducive to the achievement of development goals ... The assumptions underlying the deprivation-development thesis suggest that progress is achieved by spreading modernism to backward areas through the application of technology and capital" (LaBelle 1976a: 329). It is the self-imposed task of the more 'developed' countries to help these selected countries to acquire what they lack – partly out of self-interest, and partly out of a sense of guilt for the exploitation which had characterised the relations between the West and the colonised countries and which still characterises these relationships in many new forms.

This framework uses the language of 'needs' to identify the deficits; and such needs tend to be assessed (i.e. created) by outsiders, with all the cultural problems and dangers of the misidentification of needs in culturally inappropriate terms. Thus 'needs assessments' precede and justify development interventions which are often described in terms of 'inputs' leading to specified 'outcomes'. There is an attainable goal for development, a model of which can be seen in Western industrialised democracies. It is argued that once the identified deficits had been met, all will be well; the 'backward countries' will 'take off' and become self-sufficient growth areas within a global economy. Much of the inputs needed will come from outside of the developing societies. Indeed, behind much of this deficit frame of reference lies an assumption that the people in developing countries cannot by themselves get out of the hole in which they have become trapped. They 'need' help (aid).

Five main sets of approaches to development can be seen in this strand (see table above).

Modernisation and growth: Development in the deficit paradigm was at first seen largely in terms of economic growth. Modernisation (especially the industrialisation of agriculture and production) was (and for many still is) the key aim of development; the means to the creation of a modern economic sector (Foubert 1983). The problem was seen as one of low productivity despite abundant labour. Less developed countries were to be encouraged and helped to leap across the successive stepping stones to a modern industrialised economy in a similar but accelerated process to that which the Western societies had undergone in the nineteenth and early twentieth centuries, and in this process, helped to avoid the pitfalls which such leaps had entailed.

Needs-based development then was seen as linear, a universally valid sequence from a pre-capitalist society through a proto-capitalist stage (if necessary) to a modern capitalist system, a progression to be followed closely in all cases (Rostow 1960; Moore 1964; see Webster 1990, 1995). Developing societies were encouraged to 'catch up' with their Western colleagues. At first, aid agencies concentrated on resource exploitation, but later they encouraged industrialisation within the developing countries themselves, both for home consumption and for export. The industrialisation process might consist of 'trickle down' (E M Rogers 1976), promoting major national economic sectors in the expectation that the benefits of a growing supply-led economy would diffuse themselves downwards and outwards throughout the whole of society, especially the poor. Or it might consist of bottom-up development, promoting more integrated local and/or regional economic development which in turn would encourage demand and thus build up further economic development. In both cases, the formal employment sector was seen to be the key to development and therefore the object of development programmes; and growth was seen to be unlimited.

Human Resource Development: A second strand within the deficit approach to development spoke of needs as including modern techniques of production. This approach saw the poorer populations of developing countries as the problem. They needed to change, to overcome their resistance to change, to embrace scientific attitudes and new ways of living and working (Harbison 1965). The major cause of under-development was felt to be the complex of traditional attitudes and practices of the poor; what was needed was the acculturation of the working population, their inclusion within a formal economic sector (Inkeles & Smith 1974). Thus farmers were encouraged to adopt modern production techniques and large scale cropping for the market (especially for export). The development of factories in both urban and rural areas became a hallmark of this kind of development. To accomplish these ends, Human Resource Development became a key component of development programmes (Rogers et al. 1981). Education and training were important parts of this process of developing human potential: "It is simply not possible to have the fruits of modern agriculture and the abundance of modern industry without making large investments in human beings" (Schultz 1961: 322). Development came to be seen as "a process of enabling people to accomplish things that they could not do before – that is, to learn and apply information, attitudes, values and skills previously unavailable to them. Learning is not usually enough by itself. Most aspects of development require capital investment and technical process. But capital and technology are inert without human knowledge and effort. In this sense, learning is central to development" (Wallman 1979: 353). People were often spoken of as if they were tools, to be honed to fit their required economic functions.

Basic Human Needs: In a major reaction to this economistic approach, worried about the increasing disparities (especially in wealth) which the modernisation approach to development was leading to and which the emerging disadvantage paradigm was revealing (see below), and responding to concerns expressed by many 'developing countries' (King & Buchert 1999: 100), the deficit discourse changed course. There thus arose in the West from the late 1960s a concern with a more mass poverty (and rural) oriented approach to development rather than the elitist modernisation approach (Seers 1969; Myrdal 1971; Russell & Nicholson 1981).

At the time, this was seen to represent a major turning point in development approaches, responding to criticisms being made by the disadvantage construct. The World Bank Education Sector paper of 1974, recirculated in 1975 under the title *The Assault on World Poverty: problems of rural development, education and health* (World Bank 1975) with its poverty-focus led the way. "Questions of employment, environment, social equality and above all participation in development by the less privileged now share with simple 'growth' in the definition of objectives, and hence the model, of development toward which the effort of all parties is to be directed" (World Bank 1974: 10). Integrated rural development became a key theme. "Development ... was re-defined as progress towards reduction of poverty, illiteracy, disease, malnutrition and social inequality" (Mickelwaite et al. 1979; see Ayers 1983).

Such 'welfarism' laid emphasis on various social indicators of under-development. In an even stronger deficit discourse, ILO and other international development agencies created the Basic Human Needs school of development. There is no point, it was argued, in encouraging and enabling men and women to engage in new production techniques if their health and nutrition needs are not met. Stress was laid on improving 'the quality of life' of the poor, especially the 'poorest of the poor', as the main goal of development: "a process of change that enables people to take charge of their own destinies and realise their full potential. It requires building up in the people the confidence, skills, assets and freedom necessary to achieve this goal" (J Clarke 1991 cited in Touwen 1996). Without this social democratic form of deve-lopment (sometimes called 'welfare capitalism', Youngman 2000: 70), economic growth would not be possible. Poverty-focused growth was the aim of much development assistance at this time. Indeed, the purpose of aiming at economic growth was to meet the country's social needs: instead of economic growth being an end in itself, now economic growth has become a means to the improvement of the quality of life of 'the people' (UNDP 1990; see Leach & Little 1999: 10-11).

Post-welfare/neo-liberal development: The fourth member of this family of needs-based approaches to development within the deficit paradigm is the more recent neo-liberal approach. It is inspired by the Structural Adjustment Policies (SAP) of Western governments imposing conditionalities on aid-receiving countries (despite much rhetoric about 'partnerships'), with their insistence on the shrinking role of govern-ments, multi-party democracy and the responsibilities of civil societies in the provision of development inputs and by the movement for debt relief. Just as the Human Resource Development approach, in response to the pressures of the new paradigm of disadvantage, changed into Basic Human Needs, so the Basic Human Needs adapted into a new and very Western monetarist approach to development. Market forces are the predominant consideration rather than state intervention (Leach & Little 1999: 203). 'Global capitalism with a human face' leads to a changed role of government as facilitator rather than as provider of services, with emphasis on free markets, privatisation and partnership with civil society, and the creation of safety nets for the most vulnerable.

The language that is being used here derives in part from the older discourses of modernisation and Human Resource Management and in part from the newer discourses of disadvantage (see below pp.23-26). Thus for example, this discourse speaks of grass-roots, people-centred development. "In Latin American societies, collective protests and local movements ... have become institutionalized, ... [they] make up a Third Sector different from the state and the market. Structurally these organizations are mediators between the state and the demands of the masses, between international movements and organizations and local needs ... The national NGOs ... are becoming a new actor in the social scene. Their work is becoming ever more important at times when the predominance of neo-liberal policies is increasingly limiting state action on social policies" (Jelin 1996 cited in Jung & King 1999: 15-16). Through decentralisation and capacity building of local organisations, each community must accept responsibility for its own development.

But it is rarely as disinterested as this. The post-welfare approach seeks to encourage community participation in the form of cost- and resource-sharing; but the goals are still being set by the aid agencies and their partner governments. Civil society is to be encouraged to help the state to meet the state's targets. Participation is designed to reduce opposition to centrally planned programmes (Cooke & Kothari 2001). NGOs have been co-opted into the development programme of the international and national agencies, causing at least one African writer to express his doubts: "NGOs are one of the instruments for the continued conquest and occupation of the South. They join in the marginalisation of Third World governments and indigenous NGOs and leadership ... This way, the North's latest conquest would be complete ... all of this is usually done in the name of empowering the grass roots" (Wangoola 1995: 68).

But the thinking behind all of this is economistic: a new monetarism, stressing both the essential call for sustainable development (Carley & Christie 1992; Carew-Reid et al. 1994; Fitzgerald 1997) and also the responsibilities of civil society, the role of the market, the promotion and facilitation of demand, the increase of competition and the consequent importance of the private sector in meeting needs. On the one hand is the major change from a view that resource exploitation and economic growth could be unlimited to a realisation that resources are limited and need conservation. On the other hand, responsibility for sustainable development is thrown onto 'the people' through decentralisation (Shepherd 1998). This approach emphasises the importance of capacity building, and uses the language of comparative advantage as the basis of economic growth. Several writers have termed this discourse 'neo-liberal' (Colclough & Manor 1991; Youngman 2000; Schuurman 1993), but since this approach "sees inequality as a source of individual incentive ... rejecting the concern of welfare capitalism with the issue of equity secured through state intervention" (Youngman 2000: 70), the term would seem to be less than satisfactory. While this approach does stress such 'liberal' values as (ostensibly) 'free markets' (they are in fact anything but free), the responsibility of the individual, the importance of personal choices, and the privatisation of state services for the achievement of what remain its essential goals, modernism and economic growth, nevertheless it is at the same time working for further exploitation and the accumulation of capital in a few centres, while denying space to other forms of economic activities. The newly current term of 'post-welfare' seems more appropriate (Tomlinson 2001).

Poverty eradication: The most recent facet of this paradigm is of course the poverty eradication (sometimes alleviation or reduction) goal now being set for most donor and aid agencies (see for example DFID 1997; McGrath 2001). Most countries have been urged by the World Bank to prepare Poverty Reduction Strategy Plans as a condition for continuing inputs.

The voice of deficit development: This in brief is an outline of some of the various deficit approaches in which development programmes have been clothed. Once the deficits had been met, it is argued or assumed, all will be well. This has led to a development process based on inputs (cash, equipment, scientific information, technical advisors, training programmes etc.). The problem of under-development lies with the people (in general terms or more specifically with the poor) and with the poor countries themselves. If these could be persuaded (motivated) to change, to take up and use the inputs, then development will inevitably take place.

It may be argued that the voice behind this deficit discourse is that of the capitalist West. The aim of development is two-fold – a) the export to the West of, first, the resources and later the products of developing country economies, and b) the opening up of wider markets to goods made in the West. The major tools of this include bodies such as the World Trade Organisation and GATT. Aid is seen as investment, and lending is normally to be repaid. Such approaches are of course highly contested.

The Framework of Disadvantage

By the late 1960s, the modernisation and growth model of development came under acute attack and an alternative set of discourses to the deficit paradigm became more prominent, based on concepts of disadvantage (or sometimes discrimination, see Bhabha 1994). As with all discourses, these formed the basis of discourse communities which shared much the same set of ideologies and pursued much the same set of development practices. They were quite different from the deficit discourse communities with their ideologies and practices, and as we have seen, they influenced the deficit discourses, changing the language, some of the under-lying assumptions and some of the activities of development.[3]

The disadvantage discourses (e.g. Frank 1967; Galtung 1971; Carnoy 1974) felt that the deficit discourse communities tended to blame the victims, to demean the populations of the less industrialised nations, to assert unjustifiably that such societies could not engage in their own development, to stress their needs rather than the causes of their needs. The deficit paradigm seemed to absolve the richer and more powerful elements in society from any responsibility for under-development. The paradigm of disadvantage, on the other hand, pointed out that the causes of poverty and under-development lay outside of the poor communities, with social, political and economic systems; that even if 'the people' could receive all the inputs needed, they would still remain poor. Contrasting the deficit and the newer paradigm, Goulet and Hudson wrote in 1971,

> The first view postulates that while some nations are unfortunately 'backward', they can evolve in the direction of 'developed' nations, if they adopt acceptable behavior and modern goals. The second view rejects this language as historically unreal. Underdevelopment is not rooted in providence, inferior personality traits or traditional values. Rather, it exists because the Third World has been the object of systematic subjugation action by the dominant nations. (Goulet & Hudson 1971: 9)

The causes of under-development thus are here seen to lie in oppressive systems which deprive the poor of the needed elements for their own development, and it is these systems which need to be changed. For example, to train and assist farmers to produce more is of no value to the farmers if there is no access to appropriate markets; the provision of irrigation to large areas is of no value if control of the flow of water continues to lie with small elite groups who favour their own; the industrialisation of poorer countries will bring no benefit if the rich countries continue to deny full access to international outlets or if local corruption misappropriates the profits.

In other words, the causes of under-development are being constructed in this set of discourses as lying in oppression, not in the deficits of the poor. This discourse community asks the question, *why* are the poor poor? rather than the earlier question, *how* are the poor poor? They suggest that the reason why some people are poor is because the systems devised by the dominant groups oppress the more marginalised and keep them poor. And they see the answer to development issues such as these as lying in social and community action.

Whereas the deficit paradigm sees the world in a single normative framework which all persons and nations need to come to, the disadvantaged paradigm sees the world in terms of dichotomies – the oppressed and the oppressors; the rich and the

---

[3] The language of disadvantage is at times used within the deficit discourses to indicate multiple deficits; the key however is that the deficit paradigm is largely focused on changing the poor countries and persons, not on changing the systems, see Thompson 1983: 43.

poor; the industrialised and the non-industrialised; the indigenous and the colonisers; the literate and the illiterate; the core and the periphery etc.. And in development, they felt that both sides needed to change, not just the poor and the oppressed.

This paradigm then has moved the focus of analysis from the individual to the social, from individual choice, abilities and behaviour to a consideration of the historical and structural context within which individual action takes place. These are the development workers who construct under-development in terms of external rather than internal factors, seeking to demystify patterns of domination, as Freire put it (Youngman 2000: 3, 37; see Coben 1998; P Mayo 1999). These are the discourse communities which embraced the search for equality and which thus provoked the modernisation approaches to development to move towards a more socially integrative approach. This is the paradigm which began to explore more systematically issues of gender, colour, race, sexual inequalities, as well as poverty; that looked for good governance and human rights. This is the framework that suggests that access to education is not simply a matter of the lack of motivation of the poor but rather a matter of the exclusion of the poor through barriers which the providers of education have erected. The issue at the heart of the disadvantage development discourses is power. This was the age in which critical theorists like Adorno and Marcuse arose to power in the academic and development debates (Giroux 1983; Held 1980; Horkheimer 1972; Carr & Kemmis 1986; see Darder et al. 2003).

And, like the deficit discourse communities, as the 'disadvantage development' theorists and practitioners became increasingly dissatisfied with the effectiveness of their activities, their paradigm showed change. Two main discourses can be detected in this paradigm.

Dependency: The first is the so-called Dependency and Self-Reliance discourse, which argues that the rich keep the poor (both persons and countries) in a state of dependency, and that true development will only come about when local populations become self-reliant. Using the language of marginalisation, it is argued that the major powers in the West have created a system by which there is a continuous transfer from the poorer countries to the richer, which results in "the development of the core and underdevelopment of the periphery" (Foubert 1983: 69; Schuurman 1993: 5). Nyerere in Tanzania was one of the exponents of this view (Frank 1967, 1969; Rodney 1972; Thomas 1974). Dependency is not simply economic; it is in fact just as much or even more cultural, needing (as Freire put it) 'cultural action' to break it (Freire 1972, 1975). 'De-linking' became a key term in this strand of the discourse. The debate surrounding post-colonialism was under-pinning much of this discourse (Spivak 1987, 1990; O'Hanlon & Washbrook 1992; Bhabha 1990, 1994)

The 1970s was the age of confrontation, of dichotomy and polarities, of typifications and binary oppositions, of absolute certainty of right and wrong (Escobar 1995). The world of reality came to be seen as polarised, and the aim of development is to try to change the balance between the two opposing elements. Some saw (and still see) this as an act of redressing injustices once and for all; others saw (and see) it as a constant dialectic between the different elements in society, battling over hegemony. The discourses of disadvantage or deprivation owe much to the class polarities of Marx (Youngman 2000). It is this which lies behind the move of some people to define development more in terms of fulfilment of rights than of the provision of services.

Social transformation: The dependency discourse constructs 'the people' as a singularity. Freire for example, saw the world as a battlefield between two unitary forces, the oppressed and the oppressors, for whom the same social action process would lead to the liberation of both oppressed and oppressors. But under pressure from the third major paradigm, that of diversity or difference (see below pp.27-29), the disadvantage/discrimination paradigm too changed away from dependency to the discourse of social transformation. This laid greater stress on the diversity of 'the people', especially indigenous peoples (Youngman 2000 therefore calls this discourse 'populism') who are exploited by the rich, the powerful, the elites. Whereas the dependency discourse sees the development of the formal economy within developing countries as an essential part of the delinking process, the social transformation discourse stresses the necessity for redistribution of incomes and the consequent importance of the informal economic sectors (Leach & Little 1999: 18). For the first time, some differentiation is being introduced into the construction of 'developing countries', and the final goal of development (transformed societies) is not seen to be the same everywhere (Sachs 1993; Sen & Grown 1987; Rahnema 1991).

The process of development as constructed by these two discourse communities lies in participation in social action. The inclusion of marginalised or excluded groups is the major goal of development within this paradigm; the complete transformation of social structures and values of the elites is the process. Access for the 'excluded' continues as a key theme of development; but whereas the deficit discourses suggest that the barriers to access lie in the reluctance of the non-participants, laying stress therefore on motivating them, changing them, the disadvantage discourses suggest that the barriers to access lie in the surrounding society which – if transformed – will allow the people's natural wishes to assert themselves. What is needed is for the poor to be helped to recognise their oppression (conscientisation) and to be enabled to take action against their oppressors. Unless the poor take control and exercise the power which lies latently within their own communities, unless they liberate the oppressors by dispossessing the powerful of their power, there will be no development. The empowerment of the poor through social and community action has become in this model the answer to the problem of oppression. Unlike the deficit model, the disadvantage model takes a more positive attitude towards the target groups. Instead of not wanting 'development', it is argued that the people want development but that they are unable to act for their own development until they have freed themselves from the constraints which tie them (Mohanty et al. 1991).

The Framework of Difference

More recently, new voices have been heard constructing development in the language of 'difference' or 'diversity' (two recent case studies are in Leach & Little 1999: 95-110 and 283-299; see also 81-93; Benhabib 1996).

In part, this construction owes much to the post-modern debate on 'difference' (Lyotard, Derida, Foucault etc.). To cite one example, "The concept of autonomy refers to the existence of a multiplicity of social subjects and agents, demanding their own space, their own voice in society and exerting pressure to satisfy their particular demands. Autonomy is the concept that better than any other appears to refer to the recognition of diversity, differences, plurality" (Meynes & Vargas 1991, cited in Jung & King 1999: 20). But although undoubtedly influenced by the accompanying post-modernist relativity and increased lack of certainty, this new development discourse does not seem to have built itself solely on this basis (Apter 1987; Barnett 1988; Usher & Edwards 1994). Rather, it has emerged from ethnographic studies of different cultures and from the anthropological insights of culture as being "ongoingly built and contested" (Apple 1988: 119 cited in Youngman 2000: 36), together with an emphasis on a more fully participatory approach to development (Chambers 1983, 1997; Shepherd 1998).

The argument for the difference development paradigm goes like this (Grillo 1998; Crossley & Watson 2003). If, as the disadvantage discourse community argues, "development is not a cluster of benefits 'given' to people in need but rather a process by which a populace acquires a greater mastery over its own destiny", then universal solutions to what were once seen as common problems cannot be the outcome of the development process. There is a "difference between being the agent of one's own development as defined in one's own terms and being a mere beneficiary of development as defined by someone else". Local self-determination rather than the adoption of generalised solutions is (in this framework) the process of development. Instead of the dualism of the disadvantaged approach, the difference approach stresses the multiple nature of society – moving indeed from difference (between two forms) to diversity (multiple differences). In place of the essentialism which (for example) sees all indigenous groups or all poor, all farmers or all fisherfolk, or indeed all women, as having essentially the same identity and interests, internal as well as external differences are being stressed. Multiple identities are constructed as well as ascribed. This is the language which speaks of indigenous peoples instead of indigenous people. Such a model stresses the value and importance of cultural diversity and seeks to promote multiple ethnic and other identities within society (Stavenhagen 1986). "Western models taken as the norm for 'one world' are to be replaced by 'a prospect of a pluri-cultural world' ".

There is then, in development as elsewhere, a Third Way, between the capitalist and neo-capitalist modernisation and growth models and the social engineering 'disadvantaged' model calling for action to redistribute wealth and power. "The Third Way is about simple material living standards, local self-sufficiency, grassroots participation and 'village' democracy, living in harmony with the environment, co-operation and zero economic growth. It is also about development defined more in terms of personal, ecological, community and cultural welfare and progress than in terms of the mere accumulation of economic wealth" (Trainer 1989: 6).

In particular, this frame of reference of diversity takes an even more positive attitude towards the potentialities of those whom the other discourses construct as 'under-developed' (Kitching 1989; Sen 1999). Whereas the deficit discourse says that the people lack motivation, and the disadvantage discourses say that the people want to act but cannot because of the systems, the diversity discourse asserts strongly that the people can and often do act in their own development, but that these people define development in terms which are frequently different from those of the major aid and development agencies.

But if people are to be 'allowed' (indeed encouraged) to define development in their own terms, the result will be a wide diversity of 'developments'. It will not be the agenda of the development agency which predominates; indeed, the agenda of the development agency will not necessarily be fulfilled. Village groups may prefer to build a cinema rather than a community learning centre; men and women may use their new literacy skills for reading film, fashion and sports magazines rather than newly prepared 'post-literacy developmental literature' on health, sanitation and nutrition. But instead of this being seen as a failure, any resultant self-determined activity will be seen as fulfilling development goals as seen in terms of the participants.

The discourse of diversity does not see the world as built around polarities. Rather there are a multitude of different interest groups, different cultures, different voices all interacting with each other. There are multiple sources of oppression in society, not just one. A simple construct does not describe any society adequately; it is in fact very complex, many-hued, multi-cultural and constantly changing. Identities are constantly being formed and reformed (Rogers 2003: 49-51): 'One man in his time plays many (sometimes contradictory) parts'. People who lack confidence when faced with a written or printed text cannot be described for all time as powerless or oppressed; they often in other situations display great confidence and ingenuity in achieving their ends. Diversity and the encouragement of increased diversity are the key elements in this construct.

Development practices will thus be built on the 'aspirations and intentions' of the participants (Rogers 1992: 148-155) rather than on 'needs' (however defined). Instead of seeing the poor as lacking against some externally set standard, instead of seeing them as powerless and oppressed, within a culture of silence, this paradigm constructs the poor in positive terms, as having the ability, the desire and potential of speaking their minds and acting in their own behalf – 'walking the road' (Horton & Freire 1990) in their own way rather than in a prescribed way in order to meet their own goals rather than the goals of the development workers. These discourses speak of local control: the evaluation of development, for instance, will be undertaken by the participants, not the aid agencies, and success will be defined in local terms through the sense of satisfaction of the participants.

The chief theme within this family is participation – participatory or people-centred development (this term is claimed by several different development discourses) or people's self-development, an alternative development (Burkey 1993; Rahman 1993). The language of participation (like that of gender and environmentalism) can of course be seen in every development discourse, but participation is interpreted in different ways by each of these discourse communities (see below pp.22, 26-27). Much of the programme of development is to be found in 'the new social movements' – women's movements, CBOs, grass-roots development organisations, environmental campaigns, human rights and legal aid pressure groups, and other, often single issue, associations (Youngman 2000: 24-26; Foley 1999) which serve as an indicator of the need for and the processes of social transformation. These views are often expressed in the form of resistance, turning against both politics and parties and frequently the state (Laclau & Mouffe 1985; Carnoy 1989: 20-21). There are then multiple developments rather than a single development; development itself is a site of contestation.

The discourse involved here can be confused with the discourse of the post-welfare neo-liberal discourse – for both talk about each community accepting responsibility for its own development. The significant differences between these two approaches may on occasion be obscured by the use of the same terms but with different underlying assumptions as to control and the value systems which underpin the outcomes of the development interventions.

Conclusion: from global to local: We have seen in the development field three main families of discourses. It is interesting that these three paradigms seem to move from the global and uniform to the local and pluralist (for globalisation and local, see Hall 1999: 133). It can be argued that the deficit discourses tend to stress the global, the universal. All poor societies are seen to be the same and need the same processes; the problems of under-development and their answers are universal. The disadvantage discourses emphasise cultural elements: oppression takes different forms in different cultures. But the processes of overcoming oppression are much the same, social and community action. But the difference/diversity discourse, while still global, tends to stress the local: each community will take their own decisions based on their own experiences and expectations, their own lifeworld constructions.

CHANGING PARADIGMS AND DISCOURSES IN OTHER FIELDS

These three paradigms can also be seen in other areas of social activity (see Fox 1996).

Gender: For example, in gender debates, the same three approaches appear. Cameron (1994) has argued that in one construct, all women can be seen as having a common set of *deficits*, to lack what men have, and the process of women's equalisation is to help them to get what they need. The concentration is thus laid on women's immediate and practical needs rather than the structural issues which confront women. Development programmes are aimed at overcoming the barriers to women's participation, helping generalised women to cope with their multiple roles. The answers are functional and universal. A second approach to understanding gender inequalities is through a *dominance* discourse. Women are deprived by male-dominated structures and systems. What is needed is a change in structures. Gender is a matter of power. But a rather different stress is laid by some on *difference*. Not only are women different from men; there are many differences within the construct 'women'. Universal answers no longer hold. Women's liberation is being interpreted at very local levels (see also Leach 1998a, 1998b, 2000).[4]

Discrimination and disabilities: Much the same range of approaches seems to apply in discussions of racial emancipation and to discussions of disabilities, moving from concentrating on the immediate needs of the participants to changing the whole of society to bring about new relationships of power, and finally to seeing these in terms of the encouragement of differences rather than uniformity and integration.

To give just one example of how this works, the issue of dyslexia. At first, this was constructed in deficit terms, leading to extra training for those identified and constructed as 'dyslexics'. The dyslexics needed to change to fit in with existing society norms. Then dyslexia was constructed in terms of exclusion; those who were identified as 'having dyslexia' were constructed as disadvantaged. Organisations and institutions were required to change to accommodate them (e.g. extra time for examinations). But more recently, dyslexia is seen as an otherness, similar to other othernesses (e.g. being very tall or short) which can cause problems or issues *in certain circumstances*. The dyslexic is no longer constructed as a dyslexic; there is more to them than their dyslexia. They are now encouraged to reassume agency for their own development – to assess each situation in which they encounter problems with their dyslexia and to take appropriate (but different) action in each such situation. Universal categorisation and universal solutions are not the answer. The same range of constructs and discourses from deficit to disadvantage to difference can be seen in many such cases.

Literacy: Recent explorations of literacy reveal the same picture. For many, literacy is constructed in terms of a single and universally applicable (what has been called an 'autonomous') set of skills which many people (defined by the literate as 'illiterates') lack. The lack is both immediate and personal. Only one kind of literacy is legitimated and this norm is imposed on the learners in a one-shot literacy teaching programme which is thought to convert those who have been constructed as 'illiterates' into agency-defined 'literates' (Bhola 1984; see e.g. Ong 1982; Goody 1977). Development, in literacy terms, comes from supplying the deficits through inputs (training). The learning programme is uniform, not context-dependent. 'Participation' in deficit

---

[4] Cameron deliberately sequences these paradigms as deficit, difference and dominance.

literacy is expressed in terms of motivating attendance (access) and preventing drop-outs.

In an alternative construct (under the influence of Freire among others), literacy is interpreted in terms of power. Non-literates are defined as being oppressed by the literate; and the general purpose of learning literacy skills is to achieve 'empowerment' and to change the systems, to help the oppressed through literacy to achieve their liberation. 'Participation' in this paradigm means not just attending literacy classes but joining in the group activities rather than being passive learners. 'Drop-outs' are reinterpreted in terms of 'push-outs'.

The difference discourse appears in the New Literacy Studies. Literacy is being rewritten in terms of social practices. There is no one universal literacy; there are rather many different literacies and they form only one part of a wide range of communicative practices. Local literacies is the argument (Barton 1994; Street 1984, 1995). Literacy practices within different contexts are being examined; literacy communities are being identified (Street 2001). Literacy is part of the cultural processes within any one society. Participation in this kind of literacy discourse is seen as helping individuals and groups with the different literacies they are already engaged in, working within *their* literacy context (Rogers 1994, 2002; DFID 1994).

Changing Frameworks for Education

Paulston has drawn attention to similar "representations" within the field of education. First he identifies a representation of *orthodoxy* – "the hegemonising and totalizing influences of functionalism and positivism". In this view, "adherents of the existing orthodoxy assume their metanarrative contains truth and insights about how progress can be achieved ... and [they] force consensus, and do not tolerate and appreciate other perspectives" (Paulston 1996: 32-33). Such truths are universally valid. Thus education is the same in every society. Education through schooling is primarily to incorporate the younger generations into society, either consciously through socialisation or less consciously through hegemony. Its aim is to reproduce and strengthen the dominant culture, to provide what people lack, meet what others have identified as their needs in social terms, to bring about social change in strictly limited and controlled directions only. Education in this understanding is a universal good. Learning is behavioural change. This 'orthodoxy' view can be equated closely with the deficit set of discourses.

A contrary representation of *heterodoxy* emerged, "where critical and interpretive views successfully competed with and challenged orthodoxy" in a binary opposition. The 1960s, he argued, had "abandoned the notion of fixed intelligence and abilities, emphasising rather the power of [the] environment ... on intellectual growth", and this presented a challenge to the orthodox and universal form of education. At the school level, the expansion of primary education and its concentration on child-centred approaches are (within this representation) thought to help to bring about greater equality. At adult level, an education that springs from the people, 'popular education', will enable adults to act to transform their lifeworlds. Education in this frame is thus aimed at social transformation, overcoming inequalities which traditional schooling is perpetuating and even strengthening. Transformative learning, the making of meaning, forms a mainstay of discussions about the nature of learning. Alternatives to schooling are being sought, and many experimental reform programmes have been created. In part, this can be seen as a resistance to incorporation. Critiques of 'orthodox' education appear in "a struggle for power, an attempt to dethrone the pervasive view and replace it. ... This struggle is one of 'either/or' competition, a closed defense of the favored paradigm and total disdain for opposing paradigms ... [in] antagonistic and partisan dramas of orthodoxy and heterodoxy ... a period of combative heterodoxy" (Paulston ibid). Whereas orthodoxy (the deficit approach) tends to stress a universal educational provision through or supported by governments, the heterodoxy strand (disadvantage) tends to set out the new paradigm in terms of polarities. Dore's (1976) contrast between education for qualifications and education for learning is one example. Carl Rogers' (1983) distinction between teaching and learning is another.

Paulston suggests that a good deal of current interest in educational circles now focuses on *heterogeneity*, differences in educational provision, purposes and take up. Paulston sees this discourse as "consisting of disputatious yet complementary knowledge communities, that have come to recognize, tolerate and even appreciate the existence of multiple theoretical realities and perspectives ... what we have left is ... *difference*" (Paulston ibid, original emphasis), what others have called the celebration rather than the suppression of the other (Sampson 1993). There has been a breakdown of consensus and a stress on the relativity of experience. Increasing diversity in education with multiple providers and multiple forms of provision, different curricula and clientele, the emergence of new forms of religious education – all these reflect increasing diversity in education. Multi-cultural and inter-cultural education (Aikman 1999) are key issues – the stimulation of "cultural identity and assertion ... the idea that national unity requires a positive recognition of cultural differences between ethnic groups" (Youngman 2000: 189). Even curricula are not exempt: "All our liberal reflexes resonate when we consider the idea of schools developing and teaching their own curricula, adapted to the unique constellation of factors which make up each and every school's milieu" (Gordon & Lawton 1987: 29). The decentralisation or localisation of control and provision, the democratisation of education, the promotion of different educational cultures, the increase in participatory education are some of the emerging issues of contemporary discussion and debates.

Paulston locates these contesting paradigms of education within a wider context of changing climates. He sees these as successive stages, orthodoxy characterising the 1950s and 1960s, heterodoxy the 1970s and 1980s, and heterogeneity the 1990s, rather than as competing, overlapping and continuing frames of reference and discourses. And he goes on to suggest that these changes correlate closely with the wider 'climatic' changes in modernism, post-colonialism, and post-modernism.[5]

Now, it is true that the denial of meta-narratives, the stress on the local as·a balance to globalisation, the construction of society as a collection of organised or unorganised interest groups which bring pressure to bear on each other and on the state, and the attack on capitalism as being only one description (and a partial and inadequate description at that) of the economy, let alone of political systems, are all features of contemporary debate. But this does not mean that the diversity discourse has replaced both the deficit and the disadvantage discourses. Rather, the deficit paradigm still remains predominant, while at the same time the disadvantaged paradigm is still growing in strength (especially through the social exclusion/inclusion policies), while the diversity paradigm still struggles to get its voice heard.

Table 2.2
Summarising the three main paradigms in different development areas

development	literacy	gender	education
deficit needs; inputs; human resource development; basic human needs	*deficit* autonomous literacy; technical, universal skills; motivation and drop-outs	*deficit* practical needs; fitting in	*orthodoxy* socialisation/ reproduction; access; incorporation
disadvantage liberation, social action, transformation, critical theory	*oppression* empowerment, Freire, push-outs	*disadvantage* structural needs special development for and with women	*heterodoxy* resistance to incorporation, exclusion/ inclusion – social transformation, transformative learning
diversity participatory development; alternatives; social movements; intentions rather than needs	*cultural* ideological; local literacies; literacy practices; communicative practices	*dominance* difference from and difference within	*heterogeneity* diversity in provision; multi-cultural and inter-cultural

---

[5] Mundy has proposed rather similar phases in King and Buchert 1999: 94-96; and Bagnall 2001: 35-36 speaks of the "three progressive sentiments" which have informed "lifelong learning ideology, theory and advocacy, over the last four decades", the individual (deficit), the democratic (disadvantage), and the adaptive (diversity).

Changing discourses and the role of education

All of the different paradigms of development and the discourses in which they have been clothed have had and continue to have profound implications for the *practice of education*, especially but not only in the contexts of developing societies which is where non-formal education first emerged. The modernisation and growth discourses concentrate their efforts and aid on manpower planning, on specialist technical and higher education of elites, on human capital theories and human resource development. And Basic Human Needs with its Integrated Rural Development approaches have changed this to concentrate on mass education,[6] especially for rural areas, including adult education: as USAID put it,

> General social progress cannot be achieved by a small elite com-
> manding a huge constituency of illiterate and disoriented people.
> Success in development requires that at least a majority of people be
> supplied with knowledge and the opportunity to participate to some
> reasonable degree in economic, social and political activity. (cited in
> ODA 1986: 156)

The post-welfare discourse of today concentrates its attention on universal primary education and on continuing education (expressed often in terms of lifelong education and learning for work-related activities), with the heavy involvement of civil society (including the local community and private commercial interests) in the provision of all kinds of schooling, education and training.

Equally the disadvantaged discourses see education as a tool of development rather than as a goal of development – education for economic and social trans-formation. The Dependency Theory concentrates on vocational education and training to build up local economic capacity for self-reliance, while the social transformation approach focuses on alternative education and non-formal education. Universal Basic Education (UBE) has to some extent replaced Universal Primary Education (UPE). The difference paradigm however sees education in terms of the diversity of provision, of multi-cultural and inter-cultural education, of the involvement of civil society in education, especially community schools, an educational free-for-all.

Locating non-formal education in these paradigms and discourses

Seen within this context of changing discourses of development within changing paradigms, it is possible to see the non-formal education debate as growing up at a time when an alternative approach was emerging in the deficit paradigm, opposed to the dominant modernisation and growth approach to development and its con-centration on human resource development, elitist urban-oriented education for the

---

[6] For an interesting example of this change in terms of science education, away from science for elites to mass science education, see Leach & Little 1999: 284.

modern formal economic sector. This new construction concentrated on basic human needs, integrated rural development and social welfare. NFE was seen as the way of meeting the new developmental goals, mass education coping with the educational and training needs of the rural poor and other under-educated populations and aimed mainly at the informal economic sector.

The fact that it was quickly taken up by those working within the newer disadvantaged paradigm and then became a football between the various discourses is part of the theme of what follows. But its origin lay in dissatisfaction with the existing approaches to education in developing societies which were seen as being inadequate, partial and ineffective, and this led to the search for new descriptions of developmental education. The deficit discourses were felt to be perpetuating and even strengthening inequalities. The newer discourses of disadvantage sought to articulate the views of subaltern groups against the dominant groups in a new polarity. Agencies now tried to identify themselves and their programmes with the oppressed.

It was in the course of this contest that NFE emerged as one answer to the pressing problems of development and education. NFE did not yet know of diversity, of difference; it was born within the deficit discourses and grew to maturity in the disadvantaged discourses. I see NFE as a single discourse. It constructs the world of education into two (or at times into three, as we shall see) sectors; all who participate share this view. But it contains different and often conflicting perspectives and different action plans, and it is these which form the subject of this study.

3

The Educational Context:
The Call for Reform

... these more flexible programs are compensating for the deficiencies of the formal system which stem from its failure to adapt rapidly enough to changing needs. (Coombs 1968: 141)

The non-formal education debate then arose at the time when the deficit discourses were changing over to a changed vision of development as including the rural and traditional sectors of society and when the discourses of disadvantage were becoming more insistent in debates about development and about the role of education in developing societies. But in order to understand the nature of non-formal education as seen during the great debate, we need to see the more immediate context from which it sprang. And that context was strongly one of the reform of formal education systems within developing societies. This is clearly shown in the first of the key texts in the debate, Philip Coombs' *The World Educational Crisis: a systems approach* which was published in 1968.

Discussions of non-formal education were largely confined to the so-called 'less developed countries'; there was little heard at first about NFE under that title in Western societies.[1] Nevertheless it drew upon this Western context. Indeed, it was largely in the Third World context that Western educational reformers saw their best chances of success. This is one reason why a systems approach to education was dominant at that time. What was seen by many development workers as the slowness of formal educational systems to adapt away from a modernisation agenda in order to meet the newly identified (rural and mass) needs of developing countries coincided in the West with a sense that educational systems were not only ineffective but were positively harmful. The family into which NFE was born was the family of planners more than practitioners. Non-formal education was not a bottom-up creation: the only genuinely grassroots educational programme of that era was 'popular education' in Latin America which deserves a detailed study of its own. NFE was a creation of Western aid agencies sent out like a dove to bring peace and harmony to a disunited

---

[1] Coombs spoke about NFE in industrialised societies as being concerned with the preparation of children for formal schooling (*pre*-school), extra-curricula activities *inside* formal schooling, and continuing and further education *after* schooling, Coombs et al. 1973: 25-26.

international educational world, a panacea for all educational ills.

DISCONTENT WITH EDUCATION

It will be important to look at the criticisms which were being made about education, since for many people, non-formal education was designed to meet those failures, to fill in gaps and to provide a more effective form of education for those who were being failed by the schooling offered to them and their children.

Criticisms of education: Discontent with education in Western societies was common during the 1960s, a discontent which led directly to the student riots from Paris to the USA in the later years of that decade. But it was much wider than that. Throughout the late 1960s and the 1970s, "criticism of formal education ... continued to increase throughout the world" (Simmons 1980: 1). Such criticisms, aired in government reviews and policy documents and in the public press, were shared by students, parents and politicians alike, both in the West and in developing societies.

Some issues were common to these two situations.[2] Inequality was one of them. Writers such as Bowles and Gintis (1976) and Reimer (1971) exposed the increasing inequalities which formal education was helping to bring about in the West. There was growing concern among many aid agencies that the modernisation agenda seemed to be bringing about a similar widening of the gap in developing societies. The Green Revolution in farming, for example, tended to make rich farmers richer and poor ones even poorer. Again in both arenas, increasing resources were devoted to education, but the thrust towards a more academic model of formal education rather than to the felt needs of both society and many of the users led to increasing frustration.

Such criticisms were particularly strongly felt in the context of developing societies. There seem to have been two main strands. On the one hand, there was growing dissatisfaction among Western aid agencies with education in developing societies, especially sub-Saharan Africa. It was suggested that large sums of money had been spent in many former colonial states on educational systems, especially during the early stages after Independence, but without discernible improvement. Indeed, in some respects, there would even seem to have been a backward movement from the colonial days, as an increasing number of countries were unable to meet the growing pressure for Western types of schooling from (in most cases) expanding target groups, especially rural populations where both the population and the demand for schooling were growing fast. At the same time, the failure of the education system was felt especially acutely within these countries themselves, as Coombs pointed out (1968: 126), partly because of the high expectations of the relevance of education to national development goals, and partly because of rapidly rising costs in countries where

---

[2] I am aware that the concepts of 'the West' and 'developing societies' and the contrast to be drawn between them are constructs. I have accepted these for the purposes of this section.

resources were limited and priority choices were severe.

The view of education as a major tool of development was encouraged by the international aid agencies. The modernisation advocates saw education as creating 'pools of modernity' within traditional societies. But others saw education as being re-oriented towards the new development goals. As the head of the World Bank asked in his now famous Report of 1974,

> How can educational systems be reshaped to help the poorest segments of society? How can education contribute to rural development and thus respond to the needs and aspirations of the vast majority of the poor living in the villages[3] ... in countries where educational systems have hitherto favored the urban dwellers and the relatively rich? (World Bank 1974: i)

Whether seen as geared to high level skills and the formal employed economic sector or to the new goals of mass development, the expansion of the informal economic sector and social transformation, the failure of education to adapt to meet these goals became increasingly apparent. In particular, many liberation movements had promised the population of their countries that, after Independence, the new governments would provide wider access to the many benefits that formal education clearly brought to the elites – promises which were not fulfilled in practice (most of the benefits were retained to the new elites) and promises which they probably could never have fulfilled. Discontent sprang not just from education's failure to fulfil what were felt to be its traditional role but also from its failure to meet the expectations created by new and differing demands.

Redeemable and irredeemable criticisms: The discontent with the formal systems of education which prevailed at that time was of two kinds. One saw the problems within education as being large and complex, but education was essentially redeemable. The other saw the problems as inherently within the nature of education, and therefore they could not be cured, the whole system needed to be replaced. Positive attitudes towards formal education predominated among the former group; schooling was felt to be basically a good thing but it had many features which needed to be reformed. Education could still help to bring about the building of a better society if its failures were overcome. On the other hand, more negative attitudes towards the formal system of education predominated among the latter group. Formal education contained within it elements by which it would destroy society and the hopes of peoples. Schooling itself was the enemy. It could not be reformed; it needed to be eradicated or at least changed fundamentally. Some of course, in the lists of criticisms which they drew up, mixed up the two, but on the whole the critics fell into one camp or the other. It will be useful to look more closely at these two sets of criticisms, for we can then see how it

---

[3] The construct of 'developing societies' as consisting mainly of 'villages' (also constructed) which were invariably poor has been pointed out several times, e.g. Escobar 1995: 47-48.

was hoped that NFE would remedy the problems created by formal education.

Box 1

Nepal: a study of education in one district of Nepal in 1977 identified the following problems:

- few schools in remote rural areas, more in more densely populated areas
- girls were only one fifth of class enrolments in primary schools and lower in secondary schools
- a drop out rate of children from first year of primary school of more than 50%
- a shortage of lower secondary schools and therefore further drop out at this transfer point
- a shortage of trained teachers; the use of some untrained teachers; a lack of professional guidance
- low examination results
- shortage of books, visual aids and the material conditions in which teaching takes place

Sudan: a parallel study of Sudan taken at the same time identified the following:

- shortage of trained teachers
- the absence of vocational subjects in schools,
- over-crowding as enrolments exceed the maximum capacity of the buildings
- shortage of teaching material like visual aids

(IIEP 1981: 178-179)

Contradictory expectations: These complaints of course take many forms, for they depend on who is making them and who stands to gain from them, how far education is seen as fulfilling or not fulfilling the differing expectations of the various groups of stakeholders. Parents and students may hold differing views from each other; but their claims are likely to be different from governments, educationalists and employers, all of whom will almost certainly hold yet further expectations of what education will achieve in a changing and modernising society. And some of these views themselves will be inconsistent. For example, governments will often wish that education will socialise the students into the norms of society and yet at the same time change those very norms; above all, they want education to persuade the students to support the government. Parents will usually see education as helping their offspring sometimes to be socialised into the constraints of society and sometimes to break out of the constraints which the parents feel. Some educationalists will hope that their education will encourage individualism, while others will try to curb the differences between their pupils. Employers will look to education to provide not only trained and disciplined employees but at times a creative and self-reliant workforce. So that education (formal and non-formal) designed to meet these unfulfilled expectations will be drawn differently by different groups.

Equally, the context will create further differences. In some situations complaints arose from the fact that the educational system was expanding, in others from the fact that it was in decline. And clearly the criticisms of schooling in countries with a stable environment, seeking through government action to achieve a measure of controlled socio-economic change, will vary from the criticisms heard in situations which are less stable and where calls for radical change may be heard and indeed may be supported by external agencies. It is unlikely that a uniform approach to education will emerge from such contrasting contexts.

The concept of non-formal education emerged from all this criticism as a potential saviour of formal education. The role that NFE was called upon to fulfil was initially to provide new kinds of inputs to meet the detected deficiencies of formal education. The nature of NFE thus came to depend on how the problem was constructed.

COMPLAINTS ABOUT EDUCATION: Redeemable Education

Many educational aid agencies felt that there were huge problems with education as they experienced it in developing countries, but that these could be remedied. UNESCO, USAID, and especially the World Bank in their review papers of their programmes at the time of the great conversion from modernisation to mass rural development, drew up lists of these problems. Country after country followed them in producing their own analyses of the failures of the systems of education they ran to meet the goals set for them. Educated persons wrote to the newspapers deploring the ways in which schools and colleges failed to meet the perceived needs of themselves, their families and the wider society. From India to Zimbabwe, as in the West, students protested, often violently, and universities and colleges were closed for a time. Practitioners and consultants wrote their own assessment of these failures. One of the more devastating diagnoses was that of Ronald Dore (1976) which drew together the kinds of criticisms which had been made of formal schooling for more than a decade. But it was not the only one. In 1968, Coombs pointed to "poor internal efficiency and external productivity", and in 1980, Simmons expanded this to internal inefficiency, a mismatch in outputs, and inequalities in the distribution of opportunities and results (Coombs 1968; Simmons 1980).[4]

---

[4] These statements were frequently repeated or adapted. For example, Ahmed 1982: 135-136: failures in external efficiency (i.e. relevance), internal efficiency, and equity; Bhola 1983: 45: there is not enough, not enough money, high costs, inadequate outputs, and inefficiency. Brembeck 1974 said that formal education was too costly to meet increasing demand, was ineffective, and increased inequalities. Even today the same comments are being made:

Box 2

The major redeemable criticisms of formal education

- not keeping up with demand
- high costs: low cost effectiveness
- low quality
- irrelevant curriculum
- over-production of graduates
- educational inflation
- imbalance between primary and higher education

---

1. First and foremost, there was **not enough education available** to meet the needs produced by both an expanding population and an ever increasing demand (Dore 1976: 4). There was, it is true, in most countries an explosion of formal education both at primary and higher level (less often at secondary level) to meet both political objectives and increasing demand. The world around was changing fast. UNESCO in 1985 identified some of these changes:

- increasing populations
- increasing demand for education
- increases in knowledge
- increasing unemployment, especially among many of the professions
- increasing inequalities in opportunity, in society, in jobs and at school
- increasing bureaucracy
- the increasing politicisation of education
- changing national goals set for education
- and spread of new technologies (UNESCO 1985: 53-54).

But the demands for education which these changes were creating were being met only in part by many societies. In country after country, education was thought to be failing to keep up with growing populations and growing demand. "A major problem shared by countries all over the world, both rich and poor, developed and developing, is the soaring social demand for formal education, the enormous pressure for more and more formal education" (UNESCO 1985: 32). As the primary school system tried to expand, many devices were tried in an attempt to maintain this system, but there was never enough to meet all new and changing demands for education. And meeting such demands was always a political issue involving factors other than educational concerns.

Hoppers 2000a:5 says there is a view that formal education is too costly, unresponsive and impervious to change, exclusive, and irrelevant.

2. Secondly, it was **too costly and not cost effective**. Education of course was seen to be vital to a country's development. "Expenditure on education ... is to be thought of as an investment – investment in mankind. The returns on education, both individually and socially, are at least as high as those on physical capacity" (Vaizey & Debeauvais 1961: 38; see Schultz 1961). If education were to help society to cope with the changing world, it needed increased financial resources. Any investment needs to assess the returns; and many assessments of the return on investment in education were made at this time.

But assessments identified two main issues, high costs and inequitable funding. First, both in the West and in developing societies, costs were rising dramatically, especially as demand for more and better education escalated. Increasing costs met increasing scarcity of resources most acutely in education and in health provision, especially in countries where the lack of security made other forms of expenditure such as defence essential. In 1960, it was estimated that some countries were spending 10-15% of all government expenditure on education; by 1970, these same countries were being called upon to spend between 20 and 25% on education (Dore 1976: 4, 7).[5] The instabilities in state finances introduced by the world financial crisis of 1973 and subsequent years and the recessions of the 1980s made matters even worse in most poor countries.

There were of course huge variations in cost. Education in Africa in terms of unit costs was much higher than in Asia or Latin America for all kinds of reasons, the conditions of service for staff in terms of housing and health assistance being one of them. The costs of catching up in primary education and especially in secondary education were far greater than many of the very poor countries could ever expect to meet, with their inadequate systems for collecting national revenues and heavy debt burdens, although that did not stop the promises of universal quality education from being made by politicians. And many developing countries were (and still are) facing huge increases in population, resulting in increased demand for education at all levels. "To put it bluntly, ... schools ... have been forced to run fast just to stand still in relation to their existing enrolment ratios, and even faster to boost those ratios" (Coombs cited in ODA 1986: 11).

But never fast enough. For it was generally recognised that "the system of formal education has left untouched a large segment of the population" (IUACE 1971: 199). The equity argument was a strong one. It was pointed out that the poor were being taxed so that the state could provide an educational system which was open in practice to none but the rich or privileged. Graduates could earn far more than non-graduates and find more loopholes to evade taxation, so the gap got ever wider. The formal system of schooling was increasing the existing social divides, not leading to a reformed society.

---

[5] In Ireland, it was estimated in 1981 that if the costs rose at the same rate, by the year 1991, the size of the education bill would be higher than the total government spending in 1981 (Tussing 1978).

3. Expansion, costs and other factors led to **low quality.** Some 95% of spending in many countries went on salaries, leaving very little for other educational expenditure. Lack of finances led to poor buildings and even poorer equipment and materials. Whether seen in terms of teachers, management systems or examination results, everywhere there was detected a decline in the standard of the education provided for the students, especially in sub-Saharan Africa. And it was asserted, this led to low morale of staff and students and to high drop-out rates.

Whether or not the education provided at most of the African universities declined in absolute terms is of course disputed, but it was *felt* to decline, largely because of the failure to maintain the supply of textbooks and equipment to the establishments and staff. Despite the many individuals who came through the systems with knowledge levels, skills and academic discipline of the highest levels, producing work that ranks in every country among the best in the world, it was widely thought (especially by outside assessors) that standards had declined significantly. Some academic journals reported that many of the papers submitted to them for publication by African university staff had to be rejected, not so much because the writers were unable to produce good work but because they did not have access to some of the most important recent literature on the subject.

Box 3

A major report on education in Sub-Saharan Africa of 1984 identified the following indicators of the **low quality of education** in that region:

- inadequate buildings and equipment
- lack of teaching-learning materials
- high rates of under-trained and untrained staff and low morale
- poor supervision
- poor management
- inadequate organisation
- poor attendance and high drop out rates

The result of this was
- decline in performance standards
- examinations dominate curriculum
- elite schools progress while system schools decline
- school is increasingly irrelevant

ODA 1984: 40-41

But this problem did not lie solely with higher education. There were relatively few secondary schools in many developing countries, and the quality of primary education, especially in the rural schools, was particularly low. The rates of repetition of grades and of 'drop-outs', it was suggested, revealed the poor levels of teaching in the schools. Teachers were often inadequately trained; they were almost everywhere inadequately and sometimes rarely paid, so that their status declined, there was a high turnover rate, and recruitment of new teachers often fell short. Motivation too declined: many teachers found themselves impelled to undertake other work to supplement their incomes, often neglecting their school duties in the process. There was in many areas a substantial shortfall of teachers, trained or untrained, especially women, which added to other cultural constraints against sending girls to school and colleges. School management too was often felt to be very weak. Ghost schools persisted in many areas – empty buildings with either no staff or no pupils. Quality education was often not available to many of the people who had based their sacrificial support to the independence movements on the expectations of increased mobility for their children through education; and in many rural areas, there was no educational provision at all.

4. **An irrelevant curriculum:** Much of the anger generated in this discussion was directed at the formal education curriculum. Employers, governments and parents joined in the litany. Education was unable to provide the country with the trained workforce it required. Firms often needed to train school or college graduates when they first joined as employees: school education was thought to be too theoretical, not practical enough. The teaching-learning approaches were too input- and memorisation-oriented to create problem-solvers; they made for dependent learners. "Students are uniformly penalised for creativity, autonomy, initiative ... and independence ... they are rewarded for perseverance, ... and other traits that are indicative of docility, industry and ego-control" (Simmons 1975: 24). Many school methodologies were authoritarian and rigid, largely because of the lack of confidence of many teachers. In Ethiopia, for example, as elsewhere, it could be reported that "there was a tendency to favour rote learning as a means of instruction ... a child was supposed to be quiet, polite, shy, unquestioningly obedient and uncomplaining ... Pedagogy at all levels was based on repetition and memorisation, with strict adherence to the conventions preferred by the teacher ... expressions of individual thought were frowned upon" (Kebede 1993: 2; see also Ingadayehu 1985). As Kleis put it, the "term 'schooling' is perhaps ... better than 'formal education' to denote the particular sort of education provided by educational establishments" (Kleis et al. 1973: 9). School and college were aimed at the impersonal acquisition of knowledge through a giver and receiver relationship.[6] It was intended to foster an uncritical-obedience syndrome (Adiseshiah 1985: 1). Examinations dominated the system; there was no testing of learning abilities or problem-solving skills.

---

[6] Even today in India in particular, the word 'impart' remains the base word of all education – to 'impart' knowledge, skills and attitudes, to 'impart' literacy etc., again revealing the deficit discourse.

The cause of the failure of education to enable its participants to obtain the jobs they sought was often seen to lie in an irrelevant teaching-learning programme leading to irrelevant qualifications. "While millions of people from among the educated are unemployed, millions of jobs are waiting to be done because people with the right education, training and skills cannot be found ... [This is] one of the most disturbing paradoxes of our time" (World Bank 1974). The curriculum had become fixed and static, inflexible; there was no room for the curriculum to change as society changed. Schools had become out of touch with the society in which they stood. The content of much education was felt to be outdated; it was alien, imported from countries and cultures very foreign to the local setting (Adiseshiah 1985: 1, 6).

These criticisms of course were not left uncontested. Blaug (1973), for example, suggested that the irrelevance of the formal education curriculum was not the cause of the urban drift of the youth, nor of the high expectations of many that formal education would lead to white collar employment. These sprang, he suggested, from deeper causes in society. But the criticisms persisted. "If the goal of education is to fit the students for life and for jobs, then it had failed" (Adiseshiah 1985: 6). As Dore wrote: "Not all schooling is education. Much of it is mere qualification-earning... ritualistic, tedious, suffused with anxiety and boredom, destructive of curiosity and imagination; in short, anti-educational" (Dore 1976: ix). Schools were designed to select the few and promote those selected.

5. Over-production in some areas: But during the 1960s, even this failed. For the result of the expansion of higher education was a massive over-production of graduates. "In India in 1960, 2.5% of the unemployed were in the professional, executive, highly trained technician and managerial category. By 1968, this figure had climbed to 8.5%. In Ceylon, Pakistan and the Philippines, unemployment statistics show the same tendency" (IUACE 1971: 14). People attended higher education institutions for status and social mobility reasons, especially the urbanisation of rural populations; most students expected that higher education would lead to guaranteed employment in the formal or public sectors.

The overproduction of graduates has been seen as a major social problem in many countries (Dore 1976: 4-5). The build-up of disillusioned and discontented 'educated' youth in the towns, rootless and distant from their rural communities, was felt to be a potential powder cask for revolutionary activities, especially at a time when rioting students could be seen setting fire to their own universities. Programmes to foster self-employment, like India's NAESEY (National Association for Educated Self-Employed Youth, a credit scheme for university graduates to establish small businesses) were seen as one way to address this issue.

6. Education inflation: In part, the reason why graduates with their qualifications could not get the jobs they expected was that expectations rose. But at the same time, the jobs simply were not there. And the worse the employment situation became, the stronger became the demand for more education. The result was 'the diploma disease', educational inflation in which

> secondary leavers take jobs which formerly went to primary school leavers, and gradually a secondary certificate becomes necessary for the job. What were once secondary leavers' jobs become graduate jobs and so on. ... In response to the qualifications spiral and because there is nothing else to do, the unemployed primary leavers redouble their efforts to get into secondary schools, the unemployed secondary leavers press on to university, and unemployed graduates flock to masters programs. (Dore 1980: 71)

The value of each level of qualification was felt to have declined, making it necessary for students to gain a higher qualification if they were still to obtain the same job (Berg 1970; Boudon 1974). "As individuals ... attain higher levels of schooling, the value of that education is deflated by rising job requirements. Consequently, people must acquire more schooling simply to attain the same levels of social reward" (LaBelle & Verhine 1975: 166).

7. Imbalance between higher education and primary/basic education: This in turn led to a concentration on higher education to meet the growing demands of the wealthy and influential. "The result has been a near-exponential increase in secondary and tertiary provision" (Dore 1980: 71).

The tension between these levels of education became considerable in many contexts. On the one hand, universal primary education was felt to be essential, to mobilise the population behind the government's development policies. On the other hand, secondary and higher education were seen as the mechanisms for modernisation. Most developing countries, in response to direct local political pressure, spent far more on higher education than on primary levels. This was not just a matter of manpower planning as is often represented (King 1991). Rather, the new elites in countries like India saw this as a way of pushing governments into concentrating resources on the post-primary levels, thereby restricting entry to higher education to those sections of the population who already had access to secondary schooling and who could afford to pay for it. Time and again, for example, the government of India decreed that no more colleges would be established, that more resources would be devoted to rural and/or urban primary schooling; and time after time, such decrees were broken and new colleges were founded at public expense because of local political pressure.

The result of this was that

> primary school enrolments mark time, partly because political demands for the expansion of secondary and tertiary places are more potent than the peasants' demand for primary schools, partly because in too many

societies the primary school has become not the place where one is educated for a useful life but the place where one competes for an exit visa from rural society. Small wonder that so many disadvantaged children of the villages, with little chance of getting into a secondary school, simply drop out. What is the use of school if there is no job at the end of it? (Dore 1980: 71)

There was then a perceived internal contradiction. On the one hand, there was increasing demand for schooling. On the other hand, many among the rural poor were seen to be alienated from an educational system which seemed to offer them so little of relevance. Girls in particular were often denied access to formal education because of fears that it would change their lifeworld for the worse. The gap between the educationally rich and the educationally poor appeared to be growing wider.

Reforming the system

The formal systems of schooling then were often accused of not bringing about the required social change. In fact, they were alleged to be creating the wrong kind of social change, increasing inequalities.

But such criticisms were made precisely because it was believed that the system could be reformed. Education was not irredeemable. Indeed, it had to be, because it was seen as a fundamental part of any modern society, necessary both for socialisation and for bringing about the development changes which the age called for. And if only things could be set right, education would provide the rich harvest which people everywhere hoped for and expected, if not for this generation, at least for the next. Many schemes were launched. In Kenya, aid agencies promoted training for education management. In Uganda, distance education was used for the training of teachers. In India, projects aimed at improving school equipment and staff training were supported. All over the world, governments introduced financial measures such as cost cutting schemes and the redistribution of expenditure, cost sharing with much falling on the local community, restructuring to save resources, and activities designed to generate additional resources for education, such as pupil productivity projects. For such agencies, non-formal education was seen as one part of their strategy to reform the formal system of education, to bring it back to being a useful member of society.

Complaints about Education: Irredeemable Education

But there was a group who came to the conclusion that the problems within education were inherent within the system and process of education itself; that education could not be reformed but needed to be scrapped and another process put in its place. The arguments of this group centred round writers such as Illich and Freire.

Origins and spread of formal education: The UNESCO Faure Report of 1972 provides a summary of many of the arguments. First, the formal system of education is not a natural, universal and inevitable model. It is something which grew up in a specific place (western Europe mainly) at a specific time (relatively late, in fact, during the second half of the nineteenth century) to meet a specific need (to discipline the populace for participation in an industrial society). Such schooling set out to train young persons for a lifetime of controlled work rather than self-determining activities. Transferring the main focus of socialisation from the home to the school was part of the contemporary transition from a home-based to a factory-based economy. It is pointed out that the timing and discipline of schooling were designed to drill children into their future of working in the mills; that many school buildings, with their imposing facades and high windows from which views of the outside world were excluded, were constructed on similar lines to the factories in which the grown-up children were expected to spend the rest of their lives; and that the curriculum grossly neglected or demeaned rural subjects. In short, the formal system of education is not neutral; it is culturally determined but not culturally flexible enough to allow for local adaptations; it replicates one fixed model.

And this singular and idiosyncratic form of schooling has become dominant globally (Altbach & Kelly 1986; Meyer 1992; Serpell 1999). In the West, one compulsory and universal system of schooling replaced other diverse modes of education. And from Europe and North America, it was exported worldwide with enthusiasm. One illustration will suffice: in 1990, the World Bank reported:

> Through the influence of the UN and other international organisations, primary school curricula are remarkably similar world-wide. Regardless of the level of economic or educational development, countries now teach the same subjects and accord them the same relative importance. Approximately 35% of available instructional time is devoted to the acquisition of language skills and 18% of time to mathematics. Science, social studies and the arts are given equal weight, about half that of mathematics and one-fourth that of language. (World Bank 1990: 16)

The influence of globalisation in examinations and especially university programmes led to the export of the Western system and processes of education, divided into primary, secondary and higher, throughout the world. In 1986, one study could report that there is "an astonishing uniformity of school mathematics curricula worldwide ... faced with a standard school mathematics textbook from an unspecified country, even internationally experienced mathematics educators find it almost impossible to say what part of the world it comes from" (Howson & Wilson 1986: 7 cited in Leach & Little 1999: 316). As the Faure Report revealed, "education today throughout the world is built on one very limited approach to education; other approaches are neglected" (Faure et al. 1972: x). "The Third World has been invaded by a mythology that is irrelevant and disastrous to it. The suggestion is that a particular Western culture and a Western type and system of qualification has [sic] been imposed quite inappropriately, at great material and spiritual cost, on alien cultures facing different circumstances" (Barrow 1978: 8-9). The impact of this universalisation of one form of education was seen to be harmful: "The power of Western hegemony rests on the claims of the superiority, universality and ethical neutrality of Western mathematics, positivistic science, technology and education. These claims of Western superiority extend into social, cultural, moral, political and intellectual spheres" (Fasheh 1990: 25 cited in Leach & Little 1999: 322). With its ideology of personal growth, it introduced an element of dislocation in many developing societies (Leach & Little 1999: 114-118, 191, 316-322, 371-372).

To a large extent, this was a result of colonialism. "The spread of schooling was carried out in the context of imperialism and colonialism, in the spread of mercantilism and colonialism – and it cannot ... be separated from that context ... The structure of schooling, since it came from the metropole, was based in large part on the needs of metropole investors, traders and culture" (Carnoy 1974: 15). But this is not the whole picture, for countries which were never fully colonised such as Nepal have adopted it, and equally after Independence, the new rulers of former colonial countries have not sought to replace the Western educational system with more indigenous forms of learning systems but rather to strengthen it, to emulate their former colonial masters in a new form of oppression.

This spread of a single and universalised (i.e. decontextualised) learning system throughout the world saw an often unplanned and unpremeditated onslaught on indigenous learning systems[7] both from without and from within the culture concerned (Faure et al. 1972: 11; Merriam & Caffarella 1999; Amaratunga 1977; Brokenshaw et al. 1980; Colletta & Kidd 1980; Odora 1992; Paul M C 1999). For there *were* alternatives to this universalised schooling. Even in Europe, there were other forms of education – apprenticeship programmes with more or less formal examinations, household tutors, part-time religious schools such as Sunday Schools especially for learning certain skills later in life, and specific learning programmes for selected persons (scribes, doctors, architects, astronomers, priests etc.). In other parts of the world, there were not only informal learning systems of the family and clan and the community (Aikman 1999) but more formal planned learning systems which came under attack. In India, the traditional village education system "was largely discredited" (Acharya 1998 cited in Dyer 2000: 34). In Africa, the staged induction programmes for girls and boys with certain designated 'teachers' leading to various initiation rites largely disappeared, as they were felt to be 'primitive' (Mead 1943; Ocitti 1988, 1994; Coombs 1976: 282-283; Lynch et al. 1997: 103-105).

It is important at this stage that we are clear that we are talking not simply about the informal learning processes which exist in any society, often without agency, but about those planned learning opportunities which each society constructs at different times and in different ways for its people and which it values and seeks to preserve,

---

[7] Indigenous education "is meant to refer to any formalized (i.e. culturally codified, recognized and/or authorized) system of instruction that is not a direct descendant of modern European public schooling" (Wagner 1999: 283).

enhance and pass on to the next generation. It is not always easy to draw a distinction between these two kinds of learning activity, for the one often shades into the other. But in each society there exist indigenous formalised ways of learning. These felt the force of the hegemony of the Western industrialised schooling system and process. In Asia, the role of the guru and wandering scholar fell largely out of practice, and the ashram (both brahmin and buddhist), although it survived, was relegated to a supplementary role. The same was true of the various forms of *maktab* or *madrassa* (Quranic) schools in many Islamic societies (Faure et al. 1972 chapter 1). It is argued today by many groups that the privileging of formal Western models of education above more diverse indigenous learning systems has in some cases meant that the damage to these indigenous systems has gone too far for them ever to be recovered.

Characteristics of the formal education system: Those who made this analysis of the spread of the formal system of education from its base in the West throughout the world sometimes saw in this a hostile invasion, a virus leading to all kinds of social ills (Barrow 1978: 8-9). Lists of the malign characteristics of formal education were drawn up. Freire in the late 1960s (certainly by 1970 when his *Pedagogy of the Oppressed* became more widely available) was one of the most vitriolic. In the formal system of schooling, he wrote,

1. The teacher teaches and the students are taught
2. The teacher knows everything and the students know nothing
3. The teacher thinks and the students are thought about
4. The teacher talks and the students listen – meekly
5. The teacher disciplines and the students are disciplined
6. The teacher chooses and enforces his/her choice, and the students comply
7. The teacher acts and the students have the illusion of acting through the action of the teacher
8. The teacher chooses the programme content, and the students (who were not consulted) adapt to it
9. The teacher confuses the authority of knowledge with her/his own professional authority which s/he sets in opposition to the freedom of the students
10. The teacher is the subject of the learning process, while the pupils are mere objects (Freire 1972: 46-47)

With such a system, there can be no compromise, no measure of reform; it needs to be eradicated and replaced, root and branch. An educational system which is non-formal will be needed to remedy such characteristics.

It is not easy to describe the main elements in the critiques of formal education provided by so many writers (see for example Barrow 1978; Curle 1973; Lister 1975). But we can perhaps summarise much of the argument under three headings (see table overleaf): the process of selecting for failure; the isolation from the real lifeworld of the learners; and the setting of externally controlled goals.

Selection for failure: It was argued that although formal education is compulsory and universal, at the same time it is also terminal and selective, in the sense that there are fixed entry and departure points. The participants are forced to enter the system at a set age and to leave at a point where they are prevented from going any further by examinations or other regulations. It is essentially and inherently competitive and certificated. In other words, in that "the school system itself has different levels to pro-

Box 4

Inherent characteristics of the Formal System of Education as identified by reformers

1. Formal education tends to be for young people only. There has been some opening up at the higher levels but not at the lower levels.
2. Formal education is for ALL young people i.e. universal and compulsory: even those countries who do not provide universal, compulsory education would like to do so.
3. Formal education is normally full-time, not part-time: only at the higher levels is some part-time provision being made.
4. Formal education takes place in special establishments and is separate from life.
5. Formal education is largely based on written materials and assessment techniques rather than oral.
6. Formal education provides one kind of education for all pupils.
7. Formal education has a pre-set curriculum, which is compartmentalised into academic disciplines. The curriculum relates to a limited part of life – it omits some important parts of the lifeworld.
8. Formal education is hierarchical: teacher-pupils.
9. Formal education is individually competitive.
10. Formal education has goals which are pre-set by outsiders before the 'course' begins. These goals relate mostly to the reproduction of existing dominant group values, not to radical social change or to the validation of minority cultures.
11. Formal education is conformist; it aims to make the students conform to agreed social norms.
12. Formal education is oriented to the future – on a learn-now-and-practise-later model.
13. Formal education is selective at each stage: only some people can continue to study.
14. Formal education tends to be terminal. It says to different groups at different stages that they have 'completed' their education. The certificates awarded often reinforce this, with society recognising the judgements which the certificates imply.
15. Formal education is a self-assessing system. Judgements about the quality of educational institutions are made by the educational system itself. Formal education is controlled by professionals, not by the community.

duce workers for different levels within the occupational structure" (Youngman 2000: 34), it is designed through its certification systems to create a certain number of failures, to 'strain' the pupils and to allow an approved group through to the next stage. The formal system "channels [students] through the system with increasingly diverse – but limited – options; ... teachers and administrators authorise students to move from one level of the system to the next" (Moulton 2000: 4).

"The mood has swung from the almost euphoric conception of education as the Great Equalizer to that of education as the Great Sieve that sorts and certifies people for their slot in society" (Husen cited in Simmons 1980: 8), a "mechanism for social selection and allocation of roles in adult life" (Haralambos 1985 cited in Youngman 2000: 154). The process is largely class-based and therefore it not only reinforces the existing social structure, it exaggerates it and increases inequalities (Jencks et al. 1973: 72; Inkeles & Holsinger 1974: 66). Such writers claim that the successful succeed; the failures fail ever further. "Most educational investment enhances the power of those who already have social and economic advantages far more than it enhances the power or position of those who have not" (Simmons 1980: 8).

Bowles and Gintis were major contributors to this debate. They suggested that (USA) schools reproduced the world of work with its hierarchies, and that pupils learned the social relations and "forms of consciousness" appropriate to their future station in life. Modifications ('reforms') to the educational system were "dictated in the interests of a more harmonious reproduction" of working relationships and practices, and were intended to help pupils adapt to changes in the modes of industrial production (Bowles & Gintis 1976: 132-133).[8] In this sense, schooling ("establishment education") cannot change society: as Illich put it, "neither individual learning nor social equality can be enhanced by the ritual of schooling" (Illich 1973: 43).

Formal education was seen to be short term in the sense that it has to be completed within a specified time. In the classic formal education system, life is divided into two phases, the first phase (childhood) being one of full-time education and no work, the second phase (working adulthood) being one of work and no or little education (a 'third age' of retirement, one of no work and relatively little education, has been added more recently). Although this construction was even then being challenged by the concepts and increasing practice of lifelong education, the formal system of school and colleges seemed to operate on the basis that the students need to learn some subject or other now 'because it cannot be learned later'.

And therefore it is largely knowledge-based rather than skills or attitudes-based. "Educational thinking is still dominated by the notion that a citizen should get a fixed amount of knowledge in youth and live out the rest of his/her life career with this stock of knowledge plus the 'experience' which life imparts" (IUACE 1971: 38). Freire referred to this as a 'banking system': it fills the young with the learning which they will later use throughout their lives, as a bank account is filled up and later spent

---

[8] They would no doubt today argue that the current changes in the schools reflect contemporary changes in working practices introduced through the increasing use of ICT in the workplace.

(Freire 1972). Others have called this 'learning for certainty' – that is, the students are learning for a long working future in a static society rather than 'learning for uncertainty', for a changing and unknown future (King 1979).

Isolated from the lifeworld: A further accusation is that schooling takes the students out of their lifeworlds into special institutions; it creates a special lifeworld for the learners. In formal education, "learning is rigidly organized within a limited timespan and circumscribed space" (Radcliffe & Colletta 1985: 3537). It uses 'sole use' buildings, separate from the community. It is "education within the campus for chosen scholars" (IUACE 1971: 136). In such centres, young people are trained within an unreal world for a future existence within the 'real world'. And much of the ethos of this unreal world is urban: as several have pointed out, such schooling cannot meet the needs of the poor, especially the rural poor (Bock & Papagiannis 1976: 11).

This is because the curriculum of the formal schools has been constructed by educationalists and relates to academic disciplines, not to the 'messy problems' which life presents. It is highly compartmentalised: thus the pupils study things which are not of real life, history separate from geography separate from biology etc.. It therefore appears to be irrelevant, even if it is not. It is universal in the sense that all students follow the same curriculum.

Pre-set goals: And finally, the goals of the formal system of education have been set by 'outsiders', usually educationalists but sometimes politicians, rather than by the participants (teachers and students and parents). And the goals are (in Freire's term) 'domesticating' rather than 'liberating'. Education seeks to socialise the young, to fit them into their allotted slot in society for all time. There were those who suggested that schools inherently "get in the way of the healthy intellectual and spiritual development of the individual" (Dore 1976: 132).

Many of these inherent characteristics of the formal education system, as set out in the criticisms of the 1960s and the 1970s, have of course been recognised. Steps have been taken to ameliorate some of them, for example, by creating a more flexible and problem-based curriculum or by opening up opportunities to adults to participate in formal education at different stages in their lives. But the key issues remain – formal education, with its emphasis on certificates, creates many failures; it is largely knowledge-based for future use rather than based on experience and aimed at the immediate application of new knowledge and skills. It creates a special and to a large extent artificial lifeworld. Indeed, it was suggested, schooling creates children; it constructs childhood in the sense that schools set out how children ought to behave in society. Schools stratify and domesticate their pupils. Such schools, through their discipline and their pre-set goals to which the students are expected to conform, deny humanity, degrade their students, distort learning, increase inequality, reproduce current hierarchies and educate to increase consumption (Dore 1976: 132-133). They also impersonalise knowledge and skills, privileging some forms of knowing above others. The academic is the basis of the learning programme, not life experiences. Schools perpetuate forms of power in society.

Such a system with its inherent and inalienable characteristics cannot be re-formed: "The mere existence of schools disadvantages and disables the poor ... because they make us believe that they [the schools] are the proper and only channel for genuine learning" (Illich 1973: 89). "The school system must not be replaced by another dominant system..." (Reimer 1971: 89; see Postman & Weingartner 1971). There can be no compromise: something new is needed. Whereas the redeemable criticisms of formal education were framed in deficit terms to be remedied by inputs, these criticisms were framed in terms of disadvantage and dichotomy, needing radical change of systems.

An Alternative Education?

Those who criticised formal education were stronger on the criticisms than on the remedies. But alternative models were available. Different kinds of educational processes had been proposed by earlier writers such as Dewey and others. This trend received strength from the humanistic sciences, especially psychology and psycho-therapy. Throughout the late 1960s and into the 1970s, a polarity in relation to education emerged and battled it out. They can be seen in a number of humanistic educators such as Cy Houle, Malcolm Knowles and Carl Rogers. Houle wrote as early as 1963: "Education either functions as an instrument that is used to facilitate the younger generation into the logic of the present system, or it becomes the practice of freedom, the means by which women and men deal critically and actively with reality and discover how to participate in the transformation of their world". Instead of what he called the traditional pattern of schooling, Carl Rogers proposed in his paradigm of experiential learning a humanistic approach with voluntary learning based on the concerns and experiences of the learners, respect for learners as separate unique individuals, learning responsibility shared with all members of learning group, critical reflection on knowledge, beliefs, values and behaviours of society, self-directed learning , and the cyclic interaction of learning and action:

Table 3.1

Significant experiential learning	Traditional conventional learning
• personal involvement	• prescribed curriculum
• whole person	• similar for all students
• self-initiated	• lecturing
• pervasive	• standardised testing
• evaluated by learner	• instructor-evaluated
• essence is meaning	• essence is knowing and reproducing

Source: C R Rogers 1983

Knowles (1970) distinguished between schooling and self-directed learning. Dore too (1976) indicated two kinds of schooling, one aimed at qualifications, the other at "appropriate learning". In the former, knowledge is sought to pass an examination, not to be used. The process of schooling is done once and for all time, not continuously; and the aim is to reproduce what is learned. This is learning to *get* a job. External standards are employed to assess the achievement of the goals, and motivation of both teachers and learners relies on threats and worries since both relate in much the same way to external examiners. In the latter kind of programme, learning is sought for its own sake, for enjoyment and utility. It is undertaken to increase self-respect, not to obtain recognition from an external assessor; professional standards and belief systems have been internalised and form the basis for self-assessment. This is learning in order to *do* a job, not simply to get a job. The relationship of teacher and student is one of mutual respect.

Dore went on to argue that the need to qualify kills the desire to learn, because of anxiety, especially uncertainty about what the examiner wants, the pressure of time to cover a syllabus and other factors. This destruction of education gradually passes down the educational system. And it extends beyond school: the need to qualify with its fear of failing kills the attitudes needed to do a good job – imagination, creativity, honesty, curiosity, experimentation, the valuing of the views and experience of others, the determination to get to the bottom of something, the desire to do a good job for itself.

This debate continues – between the 'exchange value' and the 'use value' of education. Barr and Tagg (1995) draw a distinction between educational institutions which "exist to provide instruction" and those which "exist to produce learning", between the Instructional Paradigm and the Learning Paradigm, with their different purposes, criteria for success, structures, learning theory, funding and roles, similar to those of many writers on non-formal education. The Delors Report distinguishes between knowledge-dominated learning and competence-developing learning (Delors et al. 1996). Rydstrom, in a study of Swedish adult education, writes that when the various popular movements in that country such as the labour movement, the temperance movement, the churches, the co-operative movement etc., wanted to help their members gain an education to which they had not had access earlier,

> they found that ... [their members] needed knowledge of a kind that the formal school system of the times could not provide. The lower compulsory levels were elementary indeed; the higher levels academic and Latin-oriented; and the university world was hostile to the very concept of popular education....The popular movements wanted to build their own educational tradition, to shape a new kind of culture, participatory and democratic. (Rydstrom 1995: 127)

Several of those who constructed education in this vein set out the differences in parallel terms. One example can stand for all:

Table 3.2

Traditional education *emphasises*:	Alternative learning *values:*
• programmes	• excitement and love of learning
• memorisation and repetition	• holistic learning (ethical, intellectual,
• linear and concrete intellectual	physical)
development	• diversity and personal esteem
• conformity to models set by teacher	• co-operative/collaborative efforts
• individual/competitive efforts	• creativity and intuition process
• static and rigid processes, rationalist	learning, problem-centred
content learning	• teachers as learning facilitators
• teachers as information providers	• interdisciplinary learning
• compartmentalised learning	• cultural differences and
• cultural uniformity	commonalities
• isolated teaching environments	• life-based environments
• separation from community	• community partnerships

Adapted from *Lifelong Learning Comment* 1 1985

This was the picture when the non-formal education concept burst on the scene. Stark contrasts were drawn between the increasingly universalised formal system of schooling and more local forms of learning which were felt to be person-centred rather than system-centred. Many different strands came together at the same time to challenge the existing paradigm of schooling as it spread around the globe. At the heart of these lies the distinction between whether the student-learners are passive recipients of knowledge, skills and attitudes which are imparted to them through the medium of the school and the agency of the teacher and reproduced on demand, or whether the student-learners are active in creating uniquely constructed knowledge based on experience (see p.61 below).

Two characteristics of this period stand out as important for our discussion of educational reform. The first was that the debate was **confrontational**. Reform was not seen to be evolutionary but revolutionary; it was not incremental but a scrapping of what existed and its replacement by something new. Dichotomy was the name of the game. Secondly, there was a strongly **romantic** element in what the reformers believed in. It was largely liberal and humanistic, even that which was based on Marxism and class-consciousness, but it was also largely rhetorical. These writers believed that it was possible to build an ideal world; and if the educational system stood in the way, then the system should be swept away and replaced either with another system or with no system at all – with freedom (Taylor 1993: 32-33).

It will also be worth putting this debate into its political setting. This was the age of the Vietnam War and its oppositional groups, of the extreme bitterness and the patent injustices of the hysterical paranoia of the West against all forms of socialism at the height of the Cold War. This was the age of the civil rights movements, the age when youth rebelled finally against the wisdom of their elders and seniors, when utopia seemed achievable. Many people were repelled from the certainties of the dominant groups in the West rather than attracted by the certainties of revolutionary movements. It has been suggested that Freire himself was influenced more by repulsion at the injustice of Western culture and educational presuppositions than by a belief in the justice of the proposed alternatives (Coben 1998; P Mayo 1999).

Education as problem and saviour: The 1960s and early 1970s thus saw a period of extreme discontent with the nature and outcomes of the formal system of education in both the industrialised world and less developed countries – a 'world crisis' in education. The complaints of students and parents began to be taken seriously by educational planners and policy-makers. Thus it was that, although education (at least in the sense of formal schooling) was seen to be one of the tools by which dominant interests imposed their value systems on the population at large (Gramsci's works on hegemony were beginning to influence Western thought, although they had been written in the 1920s and early 1930s), a reformed *education* was also seen to be the potential saviour.

It is thus not surprising that most of this discussion took place firmly *within* one or other educational discourse, not from outside. Most of it was led by educationalists with a few politicians. They took for granted that some kind of 'education' was necessary, a good thing. It was not education that was at fault; it was schooling which needed to be replaced because it was anti-educational. If education was part of the problem, it was also part of the solution. What was needed was to make it more effective as well as more efficient. The issues related to structures, to processes, to curriculum and evaluation methods, to staffing. Even Illich found it hard to find a discourse outside of education in which to discuss education. The same categories were used, the same goals were analysed, the same language was employed in much the same way – but to different ends. And part of what was at issue was how governments, especially in developing society contexts, could deal with the increasingly vocal critics of their educational systems.

The purpose of education

The 1960s and 1970s discontent with the formal education system thus aroused intense interest in the purpose of education (seen as socially approved planned learning opportunities, whether for children, adolescents or adults). For what was at issue was a political matter. On the one hand, education was seen to be a tool used by the government and elites either to maintain the power and dominance of the elites over subaltern groups and interests (particularly by defining what is useful knowledge) or to control the pace and direction of change (development). On the other hand, education could be used by radical movements to challenge the dominant culture groups.

There were several different voices in this debate. Much of the critique of formal education came from academic educationalists and planners. But there were other critiques of formal education which were not so unfavourable. For there are other stakeholders in the formal system of education, of whom four groups may be seen to be particularly important – governments, users (parents-pupils), practitioners (teachers as well as educationalists) and employers. Each of these seem to have held differing views of formal education.

a) For government servants and politicians, because formal education is provided, subsidised or legitimated by **governments**, it is thought to serve governmental goals rather than the goals of the participants or other interests. It is therefore subject to political interference and control. Its aim is to reproduce the existing social and cultural systems and induct its subjects into the common or the dominant culture. At the same time another goal of education was to help to bring about controlled change, to achieve national goals for (economic) development and the creation of a trained workforce. It could be used for social engineering, for social control or to help the population to cope with change.

b) **Popular attitudes** (mainly those of parents and students) to education to a large extent internalised the dominant group values – but not entirely. Because education (especially in developing societies) was often thought of as a tool of modernisation, in that sense, it was seen to be an external intrusion into the existing pattern of life. Perceptions of education, the images which it conjured up, cultural attitudes to schooling and expectations of the benefits which education would bring (mainly a better job leading to an improved quality of life) all created the willingness or otherwise to participate. Motivations seem to have been for the social and economic mobility of the family rather than national developmental goals. For them, education is a human right, an opportunity to join in the processes by which some people are selected for various positions and the benefits that go with them. Education thus is one of the weapons to participate in the existing social conflicts in society successfully. These stakeholders stressed the performance rather than the structural failures of the formal education system.

c) **Employers** had a much clearer approach to the value and purposes of education. It was to meet their manpower needs, to supply them with a trained and disciplined workforce. The failure of existing schooling to achieve this goal and the inability of educational systems to move quickly enough to meet changing work requirements were constant issues with employers.

d) **Practitioners** on the other hand found themselves facing in an acute way a number of tensions, some of which are inherent in education, others of which arose from the expressed interests of the different stakeholder groups. In particular, some of these sprang from the goals which educators set for education, such as the personal growth of their pupils. For the different approaches to education which each set of stakeholders advocated created problems of reconciliation and judgements. All of these goals were contested.[9] We cannot set out all of the tensions here, but they circled

---

[9] Youngman sees these tensions in class terms: that the capitalist class seeks to use education for the maintenance of the status quo and the subordinated classes and groups seek to use it to

around the following issues:

- *whether the goal of education is intended for the growth and development of society or for the growth and development of the individual.* Some see this as a more Westernised approach, with its stress on the individual (Macfarlane 1978). Many eastern cultures appear to have less polarity between the individual and the collective than in European-derived cultures (Cooke & Kothari 2001: 96; citing Hofstede 1991 & Trompenaars 1993.)[10] But posed in an extreme form, the issue is whether education aims at helping a relatively small number of individuals to escape from the slums or whether it is intended to help the community of the slum dwellers to change the slums. These aims would seem to be mutually exclusive.
- *whether the objective of education is the promotion of conformity, the socialisation of the individual into the acceptable norms of behaviour and thinking, or the encouragement of uniqueness and self-expression.* We note here Freire's critique of education as not being neutral, as being aimed at *either* 'domestication' *or* 'liberation'.
- *whether the aim of education is the reproduction of the status quo, in the search for stability and communal harmony in a rapidly changing society, or whether the aim is the transformation of society* – and if so, towards what kind of society; whether education should promote or restrain the forces for change in society. This was the age of what proved to be the indecisive exploration of the relationship between education and (national) development and nation-building (Fagerlind & Saha 1983; Green 1990; Lowe et al. 1971).

There were of course other polarities expressed. But these are some of the most important which will lay down important criteria for our assessment of the non-formal education debate. And of course there was no consensus on them – despite the fact that some common trends can be seen.

OTHER PRESSURES FOR CHANGE

Before looking at the efforts made to reform the educational systems in developing countries in response to the criticisms being made of it, it will be useful to look briefly at some of the other pressures for change which were being felt. For NFE emerged as one of the leading educational concepts at a time when other pressures were being felt. Education is not and cannot be isolated from its social context; and as society changes, so education will change.

---

challenge the status quo and to achieve greater equality of opportunity in (and presumably through) education (Youngman 2000: 35-36). But the class discourses seem no longer to fit contemporary societies (Laclau & Mouffe 1990).

[10] This polarity is being challenged in some forthcoming work.

Among the most important of these factors were the following:

Globalisation: Probably the greatest pressure for change was the growth of international capital and all that that brought with it, including the commodification of knowledge and the globalisation of education. One result of this was the increase of interest in comparative education, and with it a belief that educational systems in developing countries were failing to meet internationally established standards.

This tendency was never of course uncontested. Indeed its very success provoked new awareness of local issues, including the needs and demands of indigenous populations. Non-formal education emerged during a major outbreak of global awareness. Indeed, its greatest advocate, Coombs, entitled the book within which he set out the terms of the future debate *The World Educational Crisis*, taking a deliberately international perspective.

Changing understandings of education and learning: At the same time, two very influential changes occurred in the field of learning:

a) *the constructivist approach to knowledge:* There was an increasing feeling that an educational system built on a view of knowledge as transferable rather than individually created would not only be ineffective but in fact would create problems. Md Anisur Rahman has summarised this well:

> Knowledge cannot be transferred; it can be memorised for mechanical application, but learning is always an act of self-search and discovery. In this search and discovery, one may be stimulated and assisted but one cannot be 'taught'... Institutions of teaching and training which seek to transfer knowledge and skills serve mainly to disorient the capacity that is in every healthy individual to search and discover knowledge creatively. It indoctrinates them, furthermore, in the value of hierarchy which they then tend to pursue with a vengeance, the humiliation of being subordinated is passed on to their subordinates. (Rahman 1993: 222)

The constructivist approach to knowledge, building on the work of educationalists such as Dewey and Kelly, was spreading strongly at this time, and learning- and learner-centred education was challenging the traditional approach to a formal education system founded on assumptions about the transfer of knowledge and its reproduction in examinations.

b) *an increasing emphasis on continuing/lifelong learning and lifelong education:* There was also at this time a reconsideration of learning contexts. It was appreciated that learning (however defined) continued for all persons throughout the whole of their lives. And the provision of continuing learning opportunities, lifelong education, was a feature of contemporary thinking at the time. It had not yet achieved the dominance it was to achieve later; it had not yet been co-opted by the modern state and the global capitalist systems which called upon it to supply an ever-changing work force to meet their needs. But it was becoming clearer that school was not the only learning opportunity which people would have. The privileged position which formal schooling occupied was to some extent being challenged by these new approaches.

Human rights and democracy: A further change was in the field of human rights and the demand for democracy. Just as economic changes altered the perceptions of the need for learning and re-learning, so too the radicalism of many groups created an increasing concern about the inequalities of educational opportunities, both in industrialised societies and in developing countries. There seem to have been substantial changes in value systems at this time, increasing emphasis on inclusion and on democratic processes. Human rights belonged to everyone, not to elites; and this meant that competences should be more evenly distributed. The demands of modern society called for universal individual competences (for example universal literacy skills) rather than an elitist approach by which competences fell to the few. Gender issues were foremost, of course, but so were national liberation movements and concern over other kinds of 'exclusion', especially disabilities, racial and colour discrimination, sexual and religious oppression. The formal system of education was seen by some as a major factor in maintaining privilege, increasing inequalities, and in creating, preserving and disseminating dominant attitudes and patterns of behaviour. It needed to be changed.

The voluntary movement: Closely associated with this was the growth everywhere of self-help groups – and these required learning opportunities to help them with their self-appointed missions, opportunities which the formal system of education could not provide. While the concept of 'civil society' had not yet spread widely, the strength of what would later be called 'civil society' groupings and 'new social movement' was rapidly increasing.

THE REFORM CYCLE

The demand for educational reform, then, at this time was very substantial. It applied to education/schooling in both Western and developing societies. It was not just "the cultural arrogance of Western experts" (Fry & Thurber 1989). It was supported by several different strands, leading to different agendas. This was why, when non-formal education came to be adopted by many as the answer, it took different forms.

But NFE was only one answer to the problems of formal education. Various proposals were made to overcome the identified failures of the formal education system in developing societies throughout the 1960s and 1970s, and a brief summary of these will help to locate NFE firmly within its context.

Table 3.3

A report on education in Sub-Saharan Africa in 1984 suggested the following reforms were needed:

- improving the coverage and relevancy of basic education
- increasing resources
- improving organisation
- changing the curriculum
- increasing access, especially of girls and women
- improving the quality and effectiveness of primary education
- making primary education a major component
- extending technical and vocational education
- developing African universities
- improving management in education

Source: ODA 1984: 34-51

The responses to the various diagnoses of the ills of formal education seem to have taken something of a cyclic form. Each successive reform provoked a response rejecting the solution proposed and thus leading to a further suggested remedy. This can be set out in a diagram as in Figure 1 overleaf. It is important to note that this is not entirely a chronological cycle, for many educational reformers went through phases of this cycle at different times. It is also important to recognise that each element in the reform cycle has political implications, each springs from and is interpreted differently within a particular local context.

To summarise a wide field very briefly, we can elaborate upon the following elements in this reform cycle.

1. First, there was a move to **expand the system** to reach the unreached, to become more equitable, to concentrate on mass education (universal primary education) rather than on the more elitist higher or advanced education. Crash courses for teachers; the use of untrained and assistant teachers and student monitors; the building of new schools and some new colleges; double shifts in some schools; the encouragement of private and self-help education, as in Egypt, India and the Philippines; increases in class sizes – these and many other strategies were employed in this process (Blaug 1973; Dore 1976: 4, 99ff).

Fig. 1 The Reform Cycle

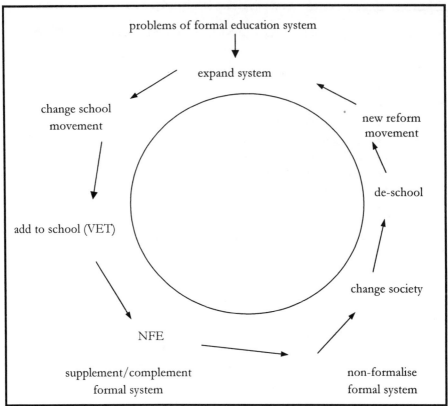

But this became no solution to the problem of quality. Indeed, by simply expanding the problems of primary education, it seemed to make matters worse. It raised in an acute form the unresolved dilemma as to whether universal primary education was a complete programme in itself or whether it was simply the first step on the ladder. What was the aim of primary education? "More of the same quality ... of schooling is unlikely to meet national objectives for social mobility and equality, nor the manpower development required for growth" (Simmons 1980: 8).

2. Attention then switched to **changing schooling** – improving quality in terms of goals (to clarify its relationship with national development, to enable education to lead to social transformation rather than simply personal transformation), curriculum (to make it more relevant), costs (cost cutting, cost sharing, resource raising etc.) and systems changes (for example, the abolition of selection, management strengthening), even examination reforms. It was argued that there should be less emphasis on cognitive elements in education; instead, schools should concentrate on developing mental abilities and competencies and on changing attitudes, both in terms of social perceptions and self perceptions. Two examples of these kinds of changes have been pointed out (Dore 1976). In Tanzania, Nyerere sought in his Education for Self-

Reliance to make the primary school a complete experience, down-grading examinations, using mother tongue instruction and learning through production activities. Cuba on the other hand, along with an expansion of primary education, "strictly limited the number of students who get more than ten years of schooling to those for whom jobs requiring higher education are available... The Cubans moved most secondary education to five-day boarding schools in the countryside, to both facilitate the concentration of students on their studies and teach the importance of agriculture and manual labor" (Simmons 1980: 4-5).

But such changes, while they sought to cure some of the multiple problems, could not deal with them all. They did not, for example, alter the fact that many people saw in formal education a way into the formal economic sector or a way of modernising society. Even in Tanzania, the new education did not meet rural needs or the aspirations of the majority population at a time when integrated rural development was the current area of developmental concern. The formal system, even when reformed, was not enough for the 'new development' paradigm.

3. To cope with this, **vocational education and training** (VET) became a focal point for reforming the educational systems in many developing countries. Some countries concentrated on adding a separate VET sector alongside the formal system; others concentrated on introducing relevant VET into the formal school curriculum (Twining 1987; Lauglo 2003). Transition from school to work became one area of developing new strategies for formal education.

But it proved very difficult to adjust VET to meet the formal school system; in particular, there was resistance to incorporating VET within the formal school curriculum. Thus it was that the reformers turned to those various kinds of education and training that were going on *outside of the system.*

4. It was at this stage that reformers created the concept of **non-formal education** ("organized educational activities that occur outside the school") to supplement or complement or even to provide an alternative to the formal education system (Dore 1976: 104-105). NFE was aggressively taken up by Western planners especially USAID and the World Bank, FAO, ILO and other international agencies. One strand saw NFE as being created alongside the formal system, both to meet the populations which had not yet been effectively reached and to supply forms of education and training which the formal system could not supply. Another saw it as a different kind of education targeted at different populations.

But the move to NFE led to disillusion. NFE did not meet the demands of the parents, nor the felt needs of rural communities. It was seen by many employers, parents and students to be second class education, inferior to the formal system (Dore 1976: 101), although its intrinsic values were heralded and feted. "An education that has readily identifiable characteristics akin to those of the formal school system, and also has official recognition by the government, will generally be perceived as being of value. The poor almost never willingly choose non-formal alternatives. It is simply that they do not have a choice and must either access such alternatives or go without education" (Wright 2001: 6-7).

5. So that some began to argue that they should try to de-formalise (Simkins 1977) or **non-formalise the formal system** of education (Dore 1976: 106). Postman and Weingarten suggested 'the de-schooling of schools' rather than the de-schooling of society – getting rid of subjects and developing a new curriculum and methodologies (Barrow 1978: 7).

But those who most used the formal system did not wish it to change; it served their purposes well. The demand for formal education/schooling continued to grow. Public attitudes thus became a major barrier to educational reform.

6. It was therefore necessary to **change public attitudes and ambitions in relation to education** as a whole. It was suggested that formal education failed only because society failed to realise the true role of education and therefore expected too much from it. In other words, society (the public) invited its failure (Barrow 1978). Social concepts needed to be altered (for example, in terms of the ambitions people set through education). 'People' should come to see that the main purpose of education was not to help students to qualify to get a job but to develop the skills and attitudes which would help them to do the job. Ronald Dore's study of the 'diploma disease' fits into the cycle at this point. Change would not be brought about by attacking the education system alone but by changing people's understandings and expectations of education (Dore 1976: 103).

But it was found that it was education itself which helped to form people's attitudes towards education. The most vociferous were the educated. Education itself therefore came to be seen as the problem rather than the people. Instead of 'blaming the victim', schooling was now identified as one of the strongest barriers to change.

7. Therefore it was proposed that **education** itself in its current form **should be abolished.** Schooling denies individual liberty and increases inequality, was the cry. Compulsory attendance distorts the learning process. Schools inculcate the worst aspects of modern society; by mixing learning and selection, they encourage inappropriate attitudes towards work and society such as competitiveness. They make people less useful, not more useful. They kill the natural curiosity which is in every individual. They are too costly for a very poor society to bear.

Despite common misunderstandings, it was never proposed that all education should be eradicated from modern societies, only that more appropriate forms of education should be developed. It was 'schooling' which the de-schoolers found unacceptable, not education. The new education would encourage students to learn from 'learning networks' in society, from work and from peer groups. The policy of governments should be to build up the learning resources in the community at large rather than confine them to schools and colleges, to help to create new kinds of educational administrators, counsellors and gurus. Illich, Reimer and others wrote in this strain.

But the conclusions of Illich and his contemporaries proved to be unacceptable to most people, impractical and unrealistic. They denied the poor their human right to the same education as the elites had. As Husen put it (1974: 4), "the task of reforming education to meet the needs of a changing society required a critical review of the institutionalized nature of schools without moving to the excess of 'de-schooling'". What was needed was a twin-track reform of schooling – to widen it and to improve its quality.

8. And so we come **back to the start**, an international Education for All (EFA) policy seeking in a wider concept of Universal Basic Education (UBE) instead of UPE to expand and at the same time reform a system which most people recognise has many major problems but which all societies need in some form or other. Thus in 1995, for example, a World Bank review paper suggested six key reforms,

- a higher public priority for education (not only increased resources for it but more care and concern for its effectiveness)
- attention to outcomes, in terms of its capacity to help its participants to find employment and of its learning outcomes
- public investment focused on basic education rather than higher education; participants in higher education should contribute more to it than those in basic education
- attention to equity for all disadvantaged groups such as girls in many societies, special populations, non-dominant language groups and others such as nomads, street children and refugees.
- involvement of households in educational management as well as cost sharing
- and the development of greater autonomy for educational institutions: "educational quality can increase when schools are able to use instructional inputs according to local school and community conditions and when they are accountable to parents and communities" (World Bank 1995).

Almost all of these were being proposed during the 1960s and 1970s, during the first 'world educational crisis' (Coombs 1968).

CONCLUSION: Where did non-formal education come from?

Non-formal education seems to me to emerge at a point within the educational reform cycle when an alternative to formal education was being sought, either by changing formal schooling or abolishing schooling. Formal education with its urban and formal economic sector bias could not meet the needs of the new mass target groups for development interventions. NFE was needed to help with this task.

But this was also the period when the disadvantage frame of reference and the discourses in which it was expressed were coming to the forefront of the international stage. NFE seemed to these reformers to be an ideal tool for their attack on privilege, a way in which the inequalities which schooling fostered could be redressed. NFE came to be acknowledged and blazoned forth as one of the key answers to the dilemmas not only of education but of social and economic development.

NFE thus grew up at a time

- when the climate was moving from a deficit set of discourses to discourses based on a paradigm of disadvantage, when dichotomies reigned, when certainty was coming to mean choosing between one of two alternatives.
- when development was coming to mean helping the masses (especially rural masses) to overcome their poverty rather than industrialisation and modernisation
- when education was in a state of discontent and different reform agendas were being proposed. NFE would need to fight its corner if it were to survive in this contest.

A sense of crisis is the key to the emergence of NFE – a crisis within education as a whole. Philip Coombs' book *The World Educational Crisis: a systems approach*, published in 1968 which first set out NFE as one of the key elements in an attack on the ill-health of the formal system of education, was simply the tip of the iceberg – highly visible and influential but based on a huge under-pinning of criticism. In that context, NFE was seen by many as the saviour of formal education. The whole debate about NFE took place within a context of formal education: it was from this that it took its nature and definitions. But since the problems with formal education were constructed by the various partners in the debate in different ways, the roles assigned to NFE also varied. We need to see NFE within the context of a wide-ranging attack on and calls for the reform of education, for it was this scenario of contest that formed the frame of reference and the discourses in which NFE was debated.

Part II

The Great Debate

We do not even have enough agreement to be able to arrive at a common mind about what it is we should be quarrelling about. (MacIntyre 1987)

As with development, we can examine the debate around the concept and practice of non-formal education in terms of discourses. These discourses not only create the categories by which to identify those educational activities which are to be called non-formal, the programmes which are to be included and those which are to be excluded. They also determine the kinds of educational programmes provided and the way those programmes are constructed and supported.

There are several family members in the discourse of non-formal education; the discourse was a site of contestation. Those who saw in NFE the answer to education's main problems were not united in either their definition of NFE or their approach to the programmes which followed. In this section, I divide up the debate about NFE into four major components:

a) the *Advocates* who saw NFE as all education outside the formal system (extra-formal)

b) the *Ideologues* who saw NFE as inherently opposed to formal education (anti-formal)

c) the *Empiricists* who looked at NFE in the field and claimed it was much the same as formal education (para-formal)

d) the *Pragmatists* who saw the possibility of non-formal elements within a formal educational situation (intra-formal).

The section then looks at the decline of the debate, and ends with a discussion of some of the key issues raised by the debate.

4

The Advocates:
Constructing Non-Formal Education

By their nature, words are imprecise and layered with meanings –
the signs of things, not the things themselves. (Gore Vidal: Kalki)

THE PREHISTORY OF NFE

The main discussions on nonformal education commenced about 1968. But the idea of NFE as contrasted with formal education was not entirely new at that time. The term had been used in a few earlier writings but without a systematic context of debate. In the late 1950s, the distinction seems to have been understood; Clark and Sloan (1958) referred to "the nonformal educational enterprise", arguing that it represented "a third force" rivalling the two forces of schools and colleges. Chauncey (1962) and Weidner (1962) also seem to be familiar with the concept of non-formal education. Miles (1964: 30-33) contrasted 'formal educational systems' with 'nonformal educational systems'; the formal included "a wide range of schools and colleges", public and private, as well as other educational institutions at 'higher' and 'lower' level. Formal education was seen as being hierarchical. Non-formal systems include "educational programs of all sorts carried out by industrial organizations" and programmes run by government agencies such as the military and Departments of Agriculture, as well as commercial and voluntary bodies and "youth-serving organizations". Like Clark and Sloan, Miles appears to distinguish between three separate "educational sub-systems, school, college or non-formal". And he also made the link between such concepts and developing societies with his reference to USAID Peace Corps programmes, both in the USA and overseas.

Such references leave it uncertain as to whether the discussants saw NFE as a system or as an educational process. Nor is it clear whether the adjective 'nonformal' was intended to qualify 'system' or 'education'. Were Miles and others speaking of a 'nonformal' system and a 'formal' system, two alternative *systems* delivering the same kind of education? Or were they talking of two different *kinds of education*, 'formal education' and 'nonformal education', each of which was delivered by a separate system? It is not clear that any distinction was being drawn between the delivery system and the kind of education being delivered. What is clear is that the contrast between formal and nonformal in education was laid out earlier than the late 1960s.

But the main debate on NFE took place within the context of a discussion of aid agencies concerning the difficulties of providing formal education in developing countries. The first use of the term 'Nonformal Education' in the same sense as in the great debate was in a report in 1967 dealing with educational planning and systems (King 1967); it contains an introduction by Philip Coombs who, as Director of IIEP, had commissioned the study.

Perhaps Coombs influenced the wording of the report, for it was Coombs who launched the debate a year later. His seminal work on education in developing societies, *The World Educational Crisis*, included a chapter entitled 'Nonformal education: to catch up, keep up and get ahead' (Coombs 1968: 138-144). This set the scene and laid out the issues facing educational expansion and reform in developing societies in the late 1960s in the light of the criticisms which we have already seen.

Nonformal educational activities

It was recognised by some of the participants to the debate that nonformal education itself (however defined) did not begin in 1968. "Although the term nonformal education is rather new, the activities to which it refers are not" (LaBelle 1976a: 278). What was new was "the discovery" (LaBelle 1982: 160) or "the recent rediscovery of nonformal education by development planners" (Radcliffe & Colletta 1985: 3537). "The term 'nonformal education' did not describe a new phenomenon when it arose. It rather gave an appropriate name to a concept that had been used by various practitioners in the field of development aid years before" (Hausmann 1995: 12-13). As Bock and Papagiannis also saw (1983), it was "a change of viewpoint of educators, politicians and academics" rather than a change in practice (LaBelle & Ward 1994: 4142). The debate gave a label to a set of educational practices and events which had been going on for many years, even centuries, before 1968 (LaBelle 2000: 22-24).

There was a tendency however to write the new discourse of NFE back into history (e.g. Loveridge 1978). Gallart (1989: 19), looking back on education in Argentina in the 1940s, wrote, "Many new varieties of nonformal education have appeared on the scene in developing countries over the past 25-50 years", i.e. well before the term 'nonformal education' was adopted (see Coombs 1976: 283). Wilson (1997: 87-88) spoke of Indonesia being the first to create a Directorate of NFE in the Ministry of Education and Culture in 1949, well before the term had come into use (it was in fact a Directorate of *Community* Education, which is a different discourse). LaBelle referred to NFE programmes in Latin America from the 1920s to the 1970s (LaBelle 2000: 22-24). By whatever definition is used, there had been in every country over many decades programmes of education which displayed the characteristics later defined as 'non-formal', although they were not of course described as 'nonformal' in their own time.

Nevertheless, several writers thought that the concept of NFE was taken up by educational planners among the donor agencies and in some of the Ministries of Education in developing countries so as to create *new* programmes. "New educational programmes have been initiated outside the confines of the formal system" (Ahmed 1982: 133). Bock spoke of "the expansion of nonformal education more recently" (Bock 1976: 352), and LaBelle suggested that NFE "became a more frequent programmatic alternative for some youth and adults" (LaBelle 1982: 160). But there are in fact few signs that this happened. On the whole, the term NFE was used mainly to identify, support and co-ordinate *existing* programmes (McCall 1970). The majority of the new programmes which emerged during the 1970s and 1980s when the debate about NFE was taking place were given other titles such as 'out-of-school-youth programmes'; and a large number of them sprang from quite different origins from that which inspired the non-formal education debate.

The term 'non-formal' was initially given to existing educational programmes by administrators and planners, less frequently by practitioners. They were mostly establishment reformers of education rather than radicals. The voice being heard at first was that of mainstream educational planning and governments, particularly inter-governmental (UN) and bilateral aid agencies and international NGOs.

DEFINING NFE

Non-formal Education then was defined as all education outside of the formal system. And those who advocated NFE as a solution to the ills of education in developing societies saw it as a discrete entity, distinguishable and manageable.

However, identifying and listing some educational activities as 'formal' and others as 'nonformal' depends on some kind of definition, some criteria by which programmes were to be allocated into separate categories. And that has always proved difficult.

Education

The first element was a recognition of the distinctiveness of programmes which were *educational* in character from those which were non-educational.

This was more important for the nonformal sector than for the formal sector, for some writers tended to include various *non-educational* activities such as cultural events or social welfare programmes as part of NFE. Coombs was inconsistent here. In one place, he wrote that he and his colleagues "equate education with learning, regardless of where, how or when the learning occurs" (Coombs & Ahmed 1974: 8), so that all learning would be seen as education. But earlier he had defined education as "any *systematic organized instructional process designed to achieve* specific learning objectives by particular groups of learners", a definition which is narrower than 'all learning' and which indicates the intention and planning of the educator and the existence of an identified group of participants (Coombs 1971, cited in Paulston 1973: 65, my italics). Elsewhere, he and Ahmed spoke of formal and nonformal education as being linked together and distinguished from informal education, since both were "*designed* to promote and facilitate certain valued types of learning" (Coombs et al. 1973: 12, my italics; cf Coombs & Ahmed 1974: 233). Both formal and non-formal programmes were thus seen to consist of *educational* activities, that is, planned and organised activities designed to promote learning, clearly distinguished from the unplanned activities by which people learn many things, and from social action and welfare. Some writers spoke of education as "organised and sustained communication designed to bring about learning" (ISCED 1975 para 6 & 55, cited in Simkins 1977: 8). LaBelle (1982: 162) spoke of 'deliberate' and systematic teaching. Carron suggested that both formal and nonformal education were united in that they possessed "a programme plan, an agency and a clientele" (Carron & Carr-Hill 1991: 20).

But if it was recognised at the time that some activities labelled 'education' can be distinguished from other learning activities by being designed and organised purposefully to promote learning, it was also recognised that there were different kinds of education. Throughout the debate, the divisions proposed by Coombs and Ahmed of formal, nonformal and informal education were adopted, at least for the purposes of argument: "We found it analytically useful, and generally in accord with current realities, to distinguish between three modes of education (recognizing that there is considerable overlap and interaction between them): (1) *informal* education, (2) *formal* education, and (3) *nonformal* education" (Coombs and Ahmed 1974: 8). This distinction has been repeated many times (for example, World Bank 1979: 16; LaBelle 1982: 162-163; Bhola 1983: 47-48). Evans (1981a: 28), drawing on Michigan State University's work, suggested four kinds of education, incidental (entirely unplanned), informal (planned on one side but not on the other), nonformal (out of school), and formal (inside school); but very few follow him in this, for they have found it difficult to conceive of 'education' which consists of unplanned learning.

Informal education?

The discussion of 'informal education' has been one thread (albeit minor) throughout much of the debate on NFE. But it contains an internal inconsistency. Informal education has been classically defined as follows:

> **Informal education as used here is the lifelong process by which every person acquires and accumulates knowledge, skills, attitudes and insights from daily experiences and exposure to the environment – at home, at work, at play; from the example and attitudes of family and friends; from travel, reading newspapers and books; or by listening to the radio or viewing films or television. Generally, informal education is unorganized and often unsystematic; yet it accounts for the great bulk of any person's total lifetime learning –**

including that of even a highly 'schooled' person. (Coombs & Ahmed 1974: 8)

This of course combines Evans' categories of incidental and informal education.

It is here that Coombs is at his most inconsistent. For despite his belief (cited above) that 'education' inevitably implies some sense of intention and planning, he and Ahmed write: "People learn primarily from day-to-day experiences and from the multitude of educative forces in their environment – from family and neighbors, work and play, religious activities, the marketplace, newspapers, books, broadcasts and other media. For purposes of the study, we called this important mode of learning *informal* education (not to be confused with *nonformal*)" (Coombs & Ahmed 1974: 232-233: original emphases). He and his colleagues recognised the inconsistency: for elsewhere they write that "formal and non-formal education are alike in that both have been *organised* by societies to improve the informal learning process" (Coombs et al. 1973: 12, my italics).

It is however hard to see, even by Coombs' own definition, how such informal learning can be called education at all, for it is not so organised or designed; it lacks intention and planning. Several writers point this out. Grandstaff for example says that "we can distinguish between deliberate educational measures and events that lead to 'informal' or 'incidental' learning" (Grandstaff 1976: 294; see MSU 1973b). Simkins too differentiates formal and nonformal education from informal education: "Formal and non-formal education are separated from informal education through being *purposefully organised and directed to facilitate particular kinds of learning*. Informal education is not organised with the achievement of specific learning objectives in view, but rather is educational in a more general and implicit way" (Simkins 1977: 8; original emphasis).

In the debate, informal education received on the whole relatively little attention, and when it did, it was mostly because such writers saw difficulties with Coombs and Ahmed. "NFE, unlike informal learning, is organised" (Radcliffe & Colletta 1985: 3557). Such writers tended to justify its dismissal from the scene on the grounds that the concept referred to informal learning rather than education (Dave 1976). "It seems doubtful whether the term 'education' should be applied to informal activities at all. Rather we should, perhaps, be thinking in terms of a context of on-going, pervasive and incidental informal *learning* within which purposefully directed formal and non-formal *educational* activities take place" (Simkins 1977: 8). Informal education was thought to lack "educational intentions" (IBE 1975: 84). Case and Niehoff write, "Informal education is a term used by some educators to refer to learning not deliberately planned or organized but growing out of experience, parental guidance, learning from peers, observations, trial and error and related sources of learning. We have not found it necessary to use this term, which we believe expands the concept of education inordinately" (Case & Niehoff 1976: 53). By 1982, Ahmed was talking of informal *learning* (Ahmed 1982: 138) rather than informal education. LaBelle speaks of a continuum of "learning experiences ... from planned, compulsory and intentional to unplanned, voluntary and incidental" (LaBelle 1982: 159). Carron and Carr-Hill (1991: 19) set this view out clearly: when speaking of 'education', they write, "it makes heuristic sense to exclude from this rubric casual learning which accompanies some other activity such as the educative value of participating in a cultural event (whether that be a football match, initiation rite or an opera)". Lynch argues that informal education cannot be called education since it is not systematically organised, has no clear goals and is not certificated: "One thing it [NFE] is not is informal education, although it may include some dimension or component which is informal ... [for] informal education ... is spontaneous learning by individuals as they interact with their social and physical environment in their day-to-day living" (Lynch et al. 1997: xi-xii). Thus some writers chose to omit the informal element altogether, while others included it in their categories but mainly in the form of informal learning (Ahmed 1982: 133-134, 138; King 1982: 177-187; LaBelle 1982; see also Brennan 1997). A few writers however use the term 'informal education' to mean what others call 'nonformal education' (Lengrand 1982: 189-207).

'Informal education' then exists in the debate largely unexplored in detail; there are no surveys of it as with NFE. It was seen as consisting of incidental learning. However, we shall see later that the term contains an element which may prove to be useful in future discussions of NFE (see below p.260 for further discussion of informal education).

Formal education

Similarly, 'formal education' was not often discussed in any detail. The term already had a long cultural history, and the context in which it was used was not always that of non-formal education. It was for example often used in opposition to adult education: Deleon suggests that some people argue that "adult education was and still remains ... only a marginal educational and societal activity. The formal educational system, as a time-bound and place-bound activity, as a once-for-all process, as a 'preparation for life', corresponds fully to and is justified by the fundamental parameters of our life frame" (Deleon 1978: 170). Formal education was a part of most of the educational discourses in use at the time.

It was assumed that everyone knew what formal education was. Coombs and Ahmed show this in their classic definition, implying that 'of course' everyone knew what it was and it did not need any further defining:

> **Formal education as used here is, of course, the highly institu-
> tionalized, chronologically graded and hierarchically structured
> 'education system', spanning lower primary school and the upper
> reaches of the university. (Coombs & Ahmed 1974: 8)**

This is the usual definition, often cited in full, abbreviated or adapted slightly. Coombs and his colleagues from time to time adopted slightly different wording: for example, in 1973 they included the words "in addition to general academic studies, a variety of specialised programmes and institutions for full-time professional and technical training", which in fact widens any identification of formal education greatly (Coombs et al. 1973; Coombs 1985a: 23). But most writers limited the formal system to the state schools and state-recognised colleges. Sheffield and Diejomaoh (1972: xi) talk about "primary and secondary schools, teacher-training colleges, universities and government-operated technical and agricultural schools". For Simkins, formal education is "all schooling, university education (sometimes excluding extra-mural or extension work), full-time further education, and/or vocational training and teacher training" (Simkins 1977: 10). Grandstaff refers to "identifiable schools", and Brembeck speaks of "the formally organized educational system with its hierarchy of grades leading all the way from pre-school to graduate and professional school" (Grandstaff 1976: 294; Brembeck & Thompson 1973: xvi).

But formal education could not be so easily defined as this. In some contexts, it was identified with those educational programmes which were subject to "state influence and sponsorship" (LaBelle 1982: 162) which might seem to exclude several forms of schools and colleges. Or it was seen as that education which was "standardised and stereotyped" which widens the scope of formal education (LaBelle 1982: 174). The International Bureau of Education said it was that form of education that claimed a monopoly (Bacquelaine & Raeymakers 1991: 15), although it can be argued that very few systems of education have ever claimed a monopoly. King says it is that education which is 'compulsory', which is hard to justify in many developing countries and would exclude all university education (King 1982: 178). Berstecher (1985) defined it as the "formal entitlement system" of education (see Lynch et al. 1997: xiii) which would exclude private schools. Harbison said that "formal education connotes age-specific, full-time classroom attendance in a linear graded system geared to certificates, diplomas, degrees or other formal credentials". He goes on: "Formal education is thus easily defined – its administration and control in most developing countries is lodged in a ministry of education; its costs are measurable; and its outputs are easily identified" (Harbison 1973b: 5), all of which can be said of any national adult literacy campaign. Bock and Papagiannis refer to formal education as "limited to those processes of teaching and learning carried on at specific times, in places outside the home, for definite periods, and by persons especially prepared or trained for the task. It is education that organizes its consumers by age-grading, grants certificates and degrees, and frequently requires compulsory attendance by pupils" (1983: 15-16).

Formal education then is usually defined through its characteristics. It was provided by those "institutions which require full-time attendance of specific ages in teacher-supervised classrooms for the study of graded curricula" (Reimer 1971: 35). Within this analysis, there is a common assumption that the age-graded hierarchy of elementary, secondary and higher educational institutions represents the formal education system, and that it can be readily identified in every society. Formal education is above all certificated: Marien describes it as all those "learning situations promising some rewards (i.e. certificates, diplomas, job access, promotion, licenses, merit badges etc.) beyond the inherent value in learning for its own sake" (cited in Paulston 1973: 66-68), LaBelle as "all that education that is certificated" which must include most adult literacy classes (LaBelle 1982: 163). Later, LaBelle and Ward speak of "schooling, meaning state-sanctioned curricula associated with credits, grades, certificates and diplomas" (LaBelle & Ward 1994: 4142). In some countries, formal education was that which had been defined by law: in Japan, it was seen to consist of "those organised programmes for educational activities ... provided in the curriculum of schools based on the School Education Law" (Moro'oka 1985: 3546).

But for most writers, formal education was defined by inference, simply by saying that nonformal education was everything that was not formal. It is in this way that the characteristics of formal education became listed. LaBelle referred to the "pre-requisites [of formal education] ... the inherent elements ... such as hierarchy, compulsion, entry requirements, standard curricula and certificates"; these enable formal education to be identified (LaBelle 1982: 163). For although "the decision about what to include will of course vary between different societies and educational systems", nevertheless formal education was thought to be recognisable in every context; it was not regarded simply as an arbitrary list of educational bodies as Simkins (1977: 10) urged.

But the difficulties thrown up by such definitions and listings were never examined. No-one asked researchers to go out and investigate formal education as a system in the way they did with non-formal education. Few asked whether private schools or correspondence courses or government-run national training programmes like the Kenya village polytechnics were formal or not. It was simply assumed that the animal existed and that everyone could recognise it and that it did not need further definition.

Nonformal education

The term 'non-formal education' did not have any cultural history; it was new. This may account for the many different definitions, as those engaged in the debates tried to overcome some of the problems inherent in the term. The basic definition was that of Coombs and Ahmed: "any organized educational activity outside the established formal system – whether operating separately or as an important feature of some broader activity – that is intended to serve identified learning clienteles and learning objectives" (Coombs et al 1973: 10-11).

In the form Coombs and Ahmed put it one year later, it has been so widely and often unthinkingly cited (e.g. LaBelle 1982: 161-162; LaBelle & Verhine 1975: 161; Garrido 1992; Radcliffe & Colletta 1985: 3536; even as late as Brennan 1997) that it almost seems not to be true:

> **Nonformal education ... is any organized, systematic, educational activity carried on outside the framework of the formal system to**

provide selected types of learning to particular subgroups in the population, adults as well as children. (Coombs and Ahmed 1974: 8)

Coombs and his collaborators themselves at times abbreviated it: "simply any organized activity with educational purposes carried on outside the highly structured framework of formal educational systems as they exist today" (Coombs & Ahmed 1974: 233). Others carried on this process until NFE became simply "organized learning outside the traditional schools and university curriculum" (Simmons 1980: 2; it is interesting how quickly the relatively modern Western system of education came to be regarded as 'traditional'). NFE consisted of "training programmes outside the formal educational system" (IBE 1987) or "all organised learning that takes place outside of school" (Brembeck & Thompson 1973: xvi; Brennan 1997). Harbison says that NFE "is probably best defined as skill and knowledge generation taking place outside the formal schooling system" (Harbison 1973b: 5). Adiseshiah defined NFE as "the organized provision of learning opportunities outside the formal educational system, covering a person's lifetime, and programmed to meet a specific need – remedial, or vocational or health or welfare or civic, political or for self-fulfilment" (Adiseshiah 1975: 26).

But the 'outside formal' definition does not fit every case, and it has been frequently adapted, usually in small ways, to meet different situations. LaBelle described NFE as "organized systematic out-of-school activities designed to provide learning experiences for selected populations" (LaBelle 1976b: 278). Dore, speaking of the "new orthodoxy of the international establishment, ... nonformal education", expanded this: "meaning all the deliberate, conscious, and organised teaching and learning (not including unorganised learning in families and factories, which is known in the jargon as *in*formal) which goes on outside of schools" (Dore 1976: 104, original emphasis). For Brembeck, NFE was wider – "those learning activities that take place outside the formally organized educational system" (Brembeck & Thompson 1973: xvi).

Non-institutional: The starting point for NFE in most cases was the formal system of schooling. Thus for some, NFE was all 'non-institutional' forms of education as against institutional education (LaBelle 1982: 161; IBE 1987: 15). Paulston and others call it "non-school education". One influential publication insisted that nonformal education must be seen as both wider and narrower than this – as "organized education without formal schooling or institutionalization in which knowledge, skills and values are transmitted through relatives, peers, or other community members"; it then added, "note: do not confuse it with 'non-school' programs or the identifier 'informal education'" (ERIC 1975, 1986, cited in Garrido 1992: 83-84, 88). Although Sheffield and Diejomoah, in an early study of NFE in Africa (1972), said that "NFE ... is roughly synonymous with the more widely used term 'out of school' education" (1972: xi), and although Evans in his influential report wrote, "The term 'nonformal' education has been used synonymously with 'out-of-school' education" (Evans 1981a:

11), others (Lowe 1985: 3557-3558) pointed to "nonformal programs which are sponsored by formal educational institutions" (Brembeck & Thompson 1973: xvi). Between 1983 and 1989, IIEP undertook a survey of vocational training programmes, both formal and non-formal (IIEP 1989). It rewrote several earlier reports in what may be called 'NFE-speak', defining NFE as "programmes or provision that does not comply with the formal or structured organisation usually encountered in formal training institutions and in the formal schooling system. Non-formal training programmes may take many forms, one of them being the flexible non-formal structure of business advisory services"; and apprenticeships and other forms of on-the-job training outside institutions of education could also be included.

Enrolment: Another set of definitions, derived from UNESCO through ISCED, saw NFE as all that education which does not have registered students. In defining adult (that is, over the age of 15 years) education, ISCED said that Adult Education should be taken as being "synonymous with out of school education" and went on to say that such adult (i.e. out-of-school) education can be formal or non-formal. Bowers and Fisher (1972) distinguished between "formal education, education for which the learners are enrolled or registered, whereas non-formal education is education for which learners are not enrolled or registered", leading UNESCO to assert that "Formal education is that for which the students are enrolled or registered (regardless of the mode of teaching used). By contrast, NFE is that for which none of the learners are enrolled or registered" (ISCED 1985). They go on, "In its common international use, 'nonformal education' usually means 'non-registered education' – in other words, education without previous application by the students or registration, and without any certificate or degree" (cited in Garrido 1992: 83; Bacquelaine & Raeymakers 1991: 16). But it is hard to find this 'common international usage'; Bowers and Fisher's definition is one which most other writers seem pointedly to ignore. Indeed, an early survey of NFE programmes reported that in their case studies, "in some cases, entrants to non-formal education projects were admitted on the basis of competitive examinations. More often, however, the procedure of admission involved an application and an interview", which seems to indicate formal enrolment and registration (Sheffield & Diejomoah 1972: 200). All adult literacy programmes enrolled and registered their students, and these are regularly included among NFE, not formal education (for the problems of defining NFE by enrolment, see Carr-Hill et al. 2001: 332-333).

NGOs: A third refinement was to stress the role of the state in formal education and of NGOs in non-formal education. It was suggested that formal education was state-provided and that NFE was NGO-provided. USAID in an early planning document defined NFE as "that portion of the total educational system which has not been incorporated under the formal education ministry or in the formal graded classroom situation" (Krueger & Moulton 1981: 13). "NFE is sometimes used as a synonym for non-state or non-institutionalized provision of basic education or skills training for adults or over-age youth" (Lynch et al. 1997: ix; see Bacquelaine & Raeymakers 1991). Some have defined NFE as those "types of learning which take place outside the institutional context of the Ministry of Education" (Goodale 1989 cited in IIEP 1999), or as all education provided by NGOs as opposed to state-promoted education (LaBelle 1982: 167). But this did not meet with any real success, for again it excluded that "NFE which falls within the rubric for Ministries of Education" (Townsend-Coles 1982b: 261; see Townsend Coles 1982a).

There were other, less widely accepted, distinctions. Several saw NFE as all **non-certificated education** as against certificated education – "i.e. education without formal credentials" (LaBelle & Verhine 1975: 161; Lynch et al. 1997: xxvii). Formal education was seen as being certificated, implying that NFE can be identified by being non-certificated. "Nonformal education programs are not schools because they do not receive or deliver the same medium of exchange – credits, grades and diplomas – that are recognized and sanctioned by the society's most legitimate and formal system of teaching and learning" (LaBelle 1981: 315). But this has never been widely accepted, because it clearly cannot apply to many of the programmes which were at the time designated NFE. Another definition (Colletta & Radcliffe 1980; Radcliffe & Colletta 1985: 3538) proposed that formal education was **cognitive education** and NFE was **skill training** (see also IBE 1987), but this too was met with silent rejection and clearly could not meet such data as the researchers were collecting.

The reason which seems to lie behind these different and changing definitions was the concern of donors and international educational planners to engage in comparative research and planning for education. And making comparisons about education in countries as diverse (educationally as in other ways) as Nepal and Nigeria and Nicaragua led to constant revisions of categories, constant challenging of existing paradigms to make them fit the messy world.

We can thus see that in defining NFE, many writers were building on an undefined formal education. NFE was almost always seen as secondary to formal education, but in the process of defining NFE, the definition of formal education followed; it did not precede NFE.

The nature of NFE programmes

Many writers saw NFE as a collection of discrete but identifiable programmes. Some take a narrow view, others a very wide view. Bhola limited the term: "The term non-formal education should be reserved for short-term classes, systematic problem-oriented training activities and teaching of social and political skills" (Bhola 1983: 48), and Paulston spoke of NFE as basic education only, "education that does not advance to a higher level of the hierarchical formal school system" (Paulston 1972: ix). Others saw NFE as covering all adult, basic and vocational education and training outside of the school system (LaBelle 2000: 21). They did not however indicate how much basic or vocational education lay *inside* the formal system or what term they would give to the many other forms of education (e.g. religious education) outside of the formal system if they could no longer be called NFE. King distinguished between adult literacy and NFE – "these two thematic areas, each very different from each other" (King 1991: 147, 180). He thus confined NFE to adult education which he saw as "including other basic skills" than literacy. But equally, he constructed adult education as wider than NFE, proposing that some adult education could be formal and some non-formal. Adiseshiah, in an interesting discussion of the development of schooling, saw NFE as widening out first through 'adult education' ("both of the general-education type ... and of the vocational-training type") and secondly through "the development of various forms of non-formal education for those who had been denied schooling, who had to interrupt their schooling for economic reasons, or whose skills faced obsolescence. Thus arose the various forms of adult literacy programmes, the farmers' training and education schemes, the correspondence courses for those living at a distance from educational centres or those wishing to learn more or afresh" (Adiseshiah 1985: 38). Exactly how adult education and NFE fitted together is not explained.

NFE for development: One key element seems to have been the attempt to link NFE with development. The newer understanding of development as aimed at the masses of the poor rather than the elites gave an impetus to this tendency (World Bank 1972). USAID spoke of NFE as a "subset of educational efforts that also have identifiable development purposes related to the contextualized setting in which they take place" (Krueger & Moulton 1981: 9). Indeed, for some, NFE is all that education aimed at development (implying that formal education was not aimed at development): "any deliberately organized educational activity outside the established framework of formal school and university systems, principally for out-of-school youth and adults, for the purpose of communicating ideas, developing skills, changing attitudes or modifying behavior related to the realization of development goals and the achievement of higher standards of living and welfare of the people" (Case & Niehoff 1976: 53), but there is no discussion of whether formal education might share the same developmental goals as NFE. As we have seen above (p.21), in the early 1970s, international development agencies announced a concerted effort to address the plight of the 'poorest of the poor' in less developed countries and chose non-formal education as their preferred tool (LaBelle & Ward 1994: 4141).

Rural education: Some, misinterpreting the studies of Coombs and his colleagues when they suggested that "conventional primary schools, oriented towards urban life and climbing the academic ladder, [provide] at best limited help in meeting the essential learning needs of the rural young" (Coombs 1976: 286), came to see NFE as 'rural' education as opposed to urban education (Johnson 1976; Dejene 1980; Hiehoff 1977; Heredero 1977; Bucholz 1987; Lamichane & Kapoor 1992 etc.). "In general, the clients of nonformal education ... are predominantly rural" (Grandstaff 1976: 303). This is a constant theme in USAID documents: "the requirements of nonformal education among the rural poor" (Krueger & Moulton 1981: 42 etc.). The role of NFE, "in addition to transforming and strengthening the formal schools, [is] to help meet the essential learning needs of millions of educationally deprived rural children and adolescents and to help accelerate social and economic development in rural areas ... An especially important task for developing countries is to bring the vast numbers of farmers, workers, small entrepreneurs and others who have never seen the inside of a formal classroom – and perhaps never will – a spate of useful skills and knowledge which they can promptly apply to their own and their nation's development" (Coombs et al. 1973: 2, 7). A focused debate centred round this issue came to a peak in the early 1980s (e.g. Barber 1981; Evans 1981c). Others widened the development agenda. NFE is that "education which teaches (rural and urban) manual skills for develop-ment ... more practical education" (Bock 1976: 351; Ahmed & Coombs 1975; World Bank 1974; Simmons 1980: 8-9; Muyeed 1982: 227-238).

The picture then we have is very confused and confusing. Several writers use quite different definitions in the same piece of writing (e.g. LaBelle 1982; King 1991).

Labelling NFE

The "problems with the NFE term" (LaBelle & Ward 1994: 4142) were recognised even by those who espoused this discourse. Coombs and Ahmed from the start sug-gested that

> these terms leave something to be desired, but they seem less ambi-guous and less distorted by usage than the various alternatives we considered. It is not without significance that the standard lexicon of education in all the major languages is tied almost exclusively to formal education and provides no precise and well understood vocabulary for discussing what we have termed informal and nonformal education".
> (Coombs & Ahmed 1974: 8)

From the earliest days of the use of the term, NFE in the field was seen as "a motley collection of relatively ill-defined, unstandardized and unrelated activities, each aimed at quite a different goal" (King 1967 Foreword) – a statement which makes one wonder why the term was ever used in the first place, if the activities are all 'unrelated'. But the use of the term created the category. Evans calls it 'a catch-all title' (Evans & Smith 1972: 12). Ahmed and Coombs (1975), in their wide-ranging survey of non-formal educational activities for rural development, included many programmes which did not call themselves non-formal, and those which did covered a wide range of activities for children and youth and adults, extending from literacy to industrial training, from youth camps to vocational education and training.

Like others, Paulston was aware that the term was too wide in its general application and sought to limit it: "If loosely defined, it could conceivably include all socialization and skills learning processes taking place outside formal education – an overwhelming field of activity": and for the sake of study and planning, he proposed to limit the term to "any structured, systematic nonschool educational and training activities of relatively short duration, where sponsoring agencies seek concrete behavioral changes in fairly distinct target populations", which would exclude much of what others call NFE (Paulston 1973: 65; see also Paulston 1972: ix). Garrido says of Hochleitner's description of NFE as "embracing all learning processes throughout life which offer access to knowledge and basic or advanced skills, whether or not such a process is institutionalised or leading to certificates or degrees", that it "sounds practically the same as plain 'education' " (Garrido 1992: 84). Brembeck speaks of NFE as "a broad amorphous term", and Harbison says of it, "Getting hold of nonformal education is a little like trying to get hold of apple sauce. Put your hand in the bowl and you don't come up with much" (Brembeck & Thompson 1973: xvi).

Creating the label: Coombs indicates that he and Ahmed looked at other terms before settling on NFE. For nonformal education was only one of a number of terms being used at that time in the search for alternative forms of education which would reach a wider clientele and which would be more effective in achieving its goals, or when considering new ways of putting right all the multiple and manifest faults of formal schooling (see above Chapter 2). Indigenous education, out-of-school education, shadow school system, educational alternatives, lifelong learning/education (Case & Niehoff 1976: 76; Grandstaff 1974b; Callaway 1973; LaBelle 1975; Radcliffe & Colletta 1985: 3537) were all terms being increasingly used at this period. Continuing education, fundamental or foundation education, recurrent education, extension education, community education (Harman 1974) were similarly being experimented with at the same time (King 1991: 164, citing Prosser 1967). Popular education was particularly well known, especially in Latin America (e.g. Bhola 1983: 45-48; Grandstaff 1974b; LaBelle 1975; Carnoy 1982). Brembeck, although using the term NFE, preferred to speak of "new strategies for education" (Brembeck & Thompson 1973; Radcliffe & Colletta 1985: 3537). The term NFE had rivals for the educational establishment's affections at this time.

Nevertheless, out of all the available terms then being used, NFE was the term which was picked up to a remarkable extent, far beyond any of the others, even 'popular education'. The number of publications devoted to NFE over the fifteen years or so after 1970 is a tribute to the energy with which the concept was pursued[1]. Even when not using the term 'Nonformal' in the title of their works, many writers expanded on NFE in their texts (e.g. Blaug 1973, Harbison 1973b, Stromquist 1985, 1988).

NFE then chimed in with much contemporary thinking. It seemed to group together programmes which hitherto had never been regarded as linked in any way. Coombs himself saw it as "simply a convenient label covering a bewildering assortment of organized educational activities" (Coombs 1976: 282; see Coombs & Ahmed 1974: 233); the only thing they had in common was that they were "outside the formal system". As Carron said, "the appellation nonformal is simply a device for

---

[1] My bibliography of articles, books and pamphlets, and informal papers etc. runs to well over 800 items.

labelling those activities outside the control or regulation of the bureaucratic school system" (Carron & Carr-Hill 1991: 20). LaBelle suggested optimistically that "After more than a decade of use, the concept of nonformal education has demonstrated its heuristic utility in describing and analyzing a wide array of out of school activities that exist worldwide" (LaBelle 1982: 173). Hunt in his study of different paradigms of development pointed out that such labelling usually leads to over-simplification and the obscuring of differences within the categories used (Hunt 1989), while Escobar suggested that labels usually establish hierarchies (Escobar 1995: 109-110).

Value of labelling: The value of providing a label, however, must not be under-estimated. A label is seen to define items by linking them together. A label provides the planners and others with a handle enabling them to get a hold on programmes which otherwise they could not bring together. It does this by emphasising their commonalities. Labels inevitably speak of those items within the label as having some features in common. All of those who wrote about NFE were looking for common characteristics within disparate programmes, even those who stressed the wide range of NFE activities. Normally such characteristics were seen to consist of the advantages and disadvantages which NFE had in relation to the formal system of education.

Coombs and Ahmed set this out well early in the debate. NFE

> is a bewildering assortment of separate educational activities, generally having little connection with each other... For precisely this reason, because it is *not* a coherent and unified system, nonformal education – at least potentially and to a greater extent actually – has a far wider scope and greater versatility, diversity and adaptability than formal education enjoys at present ... Along with the many advantages of nonformal education, however, go some important handicaps – not the least being the strong competitive disadvantages of nonformal education vis-a-vis formal education in terms of social prestige, access to good jobs and access to the public treasury. (Coombs & Ahmed 1974: 233)

But such a view depends for its validity on the assumption that there is some unity to be identified, that educationalists are able to make generalisations about "NFE as *it* actually exists around the world today" (Coombs 1976: 286, my italics). As the many comparative studies of NFE made at the time show, Coombs and his colleagues assume that there is an 'it', an entity which can be labelled NFE, despite several caveats: for example, "by its nature, nonformal education is extremely diverse in pedagogical approaches, organization and objectives. Therefore inferences about the general behaviour of costs in nonformal education would be much more difficult to arrive at than in formal education" (Ahmed 1985: 3545). NFE, they felt, actually exists somewhere 'out there' and can be recognised. Evans wrote in 1981: "Nonformal education is a definable set of educational activities which can be clearly separated from formal school structures on the one hand and from the broad range of unstructured learning activities of everyday life on the other" (Evans 1981a: 39). They thus felt that they were justified in making clear statements about NFE as a whole. Coombs asserted that "the stultifying fragmentation of nonformal education continues and worsens", while others spoke about "the institutionalization of nonformal education" (Coombs 1976: 285; Bock 1976: 351). NFE had existed for many years, but its nature and connections had not been recognised until the label 'non-formal education' was attached to these different educational activities.

The labelling of NFE then aggregated many disparate educational activities into one 'programme'. The term helped to render this 'programme' visible, to 'legitimate' it (LaBelle 1982: 160), to give it coherence and to render it amenable to analysis. It enabled NFE to be justified to policy-makers and resource-controllers. It rendered such programmes fashionable for a time. As Don Adams wrote in 1972:

> Having been publicized by the US Agency for Economic Development, certified as important by the International Bank of Reconstruction and Development, and anointed with research money by the Ford Foundation, Nonformal Education must be viewed as one of the new favored areas of inquiry in education. (cited in Paulston 1972: vii)

The New Fashion

Several strands came together to support this new discourse (Evans & Smith 1972). "As the world crisis in formal education intensified, interest in nonformal, or non-school, education has grown at a rapid pace" (Paulston 1972: ix). There was, it was reported, an "electric excitement" about the possibilities of NFE, a "phenomenal 'take off' of nonformal education", a "remarkable worldwide upsurge of interest in non-formal education" (Coombs 1976: 281,291; Coombs 1985b: 3541; see King 1991: 165-174; Bock 1976: 348; Blunt 1988: 41).

Aid agencies: The enthusiasm was indeed widespread. Coombs' own agency, the International Center for Educational Development (ICED) in USA, was at the heart of this movement. Other bodies took up the theme. ILO undertook employment missions under their World Employment Programme (ILO 1971a, 1971b), and consultancies under the title of NFE were completed for ILO (Blaug 1973). The Ford Foundation made it a major focus for its support. USAID took a lead, claiming that "even though nonformal education fits logically into this alternative development theory and related strategies, neither Unesco, Unicef nor the World Bank joined in the commitment made by [USAID] to seriously study, promote and sponsor nonformal education and to build institutional capacity and organization in both the U.S. and developing countries ... [an] emphasis ... as a Key Problem (or more recently a Research and Development) Area [which] made [USAID] unique among international assistance donors and other AID bureaus" (Krueger & Moulton 1981: 37, 49; see Hilliard 1971; USAID papers). As the British government Overseas Development Administration (ODA) put it, "the 1970s ... saw strenuous efforts to redirect USAID's assistance away from support for the tertiary sector and the creation of high level manpower towards reform and expansion of elementary and non-formal basic education..." (ODA 1986: 156). Despite USAID's claims, the World Bank in its 1974 Education Sector Paper urged the development of nonformal schemes as parallel or alternative programmes to formal education. It alleged that formal education systems "have been irrelevant to the needs of developing countries for the past two decades", and it urged a programme of nonformal and vocational education to be developed, defining NFE as "education which teaches manual skills for development". From 1973 to 1979, NFE formed one major concern in its programmes. Other aid agencies followed somewhat later: thus ODA said that "there is an increasingly important role for every variety of NFE for African development" especially in the context of helping the rural poor (ODA 1984: 12; see ODA 1975).

Academic centres: The USA benefited most from this new direction. A number of major centres were encouraged by USAID and the World Bank to take up the theme of non-formal education for research, teaching and practice in the field – including the Center for International Education (CIE) at the University of Massachusetts, Amherst (Evans, Kinsey) which set up a Nonformal Education Resource Center; a Nonformal Education Information Center at the Michigan State University (MSU) at East Lansing (Brembeck, Niehoff, Grandstaff), together with the University of California in Los Angeles, Stanford University and Florida State University. While no academic journal devoted to NFE was ever established, the newsletter *Nonformal Education Exchange* and a wide range of non-formal publications issued by MSU, CIE and other bodies served as an outlet for reports on experimentation and evaluations. Outside the USA, similar centres were established such as the Centro para el Desarollo de la Educacion No-formal in Colombia (IBE 1987). Europe did not create an academic centre, but the IIEP in Paris for a time formed the key agency for the debate and promotion of NFE in that region, as did some Scandinavian university centres. UNESCO regional studies were conducted in Africa (for example, in the Sudan and Kenya) and in Asia (India). "Nonformal education has proliferated over the past few decades", wrote Hallak (1990: 238), "radically altering the contours of the educational field".

NFE programmes: And NFE spread in the field for many reasons. Most of it was devised by Western aid workers and NGOs such as World Education (Krueger & Moulton 1981: 52). Existing programmes were reclassified and new NFE programmes were implemented. NFE appealed to governments and some parents because of its relatively low costs, especially as governments came under increasing constraints in finances after the world financial crisis of 1973 followed by Structural Adjustment pressures. It brought more partners into the field of education, opening the doors to increased influence for NGOs and other civil society bodies. It fitted in with the growing calls for decentralisation, the localisation of control and community involvement. NFE was very appealing to many interested parties.

We must not of course exaggerate the importance of NFE even at that time. Few will now agree that "the contours of the educational field were radically altered". Few will now assert that NFE activities in the field proliferated in ratio to the debate, for NFE recognised more existing educational activities than it created. Many agencies and academic studies of education in relation to development did not mention NFE. The widely influential Faure Report, to which many adherents of NFE looked for support, did not see NFE as a key strategy. The term is not mentioned in any of the section titles of the report or the index. It used the terms 'conventional' and 'non-conventional' education rather than 'formal' and 'nonformal', and spoke of promoting less formalism in educational institutions and of developing more informal paths to learning (Faure et al. 1972: 185-186), but avoided the current fashion of seeing in NFE the salvation of education. The most popular textbook on education and development (Fagerlind & Saha 1983, 1989) does not refer to NFE in either of its two editions. This can only have been deliberate at this time.

Hostility to the new discourse: For some were more than hesitant about the concept and discourse of NFE. There were "those in the Third World [who] often have not liked the term because it appears to be a North American invention whose use implies Third World dependency in the borrowing of educational theory and practice" (LaBelle & Ward 1994: 4142). Thus the discourse of NFE was not always acceptable in Latin America, for 'non-formal education' was often seen there as "an American term" (LaBelle 1986: 5). But the main hostility was found in the West. IDRC, along with other agencies of the time, preferred to refer to mass primary education or to 'popular education' (by no means the same as NFE) (King 1991: 173-174; see Boli et al. 1985; IDRC 1991). Bhola, always an establishment writer, like others talked of "alternative (or substitute) formal education" (Bhola 1983b: 48; see IIEP 1985; IBE 1987; Carnoy 1982). Others preferred the term 'non-school' or 'out of school education' (see MSU 1973b), non-traditional learning (Wedemayer 1981) or open learning (Perraton 1982). UNESCO was very reluctant to use the term, partly because its staff were wedded to their existing discourse of functional literacy and the emerging discourse of lifelong education, and partly because they saw NFE as being anti-school (UNESCO 1982, 1985). For example, in 1984, they spoke of "schooled and non-schooled programmes" (*l'éducation scolaire et non scolaire,* UNESCO 1984: they used the French terms *'education'* for schools and *'formation'* for out of school). UNESCO itself debated NFE only rather belatedly (1979-1983), seeking the co-ordination between formal and nonformal education at primary school level (UNESCO 1982: 637-638; Thomas 1980). The two main UNESCO academic journals *Prospects* and *International Review of Education* were each belatedly (1982) persuaded to devote a major part of one issue to NFE, but the term 'non-formal education' does not appear in the pages of these publications as frequently as in other journals such as the American journal *Comparative Education Review*. And when the UNESCO Institute of Education took up the challenge of NFE (1988-1990), it concentrated on non-conventional approaches to primary level education (Ranaweera

1989, Armengol 1990) and on the integration of formal and nonformal education. UNICEF too, although it commissioned Coombs and his International Center for Educational Development to prepare a report on alternative educational programmes for children (Coombs et al. 1973), carefully avoided the term NFE, preferring 'out-of-school Basic Education' (see Krueger & Moulton 1981: 40). The British government aid agency expressed its fear that, because NFE was seen to be cultural and cross-ministry, it was likely to involve donors in local politics: "it will be necessary to have regards to the tensions implicit in the inevitable involvement of a range of Ministries and other interests in non-formal education" (ODA 1976: 9 cited in King 1991: 173). Reports that NFE was sometimes rejected in the field as a second-rate education were used as an excuse to avoid the term, the concept and the identified activities (Simmons 1980: 8-10).

The voice of the planners: Such questioning reminds us that at the heart of our discussion must be an enquiry as to whose interests were being served in the taking up of NFE as the answer to the world's educational crisis. It was suggested that the 'crisis' itself and NFE were both constructed by Coombs and others as a means of preserving educational planning and especially of protecting formal schools in the light of what was felt to be the spectacular failure of educational planners to fulfil their promises (Simmons 1980: 1-12). Coombs himself wrote that because NFE was education specifically for development (investment education), therefore it needed to be organised, measured and controlled to function alongside formal education (Coombs 1968). "Coombs' call for new educational strategies coincided with, perhaps even helped to initiate, a rediscovery of out of school education" (Bock 1976: 348). Bhola suggested that it was "Western elites who first declared a crisis (the crisis of formal education), then fabricated a challenge (meeting minimum basic needs of the poor) and then gifted a solution (non-formal education) to the Third World" (Bhola 1983: 51). The problems having been constructed, NFE similarly was constructed as a solution, if not in fact *the* solution, to these problems.

But the discourse having been created, it was taken up very widely in many so-called 'developing countries'. National governments, it was suggested, saw in NFE a safety valve because many could not or would not pay for universal primary education (Bock & Papagiannis 1983). NFE was advocated as "a means to help solve their social and economic development problems", a tool by which the state's authority could be extended and consolidated (LaBelle 1976b: 280; Bock 1976: 359; Bock & Bock 1985: 3551).

NFE and the deficit paradigm: The NFE discourse fitted in with both of the two main approaches within the deficit paradigm of development, the modernisation and the basic needs approaches. NFE appealed to the Human Resource Development modernisers; they liked the way that the NFE discourse asserted categorically that "more and more people must acquire more and more new kinds of skills and knowledge, as well as new attitudes and aspirations" which it is assumed they lack

(Coombs & Ahmed 1974: 234). At the same time, it appealed to the Basic Human Needs approach because it seemed to offer a division between education for the modern formal industrial economic sector (formal schooling) and an alternative rural education for the informal sector (NFE). Thus Dore stated that "the new fashion for NFE is based on the overwhelming priority for rural development" (Dore 1976: 104).

Planning for co-option: But even at the time there was a feeling that educational planners had taken to NFE in order to co-opt it, to integrate it, linking together its disparate elements to control it (Paulston 1972: xi; Ahmed 1982: 137; LaBelle & Ward 1994: 4142). The ultimate aim was to safeguard the formal system of education from the excesses of the deschoolers. This can be seen in the fact that the early Advocates never saw NFE as a threat to formal education. It is true that they felt that formal schooling needed substantial reform, but they were "surer about what they were moving away from than about what they were moving towards" (Krueger & Moulton 1981: 2). Formal needed non-formal, just as non-formal could not exist without formal. The ideology of schooling was not challenged by the Advocates for NFE.

The emphasis in all the texts, then, especially the key texts by Coombs and Ahmed and Evans, was on the need for planning NFE in order to achieve government-set goals and to use scarce resources most efficiently: "There is a flagrant need for the various sponsors of fragmented nonformal education efforts to form themselves into a co-operative and well co-ordinated community with a sense of common purpose" (Coombs 1976: 284-285). USAID funded the mapping of NFE and the preparation of inventories of NFE in countries like Ethiopia "in efforts to administer and co-ordinate it" (Krueger & Moulton 1981: 14, 34). It was asserted that NFE needs to be planned and co-ordinated alongside the formal education system: "A merger of the formal and nonformal education sectors into a technical rational model provides one system in which one can look at the full range of learning needs as well as at all possible delivery modes and make the most appropriate match" (Evans 1981a). Countries should build up a holistic approach to education, drawing on the best of both systems. Thus Brembeck argued that "if we knew more about what each is capable – or incapable – of doing, our uses of these two modes of education would be more economical, efficient and effective" (Brembeck & Grandstaff 1974: 53).

> In broad terms, it is reasonable to assume that the formal school system should perform those functions which it has the demonstrated com-petence to perform; the non-formal system should carry on those functions which it performs well. Each system should be strengthened in its respective areas of competence. The question is not one of creating a new type of education, nor is it one of establishing a dual system in which formal and non-formal education are set up in a posture of competition or confrontation". (Case & Niehoff 1976: 29)

Only in this way would the deficit, integrated rural development model, aimed not so much at modernisation but at the improvement of economic and social life, especially the informal economic sector, be fulfilled. The World Bank summed up the value of NFE for development in its widest sense:

> Within this context, modes of delivering education – formal, nonformal and informal – are conceived today not as alternatives but as complementary activities within a single system ... Nonformal education ... is neither an alternative education system nor a shortcut to the rapid education of a population. Rather, nonformal education and training provides the second chance for learning to those who missed formal schooling; it enables the rural poor, within programs of 'integrated development' to acquire useful knowledge, attitudes and skills; and affords a wide array of learning activities directly associated with work". (World Bank 1974)

This was the revolution in education which had been achieved by the early 1970s – that few could write about education without including the extra-formal element. And academics and consultants adopted the discourse of NFE because that was where the funds were. When the funds dried up, they quickly abandoned the language of NFE.

CONCLUSION

NFE then, in its infancy, meant many things to many people. Coming as it did from within the deficit paradigm of development, there was no coherence yet behind the concept, just a series of vague, often overlapping or contradictory, perceptions of what was felt to be a newly identified field of activity. NFE could mean a system, a collection of organisations and programmes different from the formal education system. Or a process, with different teaching-learning relationships from those in formal education, a less hierarchical format. Or a concept, a subject worthy of study and writing about. Or yet a practice, a professional activity undertaken by people separate from formal education professionals. Or yet a set of educational activities distinguished from formal education by having different goals or purposes, or even separated from formal schooling by being socially purposeful, part of the radical social transformation movement.

It was this last strand which made the first move to bring some measure of coherence to this confusion.

5

Ideologues

If nonformal education is to be anything more than a new and faddish
label that obscures rather than addresses problems, it is crucial to delineate
for it some distinctive character and functions. (Grandstaff 1976: 304)

The more radical educational reformers took up NFE as one of the major answers to their criticisms of formal education (schooling). NFE would not only provide what was missing from formal education; it would reform formal education: "... exposure to programs and methods of non-formal education could have a healthy effect on the formal educational system" (Case & Niehoff 1976: 33).

This was, as we have seen, the age when the paradigm of disadvantage, with its concentration on the necessity for reforming the structures rather than just the marginalised populations, was emerging. This was an age of polarities, especially in education, what Paulston has labelled as the period of heterodoxy. Knowles, Houle, Carl Rogers and other humanistic writers of the time were casting the minds of those who followed them into contrasts and opposites. The distinction between what Evans called the didactic approach and the dialogue approach (Evans 1976: 307), between Freire's education that domesticates and education that liberates, between Dore's qualification seeking or learning seeking, was common currency.

It was therefore natural that those who saw education in these terms would cast non-formal and formal into opposing camps. And NFE was constructed in a way which emphasised the more positive or desirable side of the equation, learning rather than teaching, education rather than schooling, liberation and self-actualisation and social transformation rather than domestication, discipline and reproduction. The implication was that formal education lacked the desirable qualities of education which NFE possessed.

The radical reformers thus looked at formal education in ways which were deliberately negative. Programmes which lacked the more attractive 'non-formal' qualities were 'non-educational' (i.e. they were not achieving relevant useful learning). Formal education came to be constructed in much the same way as NFE had been constructed, not as a system which could be easily recognised within any social setting but as a 'kind' of education.

Criticisms of the Advocates

There was of course much more to this trend than just an educational fashion of the time. There was serious discontent with the deficit discourses of development which underpinned the advocacy strand of the NFE debate. First, these deficit discourses were seen to be inadequate. They argued that supplementing formal education would be enough to overcome the obstacles to development. The Advocates rarely mentioned the need for reform of the structures and cultures within which educational systems stood, which is what the disadvantaged paradigm stressed. While the deficit discourses sought the answer to the question of *how* to increase participation in education and *how* to improve its quality, the disadvantaged discourses asked *why* so many people were debarred from education and *why* education was of low quality, and saw education itself as in part to blame. One sought to enhance education through NFE; the other sought to change the whole set of systems (including education) and to use NFE for this purpose. Coombs and Ahmed, it is true, widened their view of NFE in a way which drew on the disadvantage paradigm:

> Nonformal education is one of the essential weapons to be used in this attack [on rural poverty and social injustice] ... Yet new knowledge and new skills, though vitally important, are not enough. There must be new and special flows of credit and agricultural inputs to which the disadvantaged have fair and genuine access; new work and income opportunities; ... better health, education and general welfare services ... (Coombs & Ahmed 1974: 238)

But this did not feature as the main thrust of their discourse. Coombs and his colleagues were arguing for more inputs rather than for structural change, for adding NFE alongside the formal educational system rather than radically reforming or even replacing the formal education system.

The reason why the Advocates failed to give adequate emphasis to the structural problems of development was the "set of psychologically oriented assumptions about the change process" which, it was alleged, underpinned their view of non-formal education programmes (LaBelle & Ward 1994: 4144). Education was seen largely in cognitive terms; and as we have seen, the deficit paradigm implied that if the deficits of the peasants could be met through inputs, especially education and training (formal or non-formal), this would be enough to ensure that education was effective. But radical reformers doubted whether education alone was the way to change the structures of society effectively.

NFE as Ideology

The answer to these criticisms was to treat NFE as a set of educational traits which could be identified and promoted. This ideological approach to NFE did not start from field surveys such as those of Coombs and his colleagues in ICED (1973, 1974, 1975) or that of Sheffield and Diejomaoh (1972), but from overall theoretical positions. It is noticeable that, in many of the writings of the Ideologues, there are relatively few supporting references provided except to other theoretical papers expounding the arguments being made (see *CER* 1976 etc.). Rather, such writings started from theoretical, a priori, positions, and when they did try to justify these by citing examples from the field, such examples frequently did not exemplify the claims made for them (see for example Simkins 1977, where his case studies do not illustrate his depiction of NFE). Taking formal education as their starting point, they draw a picture of NFE as the opposite of formal schooling in every respect, as "an education radically different from the borrowed model", i.e. the Western model of formal education (Amin 1975: 52).

While the initial concept of NFE came from Western societies (Coombs, Brembeck, Grandstaff, Evans etc.), not from Third World countries as some early writers suggested, it was taken up and sometimes elaborated in developing societies. Several of these countries were seeking ways of creating an education which owed less to the West. India in particular produced a large number of writings on NFE during the 1970s and early 1980s. The concept was applied specifically to groups seen as specially disadvantaged (such as women) or marginal (such as scheduled castes and tribes). One such paper (India DNFE nd) suggested that NFE was especially valid for women because

- few women were selected for formal education, most were rejected as failures
- women need to be educated in-life, part-time because of their roles
- women have much indigenous knowledge
- women have much coping to do throughout life,

views which many in India both at the time and since found patronising.

An example: One of the most extensive critiques of the formal education system in a developing society, together with a justification of NFE, came from Dr Malcolm Adiseshiah, who for a number of years served as a senior member of staff of UNESCO (Adiseshiah 1975). In India, he saw formal education as a borrowed system, devised by and effective in affluent industrialised economies and cultures but not suited to India's agri-rural economy or India's culture. It creates drop-outs, or rather it pushes out the majority of its pupils.[1] Formal education drew its top percentage from the top 20% of society, thus reinforcing the class divisions in India. Its contents were outdated, imported and irrelevant. Its examinations were no test of learning abilities, but yet they

---

[1] Surveys conducted by his Madras Institute for Development Studies revealed that in Tamil Nadu at that time, 52% of eleven year olds, 80% of 15 year olds and 97% of 21 year olds had not completed their schooling up to the level considered appropriate to each age group. 60% of all adults had never been near a school.

dominated the whole system. Education, he alleged, was making its participants unemployable; in Tamil Nadu in that year, there were 300,000 unemployed graduates. Schools and colleges had consequently become places of violence not only between teachers and pupils but between other factions as well; they served as a locus of strikes and agitation rather than places of study and contemplation. The escalating costs of the system had become insupportable: again, in Tamil Nadu, what had cost 10 crores of rupees in 1950-51 had by 1975-6 become 148 crores.

All of these issues would be solved, he suggested, by Nonformal Education. NFE would be related to the native social and economic system. There would be multiple entry and re-entry points for all. Through NFE, education would be integrative rather than divisive. NFE would be job-oriented. The content would be relevant, and the validation would be by whether the work improved, not whether the examinations had been passed. There would be no violence because the programme would be seen to be appropriate and productive. NFE would be much cheaper than formal schooling.

It is clear from this and other writings at the time that NFE was seen, in India as in other developing societies, as an answer to many of the public criticisms of the formal system of education, whether these criticisms came from students, parents, employers or governments. It is therefore not surprising that, at this stage in the debate, the various differences between formal and non-formal education should have been emphasised. NFE would achieve what formal education failed to achieve – which is why the qualitative differences between them were accentuated.

NFE as opposed to formal schooling

Nonformal education then was being constructed as the opposite of formal education, everything that formal education was not. Most of the writers never defined formal education or schooling, but they described it always in very negative terms. "One can quite easily identify the basic characteristics of the standard model of schooling" (Evans & Smith 1972: 14); and although these authors do not list these basic characteristics, in discussing programmes of education which display "the absence of all the major characteristics of formal education", they itemise some of these characteristics (ibid: 15), for example, the possession of pre-set learning goals, a guide or trained teacher, a set curriculum, an external structure providing beginning or end points, a schedule, and adequate facilities or equipment (NFE was supposed to possess the opposite of all of these). Like so many others, these authors asserted the characteristics of formal education without citing any examples of these programmes (e.g. Paulston 1972; Brembeck & Thompson 1973: 58-60).

Most of these features of the formal system of education were of course seen as detrimental to true education. Brembeck, while ostensibly searching for value in formal education as well as in NFE, saw NFE almost entirely in beneficial terms and formal education in negative terms. Formal schools are detached from their environment, they form ghettos, they segregate their pupils, they function more on teaching than learning, they defer rewards, they use methods of learning which are not part of the natural learning processes (Brembeck & Thompson 1973: 58-60). This is why formal education in many such writings was often described as 'schooling' rather than education (Carson 1984; Keil 1989).

In contrast, the positive characteristics of NFE were extolled uncritically. Different people indicated that they valued particular non-formal characteristics more than others. As Evans and Smith (1972: 18) pointed out, some valued the independence of NFE from the schooling system, others learner control, some nonformal teaching-learning methods (again not always defined) and yet others flexibility in one or more aspects of provision (teachers or timetable etc.). What comes out in most of these writings is that it is the *absence* of various undesirable features of formal education more than the presence of a defined non-formality which makes some educational activities 'non-formal'. By concentrating on NFE as meeting the failures of the formal system of education, they were in fact tying NFE closer to formal education.

NFE as process rather than system

The emphasis at this stage of the debate was thus on the nature of education within both sectors more than on systems. The definitions of what was included in and what was excluded from each category did not occupy attention so much as the characteristics of non-formal education and the contrariness of the characteristics of formal education. The correlation between systems and characteristics were rarely made and usually unsatisfactorily. Thus Brembeck (Brembeck & Thompson 1973: xiv) said that NFE programmes tended not to be part of large bureaucracies (which would therefore exclude agricultural extension, much vocational training and adult literacy programmes); that they are typically smaller in scale; they arise to meet a specific need and go out of existence when the need is filled; they have a variety of sponsoring organisations, and they can develop 'useful' forms of certification. He felt that NFE was usually more flexible and innovative and could respond more quickly in more appropriate ways to new educational demands. The use of comparative terms such as 'smaller' and 'more' throughout this statement indicates that Brembeck is making a contrast, presumably with formal education, always to the advantage of NFE. Some agencies were particularly idealistic, viewing non-formal education as being unlike formal education in that it was characterised by solidarity and companionships (collective learning), the creation of channels of communication with the community, an orientation towards the critical analysis of political, social and economic reality, group work and self-criticism, the promotion of community growth and individual growth in primary groups, and the absence of discrimination against the individual or the prioritisation of their needs (ETH Focus).

Ideals: A few of those who wrote in this vein agreed that such lists of characteristics were ideals rather than clear cut characteristics. Simkins labels his list 'Ideal Type

Models of Formal and Nonformal Education' (Simkins 1977: 12):

> It is not being argued that, to be considered 'formal' [or by implication,
> 'non-formal'], a programme must conform in every detail to these
> characteristics. If this were so, very few educational programmes could
> be characterised as formal in the strict sense. What is being argued,
> however, is that any educational programme which can meaningfully be
> called 'formal' will approximate in most of its characteristics to this
> model; and conversely any educational programme which possesses
> most of these characteristics should be classified as 'formal' even if
> such terminology is not normally applied to it. (ibid: 11)

Others wrote in similar vein. In other words, NFE was seen by some as a reform
agenda which applied not only to formal schooling but also to NFE programmes.

Listing the contrasts

Lists of dichotomies were drawn up by academics and practitioners alike. Some distinguished between the *objectives* of formal and non-formal education. Some concentrated on the *processes* within education: formal processes could be distinguished
from nonformal processes. Some emphasised *curricular* differences, between ire-
levant and relevant contents of education. Some looked at the issue of *control*, how far
the participants exercised measures of control over different aspects of the education
they participated in. Several tried to be comprehensive and include everything.
    Srinivasan (1977, 1985: 3548ff) recognised several of these categories such as
contents, methods, objectives, and control, but she concentrated most on methodologies. She set out alternatives to formal education and set these along a continuum
rather than a dichotomy. Her contrasts stretched between at one end subject-centred,
didactic, directive teaching; through problem-solving, generalised skill training;
through conscientisation/general insights forms of education, to (at the opposite pole)
learner-centred, human development, creative, self-actualising, expressive education.
But others denied that the possession of non-formal methods made a programme non-
formal: "Informal methods or activities are increasingly used in formal education programs. Hence the term 'formal education' is defined ... without reference to methods
as a determining factor. Formal education ... does not become nonformal simply
because informal methods are used" (Bowers & Fisher 1972 cited in Lowe 1985: 3557).
    Thus the tabulating of parallel sets of characteristics of formal and non-formal
education did not go unchallenged. Frith and Reed, for example, felt that there were
problems with such listings: "Various efforts to construct meaningful definitions,
descriptions and lists of characteristics of nonformal education create major confu-
sions for both theory and practice... worldwide misunderstandings and conflicts among
organisational decision-makers at all levels". Instead, they elaborated the continua
approach in their Lifelong Learning Scale running from more formal to less formal
with no less than 15 dimensions expressed in terms of distance between two points

rather than as different staging posts as in Srinivasan (Frith & Reed 1982: 16-18; repeated in Reed 1987: 25; see Reed 1984).

Many such lists were drawn up. Paulston (1972: xii-xiv) outlined ten points of contrast between formal and non-formal education, setting out the contrasts in terms of their structure, content, time scale, control, locale, functions, rewards, methods, participants and costs (Paulston 1973: 66-67). Case and Niehoff (1976: 15-21) produced a similar listing of contrasting characteristics – educational process, agency, locale, clientele, objectives, teachers, learning groups, methods, motivation of the participants, resources and methods of evaluation. Callaway (1973: 16-17) listed 12 characteristics of 'out-of-school' education.

For these writers, people who were ideological in their approach, formal and non-formal education can be clearly distinguished and are in contrast. The differences between them as listed range from the simplistic to the elaborate. At their briefest, they consist of very general distinctions: for example,

FORMAL	NONFORMAL
• System (primary, secondary, tertiary)	• No system; educational activities follow on, one after the other
• Education in preparation for life • Aimed at national needs	• Education in and through life • Aimed at personal growth

A more elaborate approach can be seen in the following, taken from an Indian government brochure:

FORMAL	NONFORMAL
Selective: a strainer, a pyramid, select first and then train; system rejects participants at various stages; once out, cannot get back in; system ends up with very few (elitist); costly	Open: can get in and out at any time; no prior selection, only self-selection by participants; no rejection, no failures, no permanent dropouts; cheap
Remote from life: a period of all education and no work, followed by all work and no education; takes participants out of life into full-time education; rejects life experience for classroom experiences; learn now for future use; curriculum academic, irrelevant, colonial	In-life education: learning to be, not learning to become something different; learning how to cope with living now; uses experience and existing knowledge; relevant curriculum, immediate application; part-time, not full-time; uses indigenous knowledge
Terminal: front-end loading education, 'banking approach'; sends participants out 'trained' for life, fully equipped, no need for more; certificated	Lifelong: education never complete because always coping with new things; not so interested in certificates; admits 'I don't know'
Results: creates dependent learners; learning stops when teacher is not there	Results: creates self-reliant, independent and continuing learners

Other lists are even more elaborate, as can be seen from the Appendix to this chapter.

Note: these tables have been constructed from a large number of comparative lists drawn from many sources rather than from any one source.

The most widely used list would seem to be that drawn up by Simkins (1977) in which he contrasted the purposes, the timing, the content, the delivery systems and the measures of control of both formal and nonformal education, always to the disadvantage of formal education and the advantage of non-formal education. Von Hahmann's characteristics of NFE run to 18 points under the headings of 'focus on the community, relevance and humanism, and flexibility' (von Hahmann 1978 Appendix).

Some features of the lists: A number of features appear from these lists. First, the assumption throughout is that NFE is not just different from but in all respects better than formal education. NFE does not just complement formal education but provides a better possible model altogether. Hilliard's characterisation of the desirability of NFE as against formal education is extreme even by the writings of the time:

> ... formal education has tended to be a solemn, monastic business, suffering from an obsession with facts, discipline, and order. It emphasises information rather than understanding; objectivity but not subjectivity, knowledge rather than behavior. Its ethos was (and still is in most places) hard and solitary labor. In our return to faith in and larger reliance on nonformal education, it is essential that the ancient ethos of nonformal education be painstakingly retained: usefulness to life, participatory learning, entertainment, using vehicles of art as well as the concepts of science and technology". (Hilliard 1973: 141)

Others carried over something of the discourses of deficit from the definitional phase, suggesting that NFE was directly related to development whereas formal education was not. Grandstaff suggested that one of the best ways to identify NFE from formal education "is to relate the concept of nonformal education to the concept of development", and he went on to suggest that NFE was low-cost, short-duration, needs-based, aspiration-accommodating, employment-linked, decentralised, and highly distributive in terms of its benefits, quite the opposite of formal education (Grandstaff 1974a: 1, 54; Bhola echoes this in 1983). Brembeck suggests that formal and nonformal education serve different purposes in development.

> Initiating change and implementing change are two quite different ends. ... Formal education may best fit the end of conceptualizing and planning change. Nonformal education may be better suited to implementing it ... The capacity of nonformal education to meet specific needs, as for example in public health education, population control, agriculture production, and village improvement, makes it a useful tool for people development". (Brembeck & Thompson 1973: xv, 60)

"The importance of nonformal education for youth and adults lies in its integration as an educational component (skill training, attitude change, literacy) into the development programmes of other sectors" (Fordham 1993: 2). These attitudes towards the relative merits of both formal and nonformal education remained for many years. Formal education is constructed then as having a number of *undesirable* qualities which NFE will redress.

Secondly, some of these lists are contradictory. While for example, a number suggested that formal education is characterised by a stress on individual and non-collaborative learning whereas NFE emphasises collective and shared learning, others preferred to look at the way in which formal education put national social needs above the individual, while they saw NFE as putting individual needs above the national.

In promoting this challenge from NFE to formal education, there was some awareness of the dangers of creating two kinds of education, urban and modernising formal education and rural and traditional-supporting nonformal education. But the pleas for integration between the two, for co-operation, for building a national system utilising the best features of both which had characterised the definitional phase of the Advocates were ignored. What the Ideologues sought was for formal education to become more like nonformal education; the programme of activity for this discourse community was to reform the formal system.

But the most enduring impression from this strand to the debate is that formal and nonformal education were seen as two separate entities. They could each be recognised – not by being related to some form of system but by the characteristics which each of them bears. They were seen to stand in opposition to each other. Dichotomy ruled.

This strand was predominant until about the late 1970s. Simkins' small but influential study and Lyra Srinivasan's handbook, both published in 1977, were virtually the last major contributions to this strand. But the ideas behind it persisted and to some extent influenced later writings about NFE such as those of LaBelle.

Note on terminology: to prevent ambiguity and misunderstanding, it is necessary to state that the term 'ideological' is used here for these views since it was used during the debates. However, some writers saw these views of NFE as 'autonomous' – that is, they saw NFE as a universal, independent of local power relationships. This alternative terminology is closer to the current use of the terms 'autonomous' (universal, outside of contextualised power systems) and 'ideological' (socio-culturally constructed, integrally related to contextualised power systems) in literacy studies (see Street 1984).

Appendix

FORMAL	NONFORMAL
PURPOSES Formal education seeks to reproduce society; it is judged successful if it re-produces itself.	NFE is most successful if it leads to desired social change.
Formal education is (in one sense) long-term; that is, it is expected to provide the basis for the future, therefore it is general in character in terms of subjects and participants.	NFE is (in this sense) short-term and specific; it meets the learning needs of individuals; it inculcates specific knowledge, skills and attitudes.
It is credential-based; the end-product is often a certificate to enable the individual to obtain specific socio-economic positions in society.	It is non-credential-based; it gives tangible rewards such as immediate improvements in material well-being, productivity, self-awareness etc..
Formal schooling relies on a system which inherently creates failures. It is socially divisive, increasing social inequalities.	There are no failures in NFE; anyone can come back at any time and make further progress along their own line of development; it is aimed at universal participant satisfaction. It can be socially integrative.
TIMING Formal education is long-cycle: usually more than one year, often ten years or more.	NFE is short-cycle: it is rarely more than two years but it depends for its length on the achievement of learning goals.
On the other hand, formal education is only for a short period (say, the first twenty years of life). A participant enters once and leaves once. It is preparatory: child-related and future-orientated; it assumes a static society for which it is preparing the participants for the rest of their lives (education for certainty).	At the same time, NFE takes place throughout the whole of life. There are multiple entry and re-entry points. It is recurrent: it depends on the individual's role and stage in life, and on the constantly changing nature of society; it is education for uncertainty.
Most formal education is full-time: usually does not permit other parallel activities, especially work.	NFE is part-time: its timing is set to meet the needs and convenience of clients.
CONTENTS Formal education (schooling) is input-centred: that is, the basis of the curriculum is a standardised package of knowledge (mostly cognitive) which is imparted to the participants; it is static, often outdated and imported.	NFE is output-centred; it consists of individualised tasks or skills-centred activities; it is not standardised, but related to the needs of participants as individuals or group.

Formal education is largely academic and compartmentalised into academic disciplines which are seen as separate from each other; it is seen as an outside intrusion into the local context (especially urban elites): it is isolated from the immediate environment and discourages social action; it is mostly an uncritical induction into the common (national) culture, a socialisation process.	NFE is more practical: it is closely related to the participants' environment (both rural and urban); it draws on all disciplines in an integrated way to solve problems rather than study subjects; it often leads to critical reflection on and social action to change that environment; it will often seek to legitimise a local culture to the national.
The clientele is determined by set entry requirements which are related to their existing knowledge; the successful completion of lower levels is required for admission to higher levels.	The entry requirements for NFE are determined by the clientele, not the system; formal entry requirements are not essential.
DELIVERY SYSTEMS Formal education is institution-based: it takes place in 'schools' which are education-specific.	NFE is context-based: it takes place in a variety of settings; its facilities are minimal, low-cost and not education-specific.
It is isolated: its participants are removed from their own environments for long periods.	It is community-based: the local environment is functionally related to learning programme.
Schooling is rigidly structured around established parameters of time and the participants' ages and performance; it involves uniform entry points; it is sequential and continuous.	NFE is flexibly structured: a variety of relationships and sequences is possible; it possesses varying degrees and types of structure.
Formal education is teacher-centred: it uses labour-intensive technology; it emphasises teaching rather than learning; control is vested in recognised authorities.	NFE is learner-centred: it uses a variety of resources and technologies; it lays emphasis on learning rather than teaching, on sharing, exploring, analysing, judging together; the staff are facilitators rather than teachers.
It is resource-intensive: it involves high opportunity costs in terms of student time; most of its resources come from outside the community.	NFE is resource-sparse: it utilises community facilities and local personnel; it employs only low-cost facilities.
CONTROL It is hierarchical: internal control is highly structured and is based on role-defined relations.	NFE is democratic: substantial control is vested in the participants and the local community.

Source: based on Simkins 1977

6

Empiricists

Most of the social and political advantages attributed to nonformal education are more in the nature of a manifesto – a formal declaration of the principles, pious intentions, and perhaps possibilities of such education – rather than an actual manifestation of those great hopes. (Bhola 1983: 50)

The third major strand in the great debate on NFE emerged about 1974 with an analysis of nonformal education which saw it, not as the opposite of, but as essentially on an equivalency with, formal education and therefore amenable to all the same tests and critique as the formal system.

A NEW ANALYSIS

There was of course a cultural change behind this change of approach to NFE. There grew up a feeling that both the Advocates and the Ideologues tended to see NFE as if it occurred in a vacuum; they treated it as if it were outside of the social and political relations, ideological practices and symbolic meaning situations in which it is embedded (adapted from Rockhill 1993: 162). They were accused of seeing NFE as a remedy brought in from outside to treat ills rather than as a part of the sick society which created and maintained it.

This awareness led a new group of writers to take a "step back from the optimism of the proponents of nonformal education" (i.e. the Advocates and Ideologues) to what they saw as a more realistic position (Bock & Papagiannis 1983: 10). On the one hand, education (including NFE) was felt to have a more limited role in development than had been ascribed to it by earlier writers. Those engaged in NFE "must ... recognize that educational inputs constitute only one rather minor component in what should be an overall strategy of change which integrates several diverse, yet functionally interdependent sectors; ... as long as nonformal education is regarded as a panacea for developing countries, such change is unlikely to occur" (LaBelle & Verhine 1975: 183). Referring to the "unattainable expectations" of many NFE practitioners and policy-makers, the International Bureau of Education spoke of the fact that "education alone cannot improve quality of life" (IBE 1987).

Bock and Papagiannis (key figures in this strand of the debate) suggested that although education has the potential to transform society, such transformation rarely results since education is usually provided and controlled by the state and the elites. In most developing countries, "education is a means of legitimating the governing elite" (Bock 1976: 359; see also Bock & Bock 1985: 3553), "... a mechanism for the ... consolidation of state authority, ... a means to institutionalize that authority" (Meyer & Rubinson unpublished paper cited in Bock 1976: 359).

On the other hand, whereas the Ideological approach developed in what Evans and Smith (1972: 12) called an "anti-school era", the new approach felt much more positively about formal education. Schooling could and should be reformed but on the whole it was a good thing. Despite some of the writings of the time, Bock suggested that the "call for expanded nonformal education has not arisen as a response to, nor does it in any way comprise, a serious attack on the traditional goals and functions of schools ... [there is] a continuing affirmation of the belief in the benign relationship between education and development as modernization. Schooling is not indicted because of the inappropriateness of its goals ... but because of its observed failure in achieving these goals" (Bock 1976: 350). It was possible to reform schooling so that it did achieve developmental goals; NFE was not (as they suggested that the Ideologues believed) the only channel for such achievements.

Critique of existing paradigms of NFE

The dissatisfaction with both the Advocacy and the Ideological perspectives was based on theoretical and empirical grounds.

In theory, these writers adopted some of the same criticisms as the Ideologues, pointing out that the Advocacy paradigm was based on a deficit model and that it was psychological rather than social in its assumptions. "The advocacy position for non-formal education has largely been assumed by those educators and policy makers who tend to affirm the assumptions underlying the 'psychological deficit' or 'functional' model of development" (Bock 1976: 350; Bock & Papagiannis 1983: 9). "The primary reason that nonformal education has not produced a significant amount of social change lies with the narrow psychological approach characteristic of most programs", its failure to seek change in "both people and the social structures which constrain their behavior" (LaBelle 1976a: 328).

These writers therefore "felt the need for an interpretive framework better able to take social structure and context into account and able to deal analytically with the 'centrality of power' in the relationship between education and social subsystems" (Bock & Papagiannis 1983: 9). But the main attack was made against the Ideological model of NFE as being over-generalised and prescriptive. It decontextualised the very programmes it sought to claim were localised. The Ideologues did not see education in its local context; they assumed it was the same in every country and society, and that it operated independently of any other factors within that society. NFE "needs to be set in its social context; ... a broader, more complex structural approach ... will allow us to view education within its societal context – not as an autonomous system, but as a subsystem continually acting upon and being acted upon by the other social sub-systems, political, economic and cultural" (Bock & Papagiannis 1983: 10, 20). "A more sociologically based set of assumptions regarding nonformal education" rather than a universalised approach was what was needed (LaBelle & Ward 1994: 4144).

Secondly, the Ideological approach was felt to be uncritical. It did not discuss the issues of real power which critical theory was raising, although it claimed that the participants controlled NFE more than in formal education. The political economy of NFE was ignored; the Ideologues did not ask, 'in whose interests is NFE run?' There was too much rhetoric around the discussions of NFE.

Indeed, the Ideological approach was partial rather than objective. It tended to minimise the commonalities between formal and nonformal education, to maximise the differences between the two. And in doing so, it had become normative. Citing one Ideologist's list of characteristics of NFE, Bock and Papagiannis comment: "We do not deny that this definition might describe some nonformal educational activities, but question whether it adequately describes all or even most nonformal educational activities, particularly in developing nations" (Bock & Papagiannis 1983: 14).

For in doing this, the Ideological approach hides the differences between different kinds of NFE. Even within one social context, NFE is very diverse. The Ideologues, it was alleged, tended to treat all NFE as the same and as being capable of being compared, even across countries and continents (an approach which Bock & Papagiannis themselves also adopted uncritically, as we shall see). "The proposed characteristics of NFE are only fragmented properties valid for a very specific context and, hence, are difficult to generalise to the entire field of NFE" (IBE 1987). "The fact that nonformal education programs can possess different combinations of these variations does little to reduce the confusion surrounding nonformal education, nor does it simplify attempts to specify the characteristics that account for its impact" (Bock & Papagiannis 1983: 13).

Empirical Surveys

But the main pressure for the development of a new approach to NFE came not from theoretical criticism but from practice. It was created by those who looked at what was happening on the ground. And in brief, they found that non-formal educational activities were simply not 'non-formal' in character as defined by the Ideologues.

The grounds for this approach had been laid by the paper by Evans and Smith in 1972[1] – although they too tried to develop a set of specific and inherent characteristics of NFE. They defined NFE as everything that was not formal. Although they never

---

[1] This paper presented at the World Education Conference in 1972 was apparently never officially published by CIE, University of Massachusetts, but it became very influential, being cited in many different publications under several different titles. See Evans and Smith 1971, 1972 and 1973.

defined 'formal education', they pointed out that the umbrella term of NFE was used to bracket "a large collection of alternatives" together; but "as the conceptual framework for nonformal education develops, it is likely that a more precise series of terms will emerge which are functionally effective in describing particular types of nonformal education" (Evans & Smith 1972: 12). They felt that it is therefore important to look at what programmes actually exist outside the formal system and to assess the nature of these programmes.

This led to several substantial empirical surveys of NFE in the field, during the second half of the 1970s and throughout the 1980s by various agencies, especially IIEP between 1983 and 1989. Some of these were very general, consisting of no more than a series of brief descriptions of case studies of NFE programmes, but others were more thorough. Bock and Papagiannis brought together a collection of case studies in their major publication (1983). More detailed research was done in some countries such as the Cameroon, where 267 NFE activities were taken for closer study (Creative Assocs 1983). In 1975, an analysis of over 2000 NFE programmes in Colombia was made (Velandia et al. 1975). In the mid 1970s, the South East Asia Ministers of Education Organisation (SEAMEO) made a survey of 60 NFE projects in that region (SEAMEO 1975). In 1983, Vargas Adams (Adams & Bastian 1983) produced for the World Bank a survey of NFE in Lesotho. Carr-Hill and Lintott (1985; see also Carron & Carr-Hill 1991) used many detailed studies in their examination for IIEP of the planning and management of NFE programmes (but they equated NFE with adult education). It became rare for country surveys of education to be conducted without including a discussion of NFE (see for example Beevers 1972; Colletta 1976; Amaratunga 1977; Gajaido 1983; Marja 1993). In 1981, for example, a survey of Nepal included a substantial section on NFE (although a parallel survey of education in Sudan had only two pages on adult education, IIEP 1981). In 1989, Gallart made a historical review of education in Argentina for IIEP, including programmes which he identified as NFE although they were not so described at the time[2].

These were not the first surveys of their kind. There had been earlier collections of case studies, one of the most important being that of NFE in African countries made by Sheffield and Diejomoah in 1972. But are were not analytical nor comparative, but simply descriptive. They tend to stress the differences between the projects they were recounting and the formal system of education. The later surveys listed above were very different in intention. Although this was not always stated openly, it would seem that the purpose behind most of these studies was to challenge the assertions of the Ideologues about the potential of NFE to remedy the faults of formal education.

Lack of data: The overriding conclusion from all of these surveys was that, despite the attempts of UNESCO, data for the study of NFE did not exist. Unlike the formal system of education, for which (in theory at least) information was collected and preserved in the Ministries of Education, no such information existed for "the wide

---

[2] Similar surveys of Hungary, Russia and Canada were made at the same time.

variety of educational activities that comprise NFE" (see Mehta 1996). In Colombia, for example, data was hard to collect, for "training cycles are fluid, dropouts are not always recorded and more often than not, programmes do not award a certificate" (Velandia et al. 1975: 153 cited in IEC 1996a). "In no country has there been an adequate, systematic inventory and analysis made of nonformal education ... It seems certain that far more nonformal education and learning are taking place in every country than are known to development planners and educators" (Hilliard 1973: 139). Thus the studies of NFE on the ground concluded that it is impossible to identify all the many varied forms of NFE which exist even in one small area (see Percy 1983 for a Western example of such an attempt); the data simply does not exist. What data there is, it has been suggested, ignores whole sections of NFE.

In addition, different definitions are used to establish what is included and what is omitted (Chu 1994, 1996) – which means that it is impossible to be really clear about making comparable judgments. Different countries choose different categories when defining NFE as "organised educational activities outside school compared to those in school" (Carron & Carr-Hill 1991). Most countries seem to have taken this definition as meaning those educational activities which can be related in some way or other to school activities. Some took it to mean 'private' provision as distinct from public provision, although the definitions of public and private are often contested (IEC 1996b: 14). For others, the emphasis was on the word 'education'; activities which did not look like education (schooling), such as farm visits in agricultural extension, were omitted from some surveys, although included in others.

Testing ideology: Although Bock and his colleagues urged that NFE was amenable to analysis "using a whole range of questions that educational researchers routinely employ regarding formal schooling" (Bock & Papagiannis 1983: 12), many of the questions asked about NFE in these surveys were in fact dictated by their concern to disprove the ideological approach to NFE. For example, some local case studies were taken to test the claims of those Ideologues who saw NFE as alternative education, the most significant being the studies made by Colletta and his colleagues on Sarvodaya Shramadana in Sri Lanka (Colletta & Todd 1983, Colletta et al. 1982). The costs of NFE were compared with those of formal schooling (see p.114 below). LaBelle and Verhine (1975; see Verhine & Lehmann 1982) deliberately set out to see whether NFE opened up alternative routes to enhanced economic activities through a series of case studies in Latin America. By 1986, LaBelle was assessing the role of NFE in Latin America in terms of social action (LaBelle 1986). IIEP carried out a survey of formal and non-formal vocational education and training in the 1980s (IIEP 1999), and the UIE also surveyed the field (Ranaweera 1990). A wide range of educational programmes which were defined by the researchers as nonformal were examined with preset questions to see *where* they were located, *whom* they served, *what goals* they served, and *what social roles* they fulfilled.

The Findings

Despite the lack of data which all the surveys complained about, and despite the fact that they noted the local variations in programmes, the Empiricists were not slow to draw sweeping conclusions from the evidence they collected from locations as far dispersed as Latin America, Africa and Asia: for example, "little NFE is directly related to production" (IEC 1996b: 19); "nonformal education has not produced a significant amount of social change"; "during the last thirty years such [NFE] efforts have not led to increased power and status benefits for participants" (LaBelle 1976c: 328, 344-5); "nonformal education is producing a quite different social product than schooling, with markedly different economic and political prospects" (Bock 1976: 357).

Dividing up the field of NFE: The major finding was that the term NFE covered a very wide range of different programmes. Coombs had written in 1968 that "in contrast to the relative neatness and coherence of the formal educational system, non-formal educational activities are an untidy melange that defies simple description" (Coombs 1968: 138). LaBelle and Verhine saw NFE as encompassing "community development, agricultural extension, vocational/technical training, motivation and consciousness raising" (LaBelle & Verhine 1975: 183). Bock and Papagiannis in their key study (1983) cited trades-training centres, on-the-job training, management training, moral or political re-education, community development programmes, literacy programmes, and alternative schools among any definition of what elsewhere they term 'non-schooling education' (Bock & Papagiannis 1976: 1). This incoherence in the field forced some to try to limit their definition of NFE. Thus in a later work, LaBelle limits NFE to "the lower end of formal schooling" (LaBelle 1976a), and Torres (1990) confined it to adult literacy and work-place vocational education and training.

Much of the work of these researchers was to see how they could divide up the field. Harbison (1973a) invoked four categories: upgrading of the existing workforce, vocational education and training intended for entry into the economic sector, socio-cultural educational programmes, and 'others' (see also Paik 1973: 175-184). Lynch (1997: 86) divides NFE programmes into those for productive employment, those for formal education equivalency, and those for community mobilisation. A categorisation (Carron & Carr-Hill 1991) which found a good deal of acceptance (and adaptation – see Hallak 1990) identifies four main groups according to what is called 'their primary orientation', as follows:

a) **para-formal:** alongside the formal system, basic, complementary, compensatory, remedial, second-chance, designed to strengthen formal (i.e. primary) education in one way or another

b) **professional**/vocational/occupational training designed to provide (further) work-related skills which the formal systems of vocational education and training cannot provide

c) **personal** development training, personal post-basic education and improvement

d) **popular** and/or progressive education aimed at social transformation (see for an elaboration of this Carr-Hill et al. 2001).[3]

Carron and Carr-Hill built this up into a matrix, distinguishing along one axis basic education and post-basic education, and along the other axis state/agency control and client control.

Such categorisation however does not fit the field as the Empiricists described it. As Bock and Papagiannis (1983) showed, nonformal vocational training can also be para-formal. And the distinction between the categories of personal growth and professional/vocational training now seems to some people to be artificial. Different programmes can be included under different headings more or less according to whim, and people attend NFE for very different reasons: "classification becomes arbitrary" although it is still often used for generalisations (IEC 1996b: 14). "Non-formal education as an educational term is loaded with different shades of meaning, and these meanings vary according to the context – revolutionary, non-revolutionary, under-developed, developing – and according to one's philosophical views of the role of education in general" (Bock & Papagiannis 1983: 14).

Providers: Although some writers (e.g. King 1991; see Hoppers 2000a: 11) defined NFE in terms of NGO provision and formal as that of state provision, the Empiricists were characterised by a tendency to swing the emphasis of their approach to NFE away from NGOs to the state. In Colombia, it was pointed out that overall 69% of the programmes selected for study were government projects; in Lesotho, some 40% were seen to be government-provided. Carron and Carr-Hill (1991) distinguished between public providers (including the state), private (which they saw as mainly commercial providers), and voluntary which they defined as non-profit and which included both welfare NGO agencies and community-based organisations, popular self-help groups. But the complicated role of NGOs, especially government-sponsored NGOs as in Egypt (see LaTowsky 1997), tends to make such a categorisation doubtful. And as Carron pointed out, the state is almost always involved even in NGO-provided NFE, either as whole or part-provider, funder or regulator (Carron & Carr-Hill 1991). It is therefore not surprising that so many projects which the Empiricists defined as NFE and chose to study were government-provided.

Torres (1990, 1991) in particular expressed the view that NFE in revolutionary Latin America was a tool of the state, both to help to cope with the demand for universal primary education ("a mopping up operation clearing some of the debris left behind by an intensely faulty formal schooling system", Hoppers 2000a: 9), and also to help the new authorities fulfil their own purposes, especially the reforming mani-festo of enhanced indigenous education and cultural revival against colonialism. Thus

---

[3] This is very close to the traditional four-fold categorisation of (Western) adult education into access, vocational, liberal and radical (Rogers 1992).

such states turned to NFE as much as to formal education to work in its favour, to consolidate the power of the new elites, to co-opt the NGOs to their own purposes, and to carry out the new state's reforming agenda. In some places where the authorities had to work with NGOs, they formed "uneasy alliances" (Boukary 1998), especially where they were unable to co-opt the NGOs.

NFE and Development: Many Ideologues had suggested (following Coombs and Ahmed) that NFE could meet the needs of those populations untouched by the formal system, especially rural areas, in a way that formal education could not. But the surveys showed that NFE tended to go where most people were. In Colombia, many more of the selected NFE projects were located in major cities (59%) than in smaller towns (24%), and many more in urban than in rural areas (17%). In Lesotho, 80% of the identified projects were in the lowlands where the population was densest rather than in the mountain areas, although government-provided NFE was seen to be as numerous in the mountain areas as in the lowlands; it was the NGOs who concentrated on lowland provision (IEC 1996b). This may of course simply reflect a tendency that it is easier to collect data from government agencies than from NGOs and from urban and populous areas than from rural and desert regions. It was also noted that in many areas, most of the rural programmes consisted of basic education; the more advanced NFE projects were in the towns. NFE, the researchers suggested, was not helping rural populations to catch up to their 'rightful' levels.

From the start, there had been a tension in NFE (as in formal education) between those who felt that NFE should aim at the overall (developmental) goals for the whole of society which governments sought to promote and those who felt that NFE should seek to help the participants to meet their own perceived learning needs. The gap between donor/government goals of "social functionality" and the personal perceived needs of individual learners was noted in several of the studies. Assessments of how NFE programmes related to national development goals were made, and the integration of the surveyed programmes into other development activities were found to vary from 44% in Lesotho to 90% in Colombia (IEC 1996b).

In Colombia, where a number of NFE projects were selected on the basis of their stated objectives, the two biggest categories were found to be community development and 'basic education' (literacy, health, family welfare), each about one third of this sample of projects. The remainder were in the 'culture' category (arts, culture and sports 17%), agriculture and artisan training (10%) and pre-school (9%). When a larger number of NFE projects were surveyed in terms of the contents of the programme, however, some 42% were in the basic education category, 20% in culture and agriculture each, 16% in community development and only 4% in pre-school (ibid). It may be that what we see here is a gap between what the organisers said was their objective and what in fact their programmes actually promoted.

Again, attempts were made to classify NFE projects in terms of content, but none of these classifications became widely accepted on a comparative basis. Carr-Hill and his colleagues suggested three main categories, basic education (lumping together literacy and health), 'modern' (i.e. programmes which promoted a development policy based on modernisation and Westernisation), and cultural education including arts and sports (Carr-Hill & Lintott 1985).

NFE seemed to play a smaller role in development than the Ideologues claimed. However analysed, the Empiricists came to the conclusion that production features relatively low in the scale. A survey of agricultural NFE (SEAMEO 1975) showed that more than 40% was in human resource development, management and personnel such as co-operatives and farmers' associations, and only 30% was in technical subjects such as crops and livestock. In Lesotho, although 64% was agricultural of one kind or another, not all of this was directly related to production. 49% was in community development, family improvement (including health and nutrition and family planning) and 21% was in literacy and immigrant education (IEC 1996b). In Africa, it was estimated that 50% of all non-formal adult education offered to women was in home economics (Economic Commission of Africa 1975, cited in Youngman 2000: 181).

It is natural that literacy features low in some countries and much higher in others; but all that we know about literacy programmes makes it clear that literacy programmes are as much a political activity as an educational activity. The conclusion is hard to escape that most of the NFE programmes which these surveys selected were fulfilling government-identified needs in basic and generalised education and in organisational skill development rather than meeting the specific needs of the participants. SEAMEO (1975) on the other hand pointed out that the arts and culture predominated in the radio programmes, just as they did in the later television education programmes in India (for SITE & INSAT, see Ahmed et al. 1991: 237-238).

Teaching-learning methodologies: Empiricists also looked to see if more informal methods were used in NFE. The fact that so many NFE projects were government-sponsored may explain why the majority of the projects surveyed used what were called 'magisterial' (i.e. teacher-centred) methodologies. Some studies distinguished between "(1) instruction in classroom or demonstration without involvement; (2) individualised, modular or programmed instruction, apprenticeship, correspondence courses and practical fieldwork; (3) group discussions, games, mutual learning and theatre". Very little difference could be found in the various regions studied: "on the whole, traditional teaching methods are preferred, and only a small minority are seeking to innovate". The most extensive survey of this comes from the Colombia report (Velandia et al. 1975: 153) where 40% of the NFE projects used 'magisterial' methods, some 33% used more participatory methods (group discussion), and some 27% used what the authors call 'individualised' methods (correspondence etc.). This seems to be confirmed in Lesotho where the NGOs were said to be rather more innovative in their approaches than the government NFE programmes were. In terms of equipment and materials (a key area of interest among many aid agencies promoting NFE), it was not easy to see much difference in the range available to NFE programmes from the equipment used by the formal schools, except there was less of it in the NFE projects. In Lesotho, 17% of projects said they had no equipment at all.

There was a big interest in the use of new technologies, especially radio and television, in NFE, (Ingle 1974; Gunter 1975; Rogers & Danzieger 1975; Evans 1976; Kidd 1982, 1984; Khan 1977; Ginsburg & Arias-Godinez 1984; Burke 1987; Nyirenda 1995; Gathu 1998). Basing an assessment of the quality of educational provision on factors such as access to equipment and staff-student ratios as compared with the formal systems, while "there are no firm conclusions", the view of Hallak seems to have been agreed by all: "Experience suggests that non-formal training programmes face the same difficulties in building up and maintaining quality as formal programmes" (Hallak 1990: 253).

Participants: Once again, the authors of these surveys complained of a dearth of available data in relation to participation, but that did not prevent them from making sweeping conclusions. Lewin (1987: 87, cited in Stromquist 1988: 7) suggests that "most developing countries have enrolment ratios in these (NFE) programs of less than 50 per 1000", and Evans described Penmas in Indonesia as "one of a very few nonformal education projects that has the potential of reaching significant numbers of people" (Evans 1983: 294). The majority of participants in the surveyed NFE programmes were among the younger adult age range; for example, in Colombia, some 50% were under the age of thirty, 20% under the age of 20. In terms of gender, there were great differences between countries. These may represent differences in provision or cultural factors, for the gap between the 9% of women in the projects studied in Egypt and the 83% in Jordan is hard to explain (Carron & Carr-Hill 1991). In Colombia, just under a half (44%) of the programmes selected for study were mixed in enrolment, rather more than one third (39%) for women alone and one sixth (15%) for men only. But it was noted there that the majority of women's programmes were located in the large cities, not in the rural areas (46% against 18%).

While most NFE projects claimed to reach the poor (more than 50% of projects in Lesotho made that claim), closer analysis suggested that the clientele were mainly farmers, artisans and housewives. There were few unemployed persons in these programmes (IEC 1996b). In Colombia, only 3.5% of enrolments were among the unemployed; most of the participants came from the three main sectors of that country's formal economy. In survey after survey, although there are few hard facts to support it, the general conclusion was drawn that those who had received some formal education participated more often in NFE than those who had little or no formal education.

Costs: On perhaps the most crucial claim of the Ideologues, the relative cheapness of NFE compared with the formal system of education, the evidence could not be found despite several attempts to explore this area (Coombs & Hallak 1972; Brembeck 1974; Ahmed 1975; Hunter et al. 1974; Manna 1975; Green 1979; Ahmed 1985: 3543-3546; Morales 1983; see Rahman 1992; Ahmed 1975, 1985, 1994, 1996, 1997). Although Coombs suggested that NFE enjoyed a relative cost advantage over formal schooling for several reasons (the use of informal facilities, the lower costs of employing facilitators, and the fact that it can often "tap local resources – financial and contributed services and supplies – that are not usually available to formal education", Coombs 1976: 290), this was highly contested. There are few assessments of the relative costs of employing teachers, although one survey in India pointed out that NGOs spent 40% of their NFE budget on the salaries of their teachers while the government spent up to 97%. Nor did it appear that NFE possessed the ability to mobilise resources. Grandstaff suggested that the true costs of each form of education cannot be measured: "We are unable to say that nonformal education enjoys any appreciable cost benefits over formal education ... [NFE] may or may not be cheaper than schooling, in crude costs" (Grandstaff 1976: 297). Coombs in his later writings (1985a: 25) retracted: NFE "has no inherent magical power to ensure low cost or efficient learning. Like formal education, it can be highly efficient in some situations and shockingly inefficient in others". The findings of these surveys are in this respect inconclusive.

NFE IN PRACTICE

The Empiricists concluded that, while it would be wrong to place too much reliance on this data, a number of general conclusions can be drawn. It is however not clear whether these generalisations would change if a different collection of educational programmes were taken for study.

Out of school education is not in reality 'nonformal': Such empirical evidence of the out-of-school programmes as exists reveals that NFE in the field does not match the rhetoric of the Ideologues. "None of the pre-determined sets of distinctions based on contents, mode of delivery, enrolment are appropriate" (Carron & Carr-Hill 1991: 20). NFE does not reach the poor or the rural populations to any effective degree. Ellis, in her study of NFE programmes in the Caribbean (Ellis 1995), pointed out that despite their claims, "many NFE programs failed to meet women's particular needs" since they did not address "issues of women's oppression and empowerment and ... gender". The arguments that NFE is more cost-effective, more comprehensive in its participant groups, more democratic in its education, that it integrates mental and manual learning, that it is lifelong rather than for youth only, do not hold up when the field is examined in depth (Bock & Papagiannis 1976: 1-3). "Some of the conventional beliefs about the participation/students in NFE programmes do not correspond very well with the scattered empirical data that is available" (Carr-Hill 1988: 17). NFE activities were not in practice more relevant, more transformative. NFE does not provide a different form of education, just a rather pale imitation of formal schooling (Torres 1991: 124 suggests some reasons for this, but these reasons are not empirically tested). Indeed, Gallart's study showed that "many initiatives that began as nonformal or paraformal education, particularly in vocational training, tended to become formal and melted into the dominant educational system"; and IBE suggested that one of the main conclusions of these surveys was "the trend towards the formalisation of NFE programmes once they become institutionalised" (Gallart 1989: 15; IBE 1987).

NFE has limited effect on development: There were other surveys at the time, mainly micro-studies and many of them themselves non-formal and unpublished. Some of the NFE programmes evaluated were assessed as showing a different picture from that of Bock and Papagiannis and LaBelle. Everything depended on how the surveyor read the situation. Crone, for example, looking at a programme in the Philippines, suggested that it demonstrated that "the use of expressive materials, discussions, problem-posing, and a non-planned/emergent curriculum enables learners to exercise considerable control over what and how they want to learn" (cited in Kindervatter 1979: 126-127). Kindervatter, in a survey of the Penmas programme in Indonesia and the Khit Pen programme in Thailand, both of them large-scale and government-run, suggested that these programmes were (in fact or potentially) 'empowering' [her word] for the women engaged in them – although there are few signs of this empowerment in her study (Kindervatten 1979; see Wilson 1997). Hoxeng, in his study of Ecuador, came to similar conclusions (Hoxeng 1973; Ecuador 1975). Some of these studies of course came out of the stables which owned the race horse.

But these were relatively few. The general conclusion of the Empiricists, on the basis of their case studies, was that NFE as currently practised did not solve the many problems of the formal system which was still expanding and was becoming ever more costly and ineffective. NFE dealt with lower status occupations, provided what was widely seen as second-class education, enjoyed "dubious recognition for employment purposes", was a surrogate welfare programme concealing unemployment (Radcliffe & Colletta 1985: 3539). The international studies by UNESCO and the more detailed studies of NFE such as those in Lesotho and Colombia suggested that

- NFE does not really reach the very poor:
- the main participants in NFE are those who already have some education (formal and/or non-formal)
- NFE reaches urban populations more than rural
- NFE teaching-learning methods are 'formal'
- the levels of provision of equipment and materials at their best only match those in the formal system and are often much inferior.

By the middle of the 1970s, it is true, the claims being made for NFE had become more modest. Rather than being the panacea for all ills, educational and developmental, it was being suggested that when well aimed, NFE has a high *potential* for contributing quickly and substantially to individual and national development, that it can reach *some* of those formal education does not reach by overcoming *some* of the cultural barriers to formal education. This is a long way from the expansive claims being heard earlier.

But the Empirical approach challenged even these more modest expectations for NFE, whether they were raised by the Advocates or by the Ideologues. For such views rely on underlying beliefs about the relationship between education and socio-economic development – on the view that education can alleviate the gap between rich and poor (both people and nations) or that it can transform societies and structures, and on a linear view of the economic society in which people progress from unskilled and unemployed to blue collar to white collar to economic and professional elites. Such views were increasingly being challenged. Education is a tool of liberation only if inequality is caused by individuals, not by social structures (Bock & Papagiannis 1976: 7-9). They acknowledged on the basis of these surveys and other experience that NFE had had "some success in training people for the lower levels of the modernizing labor market; ... [that] there is some evidence that nonformal education has had a positive effect on agricultural productivity; ... that projects which are aimed primarily at the rural poor have often attracted a large number of villagers ... [but not the very poor and uneducated] ... [NFE programmes] may have served to raise the con-sciousness of the rural participants ... [and] have served as effective vehicles for transmitting the state's nation-building messages and for helping to incorporate pre-viously marginal groups into allegiance to the nation" (Bock & Bock 1985: 3553). But that is far from a ringing endorsement of NFE as a tool for development.

Formal and nonformal are much the same: A third conclusion was that formal and nonformal education were basically similar. The NFE programmes studied were seen to be subject to many of the same control mechanisms as the formal system, and contributed to inequality rather than increased equality. "As a socially created institution, non-formal education, in common with schooling, serves many of the same societal functions, including socialization, recruitment, and mobility management" (Bock & Papagiannis 1983: 21). Education as a whole is seen as part of social institutions, part of power structures, embedded in the political and social processes of each society (Youngman 2000: 156-157). Formal and nonformal education are not autonomous systems but each is a sub-system acting on and being acted on by other sub-systems, political, economic and cultural.

NFE then has no new theories or evaluation methods. Rather, it is simply one aspect of the spectrum of purposive educative phenomena (Bock & Papagiannis 1976: 4). It serves the same functions as formal education in terms of "socialization, mobility management and transmission of cognitive and non-cognitive skills" (Bock & Papagiannis 1983: 9). "NFE, although commonly conceived as a corrective reaction against existing educational arrangements, is itself primarily a socialization agency with social features and functions like any other socializing agency" (Bock & Papagiannis 1983: 21). Like formal schooling, it "may work either to reproduce or transform existing relations of domination and subordination" (Ginsburg & Arias-Godinez 1984: 117). And it has the same exchange values as formal education (LaBelle & Verhine 1975). It is as much an instrument of the existing elites for "the coercive socialization" of members of society as formal education. It allocates class status and provides a means for overt political indoctrination and control in the same way as formal education. But there is a distinction here. Whereas 'socialisation' in the formal system means induction into the prevailing dominant culture within society, in the case of NFE, especially the state-sponsored forms of NFE, it means induction into a modern changing society.

It is important to appreciate that Bock and Papagiannis, who wrote the keynote text of this strand of thinking about NFE, used the word 'socialisation' not in the sense of 'adjusting to the existing norms of society' but as meaning 'modernising' in attitudes and practices. They denied the distinction between urban and rural drawn by writers such as Coombs and others, replacing it with a class analysis of blue and white collar workers, both urban and rural. For them, formal education enabled a few individuals to cross the divide between the blue collar and white collar sectors; some of the offspring of blue collar workers are able through schooling to become white collar workers. NFE on the other hand, aimed as it is at the blue collar sector only, actually limits such transfers or at best "puts those on the bottom rung of the traditional economy onto the bottom rung of the modern stratified society. ... It acts as an agency that defines and constrains the life chances of those it processes" (Bock & Papagiannis 1983: 12, 21).

The process by which both formal and nonformal education "produce competent adult participants" in their own society, adapting their "clients to institutionally desired values and norms" (Bock & Papagiannis 1983:15, 19) is a combination of 'direct' and 'indirect' socialisation (indirect being the unplanned and hidden curriculum aspects of education). They argue that the indirect socialisation achieved by NFE is different from that of formal education, although the direct socialisation process is much the same in both kinds of education. The NFE which they examined in the field was being used by the state in an attempt to make the poorer members of society more economically productive for the benefit of society as a whole, but because of the indirect socialisation, some of the outcomes of NFE were different from those of formal schooling. For the indirect socialisation of NFE stays firmly within the traditional and the direct socialisation is only partial. Since most NFE is uncertificated or at least "does not provide the accepted and socially valued certification" (Bock & Papagiannis 1983: 11), it provides second-rate education and training. Thus 'modernisation' through NFE, according to Bock and Papagiannis, may result in changing occupational structures but not changing power relations (Bock & Papagiannis 1976: 9-14).

Indeed, NFE can even "serve to rigidify social and economic stratification rather than promote mobility for the poor" or lower status groups; "instead of providing an alternative channel for upward socio-economic mobility, nonformal education may rigidly maintain existing channels" (Bock & Papagiannis 1976; 1983: 12). Simmons too argued "that any nonformal educational program which leads to an essentially dual system will eventually work to reinforce the status quo, and thus will neither provide mobility for the poor nor promote their interests" (Simmons 1980: 9). And because it may make existing farmers and fisherfolk better at their work, NFE "is likely to effectively defuse legitimate social discontent and inhibit the development of concerted demand for sweeping social and economic restructuring of their society" (Bock 1976: 350). This "pacifier" or "cooling off" function of NFE, "reducing social discontent", "limiting disappointment by reducing 'payoff expectations'" (Bock 1976: 367), was commented on in several writings at the time (e.g. Radcliffe & Colletta 1985: 3539; Bock & Papagiannis 1983: 12). Participants in NFE "are far less likely than school graduates to be supportive of, or participant in, marginally legal, illegal or violent political protest" (Bock 1976: 365). NFE even more than formal education serves the interests of the elites.

Identifying NFE

The Empirical approach relies on a definition which suggests that formal education and NFE can be easily identified and distinguished from each other. NFE is all those "purposive educational activities carried on outside the formal school system" (Bock & Papagiannis 1983: 13-14); "organised educational activities outside school compared with those in school" (Carron & Carr-Hill 1991: 2). Empiricists see NFE as existing 'out there', as something real and with an entity despite its diversity.

Such writers therefore rejected any ideological definition of NFE. As Paulston (1972: 484) said, "learning priorities derived from ideologies always create cultural conflicts".[4] The Empiricists dismissed the Ideologues' discussion of NFE as process and replaced it with a renewed identification of NFE as system or sub-system. It is true that some of them tried to get away from talking about 'systems' and preferred to talk of 'networks' (Carron & Carr-Hill 1991: 1) or of a complex of sub-systems which enables such writers to talk freely of nonformal education, adult education and (in Latin America) popular education as if they were interchangeable terms (see LaBelle 1987; Torres 1991: 112). NFE, they argued, needs to be seen, not in terms of its impact on individual learners and its achievements in their terms but as a social product and in terms of its impact on society as a whole (Bock & Papagiannis 1976: 22). Bock and Papagiannis (1983: 13-14) assert that defining NFE "by internal or structural features" makes it impossible to engage in comparative studies of NFE.

It is important to recognise that despite the apparent open-minded way in which those who follow this strand of NFE appear to work in the field, their empiricism is still ideologically based. Bock and Papagiannis were transparent about this. "It is clear that ... one's evaluations of the value of this educative phenomena are likely to be determined by one's analytical and ideological perspectives" (Bock & Papagiannis 1983: 168). For them,

---

[4] We do need to note that the term 'ideology' is used in the debate with two main value connotations, one extremely negative, meaning a doctrinaire approach which colours all actions and speech and is partisan, and the second more independent, meaning the 'set of ideas, beliefs and values' in use by any individual, group or set at a particular time in a particular context. In the former usage, only some people have an ideology, others are more pragmatic. In the latter sense, pragmatism itself is an ideology.

education ... is a mechanism for the transformations involved in the consolidation of state authority; they [state servants] expand and reorganize education as a means to institutionalize that authority ... Mass education is ... expanded and brought under central control as an important instrument for extending citizenship status to individuals whose principal allegiance had previously been to parochial sub-groups ... Education extends the claims of the state's authority. (Bock & Papagiannis 1983: 175-176)

They and others argue that both formal and non-formal education are used by the state in much the same way – to "legitimize the government's development plans and extend the control and authority of the state" (Radcliffe & Colletta 1985: 3539).

Paulston came to change his stance from an Ideological one (1972) to one which on the whole agreed with Bock and Papagiannis, although he stressed that some NFE programmes could work against the socialisation process. In an interesting paper, he drew a distinction between two kinds of NFE, one very close to formal education and the other quite different: between on the one hand what he called "movement-controlled educational programmes", "autonomous NFE programmes" or "bottom-up education" very different from formal schooling and often subversive, and on the other hand NFE programmes "outside of movements – i.e. the vast majority". He suggested that "all formal and adult [i.e. non-formal] education outside of movements will ... tend to reinforce the status quo of existing relations" (Paulston 1980: 55-56). Whereas Bock and Papagiannis seem to suggest that all NFE served the same ends as all formal schooling, the reinforcement of the culture of the dominant group, Paulston suggested that some NFE could be more radical, although most confirmed the status quo.

Like Paulston, LaBelle argued that within its context, NFE could be used to achieve the same goals as formal education or different goals, to confirm existing social arrangements or to challenge them. He felt that most existing NFE programmes sought to change people rather than systems, although he concluded from his case studies in Latin America that NFE in that region was more often used to challenge existing social constructions, whereas formal education almost always was used to confirm these arrangements. LaBelle fell back (as did so many others) onto asserting what NFE *should be* – a normative set of statements which tend to undermine much of his (and their) empiricism. He argued that in most cases NFE (like formal education) failed to change social structures – indeed, that it confirmed these structures. This was because such NFE programmes relied on a set of psychological individual-change assumptions in relation to development more than on a set of structural-change assumptions. But NFE 'ought' to change such structures if it is to contribute to development. LaBelle's exhortations about what he called 'a multiple intervention approach' rounded off a major empirical study of NFE in Latin America (LaBelle 1976a: 200-208). Torres too suggested that "it is of particular importance that nonformal education systems and practices be linked to cultural revival ... and to changing health practices" (Torres 1991: 121). Prescriptive approaches to NFE were hard to eschew, even for Empiricists.

Advantages of NFE

Where then lay the distinction between formal and nonformal education? And what advantages, if any, did NFE have over formal education?

Torres (1991) suggested that NFE was more versatile and quick to respond and therefore of more use to governments than formal education; that it was less hierarchical, more plastic, more open to experiment and innovation, cheaper and more relevant in its content. It was more easily controlled than the formal system, especially since its teaching personnel were only para-professionals. Blunt suggested the advantages of NFE were that it reached a target group which the formal system did not reach, that it had low costs, community orientation and flexible teachers (Blunt 1988: 41; see A Hall 1986). Radcliffe and Colletta (1985: 3537) argued that NFE "was peculiarly appropriate to certain kinds of learning" because

- it was less structured, more task and skill oriented, more flexible in timing, more immediate in goals, more decentralised and locally specific, had lower costs through the sharing of resources, resulted in tangible and immediate rewards, possessed flexible teaching methods, was learner-centred rather than teacher-centred, was concrete and experiential rather than abstract and theoretical,
- participation was based on interest and opportunity, not age and compulsion,
- the teachers were recruited on the basis of opportunity, inclination and experience more than formal training and qualification,
- and it arises from the grass roots rather than being centrally planned.

Evans however suggested that the advantages of NFE existed only when it operated on its own, but where it competes with formal education, it is always second-best and contributes, like formal education, to increasing inequalities (Evans 1981c).

And here we see the Empiricists caught in the trap of the Ideological discourses of NFE. The use of the comparative mode (e.g. the word 'more') shows that the point of reference is still formal education; and these statements, like some of those of Torres, LaBelle and Bock, are not empirically based; they are ideological and prescriptive. Such writers have not examined their own case studies which would have revealed that NFE programmes on the ground were rarely like this.

Assimilation between formal and nonformal

It is clear that most of the writers in this strand assumed the priority of formal education over non-formal. Bock and Papagiannis spoke for them all:

> Education, be it in or out of school, is a process of change, and we all of us expect to be different as a result of education. Because we have been socialized to accept education, especially formal education, as the agent of this change, it may be best if one type of education should not

be seen as different from another. Out of school education should be able to take on certain external features in efforts to reach learners in a cheaper, more efficient manner, but it may be desirable to try to maintain structures and processes for the exchange of knowledge that learners understand and expect. (Bock & Papagiannis 1983: 197)

And this led inevitably to a renewal of the demand of the Advocates (as opposed to the Ideologues) for the integration of formal and nonformal education, especially at primary education level (Brembeck 1979; Fordham 1979; see below pp.143-155). "Education will not make its optimum impact on development unless its various elements – whether formal, non-formal or informal – and the interrelationships between them are conceived and planned as part of a coherent overall educational strategy" (Wass 1976: 327). One of the fears expressed was that NFE was confirming the division of the economy in developing countries into two sectors, the formal and the informal (Bock & Papagiannis 1983: 11-12). Various writers like Kassam (1979) wrote about integrating the two sectors of education: "a realistic alternative in many situations would be a merging of formal and nonformal education in a way which maintained the relative strengths of each" (Evans 1981c: 242). In 1980, UNESCO ran a comparative project in Africa and Asia on integrating the two sectors. "The sensible course" wrote Ahmed (1982: 138) "is to adopt a pragmatically flexible merging of formal and nonformal approaches within the framework of lifelong and recurrent learning opportunities for all". The report which UNESCO PROAP produced on *Formal and Nonformal Education: co-ordination and complementarity* (Apeid 1986) was one among many such discussions.

The key areas here were adult basic education and vocational training. In both of these, it was suggested in South Africa and in Latin America, outcomes-based non-formal education gradually found itself forced to become institution-based education. Certificates were needed, and it was recognised that it was the responsibility of the state to establish the agreed outcomes, to legitimate the certificates. The picture drawn by the Empiricists was that in both, the state sought to manage the outcomes, if not all the establishments, and this led to a blurring of the formal and nonformal distinction.

This Empirical strand however still assumes that a clear body of programmes which are non-formal and which stand in contrast to an equally distinct formal system of education can be identified. But this means limiting the definition of NFE beyond what has become normally acceptable. Bock and Papagiannis and their colleagues omitted many programmes which others would call NFE and included some which appear to have had all the same characteristics as formal education. The basis for their study was highly and prejudicially selective.

7

Pragmatists

Some planners have begun to move away from thinking about non-formal education as if it were a single entity susceptible to definition. Instead, they have tried to produce an analytical framework of dimensions which will provide planners with a way of both analysing existing programs, and, more importantly, designing new ones. (Evans 1981a: 30-31)

All of the groups of scholars and practitioners who were extolling or questioning the virtues of non-formal education saw NFE as distinguishable from formal education (schooling). The Advocates saw NFE as everything that was outside of a formal system of education which they felt they could clearly delimit. The Ideologues saw NFE as the opposite of schooling in every way, capable of remedying all the ills of schooling. The Empiricists saw NFE as being a parallel system alongside formal education, facing all the same issues as formal education does, and usually, but not always, serving the same ends as the formal system. All three views were based on dualism: "the border between nonformal and formal education is quite clearly marked by the distinction between school and non-school" (Evans 1981a: 29). Even the policy of bringing both formal and non-formal systems together, the demand to harmonise and indeed to integrate them relied on their separateness being recognisable.

A fourth strand emerged during the 1980s. The movements away from dichotomies and the discourses of disadvantage, and away from the reform of educational *systems* to the reform of educational *processes*, came to affect the ways in which NFE was being considered. It was felt that the best way to do this was to concentrate on formal and non-formal elements within the educational process. Formal education and NFE came to be seen not so much as opposites or separate categories, but more as ends of a continuum with many positions in between. An educational programme was not either formal or non-formal; rather, it consisted of a combination of elements of both. An educational programme could include many or very few non-formal elements. I have called such writers Pragmatists.[1]

---

[1] We should note the word pragmatism is sometimes used in the debate without this connotation; e.g. Coombs & Ahmed 1974: 233; Ahmed 1982: 138.

It started early. Case and Niehoff (1976) spoke of modifying the 'outside-of-formal-education' paradigm of NFE; they preferred to speak of one unified 'education' possessing different characteristics. It is important to realise that this pragmatism is not the same as building a national system out of the formal, non-formal and informal sectors, which many writers spoke of, for this would preserve the distinction between the different sectors.

Those who wrote in this vein reacted against the Empiricists. First, they were hesitant about the data used in some of the empirical studies, arguing that the conclusions represented the information collected rather than the full field of NFE. The data was felt to be limited, omitting many areas of NFE and unsatisfactory for comparative purposes. They pointed out that although the Empiricists recognised that the data they used was variable, depending on the definition of NFE used in each context, they still drew generalisations from their material, comparing NFE in Lesotho in Africa with Colombia in Latin America and with countries in Asia. And the Pragmatists were hesitant about the examples chosen as exemplars of NFE, many of them national "government-sponsored technical and vocational training programs" (Bock 1976: 356); such programmes could hardly be called NFE. MOBRAL in Brazil which Morales reviewed seemed to have few non-formal elements (Morales 1983: 58). The case studies of Bock and Papagiannis and the Penmas and *khit pen* programmes studied by Kindervatten (Bock & Papagiannis 1983; Kindervatten 1979) were national systems of education with a centrally planned and uniform curriculum imposed across the regions and in most cases certificated.

THE ENDING OF DUALISM

The Empiricists had rejected the 'processes' approach to NFE: "adopting nonformal processes does not make it nonformal" (see above p.113), relying instead on identifying programmes as inside the system or outside the system. But the Pragmatists challenged this dualism. They felt that it was not as easy as this to distinguish between formal and non-formal educational programmes; the boundary between the two sectors is not clear (Grandstaff 1976: 294; see Radcliffe & Colletta 1985: 3536). The work of some Empiricists had led them to report that "there is a growing functional blur between formal and non-formal education" (Brembeck & Thompson 1973: 66). Some saw "education as a continuum" of process rather than a continuum of system which earlier writers had advocated (Bacquelaine & Raeymakers 1991: 16b; see Radcliffe & Colletta 1985: 3537). "The location of a program on the continuum can be seen as representing its distance from the technology of the formal school system." "Mobilization of new resources calls for adjustments and reorientation in the educational programme, shifting it towards the non-formal end of the formal-non-formal continuum" (Evans 1976: 309; Ahmed 1983: 41). Nevertheless, their studies depended on identifying clear boundaries in order to compare the two categories.

For the Pragmatists on the other hand, it was the approach to education and not the system which determined whether any activity was formal or non-formal (IBE 1987). The processes determined the degree of non-formality which could be found in any programme. Srinivasan (1977) argued for moving all programmes away from the subject-centred didactic model of formal education towards the learner-centred expressive non-formal end of the spectrum, an Ideological construct. Instead of seeing NFE as "a set of complementary programmes for the unreached or poorly served", UNICEF saw it as

> an approach to education ... leading to greater flexibility in organisation and management of educational programmes with a decentralized structure and less authoritarian management style. It also promotes adaptation to needs and circumstances of learners, a learner-centred pedagogy, creative ways of mobilizing and using educational resources, community participation in planning and management of programmes, and learning content and methods related to life and environment of learners. (UNICEF 1993a: 1, cited in Hoppers 2000a: 12)

But this statement reveals once again how hard it is to speak of NFE in comparison with formal education without developing a series of features which compare and contrast both sets of programmes, mainly to the disadvantage of formal education. All those who saw NFE more as a process than as a system or group of programmes still built up lists of characteristics to use as a tool of analysis to determine how far any educational programme was formal and how far it was non-formal.

But this is far from the work of the Ideologues. Instead of distinguishing between the two sectors and then looking at their characteristics, the Pragmatists looked at every educational activity to see what and how many formal and non-formal elements it contained. The relation of the programme to the Ministry of Education or to the teaching unions was less important than the nature of the activities. No programme was either formal or non-formal; each contained some formal and non-formal elements. Simkins, although his discourse was primarily one of Ideology, spoke this language as early as 1977: "Most [programmes] are not *either* formal or non-formal in any meaningful sense, but exhibit various degrees of formality or non-formality depending on the particular characteristic which is being considered. Indeed, many programmes become more or less formal over time as their objectives and characteristics evolve" (Simkins 1977: 19). But unlike LaBelle (the chief spokes-person for this strand), Simkins saw a strong polarity with 'traditional schools' at one end of the continuum and non-formal community training centres at the other end. The Pragmatists on the other hand saw schooling as that kind of educational activity which contained few or no non-formal elements.

Some therefore saw a matrix:

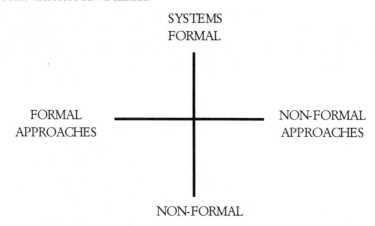

SYSTEMS
FORMAL

FORMAL
APPROACHES

NON-FORMAL
APPROACHES

NON-FORMAL

LaBelle elaborated this matrix by making it three-dimensional, adding to it Informal Education (by which he means incidental learning). He suggested that formal education regularly uses non-formal and informal approaches as well as formal – such as extra-curricular activities (NFE) and peer group learning (informal); that NFE programmes regularly possess formal features (e.g. certificates) as well as informal (participatory methodologies) processes; and that informal education regularly uses formal (e.g. workplace training) and non-formal (e.g. community learning processes such as parent-child education and training) as well as the informal learning through daily experience (LaBelle 1982: 162). Maarschalk (1988: 136) similarly speaks of formal learning possessing non-formal activities ("outside formal settings such as field trips and museum visits, where the intention is often learning") as well as informal learning ("that which grows out of spontaneous situations").

Such studies reveal the complexity to which the discourse of NFE had come by the middle of the 1980s. LaBelle saw more clearly than many others the problems inherent in the terminology which surrounded NFE, largely because of the opposition he encountered in his work in Brazil: "the Brazilians did not like the NFE term" (LaBelle pers comm.). NFE, "like schooling, ... is at the center of the contest between interest groups seeking to influence, if not determine, the means for maintaining and achieving socio-economic and political goals" (LaBelle 1986: vii). He pointed out that in South America, NFE (when used at all) covered many different strands including vocational training (human resource development), popular education (Freirean conscientisation) and even training for resistance movements.

In this view, then, formal and non-formal education do not lie in different institutions. Lynch suggests that Ministry of Defence training programmes as well as youth programmes can be seen as nonformal, just as NFE can be seen inside Ministries of Education (Lynch et al. 1997). Nevertheless there is a difference between formal and nonformal educational experiences. LaBelle feels the distinction lies in "predominant modes of learning ... In practice, informal, nonformal and formal education should be viewed as predominant modes of learning rather than ... as discrete entities" (LaBelle 1982: 162). This is largely an issue of control: formal education reflects "the interests of those who dominate the decision-making structure of the government and in most instances of the overall society"; and since it is compulsory for youth, it represents a long-term investment to maintain the status quo. On the other hand NFE has many sponsors, is open to all and can lead to immediate action for changing the status quo. Despite the evidence of the Empiricists, it is more closely under the control of the participants and challenges the "tradition of elite control over educational activity". (LaBelle 1986: vii, 8). The study of NFE will reveal social tensions in any particular culture.

With the increased control of the participants over NFE, the main element in NFE is its "considerable potential flexibility in curriculum, in who gets selected to teach and to learn, and in determining the goals and assessing outcomes" (LaBelle 1986: 6). Elements within any programme which show increased participant control, which show flexibility, can then be described as 'nonformal'; those which show rigidity and top-down control are 'formal'.

The conclusion from this is that non-formal elements exist within formal education programmes, just as NFE programmes are often made up of largely formal elements. Including informal learning in his model, he argued that all three kinds of learning programmes could (and often do) include characteristics of the other kinds of learning. "A single classroom may reflect all three modes of education [formal, non-formal and informal[2]] simultaneously" (LaBelle 1982: 163; see LaBelle 1986; LaBelle & Verhine 1975). Carron similarly argued that informal learning should be absorbed into both formal and non-formal education (Carron & Chau 1980), and Coombs in his later writings spoke of 'hybrid' forms of education (Coombs 1985a: 24). Fordham, summarising the Commonwealth Secretariat's approach to NFE, noted that some of the case studies he used "are indeed formal rather than non-formal in that they are designed to lead to qualifications". But talking of distance education, he asserted that "by serving a multiplicity of student interests and developing new programmes in response to student demand ... [they] succeed in operating in a non-formal mode" (Fordham 1990).

The implication of this move from NFE programmes to NFE processes is that the systems distinction between formal and non-formal programmes is not only inadequate as an explanation of what is going on, but it is harmful. LaBelle has recently written of this aspect of the debate (citing Tedesco 1990) that "It is time for a planned association of the formal education system with the non-formal", otherwise both will be "short lived, isolated and generally out of touch with the demands, needs and interests of the target population" (LaBelle 2000: 30). We have already seen that both the Advocates and the Empiricists were calling for a closer relationship and even an

---

[2] LaBelle in this article uses the terms 'informal learning' and 'informal education' inter-changeably, despite the fact that, in the same article, he regards all education as being de-liberate and programmatic, while these features are absent from informal learning.

integration of formal and non-formal educational programmes. But this is going further, for it is not a matter of requiring two systems to work more closely together, as suggested by Coombs and others (Coombs 1989: 58-59). Rather it is a matter of non-formalising formal education and formalising (usually in the form of institutionalising) non-formal education.

Non-formalising formal education: Ahmed in 1983 spoke of his perception that "The receptivity to non-formal features of organizational structures of education and peda-gogic methods has grown over the past two decades", but he saw it going further:

> These non-formal features can be introduced in the secondary school without necessarily dismantling the formal structure ... The attainment of [these] major goals depends on the extent to which the rigidities of the formal structures are loosened and non-formal features are adopted ... The potential [for formal schools to become directly and immediately relevant to questions related to survival and a life with human dignity] is realized to the extent that the school adopts non-formal approaches and becomes a base for non-formal educational objectives without necessarily abandoning the more traditional objectives and functions [of schooling]. (Ahmed 1983: 35, 39, 41-42)

A number of articles have emphasised the need and possibility of non-formalising formal educational programmes (see e.g. Hall & Shiffman 1996): "... an NFE *approach* can be applied not only in programmes labelled as 'NFE Programmes' but also in formal schools, contributing thus to their flexibility and 'de-formalisation'" (Hoppers 2000a: 9, 12). It seems to be particularly strong in the science education field (for example, Lucas 1983; Mocker & Spear 1982; Heimlich 1993).

This is a long way from building an educational system which embraces both formal and non-formal education. This may be illustrated by the example cited by Case and Niehoff who saw it primarily as a matter of changing the curriculum. Outlining one way in which "a non-formal education program relates to formal education" (Case & Niehoff 1976: 34), they describe how a number of rural formal schools in Bangladesh were persuaded to incorporate various farm or home-related projects into their studies in a model of non-formalisation. The International Bureau of Education identified the process of non-formalising formal schooling as the "rurali-sation of schools, introduction of productive activities, pre-vocational training" (Bacquelaine & Raymaekers 1991: 22). But for others, it meant more than changes in the content of the learning programme, in particular the development of flexible modes of delivery.

Those who urged the non-formalisation of formal education foresaw the hostility which many people would feel towards any move to deformalise the schools. "Deformalisation of schools would constitute a threat to the privileges [a] minority derives from the present schools ... any model departing from the classical school model is considered to be 'cheap education'". There is still considerable scepticism about "what formal education can learn from NFE". "This long period of recognition [of NFE] has not led to significant 'transformation' of formal education systems ... There is as yet little evidence that NFE features ... have been introduced into formal primary education on a significant scale, nor that such reforms to the extent they materialised were a direct consequence of the influence of NFE" (Hoppers 2000a: 9, 11, 12).

Formalising NFE: There was less emphasis on the formalisation of NFE during the debate, since most writers saw NFE as having more advantages over the formal system of education than disadvantages, especially in terms of its non-institutional nature. Indeed, there is some evidence to the contrary, for some writers have been hesitant about the way in which NFE has become oriented towards formal education equivalency and therefore has become formalised. Some feel that the hand of government will be harmful to the spontaneity of NFE. LaBelle in his recent work cites Messina (1993) as saying that in her chosen countries in Latin America, the NFE programmes she studied had become "compensatory in nature, did not reach a very high percentage of demand, were not efficient, were not linked to [work-related] training programmes or work opportunities and were perceived to be inferior to those programmes oriented to job training. She called for a reconceptualisation of such programmes to reconnect them with society, knowledge and work, and to *unlink them from a schooling mentality and bureaucracy*" (LaBelle 2000: 31, my italics). But there is another strand which suggests that unless NFE becomes institutionalised, it will always be unsustainable and marginalised, powerless in a society where education is power – despite the fact that Bhola pointed out several years earlier (Bhola 1983: 50-51) that "there is something paradoxical about the talk to institutionalize non-formal education, since institutionalization generates pressure towards formalization". Nevertheless, it was argued, NFE needs to be institutionalised if it is to survive as a major force in developing societies.

Here then is another approach to NFE, although is a more muted one. It lacks the certainty of the earlier positions, the urgency of the Advocates, the assurance of the Ideologues, the research base of the Empiricists. But it remains for all that a voice heard and at times adopted by some of the protagonists in the debate.

8

The End of the Debate

While local programmes remain in abundance, the large-scale initiatives and the legitimacy associated with agency sponsorship characteristic of the previous forty years, have all but disappeared.(LaBelle 2000: 21)

The great debate on NFE declined rapidly from about 1986. It had developed four main strands – an Advocacy strand in which NFE was seen as all educational and training programmes outside of the system; an Ideological strand in which NFE was seen as the antithesis of all formal education; an Empirical strand in which NFE was seen as similar to but separate from formal schooling; and a Pragmatic strand in which NFE may be said to be taking place within the formal. The distinction between formal and NFE was now minimal, consisting of approaches to teaching and learning.

After the mid-1980s, there has been relatively little serious discussion about the nature of NFE; and, as LaBelle suggested, the legitimacy of NFE was for a time seriously undermined, in large part by other discourses used by international bodies such as UNESCO, OECD and the EU (OECD 1996; EU Memo 2000; Istance et al. 2002). There have been few articles devoted to exploring the nature of NFE compared with the flood in the 1970s and early 1980s. One or two studies reminiscent of the earlier days of debate appeared (Blunt 1988; Hamadache 1991) but they are not of major significance and add little to the overall picture. There have been no special editions of journals, no conferences devoted to NFE.[1] While Torres entitled his book *The Politics of Non-formal Education in Latin America* (1990), the text of the book does not refer to NFE but to adult education, and it made no contribution to understanding the concept, although it adds significantly to an understanding of the political economy of adult education in that region. His later study of education for skills and knowledge upgrading confines its attention likewise to adult education, not NFE (Torres & Schugurensky 1994). NFE received some attention in New Zealand in the late 1980s, where in most cases it was seen to refer to post-compulsory education and usually to a mode of learning rather than a set programme ("policy development will be able to encompass all aspects of the post-compulsory sector: it will include the

---

[1] Apart from the ADEA workshops discussed below p.179. When I was at CIE in Amherst, I tried to instigate a conference on NFE but CIE did not feel it worthwhile – its time had passed.

universities, the polytechnics, colleges of education, non-formal education and training, on-the-job training, the labour market training programmes ... and also apprenticeship system" (Benseman 2000: 6 citing Minister of Education 1989; cf NZ 1985, 1989: 14; Gunn 1996; Tobias 1992, 1996).[2] Here as elsewhere, NFE as a programme seems to be equated with adult and community education. The term NFE is also used from time to time in Australia as elsewhere (Thomas 1995). One or two journals have continued to publish an occasional article with the word 'non-formal' in the title (e.g. Jilani 1998), but the use of the term in these cases seems to be more in the way of tokenism, not substantial.

Since the later 1980s, the NFE centres at Michigan State University and in the University of Massachusetts have ceased to publish on NFE, concentrating instead on international education in the formal sector than on NFE in developing societies. This reflects a change in donor interest, but it also means that the academic debate has to all intents and purposes ended. Perhaps most significant is the way Coombs himself treats NFE in his later book, *The World Crisis in Education: the view from the eighties* (1985). Instead of having a separate chapter on NFE, he includes NFE in two short sections inside chapters devoted to a review of the crisis since 1968 (1985: 22-26) and to a survey of the expansion of formal education (1985: 86-92; he also has a short section on what he calls 'the enrichment of informal education' devoted largely to the mass media, 1985: 92-97). Not only is there a shortage of space devoted to NFE in his later writings; he abandoned the concept of a non-formal educational system: "NFE, contrary impressions notwithstanding, does not constitute a distinct and separate educational system, parallel to the formal education system" (Coombs 1985: 23). Graham-Brown, in her survey of *Education in the Developing World* as late as 1991, provided a chapter entitled 'Other ways of learning: the effects of the crisis on non-formal education', but it is derivative and tends to regard NFE as the equivalent of adult literacy. Discussions of 'mass education' during this period did not deal with NFE as a discrete or significant entity at all (e.g. Boli et al. 1985; Meyer 1992; Berend in UNESCO 1985 etc.).

It may seem significant that the main international encyclopedias of education between 1985 and 1994 all included several articles on NFE, some of them substantial (for example articles by Colletta, Ahmed, Labelle & Ward, and Chu in Tuijnman 1996: 22-27, 131-135, 158-163, 878-883 which are based on Husen & Postlethwaite 1994). But these were all written by participants to the past debate, adopting their long-held poses once again, rehearsing older arguments for and against NFE. Encyclopedias tend to reflect the state of knowledge of some five or more years previous to their publication; in this case, the papers are almost all taken from or built on earlier publications and do not advance any new arguments about the nature of NFE. Only the article by LaBelle and Ward (1994: 4141-4145) seeks to explore the concepts more thoroughly. Several were repeated in later editions of these encyclopaedias, sometimes

---

[2] I owe these references to Linda Daniell and John Benseman of Auckland.

with minor adjustments, occasionally without alteration (e.g. Husen & Postlethwaite 1985, 1994, Tuijnman 1996).[3]

Some Reasons for the Decline of the Debate

It is possible to suggest some causes for this decline, but the balance between the various factors may have varied in individual cases. To look for the reasons behind this general abandonment of the concepts and language of NFE is to notice several contrary trends.

Formal fights back: There was, I think, a fight back by the formal education system. NFE was seen by many as an attack on formal schooling, and some of these rose in its defence. From an early date, there were those who opposed NFE on grounds related to its social impact. In answer to the charge of the irrelevance of formal education, "the extent of the opposition among educators and middle and upper-class parents to nonformal education is impressive. They feel that formal education *is* relevant to their occupational, personal and civic needs. Lower-income parents also object to a dual educational system that streams their children into manual jobs while still in primary school" (Simmons 1980: 9, original italics). Several writers pointed out how many parents saw NFE as 'second-rate' education (e.g. Blunt 1988). It is significant that by 1985, some studies of what in other contexts would be called NFE are referring to these as formal education.[4]

Despite possessing a small unit on NFE, UNESCO took the lead in the attack on NFE. Already beginning to move away from its earlier discourse of functional literacy to universal basic education (UBE) which "should be the top priority for educational policies in the 1970s" (Faure et al. 1972: 192), it carefully eschewed the NFE discourse. One of the clearest examples of this trend, UNESCO's Report entitled *Reflections on the future development of education* (1985) seems to have tried to avoid using the term 'non-formal' on a systematic basis.[5] Instead, it spoke of "out-of-school activities at all levels, within the framework of lifelong education", and called

---

[3] For the most recent (and indeed only) full-length study of NFE since the 1970s, Poizat 2003, see footnote on p.5 above.

[4] For example, the work of Ezeomah on education with nomadic groups in Nigeria speaks of "experiments to bring formal education to nomadic Fulani in Nigeria" (Ezeomah 1985) when many of his programmes would be called by others NFE – e.g. "the type of education suited to the nomadic Fulani lifestyle and related to their culture", p.11.

[5] Apart from Adiseshiah and Mitra, there is an occasional passing reference such as the statement about many governments formulating policies, setting targets, and defining a structural framework for all types and levels of formal and non-formal education (p.22) – a government-oriented view; or "paying attention to non-formal and informal teaching methods and to improved co-ordination between formal and non-formal education" (p.53); or "adult education, whether in formal evening schools or non-formal programmes" (p.86). These do not amount to a discourse. There is no index to this report.

for "making school and out-of-school services complementary" (UNESCO 1985: 18). Even when discussing what it calls 'new educational activities', the wording is careful. Almost the only head-on mention of NFE is half-hearted. Referring to the pleas of Malcolm Adiseshiah for the mobilisation of all forms of learning to complement the schools which he felt had failed, the report concluded: "If the situation is considered from this angle, it is difficult to see why non-formal education should not be used as *a temporary measure* to provide basic education for people who are outside the school system. But if such education is regarded as an actual substitute for the school system, the result will probably be an ersatz school, which moreover may well be more costly" (UNESCO 1985: 24-25, my italics). Even in Adiseshiah's contribution (he and his colleague Asok Mitra are the only voices through which the discourse of NFE is heard in this volume), there are relatively few references to non-formal education by name, defined as "various forms of non-formal education for those who had been denied schooling, who had to interrupt their schooling for economic reasons, or whose skills faced obsolescence" (ibid: 38).

While UNESCO is painting a state-oriented picture, there is recognition of what is called the 'democratisation of education'. But even when describing this process, NFE as such is not mentioned. The report cites with approval the description of educational planning in developing countries as including the integration of adults with children in a more flexible system of first-stage education, and the recruitment of dropouts of the educational system into a national youth employment service (Blaug 1973 cited ibid: 23). Throughout, care has been taken to avoid the words 'formal' and 'non-formal'.

The formal system of education, then, was fighting back. Whereas Paulston (1972) and others had anticipated a shift of attention and inputs from formal to non-formal education, this had not in fact taken place. "There is no reason to believe that the role of school will become less important than it is; on the contrary, it is quite likely to become more so ..." (UNESCO 1985: 25). Adiseshiah is again the only dissentient voice: "Although the school will continue to be an important locus of learning, it will in the future occupy a smaller place in the total learning system" (UNESCO 1985: 101-102). The fear of the threat which NFE could pose to schooling which this report reveals explains why UNESCO refused even to acknowledge the whole of the debate which had occupied most educational planners and policy-makers in relation to developing societies for the previous seventeen years; none of the extensive NFE literature is cited in the report except by Adiseshiah and Mitra.

The same was true of other UNESCO agency reports. A major report by IIEP in 1992 (Shaeffer 1992) did speak of "non-formal basic education" but used this term to refer to adult education (mainly literacy). UNESCO 1993 avoids the term and the discourse. Three years later (IIEP 1995b: 23, 66), IIEP noted that after Jomtien "some governments and external aid agencies place priority on the formal primary school as the principal vehicle to attain universal basic education ... Non-formal and to a lesser degree pre-school programs are marginalised ... Non-formal education [has] been traditionally under-funded, and this trend seems to be continuing" (see Torres 1993).

But this did not stop surveys of NFE. In 1985, UNESCO issued a comparative study in which the language of NFE was used (Carr-Hill & Lintott 1985) and in 1988, Carr-Hill's survey of the diversified educational field was issued by IIEP. In 1991 came Carron and Carr-Hill's research report, *NFE: information and planning issues* (IIEP 1991). All three were late contributions to the Empiricist discussion of the socio-political relevance of NFE in different contexts, based on surveys of educational programmes which they defined as 'non-formal'. But in every case, they equated NFE with adult education and therefore included some programmes others would not call NFE and excluded some programmes which were at the time being labelled NFE.

The UNDP took much the same line as UNESCO. The organisation, it reported, "remains more aligned with the development of formal education ... In the nonformal domain, human resource development, the promotion of work-related skills, and transmitting socially useful knowledge have assumed priority" (Jones 1992: 356).

The post-welfare syndrome: The language of UNDP, with its emphasis on human resource development and work-related education, reflects the new era of the post-welfare society. The Structural Adjustment conditionalities attached to aid, the monetarist approach to development, the reduction of the role of government and the emphasis laid on lifelong education and continuing education all fit uncomfortably with the more radical approach to NFE which saw in it a tool for challenging the status quo and bringing about social transformation. And this had an interesting impact on formal education. For it can be argued that, despite the protestations of UNESCO, the general acceptance, first by educationalists, later by policy-makers and politicians, of the concepts and language of lifelong education did in fact mean that schools were no longer so dominant. More attention was being paid to other forms of learning opportunities throughout life, especially those planned learning programmes which were provided and taken advantage of later in life (through and for the workplace, in particular). The knock-on effect of this was that NFE could no longer be seen primarily as a remedy and alternative to schools. The concept of lifelong education could have freed NFE from its tie to the formal system of education and given it freedom to emerge as a viable and very diverse entity in its own right. But in the end it made NFE appear simply as one among many options, and to a large extent irrelevant.

The discourse of diversity: A further factor was the emergence of the new discourses of post-modernism, especially the emphasis on diversity (see above pp.27-29). There was a general move away from the polarities of the disadvantage discourses. Life, in the so-called developing countries as elsewhere, was less clear cut, shades of 'grey' rather than black and white, and this applied to education as to other developmental sectors. As one participant at a donor conference on education in Africa said, "...even though we are dealing with the same region, the countries of the region are not necessarily the same, and educational priorities in one country may not necessarily apply to all the countries in the region" (ODA 1986: 5). Such discussions had their impact even on UNESCO. Speaking of the diversification of educational provision, "in addition to offering several types or streams of education ... within the formal school system, many countries now provide other services designed to make education more widely available to specific population groups: pre-school children, school drop-outs, young and adult workers, women, slum dwellers, rural inhabitants, immigrants, handicapped persons, senior citizens, ethnic and linguistic minorities etc.. Such services may take many forms: adult education, on-the-job training and apprenticeship schemes, correspondence courses, educational radio and television programmes, literacy campaigns, kindergartens and nursery schools" (UNESCO 1985: 89). These 'other services' were at that time being described by others in terms of non-formal education, but not by UNESCO. But in the new-speak, NFE was again one of a diverse range of learning opportunities.

There was, I suggest, a growing sense of rejection of the duality which characterised the NFE discourse. This may be indicated by the multiplicity of different terms now being used in discussions of education. New phrases emerged throughout the writings of the late 1980s and the 1990s. As early as 1982, Manzoor Ahmed was using words such as 'lifelong recurrent learning' to cover what he also called 'non-formal education' (Ahmed 1982). Others largely abandoned the term 'non-formal education', replacing it with other phrases, most of which had been in use for many years in a less prominent way, often prior to the NFE debate – terms such as popular education, alternative education, and out-of-school education, or even 'alternative formal education' (Bhola 1983; Sinclair 1990). Callaway (1973) set out-of-school education in opposition to formal education. LaBelle has at times continued to use the language of NFE but normally in the same sense as Torres, adult rather than out-of-school education. By 1992, the *International Review of Education* was referring to 'alternative educational programmes' instead of NFE, and Verhine was using the phrase 'extra-school education' (Verhine 1993). Among the newer approaches were the preferred substitutes of today, lifelong education and learning, basic education, and continuing education with their different discourses. Other less successful terms appeared for a short time but never caught on, such as 'non-conventional' (Hamadache 1994: 4132; see UNICEF 1993b) or "innovative approaches and democratization of education" (Ranaweera 1990: 2). The persistent use of the words 'educational programmes' instead of 'education' ('alternative' or 'non-conventional educational programmes') is again a reminder that we are in a paradigm of diversity rather than one of disadvantage or deficit. Those who used such terms did not see the world of education as divided into two different sectors but as composed of a wide variety of different programmes.

Participatory development: There are some indications that the participatory development paradigm played some part in this, although it is likely to be small. King has suggested that this tendency owes much to UNDP's 1987 paper on grassroots development (UNDP 1987; see King 1991: 172). But the UNDP paper was reflecting a wider and earlier discussion of participatory development by ILO and others (e.g. Oakley & Marsden 1984). As UNDP acknowledged, this new "attitude to local development programmes [was] shaped by the experience of thousands of workers in adult, community and nonformal education" at the grass roots, who however spoke with an uncertain and often contradictory voice. But however uncertain the voice, participatory development could not conceive of a world polarised into two and only two separate sectors.[6] It is this which accounts for the language of democratisation of education, of decentralisation and the growing concern for schools supported by local community involvement.

Disillusion with NFE

Perhaps the most potent source for the drying up of the flow of the discourse was a sense of disillusion with NFE. It had not fulfilled the high hopes of the reformers, and the Empiricists and Pragmatists looked at it with ambiguous eyes. The Pragmatist element in the debate provoked a disillusion with the duality between formal and nonformal education which the earlier strands had emphasised.

There were two main elements to this disillusion.

NFE as a political tool: Some people saw ideological and political issues as lying behind this decline of interest in NFE. "Some nations [in Latin America] restrict local groups in their sponsorship of nonformal education programs unless the programs serve to maintain or enhance the state's goals" (LaBelle & Ward 1994: 4145). For example, the Empiricists had revealed NFE as the site of social contest. The work of Torres (1990), speaking of both state-sponsored NFE and NFE provided by NGOs or civil society, saw both as "sites of ideological struggle", where "the struggle for hegemony in civil society" is taking place. Other writers saw NFE as having been co-opted as a tool of global capitalism, creating and confining workers within strict limits in the global economy, keeping 'developing countries' backward with a second-rate educational programme. So that those who saw in NFE a tool for resisting the globalisation of the economy and a way of spreading the class struggle found themselves out of sympathy with the way in which the concept and the discourse were now being constructed. Instead of a means of liberating oppressed peoples, NFE was seen as a way of training men and women into inferior positions and maintaining them there. "Many national and multinational firms are glad to support a program of nonformal education that teaches future workers specifically what they need to know in order to perform well in semi-skilled or skilled jobs" (Simmons 1980: 9). With the emergence of 'the new social movements', NFE continued to be an arena of contestation, some forms of NFE "challenging capitalist hegemony" and other forms of NFE promoting "learning and action which seek to reinforce the established order of power" (Youngman 2000: 215; like Torres, he equates NFE with adult education).

---

[6] Despite REFLECT, the dichotomy of Freire and the plurality of PRA are uncomfortable bedfellows.

Such statements, I think, made some aid agencies and several writers cautious about facing the issues.

NFE ineffective: Secondly there was disillusion at the perceived ineffectiveness of NFE. The work of the Empiricists, most of whom were thought to be attacking the viability of NFE when in fact they were attacking what they saw as the excessive claims of the Ideologues, had undermined the NFE concept and practice. To take just one example: when Ellis in her review of NFE programmes in the Caribbean wrote, "Few [NFE programs] resulted in any major behavioral changes. Because there were no follow-up or mechanisms to measure the impact of NFE programs, providers have no way of accurately assessing the extent to which their programs have contributed to or resulted in empowering women" (Ellis 1995), such a statement was not likely to encourage donors in their support for NFE. It was not seen as contributing to the new paradigms of development as much as had been hoped for. As a World Bank report of 1991 indicated, NFE is "too small-scale to make an appreciable impact ... too diffuse in its targeting, lacking in specificity" (World Bank 1991).

Changes in Aid Fashions

It was a complex of issues such as the above which led to one of the major changes of fashion for which educational aid programmes have been noted for many years. "Aid Agencies are always keen to support 'vogue' innovations and projects" (Wright & Govinda 1994: 17). "The pendulum of fashion has swung from NFE in the 1970s to schools in the 1990s" (Williams 1991). This change had been foretold by several writers during the early stages of the debate. Evans wrote as early as 1972: "Quite possibly, the term will fall into disuse as the field passes beyond the initial phase" (Evans & Smith 1972: 12). Another leading American educationalist expressed much the same sentiments in the same year. Speaking of the new popularity of NFE, he wrote:

> Any observer of the unseemly ease with which the priorities among national and international agencies come and go, of the ideology of currency governing the private foundations, and of the scandalous opportunism of educational researchers must feel uncomfortable. In international education, there has been a tradition of covering past failures with fanfare and promises of the great successes to come. Do we need to be reminded of the succulent fruits anticipated in the past from literacy programs, vocational schools, community education and ... comprehensive schools? Will nonformal education become just one more social movement in its Don Quixote approach to development, just another ephemeral investment of the foundations, to be forsaken when better or more prestigious entrepreneurs present themselves with alternatives? Is it just an adventitious foray of the faddist academic and professional world, as simple solutions are sought for the immeasurably

complicated problems of development and industrialization? (Adams cited in Paulston 1972: vii)

Brembeck too, talking about the way formal schooling was seen to have failed to meet the exaggerated expectations which had been imposed on it, wrote in 1973: "The same error of judgment could as easily be made now in the flush of enthusiasm for nonformal education. It too could be assumed to have magical properties which in fact do not exist, and its future could also be filled with sobering second thoughts" (Brembeck & Thompson 1973: 54-55). As early as 1976, it was seen as a "passing fad": "the wave of enthusiasm for nonformal education begins to ebb" (Coombs 1976: 293; Evans 1976: 305). "We can only hope that a few years hence we do not wistfully recall nonformal education as a good idea that never came to much realization" (Grandstaff 1976: 297).

What were regarded by many as the exaggerated claims being made for NFE by the Ideologues were felt to have detracted from the value of NFE. Equally, the work of the Empiricists suggesting that NFE was to a large extent a second rate form of formal schooling for disadvantaged populations, even if it had some advantages in terms of flexibility and outreach, had both discredited and marginalised NFE; it was out of the mainstream. Even the Pragmatists who suggested that nonformal elements could be identified within the formal system implied that there was no longer a need for NFE as a separate set of programmes. One key element in this would appear to have been the failure of the Empiricists and especially the Pragmatists to provide the educational planners with effective data on non-formal education; for without an adequate EMIS, the planners found it impossible to co-ordinate formal and non-formal education. So they turned to other forms of educational sectoral activities such as vocational education which could be counted.

Donors therefore on the whole lost interest (see Buchert 1995; Brock-Utne & Nagel 1996; Mosley et al. 1995; Verspoor 1991; King & Buchert 1999). "International agencies, once funders of NFE projects and research, have turned their attention elsewhere" (LaBelle & Ward 1994: 4145). Even SIDA, once so prominent, no longer uses the language of NFE in its programmes and reports.

World Bank: The World Bank figures are the clearest example of this. Bell's review of World Bank lending showed that over the period 1963 (when the concept and term 'non-formal education' did not even exist) to 1978, "lending for activities classified as nonformal education accounted for 11.7 percent of all sector lending. For the period 1975-78 period alone, the figure was 17.3 percent and was projected to rise to 24.6 percent in 1979-1983" (Krueger & Moulton 1981: 38). How much of the initial increase was due to recategorisation of programmes and how much to expansion cannot now be determined, although the growth of programmes *defined* as NFE in the field clearly grew. In particular most vocational training programmes were now classified as NFE, so that between 1963 and 1976, programmes which were later designated as NFE were listed as receiving 26% of the budget devoted to vocational education and training (World Bank 1991; see World Bank 2003, Annex 2). In 1987-8, the last year for which figures are available, the NFE category received 77% ($902m). NFE was clearly a major concern of the Bank officials at this time. Between 1963 and 1985, 92 out of 304 education projects approved by the Bank included NFE elements, most of them "in the mid- to late 1970s" (Eisemon et al. 1999: 361).

But since the mid-1980s, "support for NFE sharply declined" (ibid: 361). From 1987, NFE has not been identified by name in the World Bank published accounts (World Bank 1991: 66). Indeed, a review in 1987 suggested that World Bank-supported NFE projects had largely failed to achieve their goals (World Bank 1987). Lauglo has suggested that the arguments that had led to the support for NFE were no longer accepted in the World Bank (Lauglo 1995: 221-223). Certainly the Bank's policy statements of the later 1980s, such as the 1986 paper *Financing Education in Developing Countries: an exploration of policy options* with its concentration on cost recovery, a "credit market for education", the decentralisation of management and the encouragement of non-government and community-supported schools, although having the potential to increase support for NFE, actually seems to have turned away from that option (World Bank 1986; Jones 1992: 245-249; see World Bank 1995; IIEP 1995a, 1995b; Burnett 1996).

There has thus been a change in the Bank's discourse. In the 1974 World Bank Education Sector Working Paper, reflecting the new orientation of the development paradigm away from modernisation based on advanced and elite education towards mass education for rural and informal sectors, NFE was declared the first priority area for lending: "a re-orientation of the education and training systems, with greater emphasis on vocational education and on non-formal training for agriculture and industry will be required to redress present imbalances". But the 1988 World Bank Report on Education in Sub-Saharan Africa did not seem to mention the term. Rather, the Bank spoke of "the need to consider *alternative ways of delivering educational services* that shift more of the burden for learning onto the students themselves", especially through distance education in secondary education, and of *"training for those in the workforce"* (my italics). In the debate which accompanied this report (*CER* 1989), there seems again to be a reluctance to use the term 'non-formal'. Almost the only reference is to "opening up of non-formal streams through distance education courses and correspondence courses" at tertiary level (*CER* 1989: 97; see also 119, 180). In 1991, when loans were being made to Ecuador and to Indonesia for NFE, it was unequivocally stated that "no return to the Bank's earlier advocacy of NFE is being contemplated" (Eisemon et al. 1999: 360). Apart from the table indicating the sums devoted to vocational and technical education and training (World Bank 1991: 66), the term NFE is eschewed. The survey of World Bank assistance to education from 1964 to 1994 published in 1995 carefully avoids any NFE category (World Bank 1995: 148). Although the term has been used occasionally (e.g. Abadzi 1994), the Bank preferred to speak of "alternatives to traditional schooling" which it defines as "distance education, adult literacy programs – in brief, what was formerly known as nonformal education" (Eisemon et al. 1999: 362).

Since about 2001, however, the term NFE has re-entered the language of some parts of the World Bank (World Bank Tanzania 2001). The most significant seems to be the Paper on Adult and Non-Formal Education of May 2003. The definitions provided are drawn in part from the language of the 1970s and 1980s, but it would seem that both adult education and non-formal education are wider in scope than the entity 'Adult and Non-Formal Education' (ANFE). And the paper drops into other discourses, using terms such as Adult Basic Education and Training (ABET) and Adult Basic and Literacy Education (ABLE) indiscriminately. But it heralds the return of the term NFE to respectability among some World Bank policy makers (see also Lauglo 2000; World Bank 2001; Oxenham et al. 2002; Beloisya 2001).

USAID followed the World Bank. The initial impetus given to NFE by USAID has been described in detail by Krueger and Moulton (1981), particularly its funding of research and development institutions in the USA. Its concern for defining the concept, promoting the practice, developing the capacity and initiating new technologies for non-formal education established it as the leading player on the field, and its support for both the study of NFE and innovative programmes in the field are claimed to have exceeded those of any other agency. But from the mid-1980s, it too seems to have displayed growing disillusion with NFE: and once again the term seems to have been abandoned.

> The creation of a division of education and human resources in USAID in the late 1970s reflects the growing concern, held in common with CIDA, ODA and the World Bank, that the education programme should be centred on human resource needs, and that education should more thoroughly permeate activities in other sectors.

> USAID's 1982 policy paper on *Basic Education and Technical Training Assistance Strategy* adopts a human capital perspective, but along with the World Bank, places its main emphasis on the efficient use of resources in education in developing countries. While there is still a commitment to extending coverage and achieving greater equality of opportunity, it is argued that these will follow quite naturally from the more efficient use of resources". (ODA 1986: 156-157)

ODA: The UK Government's ODA report on education in sub-Saharan Africa in 1986 was to some extent an exception, but it too was hesitant: "Given the altered perceptions of the role of education, rapid changes in society, in the nature of knowledge and in occupational structures, and swift advances in technology, it is possible to argue for greater investment in non-formal education. But how far is this desirable, acceptable or possible?" (ODA 1986: 145) There are several references in this report to NFE, perhaps largely because Philip Coombs was in the chair; but even here, there is a new tone, something of a turning-away from 'non-formal' as an indicator of a tool of salvation.

CESO in the Netherlands, another agency with a keen interest in the theoretical foundations of its development interventions, showed a similar move away from NFE, although this took place a little later than some of the other agencies. In its report *Education, Culture and Productive Life* (Boeren & Epskamp 1990), which concentrated to a large extent on indigenous and traditional learning programmes, there were two chapters on NFE. One entitled 'Case studies on indigenous learning systems: implications to formal and non-formal education' suggests that both formal and non-formal education have much to learn from indigenous learning systems (which are seen as separate from both of these), but it went on: "even non-formal education seemed to have failed in enticing the people to avail of learning opportunities for personal, socio-cultural and economic advancement". The other, 'Non-formal education and rural development in Nepal', outlined a certificated integrated literacy, health and development programme for out-of-school girls aged 6 to 14 years. But by the time the report *Education and Training in the Third World* (Buchert 1992) was published,[7] there are no signs that NFE exists in any significant sense, although there are references to the formal system (e.g. ibid: 25). Instead, it talks of "the local dimension to training" (i.e. mainly indigenous) and on-the-job training such as apprenticeships.[8]

It is remarkable that in these, as in so many other publications of the time, criticisms are being made about the impact and relevance of formal Western-type education on local populations and development plans, but there is virtually no mention of NFE. And the whole of the past extensive literature of NFE is ignored. There are no references to any of the NFE texts in the bibliographies in many articles which use the term NFE in their title such as those by Wallace and Lynch (Lynch et al. 1997). It is as though the whole of this literature never existed.

The Move to Schools

By the late 1980s, then, among most of the major donors, there was a move away from expanding educational provision and a greater concentration on the quality of the education being provided (Mueller 1997; Oxfam nd). This of course reflected the Structural Adjustment Policies of this era. In particular, there was a concentration on universal primary and basic education in the early 1990s, focused round the Jomtien Education for All project. This was reflected in those who still wrote about NFE as well. In 1994, for example, when asked to write in general terms about "nonformal and alternative approaches to basic education", Hamadache could say that he would not

---

[7] There is no index to either of these volumes, so I cannot be absolutely certain about the references to NFE in these reports.

[8] There is one reference to "non-formal (vocational) training programmes" in Buchert 1992: 162-164, but the report normally uses the distinction between formal and informal vocational training (p.171). There are also mentions of "both the formal and nonformal sides of primary education" (p.191), and of "nonformal skills training" (p.194).

examine "nonformal *adult* education but only those nonformal education services for *children* at the primary level" (Hamadache 1994: 4132, my italics).

Jomtien was not a turning point in the decline of NFE. Rather, it confirmed the trends which had been going on for several years. In the lead-up to Jomtien, the International Conference on Education recommended that "the setting up of nonformal, non-conventional, innovative and flexible structures is a positive response to the formal system, provided that such structures are not of a lower standard than those in the formal schools which they should complement". This gets translated at Jomtien into "supplementary alternative programmes can help meet the basic learning needs of children with limited or no access to formal schooling, provided that they share the same standards of learning applied to schools and are adequately supported" (Ordonez 1990: 2). The term NFE is avoided. The conference itself spoke of three channels of education, primary, literacy and knowledge and skills to adults and youth, and thirdly the media. There was a noted reluctance to use the word 'non-formal'; instead terms like 'supplementary alternative programs' and 'out-of-school equivalent education' seem to have been the favoured expression (UNICEF 1993a: 1; Hoppers 2000a: 13; King 1991: 178).

Immediately after Jomtien, there was some recognition that NFE did exist. But almost the only references to NFE in the various official declarations of international agencies at this time were to 'nonformal' or 'non-conventional' approaches. Thus UIE held a series of workshops or Round Tables on the integration of formal and non-formal 'approaches' into one 'system' ("the complementarity of formal and non-formal approaches at the primary education level", "the complementarity of nonformal fundamental educational activities and formal primary education" etc., UIE 1990: 1-2). We need to note the careful use of words like *non-formal approaches* and *learning* and the phrase *'educational activities'* rather than 'non-formal *education'*. Jomtien, wrote UNESCO in 1993, surveying the EFA programme since 1990, "effectively broadened the scope of basic education to include early childhood development, primary education, *non-formal learning* (including literacy) for youth and adults, and learning conveyed through the media and social action" (UNESCO 1993: 5 my italics). "Within the perspectives of Jomtien, the importance of non-formal education for youth and adults lies in its contribution (in co-operation with schools) to meet the basic learning needs of target communities, and its integration as an educational component (skill training, attitude change, literacy) into development projects of other sectors, particularly in the informal economy, health and agriculture" (UNESCO 1991: 42). And IIEP (1995b: 23) in its mid-term review of EFA, spoke of "the broader vision of basic education put forward at Jomtien combining formal, non-formal and adult education", although the Jomtien documents do not support this statement. Such recognition of the existence of the NFE approach to education as there was appears to have been grudging.

Later conferences took up the complementarity theme of the 1990 Round Tables. UNICEF argued strongly for "a unified comprehensive system for UPE" in which "NFE and *diversified approaches to primary education* need to be seen as components of a unified system" (UNICEF 1993a: 7 my italics). The Amman conference (1996) spoke about the necessity of building "bridges and synergies between formal and nonformal education" which they saw as in very close relationship, asserting that NFE is an 'integral' part of "the education system" (cited in Hoppers 2000a: 14).

The Disintegration of the Discourse Community

The debate then broke up. The term itself continued to be employed from time to time, especially in the titles to papers and reports (e.g. Hamadache 1991). The term was occasionally adopted in relation to programmes in Europe and North America (see King 1982; Southampton 1978; LaBelle 1981; Clark 1978; Fordham et al. 1979; Brockington & White 1983; Matheson 1991; Garrido 1992 etc.) but there was no common understanding of its usage, what it was a short-hand for. Such use seems to be something of a hang-over. The important review chapter that King put into his study of aid and education (King 1991), a contribution to the Education for All debate, revealed how divided the field had become. He himself defined NFE in contradictory ways in that chapter, reflecting the divisions he found in the literature. Whether the term stood for a superior programme of education in opposition to ineffective formal schooling, or an alternative form of schooling (often inferior) for adults or for younger persons who had been particularly disadvantaged, or a particular kind of teaching-learning process which could take place in all educational programmes, or something else, needs to be deduced from the context each time. For some, it was simply an emergency (and therefore temporary) measure for children's education, "a complementary stream for meeting the needs of out of school children, youth and adults" (UIE 1990: 3; Hoppers 2000a: 13).

To take a few examples: Stromquist implies that NFE (a phrase she uses frequently) is adult education for women. She never defines the term but distinguishes between "nonformal education [which] offers a second chance [to adults] to get useful knowledge and skills" and "those nonformal education programs designed to be shallow versions of remedial primary education" (Stromquist 1988: 6). It is not clear what links these two different programmes in her mind. Her discourse is in the disadvantage paradigm. Hallak (1990), writing in the discourse of EFA, made an attempt to develop a taxonomy of education applicable to the whole world; he describes some programmes as non-formal but never defines what he means by the term. For him, NFE appears to be mainly literacy and skills training, although he adopts the four-fold categorisation of the Empiricists. Torres (as we have seen) sees at least two parallel forms of NFE, state-provided adult education (basic and vocational) to fulfil the state's purposes and "popular education which attempts to alter social order" (Torres & Schugurensky 1994: 131-152).

There are a few theoretical treatments. Van Riezen's article in 1996, Brennan's paper in 1997, Kilpatrick et al. (1998) in Australia, and recent papers by Wim Hoppers (2000) in South Africa and by LaBelle (2000) on Latin America, all show something of a revival of interest in the sector (see also Moulton 1997 & Wain 1996), but there is little that is new. Brennan (1997), for example, sets out once again the case for the Ideological position for NFE in relation to a number of programmes in the Pacific region, but his categorisation of NFE programmes as complementary, supplementary or alternative to formal schooling repeats earlier statements. The work of the ADEA Working Group on NFE includes some attempts to reconceptualise NFE (ADEA 1999, 2000b, especially Avenstrup & Swarts 2000, Hoppers 2000b, Moulton 2000). But there is a self-consciousness about the use of the term which is absent from the earlier writings on NFE: thus on occasion it is even referred to as the "so-called NFE" (Hoppers 1999: 15; Wright 2001). What seems to be happening in some cases is that the language of NFE is introduced when a sense of a radical agenda is implied: as with radical adult education, "the progressive sentiments ... persist ... used symbolically in contemporary educational discourses. But their impact on the nature of that discourse in policy and practice would seem to be at best secondary. In other words, they are admitted only after more central ... agendas have been satisfied" (Bagnell 2001: 47).

The current use of the language of NFE owes more to the discourse of lifelong learning than it does to Education for All. But in the lifelong learning discourse, NFE does not occupy the place it once did; it is merely one part of a diverse educational system which needs integration. NFE has become subject to the theorisations of lifelong education. Thus CONFINTEA 1997 spoke of various educational sub-systems (including NFE which was one of several such sub-systems), of a ladder of learning opportunities from initial formal education to continuing education within a framework of lifelong learning (UIE 1997). While there is some recognition of the discourse of nonformal education, the primacy of formal education is clear. "There has been greater alignment of programmes for adults and those for children by means of the formal educational system" (UNESCO 1997: 21).

But in general, the term NFE has until very recently been avoided. Many different terms have been adopted, often combined with the term 'non-formal' – for example, non-formal channels, delivery systems, communication, modes of learning etc. (Kassam 1982; NFL 2001; Schiele 1995; LaBelle & Sylvester 1990; Paul & Gupta 1999 etc.). The EFA follow-up consultation at Dakar, Senegal (Dakar 2000) and its sequel in 2001 (Elimu 2001: Dakar Plus One) do not use the term NFE in any significant way, nor do the UNESCO Guidelines for the country action plans (UNESCO 2001). UNICEF (1999a) tends to speak of 'adolescent education'. It is noticeable that some agencies such as the Commonwealth of Learning, when speaking of education for street children, now prefer to talk about 'open schooling' rather than non-formal education (COL 2000: 2-3). The Global Campaign for Education, which came out of the preparations for Dakar 2000, is also careful not to refer to NFE in its nine point manifesto (Global Campaign for Education 2000), speaking instead of the democratisation of education; and the parallel campaign *Elimu* of ActionAid shows that the discourses have moved on, that the concept of NFE is felt by many to be largely irrelevant to today's discussions of education in developing societies (Elimu

2000).[9]

But even if, for whatever reason, the term NFE is still being used in the new educational discourses, its meaning is uncertain and recent discussions have not clarified it. Those who try to clarify the issue are few. LaBelle in a recent contribution redefines various educational activities in Latin America from the 1920s to the 1970s, including "community-based programs, literacy, fundamental education, community development, technical vocational training, extension education, consciousness raising, population education and community schooling" (LaBelle 2000: 21) as NFE, although clearly they were not so called in their own day. He suggests that in that region the post-welfare culture has led to a concentration of NFE on the informal economy and on social movements, usually apart from and at times in opposition to governments. The main aim of what he describes as NFE in South America today is "enhancing the income and status of the poor and marginal populations", especially indigenous populations. For LaBelle, NFE is indistinguishable from many of the programmes of education for adults.

Hoppers, writing from southern Africa, takes a contrary position. Speaking of NFE as "substitute formal primary education" mainly for children, in which "teaching-learning is conventional", he argues that, in a world of lifelong education, all persons need "initial (or basic) education ... an essential foundation ... sets of essential competences ... that can be acquired by all children in a socially and culturally appropriate manner regardless of background and circumstances, ... a universal entitlement, to be credited within the context of a broad qualifications framework ..." In this context, "the old distinctions between 'formal' and 'nonformal' education need to be revisited. If 'formal' refers primarily to the notions of officially recognised creation and certification, then the common distinctions related to the content, organisational arrangements and location [i.e. the Ideological distinctions of formal and non-formal education listed above] become obsolete" (Hoppers 2000a: 22, 23, 25). All distinctions between formal and nonformal education other than certification are now meaningless, just as the distinction between education in developing societies and education in industrialised societies is also breaking down (e.g. Novib 2000).

But this still implies that any definition of NFE depends on definitions of formal education, on what is determined as the mainstream. Thus for example, some argue that formal education is what the state prescribes, and consequently NFE by definition is "learning which is not constrained or supported by prescribed frameworks" (Eraut 2000a: 12). Throughout many of these papers even today runs a strand of Ideological discussion about NFE. For example, in the ADEA workshop, NFE is said to be characterised by discussion as opposed to formal education which is characterised by teacher-talk, and that NFE has a more equal power relations between teacher and

---

[9] An interesting example of contemporary mixing of discourses is the Cape Town Statement on the Characteristic Elements of a Lifelong Learning Higher Education Institution 2001. It uses throughout the discourse of lifelong learning; but still speaks of "institutions of formal education from primary level onwards" (www.uwc.ac.za/dll/conference/ct-statement.htm).

learners, although the work of the Empiricists would suggest there is little evidence for these assertions in current NFE programmes. On the other hand, Wright (2001) sees a gap between formal and non-formal education but with all the advantages lying with formal education.

The *World Education Report* of UNESCO (2000) may be taken as an example of the language of much of today's discussions of education. Its historical review of world-wide education contains no mention of NFE. In a summary of trends since the Second World War, it suggests that fundamental/elementary education predominated from 1940s to 1960s, followed by functional literacy from the 1960s to the late 1970s, and that this has been followed by basic education, learning needs and lifelong education. It talks of mass education, popular education, community education, adult education, but the whole of the literature and the spending on non-formal education in the 1970s and 1980s are ignored. There are several mentions of 'formal education' but almost none of its counterpart. There is one passing reference (p.28b), where NFE is equated with adult literacy: "illiterate adults and others – who had not previously had an opportunity for modern education, whether formal or non-formal ...". There is a section entitled "The nonformal dimension" (pp.42-44) but in the text which follows this heading, the term 'nonformal education' is not used except in a decontextualised box containing the classic definition of Coombs and Ahmed (1974). Instead, the section talks of lifelong education, emphasising "the importance of other forms of education besides formal schooling", and it then quickly goes on to basic learning needs. It is clear that the authors of the Report cannot bring themselves to use the term 'non-formal education'. NFE in this context is no longer second-rate, marginalised, out of the mainstream; it simply does not exist. Few totalitarian regimes could have done a better task at wiping out nearly twenty years of discourse and with it the discourse community.

Yet there is still an NFE Division in UNESCO, Paris, which concentrates its work on basic education for out-of-school youth and adults. The aim of this Division is to link basic education activities with development goals rather than formal school equivalency, although its approach to certification is not clear. Its key document is a recent report *Education to Fight Exclusion* ('exclusion/inclusion' is another separate discourse with its own community, programme of action and ideology), a UNESCO special project for the enhancement of learning and training opportunities for youth. In this, it speaks of "basic non-formal education" or "non-formal basic education ... by which is meant a practical and functional mix of literacy, numeracy and life skills based on day-to-day methods of learning and working, generally outside of the school system" (UNESCO 1999a: 7). It aims to "link ... non-formal basic education [NFBE] to income generation" rather than to formal school equivalency. Most of the discourse is that of social exclusion/inclusion, but an attempt is made to marry this with the NFE discourse. "By non-formal basic education [the Project] means educational activity which occurs outside of any established or structured formal system of learning ... education where learning is improvised and adapted to each group, its aspirations and needs. The aim of this form of education is to provide young people with immediate tools, knowledge, skills and attitudes that are not possible through the formal system or are too abstract in that system to be accessible to excluded youth". NFBE "has the capacity to produce concrete results quickly ... it must not be seen as just a poor education for the poor ... It is a form of lifelong education ... [it] could have an even larger role to play in helping people to leave poverty and stay out of it. NFBE is a laboratory in which all kinds of innovative techniques in education delivery and curriculum development are being tested". In a strongly Ideological mode of thought, it urges that the main advantages of NFBE are its practicality, its affordability, its 'endogeneity', its accessibility and flexibility, and its democracy (UNESCO 1999a).

This report is a remarkable document. For apart from this paper, UNESCO appears to be unhappy with using any of the discourses of NFE, instead "arguing the need for out-of-school strategies to find their balanced place alongside school-based programmes" (Jones 1992: 355). The *Global Monitoring Report* (2002) mentions NFE only once in connection with Tanzania.

The Commonwealth Secretariat swung away to talk of 'non-formal alternatives to the school' and supports ADEA's Working Group on NFE – although like others it is not entirely clear what it means by this term (Wright 2001: 35-39). Here more than with any of the other participants in the discussion, the theme of "mainstream education" (formal education) and bringing other forms of education into the mainstream dominates in the discourse. But elsewhere, as we shall see in the Case Studies below, NFE is a term still used widely in the field, especially among Ministries of Education, and indeed its use appears to be growing. NFE has widened out to include children's education, distance education (however formal that may be) and educational technology (e.g. Perraton 1982; Dodds 1996; Moleko & Betz 1995; Siacewena forthcoming etc.). But the essence of NFE is no longer clear; and it is no longer politically or academically privileged. The value attached to knowledge in the educational world has moved to other areas of discussion (multi-grade schooling, for example, or social exclusion/inclusion). The formal system of education has taken over; when NFE is mentioned, it means either one of a considerable number of different forms of educational provision, or a minor and grudging description of alternative programmes inferior to formal schooling.

9

Some Issues Arising from the Literature

The difficulties with the term 'non-formal education' ... reflect a host of conceptual, political, cultural and linguistic issues of importance when working cross-nationally. (LaBelle 1986: 4)

A number of concerns arise during this survey of the literature, and a study of some of them may throw some light on the question of NFE as seen today. Most of these have been raised at various points during the earlier discussion but it will be useful to draw them together as cross-cutting issues.

1. Identifying non-formal educational programmes

The debate outlined above depended for its effectiveness on being able to identify which educational activities were 'non-formal' and which were not. All participants in the debate asserted that they could distinguish non-formal from formal education. Indeed, their conclusions depended on which activities they included in or excluded from their particular definition of NFE.

The distinction depended on a prior identification of 'formal' education. NFE was (in most cases) all that was left over after formal education had been identified: "It is only possible to understand NFE in relation to the education provided by the school and college system" (Carron & Carr-Hill 1991: 5).

What is the formal system? The frequently quoted definition of formal education as "the hierarchically structured, chronologically graded 'education system' running from primary school through the university and including in addition to general academic studies, a variety of specialized programmes and institutions for full-time professional and technical training" (Coombs et al. 1973: 10) seems to some to be excessively wide, since it extends formal education to include a range of 'specialized programmes and institutions' outside of the schooling system. Such a definition of formal education could include Papagiannis' Thai vocational training programme. Equally it excludes part-time education leading to standardised qualifications. But insofar as formal education was discussed, this definition was generally accepted. LaBelle however saw formal education in terms of features: it was those programmes characterised by "hierarchical ordering, compulsory attendance, admissions requirements, standardized curricula, prerequisites and certificates" (LaBelle 1982: 162-163) rather than a system.

Several writers confuse the issue with vague wording. Paulston even suggests there are more than two sectors, formal and non-formal, when he speaks of "the utility of NFE ... to formal education *and to other educational sectors as well*" (Paulston 1972: xi my italics). Sometimes the definition of formal education is made in terms of state provision. However, the term 'education' is often restricted to what the Ministry of Education offers through its schools and colleges, so that 'state education' does not include any educational activities of the Ministries of Health, Agriculture, Labour or Defence. Others speak of formal education as being 'the school system', even in contexts such as Lesotho where the school system regularly includes very large sectors of non-state school provision.

In fact, most writers make no attempt to define formal education, even when this is crucial to the determination of what they mean by NFE. To give one of many examples: "Non-formal education ... commonly conceived as a corrective reaction against *existing educational arrangements* ..." (Bock & Papagiannis 1983: 15 my italics). For these writers, formal education consists of "existing educational arrangements", whatever that may mean. It is on the basis of this vagueness that a decision is frequently taken as to which programmes may be taken as being non-formal.

Systems approach: The first approach to identifying NFE took a systems approach. Formal education was seen as all the educational programmes provided by the system of state-provided or state-approved schools and colleges. Every other educational programme was non-formal (and/or, for some, informal) education. NFE was "separate from state-sanctioned schooling" (LaBelle 1982: 163).[1]

In this discourse, NFE was defined in terms of its 'outsideness'. There was a widespread recognition of the wide range of such activities. Indeed, its diversity was what attracted attention to it. Everything which already existed or which could be created 'outside the system' was and could be included in NFE. The system came first; everything that was not the system was non-formal. And this meant that a local identification of what is formal and thus in consequence what is non-formal would be needed. Most comparative educationalists who formed the heart of this debate and who were seeking for some criteria by which international comparisons could be formulated, found this difficult to accept.

---

[1] It is noteworthy that there is no recorded use of the parallel term 'out-of-college' education, even though much of what was described as non-formal vocational education and training was provided through what were felt to be non-formal colleges such as the Village Polytechnics of Kenya (Anderson 1974) or the *vidyapeeths* in India as well as by private commercial agencies. The Folk Development Colleges of Tanzania are a prime example of this ambiguity – are they formal education or non-formal education? (Rogers 2000)

It was, I suggest, this need for comparable criteria that led to the view that the vast range of educational activities which went on 'outside the system' and which could be grouped together under the term NFE were linked together by possessing certain characteristics which were different from those of the formal system. In other words, NFE was not just *outside*; it was *different*. Coombs saw NFE as consisting of educational activities which would remedy the failures of the formal education system or which would meet "new and differing demands for education" (Coombs 1968: 183; see also LaBelle 1986: 83). He did not consider the case of those programmes which were outside his defined formal system but which did not either remedy the failures of formal education or meet new demands for education, programmes which for example replicated formal schooling exactly. What he and his colleagues were looking for was a set of programmes which were or would be different from the formal education programmes. And of course, this calls for some definition of these differences.

Prescriptive: These differences were provided by the Ideologues. These expanded on the hints of the first advocates of NFE, creating (hypothetical) criteria which would meet the failures of formal education (which they tended to call 'schooling') or new educational needs which formal education could not meet. Hence there were drawn up lists of the characteristics of formal education, and non-formal education was thought to be those programmes which possessed the opposite characteristics (e.g. Paulston 1972; Simkins 1977; Srinivasan 1977).

Despite the early insistence of the initial advocates that non-formal education included *everything* which lay "outside the formal system", the Ideologues saw non-formal education as limited to a special kind of activity outside of the system which possessed characteristics different from formal education. Activities which lay outside the formal educational system but which possessed the same characteristics as formal education possessed were ignored. Those who felt that the term 'non-formal' should be restricted to those educational activities which displayed NFE characteristics usually excluded "those programs that provide alternative means to deliver schooling – meaning state-sanctioned curricula associated with credits, grades, certificates and diplomas" (LaBelle 1986: 6) – a definition which would exclude much of what goes on under the term NFE today.

Descriptive: When, however, people began to look in the field, they concluded that in practice many programmes they defined as 'non-formal' were no different in process from the educational programmes they defined as 'formal'. And one result of this was that the field (paradoxically) became more highly segregated, not less. Writers like Bock and Papagiannis felt they could identify clearly which programmes were non-formal – "purposive education activities carried on outside the formal school system" (whatever that is) (Bock & Papagiannis 1983: 13). And because they felt that they could clearly distinguish between those programmes which were inside the system (formal) and those which were outside the system (non-formal), they also felt able to examine both sets of programmes and see exactly what they consisted of and led to, rather than argue from an *a priori* position.

We need to note however that Bock and Papagiannis' analysis was very narrowly based. Bock took a collection of primary schools in Malaysia as a case study of formal education, Papagiannis a programme of nation-wide, state-provided, government-run certificated vocational education and training programmes in Thailand as his case study of non-formal education. If they had taken other programmes for their formal education case studies and other educational activities 'outside the system' as examples of NFE, they might have been forced to draw different conclusions from their study. When they found that their examples, formal and non-formal, were very similar, they concluded that *all* formal and non-formal education experiences were similar.

They therefore asserted that formal and non-formal education could not be distinguished on the basis of any differences in process or character, only on whether they lay within the formal system or not. "'Non-formal' is a referent for education that occurs outside the school system. It does not refer to the social characteristics of the learning environment. The formality or informality of the social organization for any given purpose is an empirical question" (Papagiannis 1977: 20, original underlining).

An approach which allowed the researcher to define as NFE any educational activity 'outside of school' (even though the reasons for that definition are not always easy to follow) enabled one to look critically at these activities to assess whether they conformed or not to the prescriptive approaches to NFE. And in this context, as we have seen, the Empiricists were able to suggest that writers like Paulston, Simkins and Srinivasan had simply got things wrong. Those programmes identified as NFE performed the same roles of socialising, controlling social mobility, selecting and recruiting their participants, and providing (or not providing) modes of exchange within society, as did formal schools. Whereas the Ideologues would have asserted that any educational programme which contained these characteristics could not be called 'non-formal', that many so-called 'non-formal programmes' were not in fact 'non-formal', the Empiricists suggested that much non-formal education was in fact 'formal'.

Other writers followed suit. Lintott, Carr-Hill and Carron, without defining the formal system at all closely, felt they were able to identify clearly which programmes were non-formal and which were not. There is in these writings no hint of uncertainty, no sense that any of their identifications might be contested, no fear of acting arbitrarily. On this basis, they too found that the programmes they selected as exemplars of NFE served much the same purposes and fulfilled much the same functions as formal education. It may well have been that this arbitrary decision-making about the distinction between formal and non-formal in the end contributed to the death of the debate. If both sides were talking about the same thing, if formal and non-formal education were essentially the same, there was no longer any grounds for discussion.

Fuzzy boundaries: We have already seen that some suggested that it may not in fact be easy to distinguish between formal and non-formal activities. But that voice is not strong. The confusion is shown by Evans: "The border between non-formal and formal education is quite clearly marked by the distinction between school and non-school....[But] Certain activities may not fall clearly in either the formal or non-formal categories" (Evans 1981a: 29). "The demarcation between formal and nonformal education is fuzzy" (Hallak 1990: 241), a position which would seem to undermine the general conclusions which the Empiricists were drawing.

> The complexity of the sphere of NFE, as illustrated by the numerous forms it may have adopted, as well as the difficulty of drawing a distinct borderline between FE and NFE, explain the many definitions of NFE which have been advanced. These definitions, often formulated after the examination of a limited number of cases, merely deal with individual facets of a complex whole. ... the proposed characteristics of NFE are only fragmented properties valid for a very specific context and, hence, are difficult to generalise to the entire field of NFE. (IBE 1987)

"The ... three basic modes of education – informal, formal and nonformal – are not watertight compartments. They overlap in places, occasionally turning up in hybrid forms" (Coombs & Ahmed 1974: 233). "In practice, no hard lines of demarcation exist between formal, nonformal and informal education; while many activities may be perceived as falling exclusively into one category alone, many share aspects of two or all of them" (Radcliffe & Colletta 1985: 3536). The case of apprenticeships was raised frequently: with their 'formal' structure and certificates, were they formal or non-formal vocational training? (Callaway 1972; King 1975; Simkins 1977: 31; Wilson 1997: 99; Overwien 1997 etc.). But these hesitations did not stop them making generalisations; every writer on NFE wrote as though they felt that they could allocate activities to different categories without contestation, and on this basis proceeded to draw conclusions from what were in fact their own creations.

Process and system: Although there is a lack of clarity in many of the arguments, all of these writers were also arguing for a distinction between formal and non-formal structures and between formal and non-formal processes. The Empiricists argued that 'non-formal education' (defined as outside of the formal schooling system) could and often did show no signs of being 'non-formal' in process: "'Non-formal' is mis-leading – it suggests that there is very little or no formal structure". On the other hand, the Ideologues landed themselves in the same mire: they too argued that many educational programmes outside of the formal system could not be called 'non-formal' because they did not display any non-formal education characteristics. LaBelle (1982: 163), for example, wrote that "These [non-formal] programs evidence many formal characteristics". It is significant that most of the case studies described, for example in Sheffield and Diejomaoh (1972), were of NFE programmes which in fact seem to have been by the criteria of contemporaries very 'formal' in their implementation.

There is a major cause of confusion here. The systems approach is based on a *category* approach. A programme can be seen to be either inside or outside formal education, not half-way between the two. *Process* on the other hand is a continuum; an educational activity can be more or less formal or non-formal – it will rarely be fully one or the other.

Arguing from different premises (from process and from system) and with differing basic approaches (prescriptive or descriptive, ideological or empirical), there can be little resolution to this debate. LaBelle acknowledged this when he wrote: "The most common dilemma is confronted when individuals attempt to fit a never-ending set of behaviors and activities in the three educational modes [formal, non-formal and informal]. The result is often frustration, as everything simply does not fit neatly" (LaBelle 1986: 5). The fact that the debate, as it progressed, resulted in increased confusion rather than clarification must have contributed to its decline.

2. Relationships between NFE and formal education

Throughout the debate, the question of the relationship between the two constructed groups of programmes was constantly raised.

The question was whether NFE was a separate sub-system or a very wide and varied range of educational activities with nothing in common except the fact that they lay outside the formal system. Some argued that NFE was a sub-system among other sub-systems including formal education, and that it negotiates within society along with the other sub-systems (see for example, Evans 1981a). But others expressed fears of the creation of a dual system of education with NFE as the inferior partner. Philipps (1975b cited in Ranaweera 1990: 27-29) proposed such an unequal dual system: since in many countries it would not be possible for many years for a universalised primary education (UPE) programme to meet the needs of all children, "the role of UPE in bringing the mass of educationally deprived children above the educational poverty line probably has to be assumed by UBE [Universalised Basic Education] together with supporting services of a nonformal kind for the purposes of literacy retention and recuperation of drop-outs". This would, he admitted, lead to a dual system, one providing "a sound minimum primary education of the conventional kind" and the other for children outside of the formal system providing "a minimum form of functional literacy, similar to that which is given in adult functional literacy pro-grammes". UNESCO was hesitant about this. "The main danger is that two educational systems of different quality and prestige will develop, and thus contribute to perpetuating and increasing the existing socio-economic disparities" (UNESCO 1987: 13). But Philipps rejoined: "The existence of such a dual system may be regarded as discriminatory but surely it is less discriminatory than the unconscious present discrimination of giving children no education at all" (Philipps 1975b: 8, 158).

Coombs may have started this off (as with so many other things) when he wrote about NFE as being a 'shadow school system' (Coombs 1968; Paulston 1971). The term 'shadow' hardly suggests equality or independence. Such an approach led to the frequently expressed view that NFE (in many cases along with 'informal education') needs to be incorporated into a national educational system; that NFE was a national resource which the state should co-opt to its own purposes (see for example Courtney & Kutsch 1978), based on what each system could provide uniquely or best (Barrow 1978: 10). Ahmed drew on three main discourses of the time, NFE, de-schooling and lifelong education with a courtesy nod towards recurrent education: "Formal, nonformal and informal modes of learning can and should constitute the building blocks of a nation-wide comprehensive learning network in each country cemented into one meaningful mosaic by the concept of lifelong and recurrent learning opportunities for all" (Ahmed 1982: 139; note the careful avoidance of the word 'system'). Effective linkages needed to be built between the two sectors of education, especially in terms of training programmes, institutions, linkages between children and adult participants, and drop-outs (Hallak 1990: 248). And IBE pointed out that "in reality, positive collaboration between FE and NFE would require that they be perceived as distinct forms of a greater whole – which is education, designed to serve the needs of society" (Bacquelaine & Raeymakers 1991: 22b). Despite Coombs' growing scepticism of "the dream" of bringing together formal and non-formal education "into some neat and tidy organized package – with the aim of keeping everything well co-ordinated, well-planned and under control" (Coombs 1985a: 25), the search for integration continued, mainly at UNESCO; thus in 1987 an international symposium on the co-ordinated planning of the development of formal and non-formal education was held in Paris (UNESCO 1987).

The precise nature of the relationship between the two sectors was worked out in detail by several writers. NFE should (for the Ideologues) or did (for the Empiricists) hold a relationship to formal education of one or more of three kinds (e.g. Paulston 1972: xi; Simkins 1977: 54-55 etc.). It was (or should be)[2]

a) **complementary to the system** – that is, it provided another way in which more and more people (especially rural dwellers) could obtain *more or less the same initial education* which they had not been able to obtain or complete during their younger years. This kind of NFE is compensatory, remedial, aimed only at those who have been unable to take advantage of the formal schooling offered, and normally leads to the same or closely equivalent forms of qualification; "a programmatic way of reaching a particular population for which schools have been ineffective or inappropriate" (LaBelle & Verhine 1975: 165). This form of NFE was designed to complete the same goals of formal schooling.

b) **supplementary to formal education** – that is, NFE provided some forms of education which were *in addition to* what was provided in schools, dealing with some content not normally associated with formal education, some quick response to new demands for education or training which formal education cannot meet. This kind of NFE is aimed at all those outside of formal education, not just those who have not

---

[2] The way these terms are used here is the way the majority of writers at this time used them; some later writers use these same terms in rather different senses.

completed the initial education provided. Such programmes do not normally lead to qualifications and were seen to be primarily development oriented.

c) **alternative to formal education** – that is, NFE provided *a different kind of education altogether,* a different curriculum leading to different outcomes from formal schooling, one more appropriate to the older participants (whether adolescents or adults) who were to be found in most NFE programmes. In this form of NFE, participants would be engaged in a new curriculum, learning about subjects which were thought to be more appropriate to them than the formal education curriculum. Such programmes on occasions led to alternative qualifications, but this sector also covered traditional and/or indigenous learning programmes. Evans (1981a) called this 'replacement' education and others have seen this form of NFE as being in opposition to formal schooling.

Evans (1981a: 19ff) is the classic statement of this, but there had been earlier examples and there were many later statements with modifications in the terms used (see Hoppers 2000a: 9-10; Carr-Hill et al. 2001: 333 suggest this applies only to "developing countries"). Wilson (1997: 86-87) speaks of three major types of NFE, a substitute for, complementary or supplementary to, and oppositional to formal education. Brennan (1997: 187) uses the same terms but in different ways. Evans and Smith (1972: 10) cite a slightly different set of relationships set out in a fourfold scheme of Gillette (1977) which "divides programs according to their relationship to formal schooling: complementary, supplementary, replaces schooling, and merges with schooling". UNICEF (1993a) uses only two of these terms, complementary which it identifies with compensatory, and alternative.

Formal is normal: It is clear that all of those engaged in the debate about NFE began from formal education. This was their starting point, the given. Even Coombs, as may be seen from the space he devotes to each form of education in both of his *World Crisis* books (1968, 1985), clearly felt that formal education was more important than NFE. Paulston (1972) spoke of the formal core and the nonformal periphery. "Nonformal education ... still defines itself by what it is not, as *'organised educational activities outside the established formal system',* thus leaving the 'formal' system as the default setting". NFE diverged from the norm, and in many cases was designed to lead back to "the mainstream schooling system" (Hoppers 2000a: 9, 26 original italics). "NFE can be seen as a prop or a challenge to formal education" (Radcliffe & Colletta 1985: 3539b), but in every case, it drew its terms of reference and the criteria by which it would be judged from formal education. When the World Bank argued that NFE was meant to be "a supplement, not a rival, to the formal educational system ... intended to provide a functional, flexible low-cost education for those whom the formal system cannot yet reach or has already passed by" (World Bank 1974: 29), the Bank was assuming the primacy of formal education. "Nonformal programs are seldom designed to replace formal schools" (LaBelle & Verhine 1975: 165). Although Evans and others argued that NFE should be treated as equal to formal education, they did not envisage that the priority of formal schooling would be challenged (Evans 1981).

This does not imply that NFE was always seen to be a reflection of formal education. "The further development of NFE does not lie in the direction of attempting to make non-formal more and more like formal. The strategy should be to develop curricula, teaching-learning methodologies, and evaluation and monitoring practices which are unique and characteristic of NFE, independent of the formal models, thereby developing NFE in its own right and not as a substitute" (UIE 1990: 26). NFE was to become a home for innovation, an experimental testing ground from which formal education will benefit. But even here, the reference point is formal education, for the purpose of the innovation was to improve formal education.

3. Attitudes towards Formal Education

Negative attitudes: Behind the different positions lay different attitudes towards 'education' as a whole and schooling in particular. Those who adopted a more prescriptive approach to NFE tended to take a negative attitude towards the formal education system. It had failed to fulfil its own targets, to meet the new and differing demands for education. In many ways, it was having undesirable effects on society (increasing inequalities etc.), destructive of local, traditional indigenous learning systems, imposing global, Western and modern cultures on non-Western peoples. It is interesting that many of the alleged characteristics of formal education which were drawn up tended to be negative, while the traits of NFE were thought to be positive. The tone is reminiscent of the analyses of the de-schooling and radical writers.

Positive attitudes: On the other hand, those who adopted a descriptive approach to NFE tended to feel more positively towards 'education'. It is a process for the benefit of society; it socialises people and helps to manage social mobility (both in the sense of helping members of society to fit into accepted norms, and at the same time helping them to adapt to the changing demands of society for modernisation); it contributes to the relief of poverty. Blunt (for one) suggested that formal education is the most desirable form of education for it provides access to modern employment sectors (Blunt 1988: 43). Schooling is an essential part of modern society and cannot (and should not) be abandoned. Formal education is with us for ever and it needs to be made more, not less, effective.

Since those who adopted the more positive approach to formal education/ schooling seem to have won the day, it can be argued that what we are witnessing here is one more example of the fact that the formal education system is much stronger than non-formal education, and that it will almost always co-opt non-formal programmes. Most Empiricists accepted that NFE has positive features in terms of flexibility; and there was talk about 'non-formalising the formal system', bringing the best features of NFE into the formal educational system, to the extent that some could talk of formal becoming non-formal: "formal programmes, methods and organizations must be more flexible and nonformal whenever possible" (UNESCO 1987: 13; see Ranaweera 1990: 28). The Ideologues, on the other hand, saw dangers in the call for greater integration between NFE and formal schooling; NFE would be swamped, would lose its identity. Simkins, for example, suggested that when formal education was highly valued, NFE either became formalised or devalued. Velandia, in a study of Argentina, felt that NFE ran the risk of becoming hierarchical like formal education and in certain circumstances could even be absorbed into formal education (Velandia et al. 1975: 506). More recently, Jung quotes Rosa Maria Torres's judgment:

> Conceived as an education of and for the poor, as a second class, remedial, compensatory education ... [it] has developed in conditions of great institutional, financial, human and technical precariousness. Entire programmes that disappear from one day to the next ... Discontinuity in policies, squalid budgets, structural instability, volunteer workers or badly paid and poorly trained workers, whose training is basically learned on the job. A field of work with little theoretical development and low academic status, a lack of research and evaluation ... In short, precariousness and vulnerability all around. (Torres 1995 cited in Jung & King 1999: 26)

Such writers argued that the salvation of non-formal education may lie in keeping it separate from the formal system, distinct and distinctive, independent of all formal structures and free of hegemony – an impossible position according to the Empiricists, since NFE is itself situated in and created by a society and not independent of it. Safeguarding the future development of NFE would depend on the state and civil society recognising its socio-economic importance and providing (mainly through political goodwill) adequate resources.

4. Power and NFE

And this leads to a consideration of issues of power and NFE. For the question arises: 'importance to whom?' – the state, civil society, global capitalism or the participants, especially the 'poor', however these are constructed?

It is not surprising, since so much of the debate arose from within a context of critical theory (see above p.25), that the treatment of issues surrounding power and control in NFE was a feature of the debate. Two or three matters arose in this connection.

Socio-political issues: First, there were those who saw formal education/schooling as a natural (and to a large extent neutral) activity. They could therefore speak of NFE in terms of complementing, supplementing or providing an alternative to formal schooling without seeing in this any real threat – indeed both would gain. Neither the Advocates nor the Ideologues saw NFE as a fundamental challenge to existing power structures or special interests.

On the other hand, the Empiricists specifically set out to explore the socio-political dimensions of NFE, to see formal and nonformal education within a political and cultural context, as performing functions on behalf of interested parties, mainly the elites but in the case of some NFE oppositional interest groups. Bock and Papagiannis (1976) suggested that, since NFE lacked the credentialling powers of formal education, it was always regarded as second-rate in terms of the employment market. It could not challenge the larger socio-cultural structures and was therefore another mechanism for allocation of class status. LaBelle and Verhine (1975) saw NFE as being used on occasion to limit the access of less well educated persons into higher economic sectors. Torres (1990) saw NFE as being used by revolutionary governments to support their claims and ideologies. Carr-Hill and his colleagues (Carr-Hill & Lintott 1985, Carron & Carr-Hill 1991) suggested that NFE could be seen as a tool to pacify the potentially or actively discontented.

All of these tended to regard NFE largely as a domesticating agency, controlled through direct methods or hegemony by the elites in their own interests. But they also envisaged that, outside of the state-controlled NFE programmes, there were NFE programmes which challenged the status quo, which promoted the interests of groups within civil society. Some felt that NFE could serve either "as a prop for an over-extended but nevertheless desirable formal system or as a fundamental challenge to the political-social systems which formal schooling has come to represent" (Radcliffe & Colletta 1985: 3539). It depended to a large extent upon whether NFE was controlled by the state or by NGOs, although much NGO-provided NFE was domesticating, especially when funded by the state.

NFE then was felt to be divided between supporting or challenging the status quo. There were yet others who took an intermediate position on this, NFE as a mediator. Like the Faure Report, they saw formal schooling as a Western intrusion and NFE as the strengthening of pre-Western indigenous or native educational activities and structures. "Between formal schooling as the agent of a wider universe of knowledge which is, however, often perceived as an alien imposition, and informal indigenous education as the bearer of cultural identity and community values, nonformal education can play a harmonizing role" (Radcliffe & Colletta 1985: 3539-3540). Several writers saw NFE as consisting largely of the revival of indigenous learning approaches, but for others, "few of these [NFE] programs have been based (at least in contemporary times) on indigenous forms of schooling" (Wagner 1999: 283).

Participatory issues: A second, and to some extent related, issue concerns the claims made for NFE that it would lead to the empowerment of the participants by enabling the participants to gain more control over the programmes (Kindervatten 1979; see above pp. 116).[3] The centres of control offered to participants in the case studies taken

---

[3] Despite the work of Kindervatten and a few others, the discourse of empowerment, power within and power from, seems to have emerged largely after the end of the NFE debate and has never been happily harmonised with the NFE discourse.

by the Empiricists for study were focussed on logistical rather than content matters. For example, the University of Massachusetts' project in Ecuador, which concentrated on teaching-learning methodologies as if these were universally applicable and neutral from the socio-political contexts from which they sprang, seem to have encouraged participation without control. The methods were chosen by the (largely Western) change agents; the materials were developed by the (largely Western) project workers; the technologies were Western in origin; there was a "lack of attention to local culture" (Krueger & Moulton 1981: 52). Participation in these programmes meant active involvement in learning methodologies chosen by the educational planners and offered to the participants. Participation did not extend to facilitating the participants to determine what they should learn and for how long (Hoxeng 1973; Ecuador; Gillette 1974 etc.; see also Evans 1976; below pp.251-253).

Gender: It is strange that issues of gender were relatively limited in the great debate (see Paolucci et al. 1976; Robertson 1984). Contemporary discussions on 'Women in Development' seem to have had little influence on the NFE debate. For example, when LaBelle wrote about NFE being at the centre of the contest between interest groups (LaBelle 1986: vii; see above p.126), gender is not mentioned among the various interest groups. And this is true of most of the other writers. It was of course urged from the start that NFE programmes were particularly relevant for women, but this was a male-oriented statement patronising in its tone. Throughout the debate, the construct of 'women' was never problematised; women (like the 'people') were seen as one single undifferentiated and uniformly oppressed group for whom NFE was particularly appropriate (Kindervatten 1979 is the fullest expression of this; see Hans 1985; Jerudasa & Koshy 1976). Later the issue received more attention (Stromquist 1986, 1988; van den Westen 1990): however, as we have seen, Ellis suggested that NFE had not in fact led to women's liberation and empowerment but to confining them still in subordinate roles (see p.138 above).

Women then were regarded as the *object* of NFE, not the instruments of NFE (Derryck 1979). Even those who argued that the chief distinction between formal and non-formal education lay in participant control did not see in this a gender statement. Indeed, the voice of the debate throughout was pre-eminently a male voice. Most of the writers in the debate were men, and the specific voice of women in the debate is hardly heard. In large part, this is because education too at that time was rarely seen to have a gender dimension except in strategic terms – regretting the lower attendance of girls in schools and the lower literacy rate among women. Women were to be the recipients of the charity which NFE planners and providers could offer to them, the beneficiaries of new opportunities to engage in society on society's terms, encouraged to access the existing resources of society rather than actively transforming society. Participation meant joining in programmes designed by others. It may be that the strengthening of the feminist movement and the new concerns it came to address revealed the shallowness of the gender element in the NFE debate and contributed to the decline of the debate.

Deconstructing the debate: Finally, there was no discussion about the power issues involved in the creation of NFE as a discourse-concept itself. Whose interests was the new concern for NFE serving? There was no attempt to deconstruct the debate or to look at it from the outside except in terms of whether it were a current fashion or not. Advocates, Ideologues, Empiricists and Pragmatists all assumed that NFE existed in a variety of forms. The fact that those who benefited most from the debate were educational planners, consultants and academics, and that these dropped the discourse as soon as the funds ran out, was not pointed out. Critical theory was applied to others, not to the critical theorists.

5. Non-Formal Education and its Client Groups

Gender issues raise the question as to the main target group of NFE.

Adults: Non-formal education was often equated with adult education. IIEP (IIEP 1981: 165-176) saw NFE solely in terms of adult education. "Nonformal education is primarily directed at adults but can include the young as well" (Bock & Papagiannis 1983: 16). Simkins (1977: 63) saw NFE "largely concentrating on adults, especially those in rural areas who usually have few expectations with respect to urban employment. Attempts to offer similar programmes for young people are likely to be rapidly formalised or devalued by competition from the formal system". Indeed Evans saw one approach to NFE as implying "not working with the same populations the formal schools serve. Non-formal education in this approach must avoid competition with the schools and work with adults or with older youth who are already finished with the schools" (Evans, paper of May 1980 cited in Krueger & Moulton 1981: 43). One survey of NFE in Uganda is confined to the education of adults (Visocchi 1978). King says of NFE that it is "more concerned with adults, both young and old" (King 1991: 147). Torres (1990, 1991), like LaBelle and others, equated NFE with adult education. Many government Departments or Directorates of NFE were originally solely or primarily concerned with adult education (adult literacy), and when they were given new roles to reach out-of-school youth, this was seen as an *extension* of their existing remit. In other words, NFE for younger learners would seem to be a divergence from NFE for adults which was the norm.

Youth: But out-of-school youth, school drop-outs or non-attenders who were too old to be admitted to primary school but had not yet reached adulthood were included by some writers in the NFE 'target group'. Coombs and his colleagues could write about *New Paths to Learning for Rural Children and Youth*, as well as about *How NFE can help the attack on rural poverty* (Coombs & Ahmed 1973; Coombs & Ahmed 1974). The bi-focal nature of NFE on youth (adolescent, as IIEP 1999 defined this kind of education) and adults has been there from the start. LaBelle could write about NFE of children and youth (LaBelle 1981) while at the same time asserting that NFE consisted of "local level programs among the *adult* rural poor ... local level *community action* efforts" (LaBelle 1986: vi, 7 my italics; see LaBelle 2000 passim). The distinction between adult and young adult has always been problematic in many societies. Thailand, for example, defined 'adult' as any ten-year-old person and over who was not in school (Coombs 1976: 292).

Children: Despite King (1991: 178) who suggested that from very early NFE was seen as an alternative mode of delivery of basic education to children, there are few signs in the literature at the time of NFE being seen as a major alternative to primary education for school-age children. It was only later that the term NFE came to be used of different approaches to schooling for children other than for out-of-school youth who were past the age of entering primary school for the first time.

In more recent statements, NFE has come to be identified by some as exclusively children oriented. The Dakar meeting (1996) spoke of 'the gap between formal, non-formal and various forms of adult learning', as if non-formal is not adult education. Hoppers (2000a, 2000b) sees NFE as largely for children of school-going age, and calls education aimed at adults 'alternative education'. Just as the formal education system has colonised non-formal education programmes, so children in some contexts are coming to monopolise NFE resources. The Education For All programme shows this trend. Whereas the Jomtien Declaration asserted the equal right of both adults and children to basic education, EFA in some countries consists almost entirely of ways of extending the reach and effectiveness of primary schooling, creating alternative forms of primary education as similar as possible to formal schools with equivalent qualifications and routes and contents.

Since Jomtien, educational providers in many developing countries and their funders have been struggling with the various terms they need to use, distinguishing between basic and post-basic education and between adult and non-adult programmes. Later writers came to speak of 'nonformal *and* adult education' as if the two are not the same. So we currently end up with non-formal education being largely (but not entirely) concentrated on out-of-school children of school age and on 'youth' – those too old to enter primary school at an appropriate educational level. Some recognition of this can be detected in the papers which are accompanying the current expansion of NFE programmes, many of which distinguish what is being referred to by using terms (with or without the parentheses) such as 'Non-formal (Primary) Education', 'Non-formal (Adult) Education', 'Non-Formal (Basic) Education', even 'Basic Adult Non-formal Education' (Afrik 1995).

6. Education or Development

Throughout the debate, there was some confusion between whether NFE lay properly within the educational sector or within the development sector. Throughout it all, a deep fault line ran. On the one side were those who saw NFE as an alternative 'education'; on the other side were those who saw NFE as a tool of development. Coombs from the start saw NFE more as a development strategy, despite his starting point from the need for the reform of education (see Grandstaff 1973b). Indeed, the chief characteristic of NFE for him and his colleagues was that it was all that education which was oriented towards developmental goals such as income-generation (Wijetunga 1979; Thailand 1998b etc.) rather than educational goals. The Human Resource Development model predominated in this strand. USAID "set out to build a NFE knowledge base, examine and test promising models, disseminate ideas and information and build technical support capacity *in order to establish NFE as a development strategy* and to assist in identifying and refining roles, resources, methods and techniques which could make it most effective" for this purpose (Krueger & Moulton 1981: i, my italics). Harbison and Seltzer (1970) limited NFE to what they called "productive educative services ... that is, activities and programs within the system of non-formal education which are directly related to increasing man's [sic] capacity for work through development of the skill, knowledge, motivation and effectiveness of potential and actual members of the labor force" (cited in Krueger & Moulton 1981: 6). NFE for agriculture was a key element (Klees & Wells 1978; Loveridge 1978; MSU 1982a; see Wallace 1990). The World Bank pointed out that "much of the nonformal education which is being supported by the organization is being done under the aegis of other sectoral offices without much collaboration with educational specialists" (World Bank 1979), bemoaning the professional territorialism thus generated. NFE "must be seen as a reinforcing process for agriculture, health and energy, population, nutrition and infrastructural development, and that it not be seen as a separate sector" (USAID 1982 cited in Krueger & Moulton 1981: 45).[4] NFE is provided by development agencies as much as by educational agencies: "Typically over half the expenditures on education are made outside of the Ministry of Education". Formal education was inherently less beneficial to the newer forms of development than NFE. Indeed, several writers argued that the distinguishing feature of NFE was that "education outside the schools is usually more directly tied to development objectives and has a more immediate pay-off" (Wilder 1974), whereas formal education was not (a view disputed by other writers).

On the other hand the majority of those who supported the case for NFE saw it primarily as "a means to alleviate at least partially certain ... critical problems in the educational sector" (USAID 1971; Krueger & Moulton 1981: 3; Grandstaff 1973a). Both the Ideologues, tied as they were to formal education even though they wished to reform it, and the Empiricists who assessed NFE against formal education, on the whole fell into this category. There were of course attempts by several to claim that both could operate at the same time: that NFE was "a sub-set of educational efforts that also have identifiable development purposes related to the contextual setting in which they take place" (Wilder 1974). But this effort to bridge the fault line failed on the cutting-edge of evaluation.

---

[4] Krueger and Moulton 1981 are citing a draft of a paper prepared to be presented in 1982; hence the dates of these two documents.

7. The Evaluation of NFE

The evaluation of NFE occupied a good deal of attention in the literature of NFE but without any clear focus (see bibliography in Shavelson et al. 1985; also Ward 1973; Ward & Herzog 1974; Wilder 1977). Kinsey 1978 is one of the few who address this issue directly, and his main concern is with the use of non-formal methodologies in the evaluation of NFE programmes more than with the rationales and content of NFE evaluation. He does not address the 'what' or the 'why' of evaluation in NFE, or even the criteria by which NFE programmes would be evaluated, but rather 'how' the data is to be collected.

Evaluation was affected by the fault line between education and development as the goal of NFE. The issue is whether the evaluation of NFE is to be conducted through formalised learning tests (the educational syndrome) or through impact assessments (the development syndrome). "Aware that because classic educational evaluation models are not designed for remote rural communities in developing countries, they are of little use, ... [USAID] has not been concerned with individual learning as measured by achievement tests and learning retention scores. Instead, projects have been designed to promote basic literacy and behavior changes and as tools in community organization amenable to multiple development applications." But as they ruefully reported, they could not in the end resist the pressure from participants to award certificates based on formal evaluations of learning rather than on the use of that learning (Krueger & Moulton 1981: 9, 31, 51).

The Ideologues of course suggested educational criteria. The lists of characteristics of NFE indicate that they expected such programmes to be judged by whether or not they lived up to those characteristics. But few of these writers except Srinivasan showed signs of carrying out the field work which would justify or not their claims. Others suggested that "success... is not measured by carefully controlled evaluations but by the satisfaction of the participants themselves and the continued existence of the organizations" (Moulton 2000: 29).

The Empiricists analysed NFE programmes mainly in terms of their societal impact. Their biggest problem was the lack of data for the conduct of appropriate forms of evaluation (see e.g. Shavelson et al. 1985; Fry 1981). They did not on the whole attempt to make value judgments between programmes as to whether this programme was 'effective' or not in terms of goal-achievement, or develop criteria on which such judgments could be made. It was rather later, as NFE emerged as an alternative to formal primary school for school-aged children, that evaluations of NFE were conducted in terms of equivalent achievements in scholastic competencies through standardised tests. Several studies were made to assess whether students within NFE programmes 'performed' as well as students in formal school, judged solely by standardised tests, but there were also some wider studies (e.g. Sweetser 1999).

Perhaps the reason for the failure of the non-formal education protagonists to address the issue of evaluation in depth is their awareness that NFE calls for more qualitative forms of evaluation than the quantitative processes available, their appreciation of the difficulty of measuring qualitative changes, and their proximity to donors who demanded statistical evidence of the effectiveness of the programmes they supported (Easton 1997; Alexander 1990). Qualitative assessment and evaluation is an issue which is still troubling many educators (e.g. Crossley & Vulliamy 1997).

Today, programmes defined as NFE find it harder to determine precisely the criteria which they should use to assess their success or failure, except in terms of school tests or their equivalent (Muskin 1999; Chowdhury et al. 1994; CAMPE 1996; PPA 1997). More and more the criteria seem to be taken from formal education – and as these are themselves changing in some contexts to include more qualitative assessments, so the evaluations of non-formal education activities are also changing.

CONCLUSION

Those involved in this debate constructed NFE to suit their purposes and with it brought into play all the paraphernalia of education and development. For some, all those educational programmes which displayed non-formal methodologies and approaches were NFE; for others all those educational programmes which had developmental goals rather than educational goals comprised NFE; for yet others, NFE consisted of all those programmes provided by non-statutory bodies. In setting such limits, they were also constructing formal education. All took it for granted that non-formal education existed 'out there' rather than in their minds and discourses, and they set out to grow it, co-ordinate it, control it and use it to reform the equally constructed formal system of education.

There would seem to be two ways of looking at the end of the history of the great debate over non-formal education. One is to say (as Evans & Smith say) that the term 'non-formal education' only had

> usefulness [in] the early stages of the movement when emphasis was placed on the differences between the new approach and formal schooling. Once the legitimacy and desirability of the alternative approaches [have been] established, the term non-formal becomes more of a liability than an asset because of the confusion it creates ... A new series of terms will [need to] be generated to describe different clusters of alternatives to formal schooling ... The future will hold greater diversity, greater flexibility, and a growing understanding. (Evans & Smith 1972: 20)

An alternative interpretation of what has happened is that the history of NFE is illustrative of "the hegemony exerted by the formal system in deciding what learning is to be valued and how it is to be assessed and accredited" (Aspin et al. 2001: xxvii). What happened in and through the great NFE debate can be read in terms of formal education taking big knocks from reformers, of NFE being proposed as an alternative, of formal education recovering and launching a counter-offensive against NFE and currently co-opting NFE into its embrace. In this scenario, the victim, it can be argued, is non-formal education which (if it ever existed at all) is seen to have lost much of its distinctiveness. One argument suggests that we should give the concept and the discourse a decent burial. Another says that perhaps we should look again to see if we would lose anything of value by the abandonment of the discourse.

TIMELINE BIBLIOGRAPHY OF THE GREAT DEBATE ON NFE

Note: this is a select bibliography of the items I think are most significant. I have omitted from this list the articles on NFE in various *International Encyclopaedias*, since they were usually commissioned, or summarised works already in print, or sometimes indeed simply reproduced articles from earlier encyclopaedias with or without updating.

1958, 1964	• occasional references (e.g. Clark & Sloan; Miles)
1967	• King 1967 (first main reference)
1968	• Coombs, *The World Educational Crisis:* first major discussion of NFE
1971-75	• CIE, NFE in Ecuador project and reports
1972	• Paulston, *Bibliography of NFE* • Sheffield and Diejomaoh, *NFE in Africa* • Evans and Smith , *NFE* • World Bank, *NFE for Rural Development;* • MSU publications
1973	• Coombs and Ahmed, *New Paths to Learning for Rural Children and Youth* • MSU lists and bibliographies (1973-75) • Grandstaff, *NFE and development* • Brembeck, *New Strategies for Educational Development*
1974	• Brembeck, *NFE as alternative to schooling* • Coombs and Ahmed, *Attacking Rural Development; how NFE can help* • World Bank Education Sector Working Paper
1975	• Ahmed, *Economics of NFE* • LaBelle, *Educational Alternatives in Latin America* • Ahmed and Coombs, *NFE for Rural Development*
1976	• *Comparative Education Review* special edition on NFE • Johnson, *NFE and rural youth* (OECD) • LaBelle, *Goals and Strategies of NFE* • LaBelle, *NFE and Social Change in Latin America* • Bock and Papagiannis, *Demystification of NFE*
1976-82	• *NFE Exchange* (MSU)
1977	• SE Asia Conference on NFE • Simkins, *NFE and Development* • Srinivasan, *Perspectives on NF Adult Learning*
1978	• Kinsey, *Evaluation of NFE*
1979	• Kindervatter, *NFE for Women's Empowerment*
1980	• Dejene, *NFE as a Strategy in Development* • Commonwealth Conference on NFE: Fordham report • Paulston, *Education as anti-structure: NFE in social and ethnic movements* • UNESCO/UNICEF, Formal and NFE in Rural Development: comparative project • Colletta, two papers on NFE

1981	• LaBelle, *NFE of children and youth* • Evans, *Planning for NFE* (IIEP)˙
1982	• Altbach, *Comparative Education* (chapter on NFE) • *International Review of Education:* special edition on NFE • LaBelle, *Formal, non-formal and informal learning*
1983	• Bock and Papagiannis, *NFE and National Development* • *Prospects:* special edition on NFE
1985	• Carr-Hill and Lintott, *Comparative Adult Education Statistics* • Coombs, new version of *World Crisis in Education*
1986	• LaBelle, *NFE and the poor in Latin America and the Caribbean*
1987	• LaBelle, *From consciousness-raising to popular education* (no mention of NFE)
1988	• Blunt, Education, learning and development: evolving concepts, in *Convergence* (no mention of NFE in title but main theme of article is NFE) • Stromquist 'Women's education in development'
1989	• Ranaweera, *Non-conventional approaches to education* UIE
1990	• Torres, *Politics of NFE in Latin America* • van der Westen, *Reader on Women, Literacy and NFE* • UIE Round Table on Complementarity of Formal and Non-Formal Approaches (primary education only)
1991	• Carron and Carr-Hill, *NFE: information and planning issues* (IIEP) • Torres, *State, NFE and Socialism* • Hamadache, *NFE: definition of concept*
1993	• Fordham, *Informal, Non-formal and Formal Education Programmes*
1995	• Guttman publications on NFE (UNESCO)
1996	• van Riezen, NFE and Community Development, *Convergence*
1997	• Easton, *Sharpening our Tools: improving evaluation in adult and NFE* (UIE) • PROAP UNESCO, *Non-formal Adult Education* • International Extension College distance learning course on NFE Brennan, article in *IRE* • Lynch et al *Education and Development: Non-Formal and Non-Governmental Approaches*
1999	• ADEA NFE Working Group: Workshops in Botswana and Johannesburg and reports
2000	• Hoppers article on NFE in *IRE* • LaBelle article on NFE in Latin America in *CER* • EU Memorandum
2001	• EU Communication
2002	• World Bank paper on adult non-formal education
2003	• Poizat *L'education non-formelle*

Part III

Case Studies

This section outlines a number of case studies of non-formal education in developing societies today. These range from very small and localised projects run by community-based or non-governmental organisations to large-scale standardised and certificated national programmes for adults or for children, all of which have been designated as 'non-formal', as being outside the formal education system or alongside the formal system. It ends by looking at a programme which aims to mainstream NFE within formal education. The picture suggests that NFE today is a-theoretical, lacking any clear logic frame.

In much of what follows, I use one country's programmes of NFE to exemplify a particular approach to defining and implementing NFE, while looking at the country as a whole.

10

NFE Today: The Trajectory of Meanings

It is important to be clear about the concepts one is using, in particular in institutional building. (Jung & King 1999: 19)

The debate about the nature of NFE then has largely disappeared, to be replaced in many contexts with new discourses, especially those of lifelong learning and diversity.

Programmes labelled NFE

But interestingly, programmes labelled Non-formal Education are increasing in many countries. Divisions, Directorates or Departments of NFE within a number of governments are receiving increased attention and even some increased support. USAID for example has enlarged its assistance to the Association for the Development of Education in Africa (ADEA) for NFE by 60%, and the World Bank is expressing a revived interest, mainly in the form of Adult Basic Education and Training (ABET) (see p.139). In the Philippines, the Bureau of NFE is developing national programmes with substantial aid from the Asian Development Bank. In Botswana, the Government Department of NFE has recently received an expanded role. Throughout Asia, with the encouragement of UNESCO regional bodies, programmes labelled NFE are being expanded and replicated from country to country, for example, from Thailand to Bangladesh (Duke & Varapipatana 1982; Bobillier 2000). The pressure of Education for All (EFA) is leading many agencies to seek in NFE one means to complete tasks to which they are already committed. In Kenya, for example, programmes for urban out-of-school youth and for nomadic communities have been established under the designation of NFE (Hamadache 1994: 4133-4135).

These programmes have produced a large crop of evaluative reports and other documentation. The amount of paper-work containing the term 'non-formal education' has increased, not diminished over the last few years, although the earlier NFE Resource Centres such as those of Michigan State University at East Lansing and the University of Massachusetts, Amherst, no longer collect such material.

How then is NFE defined when such programmes, some large scale, some very small, still refer to themselves as 'non-formal'? What they mean by this term can in most cases only be determined inferentially, by looking at what they do as much as at what they say. For there is relatively little theoretical justification or even explanation of the term 'non-formal' in today's literature.

NFE discourses

What follows is based on a substantial number of published and unpublished reports and interviews with stakeholders in the various programmes. But we need to remember several points about this collection. First, it is idiosyncratic; it reflects the programmes with which I have come into contact. It does not represent any systematic attempt at a comprehensive coverage. I worry about the selection and about my interpretation of the programmes listed, but offer them as one possible approach to analysing NFE today.

Secondly, the voices being heard here do not always sing in harmony. In India, for example, the term NFE is used in very different ways by different people. There is no coherent picture even within any one country.

Thirdly, the voices being heard here are mainly those of government educational planners, with some donors and INGOs (many of which are inter-governmental agencies); and the purposes for which they speak are advocacy (especially fund-raising) and evaluation. The voices of the users and practitioners of these programmes are rarely heard.

Fourthly, the regional balance is largely towards Africa and Asia and especially Anglophone countries. In Latin America, relatively few grassroots agencies use the language of NFE when talking of particular education activities; other discourses have for long been heard more strongly, such as 'popular education' and the Freirean discourse of disadvantage. The language of NFE is to a large extent imposed on programmes by Northern agencies and academics rather than adopted indigenously. Reports of programmes there as elsewhere choose to use or not to use the language of NFE at whim.[1]

This fact reminds us that there are many identical educational programmes which do not use the term NFE. Indeed, in some cases, the term is actively avoided. The Khas Foundation in Indonesia, setting up a new educational programme, talks carefully of formal and informal education. We have noticed above (p.4) that the term 'non-formal' is disliked in some contexts because it appears to carry objectionable overtones. Save the Children (US) which formerly used the term now says it tries to eschew it: "we deliberately call them [SC community schools in Mali] Ecoles du Village ... avoiding the non-formal/formal cat fight" (Wood pers comm.). What follows seeks to explore the use of the term NFE and the concepts behind that use rather than to analyse all kinds of alternative educational activities. It is a discourse analysis, not a programme analysis.

How then is NFE defined today? What does it include and what does it not

---

[1] It is not clear, for instance, whether the use of the term NFE in Jung and King 1999 reflects local usage in Latin America or the decision of the editors.

include? What follows is a description of some NFE programmes illustrative of the different approaches to NFE today. It has been sequenced with care to show something of the trajectory of meanings being applied to the term 'non-formal' when applied to education. We can list the main usages as follows:

NFE can mean
1. a wide range of discrete and disparate activities by different agencies for adults, usually small-scale and localised
    ➤ some scaling up
    ➤ some co-ordination and integration: a NFE sector
2. institutionalisation: large-scale/national systems
    ➤ of vocational education and training
    ➤ of basic education, with accreditation and equivalency
    ➤ training for NFE
3. adult literacy
4. alternative primary education for out-of-school children
    ➤ community schools
    ➤ temporary schooling preliminary to formal schools
5. action within formal education
    ➤ reform of formal education
    ➤ informal educational activities within formal schooling
6. feeder schools within the educational system

---

1. NFE MEANS ... A WIDE RANGE OF ACTIVITIES

Coombs and Ahmed (1974: 8), when they defined NFE as all those organised, structured, systematic learning activities which took place outside of the formal system, were aware that this comprised a very wide range of activities: "... nonformal education includes, for example, agricultural extension and farmer training programs, adult literacy programs, occupational skill training given outside the formal system, youth clubs with substantial educational purposes and various community programs of instruction in health, nutrition, family planning and the like".

Coombs spoke of "that bewildering assortment of nonformal educational and training activities that constitute – or should constitute – an important complement to formal education in any nation's total educational effort", and Paulston of the "bewildering hodgepodge of education and training programs" (Coombs 1968: 138; Paulston 1972: x). UNESCO echoed Coombs' words (p.110): "This untidy melange of nonformal education activities ... are difficult to classify, monitor or analyse", since NFE in this sense is uncoordinated (UNESCO 1987: 37).

Disparate programmes: Today, some people see NFE in the same terms. A survey of the use of distance learning in NFE (Dodds 1996) reveals a very wide interpretation of the term. Indeed, some of the case studies listed in this review would be included by others in formal education such as the Certificate in Education and Development provided by the Namibian College of Open Learning (NAMCOL). Out of the 56^2 cases listed, 13 are literacy (usually with other topics included), 12 are agricultural and rural; health, co-operatives and small enterprises comprise five each, and among the rest are water, language education, environment, civics/citizenship, and women/gender education. Three are formal education equivalency programmes, and some are for teachers in the formal system. Eighteen are run by governments, 23 by other public bodies and 14 by NGOs including trade unions and churches. Clearly NFE is taken here to mean a very wide range of educational activities provided by a wide range of agencies.

Small-scale

Such activities are often small-scale and highly localised. As USAID put it, "experience acquired by all the large donors mentioned, [US]AID included, points to the fact that nonformal education is done best by comparatively small, flexible organizations closely linked to the client population and operating autonomously from government institutions" (Krueger & Moulton 1981: 42).

Latin America: A survey of some NFE activities in Latin America from a gender perspective illustrates this. There are in that region two main thrusts which sometimes get confused. On the one hand, NFE is often equated with adult education, which in most parts of Latin America seems to mean adult literacy/basic education. These programmes often reflect the dominant ideologies of the state and elites (Paulston 1970; Poston 1976; Jung & King 1999: 10; LaBelle 1986, 2000; Torres 1990, 1991). On the other hand, some NFE is linked with grass-roots movements, including women's movements: "Latin America has developed non-formal education initiatives with women over a long period of time ... [NFE is] direct work with women's organizations and groups" (Jung & King 1999: 117-118).

But the comparison with formal education is still there. A School for Skills Centre (*Centro Escuela de Capacitacion*) in Colombia for women, for example, sees itself as trying to overcome the results of the processes of "socialization, education and training, both formal and informal, in which the image and model reproduced are those imposed by a culture that makes women invisible, unequal and undervalued ... an exclusive sexist education that trains women only in matters socially and traditionally assigned to women; ... and [overcoming] the real barriers facing women from the grassroots in access to formal primary, secondary and university education" by using "NFE processes ..." (Jung & King 1999: 103, 107, 109-110). In Peru, an Institute to support the peasant women's autonomous movement (IAMAMC) uses what are called NFE processes for the training of facilitators (ibid: 131-140). The aim is socio-cultural transformation. "IAMAMC's non-formal education proposal [includes] a literacy

---

[2] I have taken the case studies from developing countries in Asia, Africa and Latin America.

teaching programme at the same time as it transforms agricultural production ... [and] a programme for facilitators to enable women to gain access to courses, workshops and projects over a period of two years. They will receive a certificate upon completion." Small scale credit will also be available (ibid: 137-138).

In Ecuador, an NGO (CEIME) is seeking to "promote an educational system that does not encourage sexist, violent and discriminatory behaviour and conduct towards women", on the one hand working with the formal system and on the other hand creating a "non-formal adult education process ... based on the 'experience learning circle'. It uses small groups and a series of training modules. The aim is both to change formal education in relation to gender concerns and to challenge it with alternatives". Since the formal system "is very authoritarian and repressive, ... facing this system with a different approach has a strong impact on all the sectors involved ... Our intervention is not neutral, it has of course an ideological bias based on a feminist position ... non-formal education provides enormous opportunities ... In the development of our work, there is no horizontal relationship, given that those who impart the training have knowledge that those receiving the training do not possess. ... our methodology is based on the experiences of those who are trained" (Jung & King 1999: 115, 117-118).

Similar localised approaches can be seen in other programmes identified in this survey. In El Salvador, the organisation Women for Dignity and Life has developed seven programmes ranging from feminist theory to literacy and midwife training. The programme is highly diversified. In Mexico, the Women's Education Group starts with "the motherhood we experience and want" (Jung & King 1999: 149-150), and develops new learning programmes. The Rural Development Studies Centre in Mexico engages in the training of rural women leaders. It recognises that education for rural women "has [in the past] been characterised by improvisation, empirical practices, and a lack of concrete results" (ibid: 177). Its programme, promoting project follow-up activities, environmental development, reproductive health practices and citizenship, aim to avoid such problems. The organisation has developed its own teaching-learning materials, and a diploma is awarded. In another programme in Peru (the Women's Training Centre), leaders are trained to promote nonformal education projects for displaced women and 'returners'. Projects start with local or regional issues such as community organisation, infrastructure, production processes and health and nutrition, "empowering women by giving skills that they can apply in everyday life". Subjects are organised in modules advancing from basic level to a deeper analysis. Local languages are used and participants share in the diagnosis of the topic, identifying needs, and designing, implementing and evaluating the project. There is here some scaling up: "the contents of the training courses, in their simplified version, are broadcast by radio" (ibid: 163-165).

NFE then is seen in parts of Latin America and among some practitioners (see also McClelland 1969; Klees & Wells 1978; Landazuri & Piaggesi 1998) as a wide range of local learning activities in the community with specific learning groups – highly participatory, centred on locally identified issues, and usually staff intensive.

Grass-roots programmes aimed at community development, group mobilisation and capacity building, form a major part of NFE. There are some signs of replicability, and recognition in the form of certificates may be given.

One approach to NFE today then is to see it as a series of educational activities which are not universalised but localised, covering a wide range of subjects with a substantial degree of participatory control by the participants. It is aimed at all kinds of learning for adults and out-of-school youth, not school-aged children. It is almost always in this context small scale.

Integration and scaling up

TOSTAN (Senegal): In some countries, steps are being taken build successful examples of localised activities into a more generalised programme. An example of this kind of NFE can be taken from a project in Senegal (Guttman 1985a). The initial participants were adults, but later the project has been extended to out-of-school youth. An informal group, inspired by the ideas of African and American scholars and an American expatriate worker, developed a comprehensive 18-month basic education programme called TOSTAN which goes beyond literacy. The language used is local, not French as in formal primary schools. A village education committee is usually established to support the programme. At first, lessons were held in a backyard but lately communities are encouraged to build special classrooms.

The project has passed through three main stages. First, working intensively in one village over a period of more than two years, "a team of non-formal educational specialists" created a programme for the women in that village at their request. The objectives were to help some adult learners to define and solve their own problems, improve their families' health, and more generally to fight the 'age-old' idea that misfortunes are due to 'fate'. The programme used a problem-solving approach, taking incidents which occurred to the participants as the basis of learning. Much of this was done outside of the group meetings. This initial stage was very intensive in terms of facilitator time and highly group-specific.

During this stage, a five months literacy learning programme was developed using a whole language approach and "linking basic education with literacy". Materials were designed and field tested by the educational experts who engaged in dialogue with the women involved. The participants were also exposed to real texts from the community "from the first day" and were encouraged to create texts.

In the second stage, the participants moved into a more comprehensive basic education programme including local environmental issues such as forestry. For this purpose, a modular structure was adopted. Six modules were developed with the villagers in national languages, each of 24 sessions spread over two months. The modules consisted of problem-solving methods, hygiene, oral rehydration, financial and material management, management of human resources, and income generation. The participants chose the days and times of meeting, established by the planners as three times a week for two hours a meeting, except in rainy seasons. The courses were

free. The community was involved, not only in helping to provide some of the resources needed such as the meeting place, but also in some activities such as problem-
solving. The learning programme was tied in with development projects chosen by the
community – setting up a co-operative, planting trees, raising funds etc.. In the village
where TOSTAN started, the villagers elected a health committee which obtained funds
to build a health hut; they wrote a play and developed a display.

In the third stage, the course was developed further to be used by other agencies
in the region – first in 19 other villages, then in 55 more villages. Training programmes were needed to induct the staff of the participating NGOs into the TOSTAN
approach and courses. The project became known nationally and later internationally:
for example, "In the Gambia, the TOSTAN mathematics sessions were adapted by the
Curriculum Development Department for primary school use" (Guttman 1985a: 30).

After the adult programme, a joint government-NGO committee in Senegal
decided to adopt the TOSTAN approach for out-of-school children in the same
villages as those of the adult learners. The curriculum for this target group is wider,
more structured, centrally determined and sequenced. It includes nutrition, children's
rights, history, geography, education for peace and civic education, vocational skills,
leadership skills and group dynamics. Health matters such as AIDS, first aid, and
malaria are included. It has again adopted a modular approach. A training centre for
the TOSTAN non-formal education approach in West Africa has been created.

Where local government became involved, it was reported that the "authorities
often want to control the organisation's actions rather than support them". To try to
protect the programme, detailed guides have been written to help to lead the trainers
and facilitators through the course. Those who developed these modules sought to
"strike the right balance" (as they saw it) between structure and flexibility, so that the
course could be used in a variety of contexts – the activities (they say) can be tailored
to local conditions. But inevitably, in the process, the programme has become less
contextualised. Topics are now determined not by the participants but by the providing
agency: thus "TOSTAN choose topics for the texts that are related to children's rights".
Classes are universally set at 30^3 learners (men and women separately). Assessment
has been introduced through short ungraded tests at the end of each module, using the
categories 'achieved; in progress; not achieved'. Each participant has a monthly
progress form. The impact of the programme is evaluated in terms of the numbers of
those in the community who vaccinate their children and use oral rehydration methods,
who show signs of improvements in health, hygiene, the management of individual and
group finances, and administration of environmental and local development projects,
and during the programme, 'dropouts' are counted.

---

[3] It is most striking that this figure of 30 adult learners to one facilitator has become so
widespread in NFE throughout Asia and Africa although there are some programmes which
operate on a lower figure. Is this perhaps the influence of Western schools where classes of 30
pupils were once the norm?

There are other programmes which seek to bring together several small-scale learning activities across a wide range of topics. In **Mongolia** for example an open learning programme for nomadic women described as "the first NFE in the country" (ignoring other kinds of NFE activities which already exist) has been developed, covering livestock rearing and processing of products, family care, literacy, survival skills, income generation, and basic business skills (Robinson 1995, 1999, 2001).

The comprehensive approach: the NFE sector

NFE then as individual, innovative, creative educational opportunities on a small scale, some of which might be scaled up, is one approach to NFE. But Coombs and Ahmed were thinking on a much grander scale than this. They saw NFE as *all* educational activities outside the formal system, including large-scale national programmes such as agricultural extension (which does not always have contextualised, participatory elements in it) as well as small-scale and localised. This is the view which many have come to support, seeing NFE as a single sector, a broad church with "a wide variety of topic areas from agricultural development to nutrition and health, infant stimulation to youth employment training, from women's education to co-operative movements" (Morolong 2000: 37). This approach can be seen in what must almost certainly be the largest NFE programme in the world at the moment, that of ADEA in Africa. It covers a large number of countries ranging from Ethiopia to South Africa (see Atchoarena & Hiti 2001: 208-213).

ADEA: The Association for the Development of Education in Africa was founded in 1988 out of earlier organisations which sought to co-ordinate educational aid in Africa. It is a committee of governments, institutions and development agencies (King & Buchert 1999: 217-219). ADEA set up a Working Group on NFE in 1996 with its own newsletter, publicity leaflet and activities.[4] Its aim is to "strengthen the NFE sector" in each country, for it argues that NFE does not receive the attention and resources it deserves and may even be under threat: "The boundaries between formal and nonformal education will become blurred and will eventually fall, but if they fall too fast, NFE will suffer" (Wright pers comm.).

Because it is inter-state, the voice being heard is mainly that of governments and international (donor) agencies, although other voices have been included in some of the seminars it has held. And because it seeks comparative approaches, ADEA is debating the nature of NFE. Various mixed discourses appear in its papers, especially those of lifelong learning and diversity, and as befits a body bringing together many officials, there is much committee-speak.

---

[4] What follows relies on extensive conversations with ADEA personnel including Dr Cream Wright formerly of the Commonwealth Secretariat who was co-ordinating secretary of the Working Group, and on printed and unprinted reports, newsletters and other papers of the Working Group.

The ADEA Working Group starts from the position that the over-arching concept is that of lifelong education, and that both formal and non-formal education fall under that rubric. It also argues that "the main responsibility for education must be anchored at the national level, with the Ministers of Education as front players" since education is aimed at achieving prosperity and peace, (ADEA President, in *ADEA Newsletter* 12.2: 7). The role of the Working Group "is to bring to the attention of Ministries of Education the work of other bodies such as the Ministries of Labour, Health and Agriculture" (Wright pers comm.). The Working Group also seeks to widen the vision of its members through comparisons between countries, for example, by exchange visits. This comparative imperative informs the whole discussion.

Nevertheless, the Working Group allows each participating country to define NFE for itself. Each country is encouraged to establish an in-country NFE working group "in order to determine who is doing what" (Wright pers comm.). This, they argue, is in line with what they see as the new (post-welfare) paradigm of development by which each local community is responsible for its own development. Indeed, part of the role of NFE is to strengthen "the growing network of decentralised training systems that provide people with the skills they need to drive local development" (NFE-WG 1: 1). The language of diversity is used to achieve neo-liberal goals.

A number of workshops have been held, reflecting the varied views of NFE of the participants (ADEA 1997, 1999, 2000). At times, NFE is seen as one among "many non-school and adult varieties of education" or as "the non-school and informal dimensions of educational systems in Africa". There is mention of 'non-formal and adult education' as if these were two equal but different parts of the whole, of "non-formal and other forms of non-conventional education", as if there were not just two sectors, formal and non-formal, but many different forms of education; but the precise nature of NFE and its relationship with these other forms remain obscure. There are "alternatives to NFE" and "alternative approaches to NFE" such as PRA and community-based activities (ADEA 1999a, 1999b). Some suggest that NFE represents different, flexible and innovative ways of presenting formal education – "alternative educational provision" (NFE-WG 1997) or "non-conventional educational provision" (NFE-WG 1999: 2). In some places, NFE is seen to be all that part of the system which is 'not formal'; but in other places, formal and non-formal education lie alongside other forms of education, as for instance, "formal education, non-formal provisions, adult education and distance learning" as joint contributors to the whole system. What distinguishes NFE from distance learning or adult education is never explained.

But on the whole, dualism reigns. Most members of the Working Group and the experts they have assembled seem to see only two sectors, formal education and everything which is not formal within one over-arching system. "Increasing resources for NFE does not affect the formal system. There is more money in the whole sector ... This means that there is little constructive engagement between the two sectors" (Wright pers comm.).

There is much stress in the Working Group papers on "the importance of NFE in achieving UBE" (Universal Basic Education: *ADEA Newsletter* 1: 1). A wide defini-tion of Basic Education is clearly taken as including both literacy and life skills. NFE in East and Southern Africa is seen as basic education especially for "minorities" through "state-NGO collaboration" which is not characteristic of formal education. "Gender equity in access to basic education and literacy" is one the key themes (Maruatona 1999). But beyond basic education, the wide range of provision within NFE is recognised, both in content and delivery systems. Faced with new demands, "a wide diversity of educational programs and modalities of provision are required which cannot be supplied by the formal system", so "alternative forms of provision under the broad rubric of nonformal education" are called for. Thus NFE covers natural resource management, crop marketing, health, credit, primary schooling [sic], income gene-ration especially for women, non-formal and community schools in Senegal, Zambia and Burkina Faso, nomadic education in Kenya and Nigeria, vocational skill training, workforce education in Namibia, alternative approaches to basic education in Kenya, training of church leaders, indigenous education, education in new technologies, continuing education, civic training, family health education, and even the training of NFE practitioners and professionals inside the formal system such as universities and colleges. It is hard to see how some of these can be described as being 'outside the formal system'.

NFE then is thought by the ADEA NFE Working Group to comprise many different forms of educational activities provided or supported by a wide range of agencies and directed towards the learning needs of many different social and econo-mic categories. There seems to be little to link these activities together. Nevertheless, NFE is seen to possess a unity defined by the unique "links which NFE has to society and to the workplace". "Nonformal education is better adapted to disadvantaged groups and offers the advantage of being grounded in the grassroots and the work-place" (ADEA Publ.). "Flexibility and responsiveness are key characteristics of non-formal education" as against formal education (ADEA WG 1999). The ideological discourse of NFE can be heard here, and there is little attempt to survey the field to assess whether in practice NFE is like this.

Despite the aim of the Working Group to achieve comparative analysis between different countries and contexts, the fact that each country can include programmes which others might deem not to be non-formal makes it difficult to achieve com-parison between the various countries of the Working Group. The justification for this *laissez faire* approach to defining NFE is that the Group believes that the main function of NFE is to fill the (state-identified) gaps which formal education cannot fill – and those gaps will vary from country to country. NFE will enable each state to meet their own new demands, the needs of their own dis-advantaged groups, and the educational and training needs of their own workforce which the different formal systems cannot necessarily meet. There are virtually no calls here for reform of formal education, although it is suggested that NFE "can contribute to the revitalization of education [in general] in Africa" on the grounds that NFE has "more effective links between education and the reality of everyday life". The NFE Working Group will seek "to identify and publicize the benefits of nonformal approaches and thus invigorate the education system as a whole" (WG Publ.).

The background to the Group is the increasing wish of governments to co-ordinate both formal and non-formal education, to mobilise NFE to meet state objectives, especially in relation to Basic Education for All, HIV/AIDS, and conflict situations. "NFE ... provides complementary approaches to ensure that countries address education and training in a more holistic manner as they progress towards the goal of basic education for all". "If learning opportunities are to achieve equity and relevance *for society and the economy*, they must be managed, funded, and judged, differently" (ADEA 1999a: 4, original italics); and it is the state which will manage, fund and judge NFE. It is therefore not surprising to read that "In almost all cases, the impetus to form a national working group [for NFE] came from the Ministry of Education", ... although "all [in-country working] groups are making efforts to include representation from various bodies involved in NFE" (ADEA WG 4: 1).

The aim is explicit: "to help African *governments* to achieve EFA through policies, regulations and measures aimed at enhancing NFE within a holistic education system" (ADEA Publ, my italics). The "interface" between the state system of formal and nonformal education is thus a key theme in the discussions of the Group which provides a forum for governments "to improve NFE and strengthen its links with formal education" (ibid). An overall survey of education in Africa (*ADEA Newsletter* 12.2 June 2000: 6-7) reveals that NFE is seen by ADEA to be a "small" [sic – presumably meaning less significant rather than in size of programmes] but integrated part of the whole and to be concerned with access. However, although sometimes seen as part of the system, NFE normally lies out of the mainstream, catering for target populations who also lie out of the mainstream (ADEA WG 4: 1). "Alternative schemes struggle in the margins of our societies – and while they often prove that they can promote learning more effectively than schools, they also remain unrecognised and thus unsupported" (WG 1999a: 2, 17). Mainstreaming NFE is a key objective (*ADEA Newsletter* 13(4): 15; Wright 2001).

Throughout the papers, there is implied recognition that formal schooling in Africa is changing. In some places, it is seen to be becoming more flexible, using local languages, enhancing multi-grade schools, promoting community involvement, reaching out to new target groups. But the discourse of NFE at times prevents these achievements of schooling from being properly recognised, for NFE is still viewed as the response to the *failings* of formal education. Thus the Working Group talks of aiming to non-formalise the formal system by promoting a flexible timetable, making sure the students have more than one opportunity to learn (that they should not miss out altogether if they are unable to fulfil learning goals once), adapting the curriculum to local interests, using local resources and using local teachers (Wright pers comm.).

But on the whole, the role of formal education has shrunk, so that it can be described as "morning learning", "single-mode and supply-led" (ADEA 1999a: 5), failing in equity, relevance and quality. Many of the innovations of formal schooling are described as NFE. The community schools in Zambia,[5] for example, with a cut-down version of the national curriculum in which seven years of full-time primary school are covered in four years part-time, and with less professional teachers and multi-grade classes, all governed by a Ministry-run 'Community School Secretariat', are called NFE. Although the Group can debate "whether these schools should be continue to be seen as a kind of 'stop-gap' measure, or whether they are in fact becoming a preferred alternative to the conventional schools", they still see them as 'outside the system'. We "need to avoid a premature absorption of these schools in the formal system when the most important lessons they can offer have not yet been deciphered"; and "we should first understand what these [non-formal] teachers are doing right that accounts for their present success before immersing them in standard training courses" (ADEA WG 5: 3).

There is however more here about institutionalising (formalising) NFE than about non-formalising formal schools. This can be seen in the expressed fear that diversity can lead to marginalisation, and the insistence that, within a diversified curriculum, "there is a need for a single system of accreditation" which must apply to both formal and non-formal education. Such accreditation need not necessarily be standardised: "it should build on the strengths of formal and non-formal education, not collapse them into *single-mode standardisation*". In particular, it should be based on equivalencies. There are "multiple and diverse learning needs, multiple arrangements and technologies for creating learning experiences; and there is a need for a system-wide framework of accreditation of learning outcomes" (ADEA 1999a: 2) with a diversity of accreditation bodies and "a whole spectrum of accreditation, from the most formal to the most *informal*" (ibid: 5, original italics). The thinking of the Working Group in this respect, according to the convenor, has changed. "Initially the Working Group thought NFE had nothing to do with the formal system; it was experiential learning, vocational training, mainly for adults. Now the Working Group starts with talking about many diverse ways of learning. Learning can be met through either formal or non-formal means. There is nothing sacrosanct about the means of education" (Wright pers comm.). A more recent statement talks about NFE as being those "means of learning which are alternatives to the formal system and which integrate NFE into the education systems" with similar accreditation and statistics (*ADEA Newsletter* 14.1 2002: 7).

In much of the discussion, then, NFE is seen, not as different education but as a different delivery system for the same education. The title of the Botswana Seminar in 1999 was 'Diversifying Education Delivery Systems'. The use of distance education, open learning, radio and television for both formal education curricula and for

---

[5] See Durston 1996. The background paper by E Mumba (ADEA 1999b) shows the discourse confusion. The title of the paper refers to 'Diversification of Adult Education provision in Zambia'; the text talks about Community Schools which cater for young children; and much of the paper concerns the programmes of the Department of Continuing Education in the Ministry of Education.

agriculture and health forms a substantial element in the discussions of the NFE Working Group.

The concepts however are confused, mixing the diversity paradigm and the dualism of NFE. Indeed, the convenor suggests that the Working Group is trying to change the thinking of its members and others to 'learning opportunities for different groups' rather than a systems approach. When the Botswana Report (ADEA 1999b) starts using the discourses of lifelong education, the arguments flow and become clearer. An early (unpublished) version of the Working Group publicity leaflet reveals this: "In every corner of the continent, individuals and groups are pursuing learning in varied non-formal ways in order to develop the skills and knowledge that new responsibilities require of them, improve on and apply lessons learned in school, or replace the formal training they may never have received". The connotations of the term 'non-formal ways' here are very different from those of 'non-formal education'; there is here no polarity of school and NFE. Justin Ellis in his paper at the Botswana Seminar uses the discourse of lifelong education only, not NFE (Ellis 1999).

Which raises the issue as to why the discourse of NFE is being used at all in this context. Both Hoppers and Youngman, in their background papers to the workshop, question this, asking whether the categories used in the 1970s are still meaningful today. It seems that the decision to employ the discourse of NFE was deliberate: the title of the Botswana Seminar included the words: "Reviving Discourse on the Formal/Non-formal Interface".

But the reason for reviving not just the discourse but with it the world picture of education divided into two (opposing) sectors which need to 'interface' is not clear. Indeed, the position paper prepared before the Seminar itself queries the relevance of the formal/non-formal debate:

> The failure of EFA – in the interpretation of (conventional) primary schooling for all – of providing all children and young people with a meaningful and effective basic education experience, forces us once again to have a hard look at what is going on under the name of 'education'. But this time the focus should not be on 'what is the alternative?' or 'which delivery system is more correct than the other?' Rather, in this time of the worldwide debate on 'lifelong learning', attention needs to focus on the increasing redundancy of the very idea of compartmentalization. In a context of greater recognition of multiple and diverse learning needs, multiple arrangements and technologies for 'creating learning experiences' and of need for a system-wide frame-work for accreditation of learning outcomes, the boundaries between formal and non-formal education, contact and distance education, in-school and out-of-school education are rapidly becoming obsolete. (ADEA 2000b: v-vi)

Why then did the Working Group turn away from the diversity discourse of the position paper and return to a NFE discourse with its implied dualism? Why did it reject the warnings of one of its own background papers? Whose interests did this serve? The key perhaps lies in the desire of governments to control and direct NFE to its own goals – as well perhaps as the desire to support Ministries of Education against other Ministries in stressing their central role in all educational activities in the country. The increasing diversity of educational provision is recognised, and there is no term within the lifelong learning discourse which enables one to refer to that 'integrated diversity' – that is, all those learning programmes which lie outside of the schools but which actually have no coherence about them other than the fact they are outside the schools; activities many of which are not normally amenable to state control except in those cases where the state pays for them. ADEA is self-proclaimedly aiming at an integrated system so as to manage this diversity; theirs is a state-controlled approach. The revival of the discourse of NFE must be seen within this context of the whole of education, society and above all the state. The division of the world of education into two sectors, formal schools and colleges which are mostly state provided and regulated, and non-formal educational programmes which ought to be state regulated, is intended to serve the purpose of political managers.[6]

Co-ordinating Programmes

Ethiopia: Ethiopia is an example of the approach which ADEA wishes African countries to adopt, perhaps because it has a long history of donor assistance to NFE. In the 1970s, USAID initiated a process of inventorying different forms of NFE in order to co-ordinate them (Niehoff & Wilder 1974; Krueger & Moulton 1981: ii, 13-15; see Ofcansky & Berry 1993; Assefa 1997). Since 1997, a drive towards the same goal emerged as a partnership between German donors and a new government. It took a wide ranging view of NFE, both government sponsored and NGO-provided, and sought to systematise it.[7]

The political background is important, with successive governments and the military engagements in which that country has been engaged for several years dictating educational policy changes. Government interest in NFE arose during the preparation of the Education Sector Development Programme (ESDP) which covered the years 1997-2001. ESDP defined NFE as basic education, literacy and numeracy, environmental education and citizenship, and health/population education. The role of NGOs was recognised: "It appears that in the next years, NGOs will be solicited to act as financiers and implementers of NFE programs in order to contribute to the achievement of ESDP". The German aid agency. IIZ/DVV agreed "to support Adult and NFE in Ethiopia in co-operation with the Ministry of Education". The Ministry established a panel with the aim of bringing together other agencies including the Ministries of Health and Agriculture.

---

[6] It will be interesting to see what happens to the ADEA NFE Working Group now that the convenor has moved to other work, whether different discourses will come to predominate.

[7] This section is based on documentation and on interviews and field visits held during a visit to Ethiopia in 2000.

The project is unusual in that it defines some of the terms it uses, reflecting the advocacy discussions with government agencies and NGOs. It cites the Economic Commission for Africa's definition of NFE (echoing Coombs, see p.171) as "any organized systematic educational and training activity carried on outside the framework of the formal system to provide selected types of learning and training to the adult sector of the population. It includes among other things agriculture extension and farmer training programs, literacy programs, occupational skill training, health, nutrition, family planning, co-operatives education etc.". But the project uses the term Nonformal Adult Education in a slightly different sense. "NFAE connotes two aspects. Adult Education in the context of work with disadvantaged adults aims at building their development capacities through organized learning and training opportunities. Nonformal Education means the mode of delivery. Thus the use of [the term] NFAE underlines the developmental dimension of adult education by nonformal approaches". In other words, NFAE here means picking up all those educational and training activities for adults which contribute to development and which are delivered by nonformal means. The important characteristics of the 'non-formal' element in NFAE "are its orientation to needs, relevance and flexibility, its success much depending on the degree of participation of the learners at all management stages" (ETH NFAE Project papers); presumably formal education lacks such an orientation to needs, relevance, flexibility and participation by the learners. NFAE does not replicate the formal education system: it "is flexible and adaptable for immediate use".

The first concern of the project was with the fragmented nature of NFAE; much that is really NFE is "hidden", i.e. unrecognised. The project seeks integration – both within the field of NFAE and between NFAE and other development sectors "because relevant learning programs for adults concern more than one sector". A new umbrella organisation to bring together professionals in the field was registered in 1997, the Adult and Non-Formal Education Association in Ethiopia (ANFEAE). In recognition of the lack of data, surveys were conducted, and a directory of "development-related adult and NFE programs and projects" was published, using the categories of general adult and NFE (literacy, vocational training, and education for out-of-school youth and street children), health, agriculture and rural industries, environment (including population education), income generation, women-specific programmes, and civic education. Miscellaneous programmes which do not fit these categories include community leadership and capacity building. It lists the providers, government and NGO. It suggests that the agricultural sector is growing; population education is a new area of NFE (ETH-BEN 2000).

Most of these programmes are aimed at immediate learning objectives; but there are a few, including the Alternative Education for Disadvantaged Urban Children, which aim to "move the children from these non-formal education programs into the formal education system" (ETH Focus 8: 24-25; FSCE 2000). Some include the training of professionals and para-professionals who provide and teach in NFE programmes.[8] There is also a programme of training of 'intermediaries' such as medical workers, development and extension agents, community leaders, school teachers and students. Some of the programmes are within the formal sector of education, so it is not easy to see the justification for calling these programmes NFE.

A small but still significant part of these NFE programmes is directed towards the young, sometimes the very young, but the large majority are aimed at older sectors and particular groups seen as disadvantaged in some way or other (illiterates, the under-served, the hungry, rural dwellers, women, older persons, displaced persons, the disabled). There are also some programmes for under- or unemployed school leavers.

A report on *Managing Nonformal Adult Education by NGOs in Ethiopia* noted that "the Ministry of Education administers a variety of parallel non-formal training opportunities" through government-provided Community Skills Training Centres set up under the earlier project. Some of these ran training courses for members of farming associations in tailoring, sewing, weaving and knitting as well as farming. The NFE Panel or Unit of the Education Bureau in each region provided 4-6 month basic education courses on a large scale – for example, 30,600 adults in Southern Region in 1995-6. The facilitators were local, grade 12 completers if possible (but most were grade 10 or even grade 8), chosen by written examination and interview and given 30 days training for their work unless they were primary school teachers. They received a small payment for their work. The timetable was determined locally by the participants or their families. NGOs provided similar programmes, for example, 25,500 adults in Southern Region in 1996. Some schools ran second chance schooling for those who discontinued their primary education (for instance, night schools), and some distance education at secondary level was provided by the NFE Panels: "the full twelve year cycle is available through evening study".

Non-formal Basic Education for adults in Ethiopia, whether provided by the state or by NGOs, is sometimes regarded as separate from the rest of NFE for adults. NFBE programmes include literacy together with the "acquisition of knowledge, skills and attitudes leading to a better quality of life". The time to be taken to complete each 'package' of NFBE depends on the rate of learning, interests and availability of the participants; and the programme is to be evaluated by "whether or not it has produced changes ... in the lives of the participants, i.e. by whether trees are planted, vegetables grown and used, toilets built, health improved, community development participation increased" rather than by educational tests.

NFE in Ethiopia is thus regarded as a very wide range of activities, mostly for adults; it is provided by a wide range of agencies. It is rarely related to formal education, and is not directly designed to overcome the failings of the formal system.

The development paradigm behind this joint Ministry-INGO project is that of deficit rather than disadvantage, despite the language used. The NFE project in

---

[8] The IIZ-DVV NFE Project has changed its focus during the last year or so. The project now concentrates on training of trainers, increasing the capacity of the Community Skills Training Centers, and a small number of pilot projects to point the way to more effective NFE.

Ethiopia seeks to provide inputs to bring the poor and under-educated up to the level of the rest of society rather than seeking ways to change the society. The voice is that of planners – to recruit the whole of NFE to the service of government and to promote its efficiency in terms of national development goals after years of war and famine. The nature of the initiative seems to have come from external development agencies and donors, steeped in the Western discourse of NFE from the 1970s and 1980s.

Growing institutionalisation: Africa

A brief survey of some of the other African countries within the ADEA programme will reveal more mixed views of NFE (see Kassam 1982; Maclure 1994; Thompson 1995; Wood 1974).

In **Botswana**, the Department of NFE within the Ministry of Education was created in the 1980s from the former Botswana Extension College (Botswana 1997), charged with "the eradication of illiteracy". Defining NFE as "educational and training programmes generated outside the formal institutional education system for the whole population or specific groups" (Botswana 1992: 25), it ran three main programmes for adults – literacy training (many in the workplace), income generating skills training, and 'distance education', partly in the form of study centres which enrolled students for Junior Certificates and GCE examinations through correspondence and some face-to-face teaching, and partly in the form of radio and some television programmes. DNFE is thus responsible for programmes in home economics and correspondence courses. "Mobility between formal and non-formal education [is promoted] by establishing equivalence of certificate procedures between the two". An Adult Basic Education Certificate, equivalent to ten years of formal primary school, has been proposed (Maruatona 1999: 6). The clientele for these programmes are adults and adolescents; but since 1998, DNFE has been charged to develop new programmes for out-of-school children. The bi-focal approach, formal and non-formal, is clearly a feature of this programme (Botswana 1992, 1994), but it omits other forms of NFE such as health and agriculture (Carr-Hill et al. 2001: 341).

Different governments have followed slightly different routes. **Ghana** which has had a long history of NFE work (Amaratunga 1977; Evans 1981b, 1983; Kinsey & Bing 1987; Robertson 1984; Sine 1979) has established a large Department of NFE in the Ministry of Education (ACCESS 2000; www.ghana.edu.gh). A new education policy in **Uganda**[9] lays considerable emphasis on Basic Adult NFE, distinguishing "adult literacy and non-formal basic education" and continuing education (see Hoppers 1985; Mucugunzi 1995). One strand is COPE – Complementary Opportunities for Primary Education which includes not only literacy but also a family health curriculum. Increasingly, NFE is seen in Uganda as community involvement in the provision and management of what may be seen as alternative primary schools. An

---

[9] This is based on presentations made at a workshop in Addis Ababa November 2000 (ACCESS 2000) and a visit to Uganda in 2000.

interesting variation is the offering of two forms of certification, a formal school entry certificate and a capacity building certificate (mainly vocational training); the selection of which students may be offered for each certificate is usually undertaken by the teachers. NFE does not seem to be clearly distinguished from, and certainly not opposed to, formal education; rather, various strands of education, one of which is non-formal, make up the whole sector. **Sierra Leone**, recovering from years of civil war, views NFE in terms of adults and young adults. The NFE Division in the Ministry of Youth, Education and Sports, organises adult literacy and basic education (called Adult Non-formal Primary Education) and vocational education and training (VET), as well as a three year programme for children "who live in areas where they do not have access to formal schooling" leading to entry to formal schools or to VET. There is also NFE for agriculture through the Ministry of Agriculture extension teams, and camps for internally displaced persons and resettlement communities (Musa 2001).

Nigeria[10] sees NFE in very wide terms. The country prides itself on the "great strides made in Western-type education", so that formal education is defined as pre-primary, primary and secondary schools (grammar, commercial and comprehensive), teacher education and tertiary (polytechnic and university) institutions. There is however a recognition of the need for reform of formal education to respond to national needs, especially in terms of textbooks, the curriculum, languages and in outreach, particularly to nomadic groups (Ezeomah 1985; Pennells & Ezeomah 2000). The disparity of access is recognised as a political problem. The low quality of formal education, especially in terms of teachers, buildings, equipment and funding, has resulted in a loss of faith in the system, so that elites use private education, and dropout rates in state schools are high. The earlier concentration of government on UPE has changed to one on UBE, but this too appears to imply mainly programmes for children, early childhood development, functional literacy and life skills, nomadic education, education for out-of-school youth, non-formal skills training (i.e. work-related training) and apprenticeship training, as well as formal schooling. The meaning of the term 'NFE' and the distinction between NFE and adult education are not at all clear. But some polarity can be seen, for there is a demand for the co-ordination of formal and non-formal education, which seems to include virtually all forms of education for adults, whether provided by public or private agencies, such as extension classes, evening classes, women's centres, vocational training centres, co-operative education, community development programmes and courses offered by private institutions. The language used to describe these programmes is sometimes confused (Omolewa 1998; Anyanwu 1984; Filson 1991).

Swaziland too distinguishes between NFE and adult education[11] (Swaziland nd). The clientele in the government NFE programme are adults and children from the age

---

[10] Based on documents and a visit in 1998.

[11] See also Rwanda where a government official can say more informally, "I'm in charge of adult education, but from time to time we get involved in NFE", meaning the non-formal education of children (pers comm.).

of seven upwards. The distinction between formal and non-formal is not clear, for the programme includes correspondence courses aimed at junior secondary and 'O' level students, using radio together with postal tutorials. Training in practical skills for self-employment is provided through rural education centres, most of which have been initiated by NGOs but are supported financially by government. The curriculum for these centres is described as a combination of problems common to all areas of rural Swaziland such as literacy, farming and household crafts, and skills for developing local enterprises appropriate to the locality served by the centre. The aim is "to make the individual learner better equipped to establish for himself [sic] and for the community and the nation a more productive way of life".

In **Kenya** NFE is alternative schooling – "non-formal schools managed by local committees" (Wright & Govinda 1994: 66; see Nyamu 1999; Gachanja 2000). The national policy, as elaborated by the Directorate of NFE in the Division of Basic Education in the Ministry of Education and Human Resource Development, and the Policy Guidelines published in 1998 both take a very broad definition of NFE; it includes non-certificated and certificated courses for youth and adults, literacy classes (especially for women) through NFE Centres as well as courses to alleviate the unemployment of graduates and secondary school leavers. There is talk about "alternative basic education"; but the formal – non-formal polarity is still clearly apparent. "NFE is a justifiable alternative delivery system of education to the formal system of education.... Learners shall be free to link with either of the two systems of education (formal and non-formal) without intimidation", although in practice the majority of "these non-formal schools are not officially recognised and therefore are not even registered. The students do not have access to the means of being granted a certificate or further schooling opportunities" (Wright & Govinda: 66). NFE will complement, not replace, the formal system, despite the fact that it is seen as more cost-effective than formal schools. The joint UNICEF-Government of Kenya Project on NFE planned since 1994 is aimed at young people (especially girls) aged between 6 and 17 years with an elaborate curriculum consisting of nine academic subjects, 7 practical subjects and two technical subjects. It includes HIV/AIDS, environmental issues (mainly urban slums) and gender. A national equivalency programme up to the level of the Kenya Certificate of Primary Education and beyond, using the standard secondary curriculum, is included in the project. The tone of some of the Kenya papers is ideological rather than empirical. There is much criticism of formal education and an interest in 'alternative routes to learning' as well as increasing flexibility in formal schooling. It is clear that the government intends to take responsibility for NFE throughout the country (Kenya 1999: 10; see Kenya 1998). It is encouraging community schools, and some non-formal primary schools have been established with flexible timetables and no uniforms. Boarding schools are regarded as non-formal since they meet the needs of nomadic groups. And beyond that, *jua kalas* (village polytechnics) are providing apprenticeship and skills training as well as literacy.

In **Lesotho**, distance education and the control of NFE are the two key features (Moleko & Betz 1995; Morolong 2000). The Lesotho Distance Teaching College set up within the Ministry of Education in 1979 "to bring education outside the formal school system to residents of Lesotho" is charged with responsibility for "basic and non-formal education programmes". It is noted that NGOs are providing the same kind of programmes – "these suggest a duplication of effort". The development of a clear policy on NFE, aimed at promoting basic life skills and improving the workforce, and the compilation of a directory of NFE programmes and agencies (as in Ethiopia) are part of the government plan for NFE.

The reaction of **Namibia** to the ADEA Working Party on NFE is revealing. Different interests in the country have different approaches to NFE (Macharia et al. 1990). On the one hand, the paper by the Ministry to the ADEA workshop (Ellis 1999) hardly mentions NFE, preferring the discourse of Lifelong Learning. It speaks of opportunities for learning "through open learning institutions, ... through the media, access to libraries and the Internet, national service schemes, agricultural and health extension programmes, skills training centres, political activism, and engagement in arts and cultural activities...". It does refer to "formally designated settings for learning" and to "learning opportunities outside of formal school and university programmes", but it points out that "a preoccupation with formal education has ... sometimes blinded us to the whole context of learning ... Part of the change of concept is to think about learning, and not just about education in the sense of what happens in schools, colleges, and similar bodies" (Ellis 1999: 3). This view is not one of polarity but of diversity which needs to be linked together through a system of equivalency of qualification. The new educational policy talks of adult education rather than NFE, and discussions of NFE tend to concentrate on the Adult Upper Primary Education Programme.

However, under the pressure of ADEA, the government has set up a national Working Group on NFE, probably because this is the terminology which is being used by donors. A "study on the status and nature of NFE as viewed by officials in the formal education sector" [the wording appears to be significant] has been started to explore the possibility of "interaction and synergy between formal and nonformal education". NFE in this context includes in-service training of formal school teachers, school management training, as well as the use of radio and television for schooling, some of which elsewhere would be seen as being within the formal system of education. Community-based skills development centres for out-of-school youth and parents are being created, aimed at the informal economic sector and subsistence farming.

The term NFE is used in Namibia outside of government circles (Namibia 1991, 1997; Frindt 1997). As early as 1976, the Council of Churches of Namibia set up an Adult and NFE Unit to promote correspondence courses at an advanced level for those deprived of the opportunity of further schooling by the apartheid regime. More recently, an impact study of non-formal basic education in Namibia was conducted by the University of Namibia (UNAM), and a report on Developing Professional Adult and NFE Programmes in Namibia was issued leading to the establishment of a Department of Adult and Nonformal Education within the University, running Diploma and PhD courses in NFE. NFE is described as "that education which meets the learner needs quite outside the constraining boundaries of the formal system of education which normally excludes and de-skills" (the works of Illich and Dore are cited in support of these views about the constraints of formal schooling, but there are no proposals to reform formal education in response to these criticisms).

The ideological tone of this report is clearly apparent. NFE is seen to be divided into two components, government programmes (which include higher education programmes about NFE) and NGO programmes. The government programmes cover adult literacy, skills development, and distance education through the Namibia College of Open Learning (NAMCOL) leading to the Junior Secondary Certificate, GCSE and the Certificate in Education for Development, together with educational broadcasting. The university itself has an outreach programme through its Centre for External Studies, described as being outside the boundaries of the formal system (which is not defined). Ten major NGOs are listed, but the discourse of NFE is not obvious in their programmes, which include English language training for school and other teachers, and management, business and computer training.

NFE is however distinguished from the formal system, and there are calls for the strengthening of links between the two, such as the use by NFE of formal school buildings. Most government NFE programmes provide equivalent qualifications: the National Literacy Programme of Namibia (NLPN) ends with a certificate equivalent to Grade IV of schooling and leads into the upper primary curriculum. "It is possible that especially youth who go through the NLPN can 'return' to formal schooling on successful completion of their training" (Indabawa 1999: 13; the use of the words 'formal schooling' here instead of 'formal education' again draws on the ideological strand of the NFE discourse where 'schooling' is seen as the enemy of 'education'). While NAMCOL (which is itself seen as an NFE institution) will prepare students for formal tertiary education, the UNAM paper suggests that NGO programmes of NFE usually have fewer links with formal education, since most of their courses are uncertificated.

Confusion of discourses

The ADEA approach then appears to encourage confusion both between countries and inside countries within the region. The adaptation of this image to the discourse of Lifelong Education (which several countries in the region have started to use and which has no such polarity) is clearly not easy. But there is a general tendency to see education as divided between two (unequal) sectors in tension with each other and needing government help to develop closer links so as to serve the needs of the nation.

What is striking is the effect that donor pressure is having on the discourses of some agencies (see for example Closson et al. 1997). Two evaluations, PADLOS (a five country survey of community development activities) and ABEL (an eight country survey of 'Achieving Basic Education and Literacy'), both of which had been started prior to the ADEA Working Group on NFE but whose reports were later submitted to the Working Group, have clearly been reclothed (uneasily) in the discourse of NFE – forcing the material of these evaluations into the polarity mould. The PADLOS study analysed "how a variety of local communities and associations ... have met the challenges of social and economic decentralisation, assumed new development functions on their own, and mobilised the skills and knowledge necessary to do so". The areas covered included local resource management, crop marketing, health service delivery, financial intermediation and primary education. In doing this, "varieties of nonformal education have ... been the means by which members of the groups have acquired the necessary competencies". The ABEL project looked at "a number of diverse varieties of nonformal education" covering literacy, income generation skills, workplace learning, and the training of church leaders. It is ironic that one of these agencies is Florida State University, one of the prime movers of the earlier NFE debate but an institution which had abandoned that discourse when donors pulled out of NFE in favour of a popular education discourse which talks of "using literacy to empower community leaders (action research)". The concerns of these reports fit uneasily the dichotomy of formal and non-formal education. The pressure of donors on the discourses used by consultants who need to earn their money is large.

A construct of NFE as a wide collection of disparate and discrete programmes covering a very wide range of learning areas would seem to characterise views about NFE in other parts of the world. In one major study in the Caribbean, NFE seems to be equated with all the many forms of education for adults, not for younger persons (Gordon 1985; see also Shorey 1983; Ellis 1995; Jones & Ellis 1995). In Sri Lanka, NFE is again of a wide nature including programmes for Muslims and tea plantation workers, using NGOs (Amaratunga 1977; Mahroof 1993; Jilani 1998; Coletta & Todd 1982; Colletta et al. 1982; Kulatunga 1997).

2. NFE AS NATIONAL SYSTEMS FOR ADULTS

The purpose of ADEA would appear to be to encourage the institutionalisation of the many different NFE programmes, partly to make NFE sustainable (Krueger & Moulton 1981: 11) and partly so that governments can more easily identify and control it. Two countries have gone down the road of institutionalising NFE, Thailand and the Philippines.

Thailand: Thailand divides education into formal and non-formal education as part of a strategy of lifelong education. It has had a Department of NFE since 1979 (Krueger & Moulton 1981: 23-25; website www.nfe.go.th).

The establishment of this Department needs to be set into its historical and political context. During the 1930s, it is argued, adult literacy programmes had been run in Thailand as part of the gradual transition of the country to democracy. During the nationalist and autocratic regimes of the 1940s, a Division of Adult Education (DAE) had been established in the Ministry of Education in order to mobilise literacy activities for national control purposes. Its aim was "to eradicate illiteracy" from the population over the age of 10 years, through adult education as "a normal and integral part of the national education system".

From the 1950s, Westernisation proceeded apace in Thailand, including the UNESCO Functional Literacy programme. As the World Bank became more heavily involved during the 1970s, so the discourse of NFE began to be heard, and the adult literacy programme became linked to Human Resource Development, vocational training for the employed sector (UNESCO PROAP 1997: 10). The movement drew on the *khitpen* philosophy which it is claimed is opposed to formal education philosophy (Kindervatten 1989), but the activities were those of Western development workers – community development, family planning, vocational skill training, and learner-centred methodologies. It followed an educational reform cycle which closely paralleled that seen above (see p.64) – expansion of the system, vocational training, community education, then NFE. The Third National Plan (1972-76) echoed the work of Coombs and Ahmed in seeing NFE as primarily directed towards adults in rural areas. Behind this lay the US determination to build barriers to communism.

In 1976, the military government drew back the adult education programme towards a concentration on vocational skills, and it was in this context that the Department of NFE (DNFE) was established in the Ministry of Education. It had three main programmes – basic education (literacy, primary and secondary) for adults and out of school youth; vocational education and training; and 'informal education' (libraries, village reading centres, television and radio, science education centres). NFE was to be a national "adult basic education system which paralleled the graded primary education system for children". A "new vision for non-formal adult education" was being created to "promote lifelong learning, decentralization, labour force education and networks" (UNESCO PROAP 1997: 10). After the restoration of civilian government, the pressures of Structural Adjustment led to a cut in the budget of DNFE despite the period of economic growth.

The Department works through a National Council which draws together many agencies such as the Ministries of the Interior, Health, Agriculture, Industry, and Defence, as well as private agencies. "NFE is not an isolated system"; its aim is to reach out to the most disadvantaged groups, "to provide education for out-of-school and the under-privileged population with non-formal and informal approaches *and to strengthen the formal education system* with the emphasis on the area of Science and technology" (Thailand DNFE 1993: 1, my italics). The "programs tended to be standardised and insufficiently responsive to the varying purposes and social conditions of the learners". In 1984, NFE received 1.76% of government spending on education but was expected to raise substantial sums from other sources. Under pressure from the World Bank programme (1977-83), NFE was decentralised and more flexible programmes were introduced. A national system of Village Reading/ Learning Centres, and Provincial and Regional (*Tambon*) NFE Learning Centres were set up with "responsibility for conducting research into the educational needs of their regions, producing nonformal education curricula, texts and learning materials relevant to the ethnic and occupational structure of the region" (Armstrong 1984: 456; see Guttman 1995b). A satellite-based Distance Education programme was launched to give wider access to both formal and non-formal education provision for adult learners. "By 1999, some 15,460 televisions and decoders had been installed in local schools and NFE Learning Centres across the country, laying the infrastructure for what promised to be a truly national system of adult distance education".

The term 'NFE' in Thailand thus does not delimit those programmes 'outside the formal system' (unless one defines the formal system very narrowly); rather NFE is part of the national system. One sign of this is the keeping of careful data on NFE by the Ministry. Drawing on the ideas of the former Centre for Educational Innovation and Technology, now inside the Department of NFE, the government sees NFE as the sector for providing different ways of access to educational opportunities and for improving the efficiency of formal and non-formal delivery systems, particularly as there are moves towards increasing privatisation of public education. There is no ideological approach to NFE.

There is however some confusion as once again the discourse of lifelong education creeps in. The Development Plan for 1997-2001 speaks of "adult literacy, basic and non-formal education", not making it clear if these are all the same or different aspects of education. DNFE is organised into three 'frames' (Thailand 1998a: 12):[12] *General (formerly Basic) Education*, a formal equivalency programme from literacy to upper secondary; *Vocational Education and Skills Training*, both short course and longer term certificated vocational programmes; and *Information Services*, a news and information programme. It is intended that all three will be inter-related, participants moving between different programmes as they felt appropriate. The main participants are youth and adults, not children.[13] While possibilities of transfer between the formal and non-formal sectors exist, this is not the main purpose of the programme.

The language used to describe these three sectors is mixed. The first frame concentrates on NFE (described as basic education aimed at "minorities and the disadvantaged", literacy, and general NFE at primary, lower secondary and upper secondary levels with continuing education, quality of life and job performance elements, using a variety of approved NFE curricula) through classroom, distance education and self-learning activities. The contents include drugs, HIV/AIDS and the environment.

The second frame provides vocational education and training courses for small groups of adults at their request, together with more generalised short courses (100-300 hours) and longer term (three-year) certificated courses from lower secondary level leading to vocational qualifications equivalent to grades 9 and 12 of schools and recognised for employment. It is built on the earlier nationwide programme with its

---

[12] This follows the criteria set down by the Jomtien conference of 1990.

[13] Recent figures for participants are 0.05% under the age of 15, 66.3% between 15 and 25, 31.9% between 26 and 49, and 1.33% 50 and over: figures from Thailand DNFE 2000.

common curriculum and agreed certificates. The third frame sets out to support and promote informal learning systems by providing access to knowledge and information necessary for earning a living and improving the quality of life, and helping people to catch up with the news and to adapt to a technological society through public and village libraries, reading centres, community learning centres, science centres and radio and television programmes. Included in this aspect is a major responsibility to support, co-operate with and encourage the formal school system with innovations (for example, the development of teaching-learning activities in educational technologies). DNFE is responsible for providing "a quality and standardised education" through a variety of means.

The use of distance education is part of the remit of DNFE, but since there has been growing pessimism about distance education, the focus has changed towards 'self-learning', especially through access to the world-wide web. More recently there has been a cut in DNFE resources, aimed at community libraries, HIV/AIDS and drug education, with an increase in the provision for vocational training (especially in rural areas), entrepreneurship and job counselling. A curriculum for industry has been developed; scholarships for unemployed students and mass campaigns on 'how to survive' in the new economic climate have been launched.

There is here (as in ADEA) a tension between the language of lifelong education and that of NFE. One of the objectives of DNFE is to promote lifelong education. The provision of many different opportunities for learning forms part of the discourse of lifelong education. But at times the separation of education into two distinct sectors can be seen: "The certificates awarded by the [Continuing Education] program have the same rights and qualifications as those from the formal education system". Some suggest that NFE in Thailand (e.g. Alexander 1990; Wilson 2001) is felt to be a valued and relevant parallel system which complements all levels of the formal system; that there is transferability between the two sub-systems, with recognised qualifications in both, and flexibility, that participants can ask for and obtain tailor-made courses. NFE is primarily for out of school youth; indeed, at times a distinction is drawn between 'non-formal' provision for youth and 'informal education' provision for adults. The contradictory desires to co-ordinate and co-opt NFE to the purposes of the state, to keep control while at the same time decentralising its management, and to adapt it to the concepts of Lifelong Education are creating tensions.

Similar approaches can be seen elsewhere in Asia. In **Indonesia,** where there is a large NFE programme, the World Bank has been supporting NFE projects since 1977 (Krueger & Moulton 1981: 15). A further loan in 1991 for the Third Nonformal Education Project targeted primary school dropouts and adult literacy, leading "to the completion of a primary school equivalent diploma" (Eisemon et al. 1999: 360, 365; for NFE in Indonesia, see Colletta 1976; Dilts 1982; Indonesia 1982).

The Philippines:[14] The Philippines has taken institutionalisation of NFE even further (Piquero 1998; Guzman 2001, 2002). This country, with its more than 7,000 islands, has recognised NFE officially, like Indonesia (Eisemon et al. 1999: 360). It has been influenced for many years by the discourses and concerns of UNESCO through the regional office for Asia and the Pacific, and this is reflected in the language and practices used. In 1977, under the influence of the Faure Report, an Under-Secretary for NFE was established in the Ministry of Education, Culture and Sports: "This decree reinserted non-formal education into the educational system" (UNESCO PROAP 1997: 8). In the 1987 Constitution, there is reference to "non-formal, informal and indigenous learning systems", but no further definition. Steps were taken "to promote the visibility and advantages of the non-formal sub-system" (Gonzales & Pijano 1997: 3).

In 1989, the Asian Development Bank made an agreement with the Government to set up a National Centre to promote NFE, although it took a number of years before the institution became effective, and its shape changed significantly from that which was at first proposed. From the start, a very wide definition of NFE was taken, wider than in Thailand: family life and health, population, nutrition, community organisation and leadership skills, vocational and livelihood skills, functional literacy and basic skills, values education (effective citizenship and environmental education), and continuing education (higher-level skill development and professional upgrading), all being provided by a multitude of agencies, public, private and commercial (ADB 1989).

EFA in 1990 "gave the non-formal education sub-system its greatest boost". It became recognised that the formal system with its traditional "rigid curriculum, time, resources and accessibility" (Philippines 1999: 5) could not meet the broad learning requirements of individuals and communities; a variety of educational projects and delivery systems were needed "to supplement, complement and enrich formal education" (Gonzales & Pijano 1997: 4). Since increased spending education "has not yet resulted in significant improvements in equity, quality or efficiency of the formal school system" (ADB 1996: 2), higher and technical education were reformed in 1994, and new agencies were set up with a remit to encourage NFE programmes.

As elsewhere, two discourses were being used, and this resulted in an ambivalent attitude to NFE on the ground. One was the language of lifelong education/learning. For example, "the lifelong learning sub-system leans heavily on formal and non-formal education". The aim of the government was the development of "an integrated fully developed system of learning opportunities that are available to all citizens everywhere throughout the lifespan". In some writings, NFE is one strand placed alongside "informal and indigenous learning, self-learning, independent study, out-of-school study programs, especially community needs" rather than embracing all of these. NFE in this model is one strand of education by which those unable to take advantage of the mainstream schooling system could obtain equivalent accreditation. The 1991 Com-

---

[14] See sites http://www.lifelong-learning.org/frameset.htm; http://accu.topica.ne.jp/litdbase

mission on Education even saw 'lifelong education' replacing NFE: it argued that since the NFE alternative system of schooling was proving to be "inadequate", there should be developed "alternative learning modes through more diversified equivalency and certificated mechanisms; non-traditional education services through alternative delivery systems", while NGOs and People's Organisations bring in "counter-education, literacy and other political educational efforts" (UNESCO PROAP 1997: 9).

The organisation which the Commission proposed to develop with the assistance of the Asian Development Bank in order to promote all these alternatives was called the National NFE Center when it was first set up. For the discourse of NFE with its dichotomous world picture is also used. The education system of the Philippines in this model is seen to consist of two major sub-systems, formal schooling ("which involves preparation for adult life and ... ends when one receives a diploma") and NFE (directed towards "adults, the disabled and out-of-school youth"; there is reference to pre-school children and one reference to ten-year old children in literacy programmes, but these do not form any clear focus for the NFE programmes). NFE is different from the formal system in clientele, organisation, activities and delivery methods. It addresses the specific needs of those outside the formal system (the Ideological position on NFE is heard here).

It was recognised in the Philippines that "the strongest proponents and most active implementers of NFE" were the NGOs (including "church organisations, civic groups and foundations"). They were running "seminars, workshops, community assemblies, television and radio programs, correspondence courses, home visits, self-directed learning modules and practical work ... Variety is the key" (Gonzales & Pijano 1997: 5). However, the fact that some formal education agencies are also involved in NFE is recognised by the statement that NFE consists of organised and systematic learning conducted *largely* outside the formal system. Thus a number of schools, particularly private schools, offer night classes and other forms of extension, as do many of the higher education institutions. In 1979, the Private Institutions and Schools National Association in NFE was formed. This "integrated under one office the efforts of a conglomeration of private schools undertaking non-formal education projects". The Accrediting Association of Schools, Colleges and Universities urged its member schools to initiate and implement non-formal education ("service to the community... programs beyond its walls") as part of its accreditation schemes. Some large NGOs were established in the mid-1980s.

███████████████████████████ **NEWS RELEASE** ████████

ASIAN DEVELOPMENT BANK
2330 ROXAS BOULEVARD, METRO MANILA PHILIPPINES
Tel. 834-4444 (local)/(632) 711-3851 (international) Telex: 63587 ADB PN/40571 ADB PM/23103 ADB PH Fax (632)741-7961

███

ADB News Release No. 182/89
25 November 1989

For Press Inquiries only
Contact Ian Gill
Tel. 834-4878

ADB TO PROVIDE TECHNICAL ASSISTANCE GRANT OF $320,000
TO PHILIPPINES FOR A NON-FORMAL EDUCATION PROJECT

The Asian Development Bank has agreed to provide a technical assistance grant of $320,000 to the Philippines for a Non-Formal Education Project. The grant will be financed by the Japan Special Fund.

One of the Project's objectives is to establish a National Center for Non-Formal Education (NCNFE) with a supporting network of regional and divisional units. Another of the Project's aims is to improve access to, and strengthen the quality of, non-formal education (NFE) programs in literacy. While the Philippines already has a high literacy rate of around 80 per cent, the Government gives high priority to achieving universal literacy.

Non-formal education is any structured educational activity which takes place outside the established formal system. Typically, NFE activities cover literacy programs for illiterate adults and out-of-school youth; livelihood programs to provide basic income-generating skills to unemployed persons; community development programs which include health, population, education, nutrition, community organization and leadership skills; values education which aims to develop skills and attitudes required for effective citizenship and including such areas as environmental education; and continuing education which includes higher-level skill development and professional upgrading.

Though NFE is available through several government departments and a wide range of non-governmental organizations, the Government wishes to address several key NFE issues such as policy and planning effectiveness, coordination among agencies, quality of programs, monitoring and data collection, and funding

The NCNFE will be a semi-autonomous body governed by a board chaired by the Secretary for Education, Culture and Sports and comprising representatives of other government departments and non-governmental organizations.

The center will support NFE activities by facilitating planning and coordination of NFE at national and local levels, providing training for NFE personnel in management and program implementation, developing instructional materials, serving as resource centers, establishing a system for collecting, analyzing and disseminating basic NFE data and conducting basic research, monitoring and evaluation activities in NFE.

Under the assistance, comprehensive data on NFE will be collected and analyzed and a project will be prepared. The assistance will take about five months to implement and will be carried out by the Department of Education, Culture and Sports through the Bureau of Non-Formal Education and the Education Projects Implementation Task Force.

The dual discourses led to a double plan of action, as reflected in the aim of the new National Centre, to integrate "all programs of various government and non-government entities involved in non-formal education ... especially the nation-wide training programs" provided by government agencies such as "literacy, industry training and upgrading, and value enhancement for development". On the one hand, the Centre was intended to co-ordinate all existing forms of NFE; on the other hand, it was formed in order to build a new nation-wide training programme.

The first aim of the Government was to co-ordinate NFE throughout the country, despite (or perhaps because of) its large NGO provision. As elsewhere, it is assumed to be the responsibility of Government to manage NFE. There was general recognition of

> the existence of a large number of Government and NGO-supported community-based training programs which are de facto providing nonformal education for the poor, although their contributions are not included in the official statistics. ... The Government recognises the need for, and is committed to, forging partnership with such [agencies] and promoting their NFE activities in order to expand the outreach and improve the effectiveness of NFE programs. ... The [ADB] Project would enable the Government to expand nonformal basic educational services to the poor and under-served communities by harnessing the considerable existing capacities and experiences of community-based organisations to ensure the relevance of the nonformal education activities. (ADB 1996: 2-3)

Among the 'problems' of NFE, apart from lack of funding and lack of impact (a report in 1990 suggested that whereas formal education reached 57% of its target group, NFE reached only 8% of its target group), the lack of co-ordination and systematic planning, together with duplication and overlap, both between government and NFE agencies and between NFE agencies themselves, were some of the most acute.

But there was also a need to create new NFE to accomplish state purposes. "There remains a need for the educational system broadly and especially institutions of higher education, to redirect programs and services in an effort to balance these with the larger society's need for lifelong learning opportunities ... for innovative programming and services". NFE needs to concentrate "on the acquisition of skills necessary for employment and competition".

Initially, it was intended that the National Centre would be more or less independent of government in order to mobilise the NGOs, but in the end the means the Government chose was a Bureau of NFE, alongside new Bureaux for Elementary, Secondary, and Sports Education within the Department of Education, Culture and Sports. The Bureau is intended to be an advocate for NFE, pointing out that most government resources still go to formal education. It brings together public and private sector organisations especially government agencies such as Health, Agriculture, Trade and Industry, Defence, Social Welfare and Development, National Manpower and the Youth Council at national and local government level. It aims to increase the capacity of the Department "to manage a decentralized NFE program ... and to assess, research and formulate policies for NFE" as well as formal education (ADB 1996: 3).

The Bureau has three main divisions: *functional literacy* for adults and out-of-school youth which is in process of shifting from centrally planned and government-implemented to community-based and government-co-ordinated activities; *continuing education* developing a new curriculum based on Essential Learning Competencies and equivalency testing and accreditation for out-of-school youth up to secondary level (a nation-wide Alternative Learning System using self-learning materials and other delivery systems) and using the NFE Testing and Research Center; and *capacity-building,* a programme of training and staff development which uses the formal system of education through fellowships and scholarships.

While the Bureau promotes adult and youth literacy programmes, it also has other interests, and many of these relate to formal education. NFE in the Philippines is to some extent aimed at non-formalising formal education: "In a rapidly changing world, colleges and universities need to cater to the demands of a more diversified clientele and respond to the growing needs of the labour market". Not only are the schools, colleges and universities encouraged to engage in outreach (extension), but distance education programmes (Continuing Learning Delivery System) help young people to access the secondary school curriculum and take formal education certificates. Indeed, NFE seems to mean in some contexts anything that is not "classroom style education" (Gonzales & Pijano 1997: 7,8). To a large extent then, NFE in the Philippines has been co-opted to help the formal education system as much as to provide an alternative to it.

Perhaps the most significant element in the Philippines programme is "the expansion of certification and equivalency programs which are administered by the formal education sub-system into the non-formal sector" (Guzman 2001). Some students are enabled to enter or re-enter formal schooling. The Commission on Higher Education is encouraging higher education institutions to strengthen and expand equivalency and accreditation in higher education in relation to a work environment. At the same time, the school-industry-government links which lead to the "dual training system" come within the purview of the Bureau for NFE. And since it is also responsible for degree updating and the renewal of professional licences through Continuing Professional Development programmes, it is clear that NFE in the Philippines works closely with and inside the formal system of education.

But in general, the Bureau sees its main role as providing a system of education and training alongside the formal system. The Alternative Learning System is "parallel with and comparable to the formal school system" but it is separate. Certificates under the Accreditation and Equivalency Program using an Educational Placement Test have been created by government and are nationally available. Accreditation for learning outside the formal system and for employment are being promoted. The difference between formal and non-formal is not always spelled out, but it seems to mean a different curriculum which "reflects technical, economic, social and cultural issues" (it is not clear how formal education does not reflect these issues), "non-traditional delivery methods" (which formal education is developing), locally adapted learning materials, at least for literacy programmes, and self-learning programmes at functional literacy and continuing education levels.

Thus in this model, NFE means providing an alternative to formal schooling in the Accreditation and Equivalency System for youth aged 15 and above (called the 'NFE A and E Program'). This has flexible entry and exit points; a new curriculum designed to be different from but of equal standing with the formal system, incorporating communication skills, problem-solving and critical thinking (mainly numeracy and science), use of resources, productivity (mainly skill training), development of sense of self and community, and world vision; different teaching-learning materials, and testing (two levels of certificate equivalent to the elementary and secondary systems); and "it utilizes a range of innovative nonformal learning strategies including self-instructional modules, facilitator-aided sessions, individual tutorials, self-study groups and audiotape-based instruction. These multiple learning options give learners as much control and choice as possible over what, when, where and how they learn" (Philippines 1999: 2).

The language used about this separate system is sometimes ambiguous. On the one hand, "It is a viable parallel and comparable system for learning accreditation" (ADB 1989: 6). On the other hand, "the NFE A and E curriculum framework is truly nonformal in its focus of content and competencies, learning approach, sociology, psychology, and philosophical dimensions. It is comparable but not equivalent nor parallel to the formal education system, emphasizes functionality, competency-based, incorporates the four [UNESCO] pillars of learning – learning to know, learning to do, learning to be, and learning to live together ... The competencies and levels ... in the NFE A and E Curriculum Framework are comparable in a general way to the formal school system but not parallel in terms of specific content. There [is] no attempt to make the nonformal curriculum a replica of the formal curriculum or to make it parallel to or equivalent with the grade or year-levels of the formal school system ... [It] is responsive to out-of-school youth and adult learner needs and goals ... [It does not possess the] subject approach of the formal school system". But the two systems interface; the NFE certificates ("signed by the DECS Secretariat which [are] deemed as a comparable qualification to the elementary and secondary certificates of the formal school system") are intended to be of equivalent value to the Elementary Level Certificate and the Secondary Level Certificate and provide the possibility of entry to grades 6 and the fourth year of high school. These NFE certificates are open to any person to take, whether registered as a student or not.

The NFE Bureau recognises however the "social bias so deeply rooted in Filipino culture that any learning experiences, opportunities and pathways outside of the formal school system are [felt to be] second class, inferior or inadequate" (Philippines 1999: 10). The publicity leaflet speaks of "shattering the traditional concept of nonformal equivalency programs". Traditional NFE, it argues, is based on rigid course structures and curricula similar to elementary or secondary school children in a formal class. This more recent programme is premised on flexibility and a nonformal curriculum as well as a range of innovative nonformal learning strategies.

A programme organised by one national NGO illustrates how this alternative system works. The Association of Non-Traditional Education in the Philippines (ANTEP) emerged from the Catholic Education Association and the Association of Christian Schools and Colleges in the 1980s. The programme they describe is run in a local community by students from a neighbouring college. Classes are held in chosen community buildings, 30 learners to one teacher. ANTEP has drawn up a new curriculum which interestingly starts with an exploration of the self, then looks at the community and finally looks at the world (including mastering the world – skill training comes after personal self-enquiry). This programme, aimed at adults, is however largely taken by younger persons with a view to obtaining employment or access into the formal system. Several participants have transferred to high schools on completing the appropriate NFE tests (ANTEP; Cruz 2000).

NFE in the Philippines on the whole now means more the creation of a new national programme helping adults and young people to obtain an education which is different from but equivalent to formal schooling than the co-ordination of existing community-based learning programmes. It seeks to influence formal schooling so as to introduce more innovative modes of learning, and above all it seeks to develop alternative certification processes which will carry exchange value and social capital.

What is clear is that there is a polarity here. Although the discourses of lifelong learning are used at times and the diversity of educational provision is perceived, the formal system is so strong that the main approach to NFE is not to increase diversity to do many different kinds of educational and training tasks, but to set up an alternative system alongside formal education. The government is actively creating NFE in an imitation of formal schooling. While academics may use the discourse of lifelong education, the educational planners at government levels seem to prefer that of NFE.

Training for NFE

The institutionalisation of NFE into large-scale systems requires some training for the large numbers of practitioners who make their career in such programmes. NFE currently lacks systematic academic research despite its widespread appearance, but there are a number of formal training programmes located in universities and some colleges specifically devoted to teaching NFE.

Nepal: Nepal is one of the countries which has a formal education course in NFE.[15] The University of Tribhuvan, through its Centre for Educational Research, Innovation

---

[15] Jimma Training College in Ethiopia developed a course on NFE in 1999 to produce Adult NFE co-ordinators "capable of initiating and managing community-based education and training programs that contribute to the development of individual and community life" (Jimma 2000); other academic programmes specifically devoted to NFE include Namibia (NamCol and UNAM), Kenya (Kenya nd), S Africa (Kotze 1991) and some in Northern locations such as Harvard (USA), Reading (UK), East Anglia (UK) etc..

and Development (CERID), has developed a training programme in NFE which is offered in modular form in its B Ed degree, "so that education students can make a choice between formal and nonformal education when they choose their profession". The course draws heavily on the early writings on NFE and thus speaks of formal, nonformal and informal education in the words of Coombs and his colleagues. The tone is Ideological in the approach adopted to the course content and the works cited.

The course has been formally recognised by the government which has set up a National NFE Council. Both in the university course and in government circles, NFE is seen almost exclusively in terms of literacy. Thus NFE "activities were initiated by the Ministry of Education and Culture and remained limited to literacy programs until the 1960s when other ministries like those of Agriculture, Health, Panchayat and Local Development carried out various nonformal education programs *with literacy as one of the important components*" (CERID 1994: 2, citing Pande 1989, my italics). Thus agricultural extension is not seen as NFE unless it includes literacy. The Basic and Primary Education Programme (BPEP) which is run nationally by the govern-ment is seen as part of NFE even though aimed in part at children. However, other government programmes come under the purview of National Council – the Women's Education Programme, the School Environment Improvement Programme, and Community Reading Centres (post-literacy centres). The University course includes as examples of NFE functional literacy, community development, income generation and women's empowerment programmes.

The practitioners mentioned as possible clientele for this distance education course are in many cases the staff of local NGOs. Many of these "started as formal school teachers and there was an understanding that [CERID] wanted to do something to help prepare people already working outside the formal sector ... especially staff members working in rural areas" (Deyo pers comm.). It would seem that CERID has taken up the discourse of NFE because at the time when the course was first devised the language of NFE rather than lifelong education was widespread among both government and NGOs,[16] and therefore positions within the staffing of these organisations would be open to graduates from this course. The development of existing staff as well as employment opportunities for new staff were part of the driving forces in retaining the discourse of NFE.

3.   NFE AS ADULT LITERACY

UNESCO-PROAP: In 1997, the UNESCO Principal Regional Office for Asia and the Pacific launched a four-country study of the Impact of Non-Formal Adult Education in the Asia-Pacific Region (UNESCO PROAP 1997). In this, "Adult NFE" was seen as coterminous with adult literacy; the wider view of NFE seen in other countries, especially Africa, is not apparent here. India took the National Literacy Mission as its

---

[16] A private 'National Resource Centre for NFE' was established in Nepal at about the same time.

case study, not its NFE schools, because of the limitation of the project to adults; Nepal took the government and NGO adult literacy programmes despite the wider view of NFE taken by the University of Tribhuvan; the Philippines took the mainly voluntary adult literacy activities; only Thailand saw NFE as somewhat wider, but still mainly as government-provided or government-supported basic education for adults (their sample included some secondary education).

The need for the collection of comparative data clearly imposed some uniformity and the compression of programmes into a particular analysis. For 'education' is seen here as being the kind of education and training given in the schools, especially primary schools, and therefore NFE for adults has become the provision of alternative schooling at basic level for adults. The other forms of NFE for adults (health, agriculture, income generation etc.) have been excluded unless they form part of a literacy learning programme.

It is not clear why UNESCO PROAP used the language of NFE in this particular case, for throughout Asia, PROAP with ACCU were setting up Community Learning Centres without using the discourse of NFE. NFE, it concluded from its studies, as provided or supported by governments, "is 'education' in a multiplicity of locales [which] involves discussion and mutual sharing rather than formal lectures and didactic presentations ... is continuous with the whole of one's life, and ... can be tailored to the needs of different ages, groups and professions in society" (UNESCO PROAP 1997: 38). The language of the Ideologues can be heard here, for these characteristics were hardly features of the adult literacy programmes in the four countries described.

Nepal: NFE in Nepal has become virtually synonymous with adult literacy. Two examples may be taken.[17]

For *the international NGO CARE*, "NFE seeks to increase literacy among girls, women and disadvantaged groups"; training programmes in family planning, income generation etc. are not seen as NFE. Much of their NFE programme is aimed at out-of-school children, a preparation for formal education rather than as an entity in its own right, and thus it uses the formal school curricula and materials. (One local project has been experimenting with the 'language experience approach' to literacy which does not use the formal school curricula, but this is not yet widespread and seems to form part of the adult programme rather than the child programme). Enrolment is officially limited to those aged eight and over who have never been in school, but younger children have been admitted. Courses last for 6-7 months, and it is reported that two thirds of those children who complete the CARE NFE programme enrol in formal

---

[17] This is based on several reports from CARE International, from CERID, from Save the Children (US), and on personal interviews during visits to Nepal. It must be remembered that there are very many other literacy programmes in Nepal as elsewhere; I have chosen these not because of any merit but because they call themselves NFE, and thus help to reveal what practitioners in Nepal regard as NFE. My concern here is with perceptions of NFE, not the practice of literacy.

schools after a bridging course (CARE Nepal 1996). The NFE programme for adults (defined as 15-45 years – but several participants are younger than 15 years) consists of two courses, the Basic Literacy course and the Advanced Literacy course. The Basic course uses the government's national adult literacy course and materials, but the Advanced course has developed its own course and materials. The main area of non-formality in all these programmes is that the teachers are locally recruited with school leaving certificate or eight years of primary education or even less, and receive only a short-term training programme; they receive twelve days of training and a 6-day refresher course after two months. Despite its claim to flexibility, "all classes start in January", and "300 hours is considered a minimum for literacy classes". Evaluation is by examination. There is little community involvement after the start of the programme except that "participants have to start a savings fund".

Save the Children (US) also runs a programme labelled NFE alongside its other programmes such as 'early child development' (Rheinhold 1993). This is much the same as that of CARE, although it includes with its literacy training "useful daily information relevant to the needy communities" such as income generation training. It too has basic and advanced classes, each lasting 6-7 months in the year, with its own curriculum and materials. It runs programmes for out-of-school youth – "second chance at schooling and with a class schedule that makes a more appropriate fit with her other daily activities". Indeed, it is reported that some children spend one or two years in formal school, then attend the NFE classes, then go back to formal school.[18] The non-formal elements are described as being a relevant curriculum, community initiative and ownership, local management, monitoring and training, integration with community development, increased awareness, taking into account the expectations and abilities of the participants – thereby implying that formal education lacks these.

NFE then in Nepal, as revealed in these cases, appears to be seen as the provision of literacy to young people and adults in alternative formats from that of formal primary school. 'Education' in this context is limited to basic skills rather than regarded in a wider sense of including access to higher levels of formal schooling and college education or continuing professional development or lifelong learning.

4. NFE AS ALTERNATIVE PRIMARY EDUCATION

Nepal illustrates the approach which equates NFE with literacy, especially adult literacy but with some basic education for younger persons. Bangladesh takes this further; NFE is seen as an alternative form of primary education (see MSU 1980; Sedere 1998); and this view has come to predominate, so that today for many people –

---

[18] Almost every country reports that children (sometimes school-going children) attend and sometimes predominate in NFE programmes for adults.

perhaps for most – NFE means a new form of schooling for school-aged children.[19]

Bangladesh: In Bangladesh different voices provide differing definitions of NFE. There is in some circles a recognition that "NFE's scope is too wide, which includes literacy education, awareness education, alternative primary schooling, vocational education, entrepreneurship development education, professional career development and continuing education" (Hossain & Rahman 1995: 18; see also Sharafuddin 1995: 8; Ahmed Z 1997; Alam & Rob 1991). However, the wide definition of NFE which many African countries hold is not generally accepted in this country: rather NFE is

> not an unorganized and unstructured learning process. It is a combination of formal and informal education, an alternative to the formal system, having more flexibility and open-endedness. It is an intentional learning mechanism guided by pre-determined goals which seeks to bring about changes in knowledge, attitudes, values and skill regarding both literacy and communication. So, nonformal education is a matter of knowing how to read, write, calculate, analyse and empower in daily life. (Hossain & Rahman 1995: 18)

Bangladesh has developed NFE, whether provided by state or NGOs, into a complete alternative system of education; one report breaks it down into NF Primary Education, NF Adolescent Education, NF Adult Education, and NF Continuing Education. Formal schooling and NFE make up a "single system of sub-systems" (Hossain & Rahman 1995). As early as 1989, the Nonformal and Alternative Approach to Primary Education was being adopted by various NGOs widely in the country (Haq 1989; see also Chowdhury et al. 1994; FREDP 1979). Part of the cause of this is the recognised problems which the Government of Bangladesh has in providing universal primary education for all its children in the light of the increasing population and the other demands on the government's resources, including coping with natural disasters.

Non-formal primary schools

The tone of the discourse is Ideological. Thus the value of NFE is contrasted with the problems of formal education. NFE is cost effective, innovative, goal-oriented, with both short-term and long-term impacts (Hossain & Rahman 1995: 18). The National Education Commission (1974) saw NFE as mainly concerned with methods, and suggested that "This kind of education can be regarded as an alternative, or complementary, to formal education ... The inadequacy of opportunity and resources in the field of formal education, the remote connection between formal education and life, and the lifelong need for acquiring learning have all contributed to the importance

---

[19] I note that during a discussion at the recent Oxford Conference, this approach was labelled "the new NFE".

of nonformal education" (Bangladesh Education Commission report 1974 cited in Sharafuddin 1995: 6). A more recent assessment comes to the same verdict: "In view of the prevailing situation in Bangladesh, the formal schooling is simply unable to cope with task of providing Education for All, and nonformal education appears to be a viable alternative which is being effectively utilised by several NGOs. The government has also seen the value of nonformal education, and a Directorate of Nonformal Education has been created" (Sharafuddin 1995: 8).

A large number of government and non-government agencies, including political parties, provide programmes which they designate as NFE. And despite significant differences between these agencies, the most striking feature is their basic uniformity – they provide alternative primary schooling on a large scale for children of school-going age and others. It is significant that most agencies keep their other education and training programmes outside of the confines of the NFE heading. It is likely that the reason for the retention of the designation 'non-formal' so strongly in Bangladesh is that almost all the programmes of adult education run by both government and NGOs started soon after the War of Independence in 1971, and that the discourse of Freire ("oppressed and oppressor") had a particular resonance in that context (Abed pers comm.). The continuation of that terminology has been accepted by the donors, although the concept itself has shown considerable change over the last 30 years or so. The emergence, in Bangladesh as elsewhere in Asia, of private education, both at school and university level, has not affected the ideas of NFE among the main providing agencies.

The Directorate of NFE, created in 1995 after many years of government experience with first the Mass Education Programme and then the Integrated NFE Programme (INFEP 1994), has a massive programme of NFE throughout the country running "parallel to the mainstream primary schools in the country". Some non-formal schools provide two years of education for children aged 6-7, to prepare for class III of formal primary school; others designed for children aged 6-8 or 8-10 are aimed at class IV, the three year formal curriculum being covered in just over two years. Some have a three year course for children aged 6-10 covering classes I-V. There is also a Non-formal Adolescent Schooling Programme, a one-year course for those aged 11-16, with skills equivalent to class III of formal schooling. There is an adult literacy programme of nearly a year for men and women aged between 15 and 35; this usually includes skill training for economic and/or community development alongside literacy learning.[20]

Much of this alternative educational system is delivered through NGOs – more than 400 such bodies are registered with CAMPE (Campaign for Popular Education – despite this title, the discourse of 'popular education' is hardly used in Bangladesh) set up in 1990 as the over-arching and co-ordinating body (Hossain & Rahman 1995).

---

[20] At the time of writing, it is reported that the Directorate is being closed and new arrangements are being made by the government.

BRAC: The Bangladesh Rural Advancement Committee is the largest such body and also the best known internationally (e.g. Lovell & Fatema 1989; Prather & Ahmed 1993). Although its annual report includes both adult literacy and continuing education under a general rubric of NFE (BRAC 1997: 7), the staff are quite clear that the term 'non-formal' is only used in the context of 'Non-Formal Primary Education'. The Non-Formal Primary Education programme started in 1985 with 22 pilot schools, and there are now in excess of 34,000 such schools scattered throughout the country, 8000 of them for adolescents aged between 11 and 14, 1500 in urban areas and 24,500 in villages.[21] A total of 1.2m pupils are in these single-teacher non-formal primary schools. The programme is funded by external donors. As BRAC's Founding Director has said, "Rapid scaling up was a problem", particularly the development of de-centralised structures (Abed pers comm.).

The schools are uniform across the country. When asked about the 'non-formal' elements,[22] the staff identified four:

a) *flexibility* – in timing and location. A local management committee is first established and parent-teachers meetings are also to be held regularly. These bodies help to determine the hours, the place of meeting and the holidays. Despite this local involvement, it is noticeable that all BRAC schools have the same pattern, 2-3 hours of classes per day, 6 days a week, and a total of about 250 days a year. Once the dates have been decided locally, they tend to remain fixed. In many villages the non-formal primary school assembles for much the same time and days as the formal schools which function according to dates which are determined centrally and sent down to the village schools. The location of BRAC schools can be in any building so long as it is central, on the basis of "education going to the people, not people to education". But again, it is noticeable that many of these non-formal primary schools meet in buildings which are sole-use buildings, specially built by the local community to house the school.

b) *curriculum* – a stream-lined version of the state curriculum of Arithmetic, Bengali language, Social Studies and (from the second year) English and Religion, operates in these NFPE schools, both simplified and speeded up. However, many of the state's teaching-learning materials form the basis of this curriculum.

c) *assessment* – it is argued that formal tests are replaced with informal tests. But a nation-wide 'Assessment of Basic Competencies' based on norms for all 12-year olds and aimed at testing literacy and numeracy skills and functional competencies such as oral rehydration therapy is used in BRAC schools. At the end of the course, the pupils take formal state examinations and have often been very successful: it has been recorded that some state schools ask BRAC pupils to take their examinations in the state schools so that the formal school pass rate can be increased.

---

[21] The latest (2001) unpublished figure I have seen is 34,141 NFPE schools. There are also some 500 other schools in the total BRAC programme – schools for garment factory children, schools for 'hard to reach children', and a few schools within the Health and Population Division of BRAC.

[22] Based on interviews with senior staff at BRAC headquarters in Dhaka and some field visits.

d) *the teachers* – these are local persons, normally with nine years of formal primary schooling. They are paid 600-650 *taka* a month instead of 2000 *taka* or more which formal school teachers receive.[23] BRAC comments on the scarcity of such teachers in some villages, but at the same time points out that for many of these facilitators, there is little in the way of alternative employment. They receive 15 days residential basic training, 3 days of orientation each year and one day per month 'refresher' – in all, 90-100 days spread over four years. This training "rests on the principle of 'distributed training' throughout the school term rather than providing a lengthy training course at the beginning of the teacher's career". The training covers the curriculum, the writing of lesson plans to be submitted to the supervisors, and participatory and learner-centred methods.

Among the distinctions which BRAC claims for its schools compared with formal schools are their smaller class sizes, informal teachers and more informal pupil-teacher relationships, more general informality (for example, no uniforms), and adequate supervision (one supervisor to about 15-17 schools). "BRAC's education programme can be distinguished from the formal system in numerous ways: class size of NFPE is only 33, parent-teacher meetings are held regularly, school hours are fixed in each season with the advice of parents, a decentralised management system works in the programme and supervision of school is regular. In contrast, in formal schools the class size is almost double, parent-teacher meetings are rarely held, school hours are fixed at the same time throughout the whole year and the management and supervision of school is very weak" (Nath et al. 1999: 8-9).[24]

The same is true of the other NGO providers of Non-Formal Primary Education in Bangladesh. What they provide is flexible and accelerated schooling. These claims have not been fully tested empirically,[25] for most of the published evaluations have concentrated on the 'success' rate of these schools compared with the formal schools, judged in terms of state examinations, comparative testing and/or transfer into the formal system (e.g. Nath et al. 1999; CAMPE 1996; Khare & Grewal 1997; Nath & Chowdhury 1998; Nath 2000). The aim of these non-formal schools is to encourage the pupils to enter formal education, and it is suggested that more than 90% of the pupils do so, although a high number of these drop out very quickly: it is suggested that the main reasons for this are economic factors and the different climate in the formal school classrooms (Nath 1999).

The distribution of this alternative non-government system of primary education is related in some senses to the state system, filling in the gaps and picking up the dropouts and out-of-school youth. Competition is avoided. However, there is considerable demand for NFPE schools; in some areas, parents have been known to falsify

---

[23] These figures are the latest I have and may no longer hold; but the level of disparity will be much the same today.

[24] It must be remembered that these papers were written by a BRAC staff member, not an outside objective observer.

[25] The author conducted an evaluation of the Proshika NFPE programme in 1997 for DFID; the findings have not been published.

their children's ages to get them into the non-formal schools (perhaps largely because they are cheaper). It is clear that for some parents, a BRAC or other non-formal primary school is the school of first choice, after which the child moves into the formal system (BRAC 1995b: 5). Several non-formal schools report that some children attend both kinds of schools where timing makes this possible. Some parents are said to be pressurising their local state schools to become like the BRAC school, but which features they wish to be changed are not known.

The relation of the non-formal school system to the state schools is complex. "NFPE complements the Universal Primary Education Programme of the government by providing basic education to the poorest children of the country" (BRAC 1997: 31); and there have been calls for greater collaboration between the two systems (Nath et al. 1999: 21). Sometimes joint training sessions for teachers are held. But at the same time there is a polarity. The possibility of some BRAC teachers being taken onto the state pay-roll is being explored. The issue of sustainability is of course a major concern: "BRAC is only piloting NFPE; this is the responsibility of the Government. We are covering a gap. It is not a parallel system but complementary, supplementary. Eventually the Government of Bangladesh will have to be in charge" (Abed pers comm.), although BRAC is not clear exactly what would be lost if such schools were taken over by the state. The 'terms of reference' of the BRAC schools are those of the formal system; they exist only to provide an alternative path to reach the same goals, to draw more young people into the formal education system (BRAC 1995b, 1996).

In return, BRAC is considering offering to take over some dysfunctional state schools and even to open some 'formal schools' in areas which may need them. In part, this is because of the problems of being able to deliver the upper primary curriculum, especially in mathematics, English language and science. There are (so they record) still some 30,000 villages in the country with no schools: "if we open schools, the villagers can access the rest of BRAC services" (Abed pers comm.).

There are other kinds of non-formal educational possibilities created by the flexibility of an NGO and by staff commitment which would not be possible to state officials. For example, one BRAC staff member arranged for some girls who had recently ended their BRAC school classes but had not been able to enrol in the state school to have additional evening instruction once a week with a volunteer teacher with materials provided by BRAC (BRAC 1997: 35). But such instances reveal the potentialities of the BRAC system rather than the norm. Provision for follow-up is provided by less than successful village libraries which are "open only to the graduates" of BRAC schools who pay a fee for the privilege and who may in some cases receive some income-generation training.

An adolescent programme was started in 1987: "Since 11-14 is a critical age bracket encompassing the teenagers, we felt that they should be dealt with separately rather than with adults" (BRAC 1995b: 1). In all respects these are similar to the non-formal primary schools; the curriculum is the same but with the addition of skill training and health issues.

BRAC then sees NFE as alternative primary school provision in a country where the provision of state primary schools falls far short of the need or even the demand. The provision of universal primary education is felt to be the most urgent need of the moment, especially under the pressure of the international agencies advocating Education for All.

Other NGOs: Many other NGOs in Bangladesh have followed the example of BRAC, often on a large scale and with some differences. **Proshika** started its programme in 1993. The term 'NFE' is kept strictly for primary schools: under its Universal Education Programme, there are Non-Formal Primary Schools and Adult Literacy classes which are not designated as NFE, and its other educational programmes (Development Education, human development training and economic development training) are not called NFE (Proshika 1994, 1995; Rahman 1994).

By 1997, Proshika had established some 4000 schools for children aged 8-11 (older than primary school enrolment so as not to challenge the state schools). Like BRAC, they concentrate on the curriculum up to Grade III and are faced with the same demand to upgrade them at least to Grade V (in three years) and even higher, so as to ensure access to formal schooling. The courses are accelerated: "by reducing vacations and holidays, each academic session is completed in nine months". Proshika has adapted "most of the essential learning contents of the government primary school curriculum ... children who complete this course will be qualified for getting them-selves admitted into secondary schools". The non-formal curriculum omits religion but uses the government textbook in English language. Teachers (facilitators) are again local persons with school-leaving certificate (wherever possible), receive 15 days initial training and four days at the start of each academic year, and have a one-day workshop when they collect their monthly wages. The emphasis (as with BRAC) is with whole-class teaching, but (looking over their shoulder at the formal school) the staff can claim in Ideological terms,

> The traditional classroom culture does not exist in Proshika's schools. The learners sit in a U shape and the teacher is always busy ... helping them. The teacher feels herself/himself to be a co-learner, and the learners sometimes play the role of a teacher. The process of teaching is given emphasis rather than the teaching of content. The learners do not memorise everything like parrots. The active learning process is maintained in teaching the children. It helps them to be independent and creative learners. (Rahman 1996: 3)

In practice, not much of this can be seen in the NFE classrooms. There are few signs here or in BRAC of the teachers contextualising the curriculum to their immediate environment (very few out-of-classroom sessions, for example). The local community is involved through a village education committee; and parents too engage with the school (a small payment per month is required for each pupil). Proshika argues that their schools form a system which "is equivalent to the formal system – not alternative, not 'consolation'".

There are many other such programmes. GSS developed in their non-formal primary schools an innovative curriculum and in particular training of teachers and teaching-learning methodologies and materials based on Western school approaches. Dhaka Ahsania Mission has a large Non-formal Primary Education provision, as do other NGOs such as the Bangladesh Association for Community Education whose schools are aimed at children aged between 4 and 7 years (BACE 1989).

In Bangladesh, then, the over-riding impression is that NFE does not mean all education and training for children and adults outside of the formal system. Rather, 'education' means (primary) schooling, and non-formal education means primary schooling for the unprovided-for children. The tone of most of the language used is that of formal education.

Why then use the term 'NFE'? First, because the state wishes to keep the distinction between state-provided schooling with professional teachers and the more informal educational state and NGO provision for many rural and some urban areas so far deprived of a more professional provision. This is particularly true when the NFPE system is so large. BRAC for example in 1997 had a total full-time staff of 25,000 and an annual turn-over equivalent to US$1.3 million. The government is keen to see NGOs help with the provision of universal primary education; but at the same time, it is not keen to see the NGO system as strong as the state system. Secondly, the NGOs have retained the discourse which they adopted enthusiastically in the 1970s; they see no reason to change it to one of the more recent discourses such as lifelong learning; it meets their needs. Thirdly, most of the donors supporting these programmes (but who have largely abandoned the discourse of NFE elsewhere) are happy to retain it so long as it is confined to alternative primary schooling, especially after Education for All has given an additional thrust to children's primary education. NFPE in Bangladesh is not anti-school. It may identify some weaknesses in the primary school system, but it imitates the formal school in a way which flatters these schools. NFPE serves the interests of the state and of the EFA advocates; it is a way of harnessing NFE to the formal education agenda. NFE in Bangladesh means non-formal schooling.

Pakistan: "The Bangladesh Rural Advancement Committee's ...so-called informal schools in villages ... are seen as a successful model, now being popularized by the World Bank, and are being adapted in many countries, including Pakistan" (Heward & Bunwaree 1999: 209-210): in Pakistan, schools built on this model are sometimes called Informal Schools. The reason for the change of terminology is not clear, for some of the NGOs running such programmes use the language of non-formal education (Akbar 1997; Pakistan papers; Ahmed 1995; Khaqwaqja & Brennan 1990; Qayyum 1981; Sinclair 1990). In 1994, the British Council with the support of the government Co-ordinating Committee for NFE brought together many workers in this field in a workshop on 'Literacy Practice in NFE' (British Council 1994).

The government recognised such schools by establishing a Department of Primary and Non-formal Education within the Ministry of Education, and an Experimental Pilot Project Integrating Education and Development was launched (Saghir 1987), starting with schools for dropout children and widening under the READ Programme (Rural Education and Development) to include women's education centres, community viewing centres, adult literacy centres and some religious schools.

NGOs were supported in the provision of non-formal schools. The NGO Bunyad Literacy Community Council (BLCC) in Punjab[26] reports that "a common element of most of [its] projects/programmes is non-formal education". It uses the term NFPE and NFBE interchangeably for its 500 primary schools catering for some 20,000 girls aged between 6 and 14 and some 45,000 adults. It also provides non-formal secondary education for girls as well as a school enrolment programme. It sees NFE as "rural community-based education [in] settings often deprived of the most basic services ..." (Jamil 1995: 1).

Many of these schools are provided and supervised by local NGOs. They are managed by a village education committee and a mothers' committee. The community provides the school space and utilities (Rahman 2000: 5). Like the BRAC schools, they have an accelerated learning programme, covering five years of formal schooling in two and a half years of part-time schooling. BLCC uses the state "textbook syllabus" repackaged, and includes other subjects such as oral rehydration, health and nutrition, income generation skills and community studies. The teachers have lower qualifications than the formal school teachers and are paid Rs600 compared with the Rs2400[27] and other benefits of the formal school teachers; but BLCC has introduced a Teachers' Empowerment Fund to assist its non-formal teachers, and has begun a scheme to certificate its teachers and open access into formal training through the Allama Iqbal Open University in Pakistan. Bunyad sees in these schools a "Non-Formal Basic Education revolution" (Jamil 1995).

ActionAid has opened a Non-formal Programme of community schools "to help children enhance their responsibilities and take part in community development, [to provide] opportunity of basic education to the deprived and destitute children, and to promote enrolment of students in the formal school system" (Saeed 2000). As the Pakistan Literacy Commission has stated, the aim is "to achieve Universal Primary Education through the NFE System – the right of every child". The non-formal elements are listed as being community demand, home-based schools, the size of classes (some 30-50 children), community-provided school accommodation, free schooling, teachers identified by the local community and "not transferable", and flexible location, timing and vacations (Pakistan 2000). The movement is growing.

---

[26] This is based on documentation from BUNYAD and on an evaluation of the NFPE schools conducted in 1995.

[27] Latest figures available.

Community schools

Many other examples of alternative primary schools labelled 'non-formal primary education' can be cited further afield, including Africa. The model has chimed in well with a trend towards community supported schools as a result of post-welfare thinking and Structural Adjustment Policies. It has been suggested that community schools and community participation in education is the developing world's contribution to the global education scene, in contrast to the charter and voucher school movements of the West. "The Community School is the interface between traditional schooling and non-formal education" (King 1976: 12), although others have argued that community schools will always remain part of any government formal educational system (Singleton 1974). Hoppers (2000b: 10) calls this the Basic School Movement.

Mali: One example will speak for all, although local differences exist. In 1992, Save the Children (US) "launched an innovative non-formal primary school" programme for out-of-school youth and dropouts in both Mali and Burkina Faso. By 1996-97, there were 386 such schools, and in 1998 some 740. Donor support is huge – USAID put in US$6.8m, although it is suggested that this scaling up may lead to increased formalism (Boukary 1998: 28).

The context is significant (Puchner 2003), Francophone Africa and a region of many languages and tribal groups. Formal education is changing with bi-lingual and double-shift schooling and improved school management systems. But these reforms have had little effect so far. There are therefore calls "to de-institutionalize formal education and substitute community-based non-formal education systems which emphasize instruction in literacy, health and agriculture". Community schools are pioneering this decentralisation of the management of schools and the participation of parents and local communities in sharing the costs of education: "experimental schools have become a venue for a differentiated education system" (Maclure 1995).

The *Save the Children* schools were consciously "modelled after the BRAC schools", although the differences are not ignored (they are set out in Boukary 1998). They are intended for school-age children who cannot get to formal schools. The communities are involved, particularly by providing the meeting location and (at least in principle) meeting some of the costs. The community is charged with providing well-behaved pupils, and there is open discussion about problems "unlike state schools". The non-formal schools for children aged six years and upwards meet for three hours each day throughout a year determined by the local agricultural seasons. Instruction is in the local language rather than French, and the initial curriculum consists of relevant life skills. The schooling lasts for a cycle of three years; some have been upgraded to six years in response to local demand, but these introduce French as the language of power and employment and a more formal curriculum, and therefore rely on teachers brought into the community from outside.

It is the agenda of reform perhaps which accounts for the continued use of the NFE discourse in this region. "Inspired by the rhetoric that came out of Jomtien ...

where it was declared that basic education is to 'be seen, once again, as the responsibility of the entire society' and NGOs have a preponderant role to play in its development, an increasing number of NGOs are engaged in experimentations with non-formal primary education systems that are more attuned [than formal schools] to the cultural, social and economic environments of the beneficiaries as well as foster an unprecedented community participation in the management and financing of education" (Boukary 1998: 4-5). The key is responsiveness and cost-effectiveness.

Initially these schools were regarded as temporary expedients to fill the gaps until the state can take over. But they have moved away to a longer-term view: "Institutionalizing these schools in rural communities has become the main focus" (Boukary 1998: 10). The issue is one of sustainability – how to maintain these schools once the donor agency has withdrawn. In Mali, there is greater stress on the responsibility of the local community to manage and eventually to provide the school than in Bangladesh.

Save the Children (US) intended their village schools to be a full educational experience in its own right; but increasingly, under local pressure, they are becoming focused on providing entry into formal schools, or even to replicating formal schools in themselves. The approach is conscious – "to adapt formal school to local realities without reducing quality". It is significant that one parent (quoted in Muskin 1999: 46) can say, "We desire for our children a formal education in Bambara because this favours more open-mindedness among the children as regards both the local and the larger, outside communities, more than does the government school".[28] "In practice, these are non-formal community-based schools, but increasingly they align themselves more with the formal system at the request of parents who control the schools through management committees" (Wood pers comm.). "There is a different route to the same examinations through community schools" (Wright pers comm.).

In this, Save the Children (US) sees its role as one of developing partnerships, not least bringing together the local community and the state, where previously there was mistrust. It works in part through local NGOs, strengthening their institutional capacity to run such schools. But the project admits that (unlike BRAC schools) relations between the state and the NGO are "fraught with problems", including lack of information, fear of competition for pupils, suspicion of unqualified teachers (the use of the title 'teacher' has particularly caused tensions), and dislike of some of the participatory teaching-learning methods employed in these non-formal schools. The issue of the use of local languages for instruction has caused disagreements. As the Ministry of Basic Education has said, "Is this a way of assuaging the aspirations of village children by imparting a second rate education? ... Is there a possibility to

---

[28] It would be interesting to know the original words of this quotation since it is translated by the author from field notes; what did this parent mean by 'formal education' in this context? The author avoids the use of the term 'non-formal' but uses 'formal' frequently; and the paper shares the same world view by talking throughout of the dichotomy between government schools and community schools. Elsewhere it speaks of community schools as providing "a formal education to previously unserved children" (Muskin 1999: 51).

harmonize the curriculum of village schools with that of the Fundamental schools?" (cited in Boukary 1998: 25). On the whole, NGOs are not highly regarded by the Ministry in Mali, since "they do not have a base in the democratic structures of society like the government". Within the communities, these non-formal schools have been valued and supported (the children attend regularly) on the grounds that they do not alienate the children from the local community, so that graduates from these schools would be able to help with local community tasks such as filling in government forms and recording marketing; and they are cheaper than state schools, attracting donor support in a way which state schools do not. But they have not always united the community; the gap between richer and poorer parents has often become wider.

The debate in Mali is largely concerned with quality in education and how this may be measured. Traditional measures such as school inputs (buildings, teachers and their training, textbooks, equipment, etc.) have largely been rejected, especially by the NFE schools. Other measures used include internal efficiency (certificates, dropout and repetition rates) and external efficiency (e.g. increased income, employment, improved standards of living). In these measures, non-formal schools with "the possibility of purposes that diverge from the conventional educational aims of more formal schooling and modern sector employment" appear to have some advantages over formal schooling (Muskin 1999: 36-39; Hoppers 2000b: 12-13).

World Education in Mali has pursued a different route by working with a group of 500 existing state schools, increasing their resource base, improving the buildings, training teachers into a more professional cadre, developing what are felt to be more appropriate teaching-learning materials and creating local school management committees; some staff refer to this as NFE (pers comm. World Education staff 2000).

The NFE activities in Mali led to a lively engagement between government, NGOs and local communities on policy issues relating to schooling. But they also need to be seen in a wider context. NFE in Mali is part of the World Bank, USAID and international development agency pressure on the state to increase provision through community involvement including cost sharing, and to reform the educational system to achieve quality as measured by Western standards – "blazing the trail for both the NGOs and the Ministry of Basic Education". The voice is in large part that of the international educational reformer once more, directing education to externally determined development goals, while at the same time claiming to represent the true voice of the people.

Temporary schooling

PEER: One of the more significant (but short-lived) approaches to NFE recently has been the UNESCO-UNICEF approach which saw NFE as a temporary but necessary device to cope with emergency situations (Tawil 1997; for a more recent approach, see REP 1998; Sinclair 2002). The Programme of Education for Emergencies and Recon-struction (PEER) started in Somalia in 1993 and was developed in Rwanda and in the Tanzanian refugee camps. The process was conceptualised (IBE 1996: 4-5). NFE was to be developed in any emergency situation such as a war or natural calamity after a needs assessment had been made. Emergency educational material was to be stock-piled; suitable persons would be identified to serve as 'teachers', and they would begin work at once with both children and adults, receiving in-service demonstration and training while engaged in this activity. This would continue until a *post-emergency situation* had arisen, on which 'normal service' (i.e. formal education) would be resumed through the use and/or production of a "more normal curriculum" and the identification of professional and trained teaching staff; a "formalized classroom situation" would be created, and the teachers would receive in-service training. Formal schooling would continue until repatriation or resettlement would have taken place.

The PEER programme became highly formalised. A generalised curriculum (including education for peace) was drawn up, and textbooks were produced for all emergency situations. A teacher emergency package and a programme of teacher training were developed. In Rwanda, there was an element called "the recovery of non-formal education with an emphasis on youth education and designing/adaptation of educational materials for literacy and post-literacy". The PEER organisers foresaw a time "when such conditions are no longer present [and] it would be time for the PEER operation to cease, yielding place to a more traditional and permanent UNESCO presence" (IBE 1996: 6).

NFE then, in this *avatar*, is simply a temporary relief education, inferior to formal schooling which is the normal model. It needs to be replaced with its superior relation as quickly as possible. This area of work has attracted a good deal of attention in very recent times, especially by UNICEF (Retamal & Aedo-Richmond 1998; Pilar & Retamal 1998; Pigozzi 1999; Fountain 1999; Davies 2003: 154-164) but the language used in the more recent discussions does not refer to NFE.

5. NFE AS REFORMING EDUCATION

NFE in other contexts means reforming the formal education system. India may be taken as an example of this.

NFE in India: Many voices speak of NFE in India (see India papers cited in bibliography; MIDS 1987a, 1987b; Iredale 1978; Naik nd; Naswa 1997; Shirur 1995; Singh & Shukla 1979; Stone 1983). Even different government officials define NFE in different ways. The Fifth Plan (1974) made only a passing reference to NFE, but later in the 1970s, a Directorate of Non-formal (Adult) Education was formed within the Ministry of Human Resource Development. The publicity leaflet it drew up used ideological terminology:

> The curriculum [of NFE] is flexible, diversified and responsive to contemporary national problems, current community issues and prevailing learners concerns. ... Learning in a nonformal education

programme takes place through democratic discussion and dialogue, critical analysis of factors in the environment, self-analysis and reflection leading to understanding ... In no case should it be authoritarian and imposed, abstract and theoretical, mechanical and routine, unrelated to the concerns and interests of the learners... .

In the *National Education Report* (India 1995: 533-544), NFE was "conceptualised [as] a non-formal stream of education for social justice by mobilising the university system ... an individual can join at any age, at any level and at any time of the year to achieve an education at his [sic] own pace ... Instruction and evaluation ... is at the convenience of the group of people involved and based on problem-solving and application to daily life situations".

The adult dimension: Initially, the main focus was then on adults contrasting NFE with schools for children. In 1978, the Rural Functional Literacy Programme incorporated what were called NFE projects (Govinda 2002), and in 1987 a national seminar was held on Development-Oriented NFE Research, again seen as adult education (MIDS 1987).

Similarly, in 1980, UNESCO conducted a study of Formal and Non-Formal Education in Rural Development through a sample survey of Karnataka (UNESCO 1980). The researchers took two formal educational programmes (rural primary and high schools) and six NFE programmes. The NFE activities included *vidyapeeths* (described as residential rural polytechnics run by the State Adult Education Council, vocational training institutes with cultural and civic elements in the curriculum, mainly for adolescent youth but without certificates), *mahila mandals* (autonomous women's groups with training in tailoring, dairy and childcare – again without certificates), adult education (literacy) centres managed by the State Directorate for Non-Formal Education), Farmers' Training Institutes (State Ministry of Agriculture), and children's health centres (*anganwadis*) (State Ministry of Health) – all of these provided and run by government; together with one NGO programme, the Mysore Resettlement and Development Agency running short-term agricultural and rural training activities (especially health), mainly for youth. There was also a short residential course on youth leadership for those aged 15-35. When the participants were interviewed about the advantages of NFE, they echoed the views of the planners – there were no examinations, the programmes were less costly than the formal courses, and the courses were more directly related to development.

There was thus in some circles a sense of the adult dimension to NFE. In 1995, in its mid-term review of the Education for All programme, the Ministry wrote of "the need for making available non-formal, flexible and need-based vocational programmes to school drop-outs, neo-literates etc. ... The government is alive to the problem of unreached areas and disadvantaged groups which may have inadequate access to education. The non-formal system is intended to increase participation of these groups" (India 1995: 11, 13; see India 1996). When PROAP called representatives of the government to their joint impact survey, NFE was defined by the Ministry of

Human Resource Development as the National Literacy Mission, i.e. adult literacy rather than the state-sponsored NFE system for children (UNESCO PROAP 1997). Other voices too have been ambivalent. Elias saw NFE as adult literacy but adult literacy programmes which were conducted in a participatory way: "Innovative non-formal education is a process of participatory learning and sharing of experiences and reflections among the participants" (Elias 1994: 10). In other words, there are formal adult literacy classes and non-formal adult literacy classes. *The Indian Journal of Adult Education*, in its many articles using the language of NFE, tended to define NFE in terms of adult literacy.

NFE and children: The government however came to regard NFE as state-provided alternative elementary education for children as part of its responsibility for developing "a systematic programme of Non-formal Education as an integral component of the approach to achieve universal elementary education".

It was the National Policy on Education of 1986 which gave NFE the thrust towards children's education: "NFE shall strive to reach school dropout children from habitations without schools, working children and girls who cannot attend whole day schools" (it is interesting that children who have been unable to attend schools through no fault of their own are still constructed as 'dropouts', representing a transference of blame). A scheme for assistance to voluntary agencies for non-formal schooling for school-age children was drafted (this approach to NFE was reinforced by the National Education Policy of 1992). "In 1987, the Ministry for Human Resource Development made funds available for NFE ... programmes to be implemented by the voluntary sector" (Ramachandran 2003: 307). This was however only one of a number of initiatives including a separate programme of Innovative Education.

Contrasting NFE elementary education and the National Literacy Mission ("these two innovations"), the National Policy on Education in 1986 urged that NFE programmes should be characterised by a flexible curriculum, different materials, a shorter duration than in formal schools and more convenient times, for example afternoons for girls and evenings for working children (Mukherjee 1997). NFE Centres (they are deliberately not called schools) were established usually lasting some two hours every day at a time to suit the children. They worked with a curriculum lasting two years, four semesters of six months each. Local facilitators were chosen and paid Rs200-400 per month as against Rs4000-6000[29] for formal school teachers. "The village community is expected to provide for space and make other arrange-ments". New teaching-learning materials and new tests and certificates were devised, providing access into formal schools. By 1995, some 277,000 such centres had been established, some 80% of them by the Government of India (GOI) and others by NGOs with government support, almost one third for girls, with a total catchment of some 6.8 million children. But there is no firm data relating to this alternative system. "NFE centres are established in places where they are least required and are admitting

---

[29] Latest figures available.

children who would have profitably attended a formal school or are in a position to pay for their learning. They have become competing centres for primary schools and naturally have been losing out in the competition against a more resourceful competitor." Cheaper teachers were seen by the formal system as a threat.

Mukherjee suggests that non-formal primary education can be seen in one of two ways – as a variant of primary education, the variations being the concise two-year curriculum, flexible hours of working and learner-friendly locations; or secondly as educational programmes with a localised curriculum, meeting local needs rather than universal primary education needs. He draws an interesting parallel with autonomous and ideological approaches which are now seen to characterise approaches to literacy (Street 1984, 1995). Formal education is autonomous – the same everywhere, taking its point of reference from within itself. NFE, he suggests, should be contextualised, set within existing local cultural systems. However, he goes on to suggest that there is a need for a national system of NFE, that NFE schools should be institutionalised, for as it currently exists, NFE "is not a credible alternative to the primary school system" (Mukherjee 1997: 19).

This disillusion with NFE seen as schools for dropouts is a marked feature of a recent survey of alternative ways of "getting children back to school" (Ramachandran 2003). "Unfortunately large-scale, non-formal education and alternative schools with parateachers are more concerned with physical access. Investment in improving the capacity/calibre of teachers ... has taken a back seat; ...the quality of education being imparted in the NFE centres was not preparing children to gain admission into mainstream schools... the steady decline in the number of NFE centres has been due partly to the inherent weakness of the model itself ... the NFE model was really an apology for school..." (Ramachandran 2003: 12, 89, 311, 318). Rather than a uniform pattern of non-formal schools, what is needed is a large number of variant ways of attracting children back into the mainstream. The language of NFE is not seen to be relevant to these alternatives; the most useful discourse is that of diversity, local answers to local problems. By tying NFE to one form of schooling, and that a discredited form, the discourse and the values which it incorporates have also lost credibility.

Reforming formal schools: In the search for new alternatives (alternatives to NFE) to reach unreached children, those who worked in this area found it necessary to seek for changes in formal schools. Ramachandran (2003) provides many examples of this without using the language of NFE, keeping that simply for the government NFE programme. Most of these attempts to reform formal schooling have been undertaken by NGOs. The government itself ran Operation Blackboard and since then the District Primary Education Programme (DPEP). But most of these activities have been undertaken without recourse to the NFE label. However, one or two have called themselves Non-formal Education.

PROPEL: One of the clearest examples of such attempts to reform formal schools is the PROPEL project in Maharashtra, the third phase of a NFE project first created in 1979 (Naik 1985, 1989; Guttman 1995c). This action-research programme stressed the need for non-formal arrangements for reaching out-of-school children; but it also saw the necessity of working with the full-time formal schools to stem the dropouts and improve retention and achievement rates – "to make rural primary schools more responsive to the needs of universalization". Although primarily aimed at illiterate older children aged 9-14, much of its work covered younger children. PROPEL (run by the Indian Institute of Education, Pune) developed an innovative curriculum separate from the universalised formal curriculum, together with non-formal teaching-learning techniques and materials. It used local teachers and "stress-free" testing. It aimed at low costs and substantial community involvement. The first phase saw some 263 local schools set up enrolling 4332 children (3237 girls): "these numbers proved the assumption that NFE could help educate girls..." (PROPEL nd: 3). The second phase was on a smaller scale and consisted of encouraging and facilitating local community leaders to work with both non-formal and formal primary schools in their area, developing "a new concept and arrangement for primary education in which the formal and non-formal channels had to be complementary" (ibid: 4). The third phase consisted of working with local communities and "enabling [them] to participate in properly planned multifaceted action for 'education for all'".

The philosophical basis for this was of course Gandhi, who

> had emphasized the need to work outside the educational system even with the ultimate objective of reforming the system itself. The pro-grammes of non-formal education provide a good basis for these efforts. To the extent that these outside efforts grow and succeed, the conditions within the system will also begin to change, and it is the simultaneous action both within and without the system that will help us to bring about the essential educational transformation and provide good education to all the people. (Naik 1978 cited in PROPEL nd: 5)

PROPEL set up "an alternative system of non-formal primary schools which function on a part-time basis so that they can be availed of by the children from the poor families who cannot attend full-time formal schools". The project aimed to devise "an experimental pattern of inter-linked systemic factors related to the realization of the goal of 'education for all' at the grass-roots level. ... In the PROPEL project the alternative channels of full-time formal education and part-time non-formal education have begun to come closer together in a relationship of complementarity" (PROPEL nd: 5, 10, 14).

We have come a long way from NFE as an independent system of adult literacy classes which does not touch the formal school system at any point. At times, the project sounds ideological: "Non-formal education has been defined as an organized and systematic learning-arrangement which responds to the needs and convenience of the learners". The characteristics are an alternative pedagogy based on individual as well as social learning, decentralised planning and management, more developed supervision of both the pedagogical process and the development of the teachers, an aim to change attitudes in the community away from simple literacy-numeracy towards the liberation of the learner's intellectual capacity to reflect on problems and to take action on them, home-support for the child's learning, and mobilisation of the community to accept "primary education, whether full-time or part-time, as its own and permanent responsibility". New curricula, methodologies and materials are needed for NFE. Evaluation is seen as reinforcement of achievement rather than testing of capabilities, using peer and self-testing, daily demonstrations to the family and periodical demonstration to the community "for deriving from it the emotional satisfaction which leads to further learning and feelings of self-esteem" (PROPEL nd: 22, 26). (A formal test was however administered in 1992 comparing the children in formal and non-formal schools.)

As part of its intention to help reform formal schooling, the project developed a training programme for primary teachers based on the project. "The core of this programme is non-formalizing the formal school so that not only would the dropout be stemmed and primary level achievements taken to higher levels, but to make teaching enjoyable for the teachers themselves ... Offering full-time formal education in a part-time arrangement does not make it non-formal" (ibid: 37, 21); what was needed was a changed education.

Lok Jumbish:[30] It is a small step from here to Lok Jumbish in Rajasthan, one of the more significant NFE projects in India (Govinda 2002: 350-362). The aim is clear: "breathing new life into (some) existing schools". Lok Jumbish works with the dysfunctional formal school system to improve quality (for example, by overcoming the problem of absentee teachers). Encouraging local communities to take over responsibility for such schools from the state, new teacher-training programmes, curricula and materials, active-learning methodologies and new assessment processes have been developed, "mostly non-formal". Co-operation between teachers and the local community is being built. Different delivery systems are created to meet local needs (for example, the desert and the fertile areas of Rajasthan have different cultural patterns). Meetings are held with the community to determine a local mode of working. In most cases, the existing school building is taken over, although at times a non-formal meeting place is utilised. School hours are adjusted, part-time teaching introduced, and teachers are drawn from the local community. Working within the *panchayati raj* (local government) system, a core group from the community engage in school mapping, identifying barriers and possible solutions to them, promoting motivation of both parents and pupils. A Village Education Committee is formed and a

---

[30] Based on documents and a visit to Lok Jumbish in 1996. A similar project is the Escuela Nueva in Colombia but significantly this does not use the language of non-formal education (Colbert 1999).

village education fund set up. The Committee keeps the school register.

Lok Jumbish suggests that "Many forms of NFE can be implemented outside the mainstream education system". Thus Sahaj Shiksha (SS) has been launched on the basis of an "equivalence with the formal school system ... transfer from SS centres to schools ... and efforts to ensure that the quality of instruction in SS is equivalent to the school system ... Formal education and NFE systems [can] learn from each others' strengths ... [with] flexibility in all organizational aspects" (Govinda 2002: 357). Residential programmes of two-three months for girls aged 9-14 have been held using seasonal hostels, bringing them up to Standard V over an 18-month period. Attempts are made to develop different educational strategies for tribal communities because of language needs and the mobility of many groups.

Relationships between Lok Jumbish and the state educational system are not always harmonious, partly because of a fear of the more flexible (and apparently less professional) programme, partly because of personalities which play a part in many localised NFE programmes. The popularity of Lok Jumbish suggests some threat to education personnel, especially the formal school teachers. And the fact that on the whole the Lok Jumbish organisers are looking for concrete indicators of social change (family planning, changes in attitudes towards and activity among women, parent support for schooling, reductions in Hindu-Muslim tension etc.) rather than or as well as performance in formal tests does not endear this project to the formal system. But Lok Jumbish is very clear: like World Education in Mali, it is supplementing and seeking to reform the government system, not building an alternative system. The contrast here is not between two systems of education or even two educational programmes but between two approaches to education within the same system; and resistance is marked within the formal part of that system.

Informal educational activities within the formal system

NFE then may be seen inside the formal education system.

South Africa: Two examples can be seen in South Africa. There seem to be two main approaches to NFE in this country. At least one writer suggests that NFE in South Africa is to be distinguished from both adult basic (compensatory) education and from skills upgrading education (Millar 1991).[31] But even this more limited definition is wide-ranging, including military education, religious education, worker education, civic education and sports (Dovey 1993, 1994, 1995). NFE thus constitutes an arena in which there is a constant battle between the hegemonic forces of those who are engaged in economic and cultural production (mostly state bodies but also commercial interests and much of the media) and those who resist such co-option (mostly NGOs). In other words, some of the battles of the apartheid era between the state and major

---

[31] I owe this reference and the construction put upon it to an unpublished study by Jane de Sousa 2001.

economic interests and the forces of liberation from unjust political and economic systems are being continued within this discourse of NFE.

But the dominant interpretation of NFE within the country (as within ADEA) resides within the human capital approach to education; and most people see NFE as access to formal schooling systems and equivalent qualifications. The context within which this takes place is of course important. The attempts of the government of South Africa to overcome the injustices and faults of the apartheid system as it applied to education (as to all other aspects of society) through a national policy of truth and reconciliation mean that education, both formal and non-formal, is highly regulated in that country. "The legacy of apartheid has left South Africa with approximately 70% of its 12th Grade African learners being over 20 years old" (Millar 1991). The development of an appropriate nation-wide curriculum for such adult learners has occupied both state and NGOs. A national attempt to develop an inclusive NFE programme within the system resulted "in the creation of a new Secondary Education Curriculum for Adults" (ASECA) with formal education equivalency. Although "accepted as part of South Africa's National Qualifications Framework, that curriculum still cannot be taught in schools. Thus the divide between formal and nonformal education proves once again difficult to bridge" (*ADEA Newsletter* 3: 3; Rabinowitz 1997; ASECA 1998).

A second example comes from the PROTEC project, supported by LinkAfrica. An Institute of Engineering decided to upgrade the skills and knowledge of high school students. Some 22 centres of technology have been created with over 5800 students. The aims are to develop awareness and interest in technology among high school students, and to increase their mathematical and science performance and other skills such as language, life skills, leadership and study skills. The achievements of the PROTEC programme are measured through examination results, but the chief purpose is to get disadvantaged (mainly black) students into technology careers.

The project uses the language of NFE in its exploration of the relation between its activities and the schools with which it works. "PROTEC remains a non-formal selective entry education organisation". Initially, it aimed to expand into a separate network across the whole country, but later it changed its aim to get its new technology curriculum taken on inside the formal sector.

> Although this seems a positive goal, it brings out the problem of integration between the two sectors. It is difficult to see how schools with few resources, under-trained teachers and de-motivated pupils will be able to use the PROTEC model. Such activity-based learning requires materials and teaching skills not resident in the majority of the formal secondary schools. Nor would [there be anyone] to support the teachers who would be using the curriculum ... The strength of PROTEC has been built on complementing the formal sector rather than entering within it. At the moment, the government is attempting to create an integrated system of accreditation (the National Qualification Framework) in an attempt to articulate formal and non-formal education.

This seems more appropriate than using a curriculum developed in one environment for another ... With [the government's] commitment to vocational education provision, PROTEC will flourish in the near future in South Africa, if it can appropriately integrate or articulate with the formal sector. (PROTEC nd)

This dichotomous approach suggests that "the pre-liberation approach to non-formal education in very narrow terms as job-specific vocational education" (NEPI 1992: 53) has changed little in the new era.

6. NFE WITHIN THE SYSTEM – FEEDER SCHOOLS

ACCESS: A rather different approach but one which again sees NFE as schooling for children linked to the formal state primary schools is the ActionAid programme entitled Appropriate Cost-Effective Centres for Education within the School System (ACCESS 2000),[32] operating in a number of African and Asian countries. ACCESS has taken the community-based non-formal school further than BRAC, trying to make it an integral part of the formal educational system in the role of feeder schools to the state primary school (see Action Aid 1997a, 1997b).

ACCESS has examined the conceptual basis of this form of NFE in depth. It argues that in the traditional approach, non-formal schooling must of necessity be non-state primary education, for all state primary education will be part of the formal system. ACCESS adopts a different approach, seeing NFE as flexible schooling within the state system, and defining the differences of NFE schools from the formal primary schools. There is a good deal of the Ideological language used in this approach.

In its policy formation, ACCESS accepts the key non-formal elements of BRAC. It aims to have a flexible timetable and calendar, and the schools meet part-time. They are to be located close to or in the village itself, using informal (low-cost and low-maintenance) premises rather than sole-use premises (BRAC uses sole-use premises in most cases). The teachers are para-professional ('lay teachers') with on-going training and support. The curriculum is stripped to the basic essentials, is practical and localised. Local languages are used and localised teaching-learning materials are produced. In Ethiopia for instance, teaching is undertaken on four days and teachers meet on the fifth day to prepare local materials. Teaching methodologies are child-centred and promote active learning. There is substantial community involvement, and the pupils are involved in the school government. Assessments are in most cases informal and internal, but final examinations are those of the formal system. The whole NFE system is said to be cheaper with lower administrative overheads.

---

[32] This section is based on a great deal of documentation relating to ACCESS in ActionAid London, in Ethiopia and in many other countries, and on a two-week workshop on ACCESS in Africa and Asia held in Addis Ababa in November 2000 for which many country papers were prepared.

ACCESS is constantly seeking to improve its performance. ActionAid is aware that many of its NFE schools are not like this. They are very variable. In many cases, there is inadequate quality control. Above all, NGO-provided primary education has its limitations, especially in terms of coverage, sustainability (including long-term funding) and uniformity. NFE needs to be scaled up in order to avoid the variations between NFE schools which depend more on the ideologies of the different NGOs than on the locality in which these NGOs are working. ACCESS suggests that NGOs often have a good record in short-term impacts but the longer-term impacts are more questionable; they tend to perpetuate the dualism between themselves and government, and this can hinder government working with civil society.

ACCESS in almost every country in which it is being implemented talks in terms of non-formal education. But several planners in ActionAid point out that using the existing language of NFE creates a division between formal and non-formal education. The traditional view of NFE as 'outside the system' makes it hard to build linkages between the two. There can be a lack of recognition of the achievements of each sector and consequent failure to transfer effectively from non-formal to formal education. NFE suffers from the lack of career paths for teachers (these programmes see a high turnover of NFE teachers). There is poor documentation for NFE, especially on cost-effectiveness. Community involvement not only often reflects all the problems and inequities and conflicts of local communities but fails to see and affect the wider context. The programme claims that many parents are alienated from NFE because they see it as second-rate, not 'proper schooling'. And because of the gap between NFE and the formal system, there is very little NFE can do to influence and reform formal primary schools. Indeed, the very existence of NFE on the community school model (and its claimed successes) actually reduces the incentive to governments to expand or reform the formal schooling system.

ACCESS argues that all primary education should be the responsibility of government and that NFE should therefore come into the formal system. Like others, they talk of non-formalising the formal system but they also talk about formalising NFE. Both should be brought together under one control. The piecemeal approach which NGO control of NFE encourages must be changed into a comprehensive approach. In other words, a single system should be created, but the flexible elements of NFE need to be preserved. ACCESS in Ethiopia sees its role as being to "mainstream the best practice of NFE into the government system", while keeping the best of the formal system. Mainstreaming does not mean making formal schools more flexible, for if that happened, there would be no difference between formal and non-formal (flexible) schools. Rather, the non-formal schools should seek to reform the formal in other ways, keeping the distinction, so that pupils can move from the one to the other within a single system.

The way to do this, they argue, is by seeing the formal primary school as at the centre of a network of smaller non-formal feeder schools, outposts, satellite schools, outreach centres, all closely linked to the central primary school. These will then all be part of the system of education. ACCESS claims to be a strategy to abolish the formal/

non-formal divide. But the programme retains the discourse of formal and non-formal, although the promoters recognise not only its dangers but also the existence of other discourses (community learning centres, community schools etc.). The reason given for this is that they see NFE as the answer to the problems of formal education – its elitism, the dropouts it creates, its rigidity, its inaccessibility both in terms of physical distance and social distance, its over-regulation and bureaucracy, its corruption, incompetence and authoritarianism, and above all, its inadequacy to meet the needs of many of the rural and urban population.

ACCESS sees some of the problems of this approach – that it confines NFE to the very young; that there is a danger of bureaucratising NFE. The gap between micro-level engagement and national policy-making is one which needs to be addressed. There is still no incentive for the formal system to reform itself, and there is a real danger that the formal system will determine what is done in the NFE schools rather than the other way round. Above all, the dualism inherent in the NFE discourse continues. However, this may be regarded as an advantage, not a disadvantage, for it will retain the space which NFE has to be creative, innovative and critical of formal schooling. NFE must seek to reform the formal system, not ignore it. NFE should not seek to implement "ideal alternatives rather than struggling to alter the realities of the existing structure" (ACCESS 2000: 9).

It is noticeable that new terms are creeping into the discourse – terms like accountability, entitlement, democratisation of education, as well as older terms of empowerment and participation. But behind this, the voice is the voice of the external reformer, the Ideologist. ACCESS has nothing to say about other areas of NFE. According to the ACCESS programme, NFE is the first and fundamental building brick of the formal system; it is needed not only in those areas where the formal system is inadequate but even where it is strong. For NFE brings to the formal system the practice of flexible schooling.

The government of Ethiopia (and it would seem other governments) are hesitant about the ACCESS approach. They are uncertain about how to accept the ACCESS pupils into the formal system; about the relationships between the ACCESS teachers and the professional teachers, and especially about how the non-formal schools can work with the state primary schools. They feel that they are being forced into adopting particular reforms of their system at the instance of NGOs. While they see some value in ACCESS schools in very remote areas without a state primary school, they see no place for such feeder schools in the towns where all children are within reach of a state primary school.

CONCLUSION

This sample of NFE programmes today shows a wide variety of meanings with no clear unifying principle underlying the use of the term 'Non-Formal Education' to cover all such cases. Not even Wittgenstein's 'family characteristics' approach to categorisation can help to reconcile the various views of NFE. For some, it is a wide range of different small-scale educational activities with different curricula for adults, characterised by extreme diversity and lack of co-ordination but useful to achieve the nation's developmental goals. For others, it is an alternative delivery system for the state's educational programme, providing different routes for different age groups to the same nationally recognised qualifications. For yet others, it is a national system providing adults with literacy and/or vocational training, or children with a simplified and flexible but yet uniform alternative basic education. For some, it is the province of NGOs, simply because it is "outside of the formal (state) system". For others, it is a useful tool of the state, largely provided and managed by the state and certainly to be co-ordinated and controlled by the state through a process of institutionalisation. For some, NFE is an attempt to create ideal forms of schooling for children, apart from the formal schools. For others, it is a direct attempt to reform formal schools by making them more flexible and responsive to local demands.

Which raises the question of why NFE seems to be growing today – or rather, why the language of NFE is still being used to label programmes of education, training and schooling in many parts of the world. In particular, why are many governments now so much more interested in NFE than they have been in the past?

It may be that the concentration of NFE on children has led to increased government interest in NFE. For NFE today seems to have lost much of its adult dimension. And the changing role of governments as facilitators rather than direct providers is a greater motivator. Governments are increasingly called upon to enter into partnership with other agencies. They have then become increasingly keen to co-opt NFE to help with both their national development goals and their EFA targets.

> The policy issue ... appears related to ... equality of access, since many NFE institutions have been established to serve those to whom access was denied by the formal educational system, either initially or historically. In the poorest nations, governments have been unable to provide equality of access to large segments of their national population. Economic conditions, demography and geography militate against the provision of equal access to formal education. (Wilson 1997: 91-92)

To meet such needs, governments find it useful to work with NGOs in the provision of education, but they categorise all educational programmes other than their own as NFE, they bring them into play but at the same time keep them distinct.

Thus the programmes of NFE reflect the changing relations between NGOs and the government in education. Many NGOs are now keen to work closely with the state rather than in opposition to government, just as the state is seeking to co-opt civil society to its goals.

There may be a further reason. Just as human rights are beginning to be seen as relative rather than universal, so there may be seen an increasing concern with education as localised rather than global. Issues such as decentralisation and democratisation of education are one aspect of this. It is interesting to see that the view which Coombs held as early as 1968 that the absence of overall planning in NFE provision leads to ineffective programmes and often wasted resources is now widely held in many developing countries by both providers and state planners, at a time when increasing diversity in educational provision and the value of loosening the control of the planners are key themes in other parts of the world.

NFE then (at least in terms of child education) is now seen to be useful to the state, not a challenge. It has been co-opted as a means of completing the state's Education for All commitments. And this is not just providing an alternative way of meeting the expectations of many parents. Rather, it can equally be seen as a means of breaking the monopoly of the formal school professionals (especially the teachers) – a way of introducing para-professional (and much cheaper) teachers into the system; a way of passing a good deal of the costs of and responsibility for providing primary education down to local communities; a way of getting out of or at least modifying the over-elaborate and over-expensive schooling systems which their colonial oppressors burdened the newly enfranchised governments with when they left. It may be that the pressures of UPE explain why some governments have recently espoused NFE. Nonformal schooling is useful, not just to reform the formal education system but to break its monopoly. And while NGOs (especially international NGOs) still talk about access and social exclusion/inclusion and equitable education, governments are more concerned with costs and with meeting internationally set targets of participation. The language and the practice of NFE are helpful to them in this.

But not all governments see NFE in this way. Some fear it as backdoor privatisation of schools. Some fear the role of NGOs in the provision of NFE, unhappy in their relations with civil society. Some fear the radical agenda of some NGO non-formal education programmes. Many fear the para-professional teachers within NFE. But others have indicated their willingness to overcome such fears. Behind this lies a feeling that NFE teachers are usually temporary and can be sacked, unlike the trained and salaried teachers who are often hard to sack and discipline; the inclusion of numbers of NFE teachers can pose a welcome threat to teacher unions. For both groups of government agencies, it is still useful to identify some educational pro-grammes and to tie the label 'Non-formal Education' on them.

ACCESS can be seen as the ultimate in the institutionalisation of NFE. ACCESS sees NFE not as education outside of the system but as lying within the system and an integral and essential part of the system. One way of looking at this is to see it in terms of formal education having captured non-formal education, making it more like itself, recreating NFE in it own image. NFE has become a useful tool of the state at a local level.

Part IV

Towards A New Logic Frame

This section sets out a possible new logic frame for Non-formal Education today.

It points out that the term NFE covers both small-scale very localised learning programmes and large-scale national programmes of flexible schooling.

It discusses whether we need the discourse of NFE at all, either as a tool of analysis or as a tool of planning – or if it should be abandoned. It suggests that the traditional dichotomy of formal and non-formal no longer fits the diversity of education today, since the term is used to cover both what may be called flexible schooling and participatory education.

The section explores what is meant by participation in educational programmes. It advocates an analysis of education in terms of contextualisation, and suggests that the planning of educational programmes needs to be based on the combination of both contextual and decontextualised approaches.

It concludes by suggesting that a better formulation might be to reserve the term 'non-formal' for flexible schooling and use the term 'informal education' for the more highly contextualised/participatory programmes.

11

Re-Conceptualising Non-Formal Education

For Men associate by Discourse, and a false and improper Imposition of
Words strangely possess the Understanding, for Words absolutely force
the Understanding, and put all Things into Confusion. (Francis Bacon,
Advancement of Learning 1620)

The situation we are faced with today is one of a growing programme of Non-formal
Education but increasing uncertainty as to the language in which these programmes
are clothed.

ADEA informs us that in Africa a "new generation of NFE activities [is]
emerging continent wide" (*ADEA Newsletter* 4). NFE programmes are being launched
and new departments to handle them are being created. In several countries, this
increase has been caused by and in turn has led to considerable institutionalisation of
NFE under government and donor agency influence. Some countries are promoting
national standardised programmes leading to certificates. Others seek a closer
relationship with NGOs in the provision of educational opportunities. Large-scale
programmes labelled NFE are receiving substantial donor funding.

We have already seen that the renewal of the use of the term NFE after several
years in the wilderness is striking. CIDA (2001) for example, speaks of the "children,
adolescents and youths [but not apparently adults] who have been excluded from
existing formal and non-formal educational opportunities"; so that one of its aims is
"continuing support for non-formal education". The World Bank has used the
language of NFE in a number of recent papers (above p.139). The term has entered
many fields, especially science, environmental and distance education (Meredith et al.
1997; Edwards 2000; Re'em 2001; Bainer et al. 2000; Clover 2000; Romi 2000;
Mohanty 1999; Robinson 1999 etc.). Not only is the term used in many 'developing
countries' in a variety of contexts (e.g. Kapoor 2000; Adegbija 2000; Mohsin 2000;
Rajan 1999; Pillai 1998; Kumar 1998; Dhaka Ahsania Mission nd etc.), but the
language of NFE has become common in Western contexts as well as developing
societies (Surrey 2001; Svetlana & Jelenc 1993 etc.).

But there is much uncertainty as to what Non-formal Education in this new context means, both in the field and in policy documents. In practice, NFE today can range from the small-scale individual or small group educational activities to large-scale national programmes; from highly contextualised to standardised programmes; from adult to children's education; from temporary learning programmes introductory to formal schooling to a permanent alternative to formal schooling; from literacy and basic education to post-initial, vocational and advanced continuing professional development; from state programmes to those offered by commercial agencies; from quite separate educational activities to practical exercises inside schools. There is no consensus about what NFE means. UNESCO has a comparative NFE-MIS project in Tanzania, India and Cambodia but it is not clear that each country means the same thing by the term NFE (GMR 2002: 59).

Equally, policy statements are unclear. The definition in the EU Commission's statement (EU Comm. 2001: 32-33) is not the same as in the EU Memorandum of 2000; and the authors admit that "definitions remain largely informal and pragmatic, wedded more closely to action than to conceptual clarity" (EU Memo 2000: 8-9). One example of this can be seen when the EU talks about accrediting non-formal learning (EU Comm. 2001: 16-17, 32-33; see also EC 2000).

And current usage is largely uncritical – it rarely tries to define what NFE means. The ADEA NFE Working Group did make an attempt but in the end gave up against divergent meanings and allowed anything, however contradictory, to go under the term NFE. Confusion reigns. For example, the UNESCO Literacy Decade (UNESCO 2001a) uses the discourse of (one undifferentiated) basic education, but at times slips in words and phrases drawn from the NFE discourse: for example, "Literacy ... is developed both in and out of school, through formal, non-formal and informal learning systems", identifying NFE with programmes for "illiterate youth and adults" and schooling with programmes for children. But elsewhere in the document it calls for a "break with conventional dichotomies such as ... formal/non-formal dichotomies" and instead sets up wording such as "Literacy education takes place both in and out of the school system", a phrase which it urges as an improvement on the parallel phrase "Literacy education [is] associated with out-of-school groups and non-formal programmes". There are times when it uses the old categories: "Literacy for All requires adopting a holistic approach to learning that articulates, both conceptually and operationally, child and adult literacy, formal, non-formal and informal education". As we have already seen (above pp.139-140), the recent World Bank working paper treats 'Adult and Non-Formal Education (ANFE)' as the overlap area between Adult Education (which is wider than ANFE) and NFE (which also is wider than ANFE) – but none of these terms is defined, and other terms are also used such as basic education for adults (World Bank 2003).

In part, this use is simply the old discourse continuing to be used uncritically: like other discourses, "some connotations of the term that once were more pertinent ... still linger on, as it were, as subterranean bases of the current usage of the concept" (Cooke & Kothari 2001: 172). The words remain "without any real thought of what that means beyond some vague notion; ... the language has remained the same but the context of shared beliefs and values in which it was used has passed. The language that was meaningful to an older generation is no longer meaningful" (Jarvis 2001a: 73). But equally, some of this revival of the language of NFE is deliberate. Many of those who have come to NFE programmes from formal education recognise the need for marking the differences between education in formal contexts and education in more informal settings (Rogers 2003); the language of NFE helps with this recognition. The ADEA workshop in 1999 in Botswana was significantly sub-titled '*Reviving* Discourse on the Formal/Non-formal Interface' (my italics).

But one of the most striking features of the contemporary usage of the term NFE is that the writers do not cite any of the NFE literature surveyed above. The whole of the earlier debate is ignored, the heritage is treated as if it never existed (see, for example, World Bank 2003). The new usage of the language is cut off from its roots. The result is that the concepts of NFE are mixed up with other more dominant discourses, particularly the discourse of lifelong learning/education. As we have noticed (above p.4-5), this newer discourse with its sense of a unified education stretching throughout the whole of life (both lifelong and lifewide) has created the need for some kinds of distinction within this unity, and this has led to a revived use of the terminology of NFE but without the whole discourse. A few attempts have been made to harmonise the discourses of NFE and lifelong learning. Atchoarena (1996: 177) notes that "lifelong education describes the processes for promoting, supporting and improving learning that ... acknowledge the contributions of non-formal and informal educational influences"; and Percy (1997) speaks of "formal, non-formal and informal lifelong learning: reconceptualising the boundaries" (cf ALICE 2000; see also Eraut 2000a, 2000b) – but this is not yet general.

Some people then see a need for a reconceptualisation of NFE. As Wright has pointed out:

> In many ways most formal education systems have been able to learn lessons over the years from successful strategies and practices in non-formal education.[1] By the same token, many non-formal or alternative forms of education have sought to emulate key features of the formal system, and some were even modeled on it in the first place ... It has been argued by various interested parties ... that this distinction is redundant and that the very concepts of formal education and non-formal education are themselves obsolete. Others have suggested that perhaps we need to revisit the whole range of concepts such as formal, non-formal, informal and alternative, to be clear about these widely used labels that influence and affect so much of what we do and how we perceive education provision in its various forms. (Wright 2001: 4)

---

[1] This view is strongly contested by writers such as Wim Hoppers.

Rosa Maria Torres has dealt with this more fully than anyone else:

> The concept of non-formal education ... was born out of the in-sufficiencies within and criticism of the formal educational system. The term NFE became associated with out-of-school education and was applied to a particular approach to education characterized by greater adaptation to the needs and circumstances of learners, creative use of educational resources, community participation, decentralized and more flexible organization and management, and less authoritarian management and teaching styles. Over time, formal and non-formal education often opposed rather than complemented each other. Many saw out-of-school education as the natural place for innovation and for diversification of education and learning strategies, and in-school edu-cation as inherently rigid, homogenous, static and resistant to change.
>
> This situation however does not hold any more. School systems have been experiencing innovation and important changes over the past few years. In many countries, especially in Asia and Africa, the term *non-formal* is also used today to refer to schools and school education policies and programs that feature some of the characteristics once attributed to NFE and out-of-school education. NFE practice has also shown it is very difficult to transform conventional educational think-ing and practice even outside school doors. Building bridges between NFE and FE, rather than developing them as separate systems, has been and continues to be an important goal in many parts of the world.
>
> ... the distinction between *formal* and *non-formal* education has become unclear and to a certain extent irrelevant. ... It is to be expected that in the next few years, and within the lifelong learning paradigm, conventional classifications will regroup around new categories ... All over the world, programs exist that resist traditional classifications. They are challenging the formal/non-formal, school/out-of-school barriers, building bridges and creating hybrids ... (Torres 2001: 50)

The need for reconceptualisation

Does this confusion of discourses matter? Throughout this study, I have frequently asked myself if the obsession with meanings and linguistic consistency is a pre-occupation of a few academics based on Western philosophical history, not shared by the majority of the world who use words partly creatively and partly by rote. But I would argue that it does. For if any discourse is to be useful, as Kuhn has shown us, it must either 'fit' or 'work'; it must serve as a tool of analysis or as a tool of planning – or preferably as both.

a) If the language of NFE is to be useful as *a tool of analysis*, it must help us by describing situations intelligibly. The discourse we use is the best approximation we can create to describe reality as we see it. Such descriptions will of course always be contingent, they will change and be contested. We construct or adopt it because it is in our interest to do so. Nevertheless, we must feel that it fits or it will cease to be useful to us. If the discourse of NFE no longer fits perceived reality, it will be less useful as a tool to assess what is happening.

b) Secondly, if the NFE discourse is to be useful as *a tool of planning*, of developing new educational activities, it must be clear about its aims. I have argued above (p.7) that the effectiveness of what we do depends on the clarity of the logic frame which we hold. I do not believe that we can be effective in NFE if we are unsure of what NFE is. The lack of theory, the gap between our espoused theory and our theory-in-practice (see above p.6) will inhibit our work. For it seems to me that the purpose of all discourse is not simply to change the way we look at the world; it is also to help us to change the world as we see it. If the NFE discourse is confused, it will be less useful as a tool of planning educational programmes.

We therefore need to ask whether the NFE discourse is the best way to construct education today. Or are there better ways which will more effectively help us to see and to alter the world we inhabit, new discourses to meet new perceptions of reality? Would we lose anything of value if we abandoned the discourse of NFE entirely?

Whose voice? It all depends of course on whose voice is being heard – whether that of government, donor and aid agencies (which is often much the same as that of government) and/or of policy-makers and providers; or of educationalists, academics and researchers; or of practitioners, teachers and local level managers; or of the participants and/or parents? Whose interests are being served?

I am very conscious that my voice is primarily that of a practitioner and researcher, one with interests in maintaining an approach to education to which I have become wedded after being engaged in it for many years, one with a liberal approach to adult education in which the participants achieve what *they* set out to achieve through the learning programmes that I am charged with planning and implementing for them. I am committed to serving the agendas of government, of donor agencies, of commercial interests or of educational institutions, *only insofar* as these agendas are committed to helping individuals and groups to fulfil their own aspirations, even if this means challenging the existing dominant interests. My voice will inevitably be different from that of many of my readers – but I hope these pages will challenge them to find their own voice in relation to NFE.

THE PROBLEM WITH THE NFE DISCOURSE

We therefore need to look at the discourse of NFE to see what it implies. For the NFE discourse constructs the world in quite specific ways.

1. The discourse divides the world of education into two unequal parts, formal and non-formal – and normally only two. There is rarely any space for a third element. We have seen above that 'informal education' as at present constructed normally means unstructured learning and not an educational process at all – but we shall return to that later.

2.   The discourse labels both of these sectors, one as 'formal' and the other as 'non-formal'. Such labelling groups many different programmes together. It imposes an artificial unity on both of these two sectors, obscures their internal differences and exaggerates the differences between the two sectors.
3.   In most forms of the NFE discourse, these two sectors are set against each other. Each is judged against the other, not against any other standard. Formal and non-formal education form a dichotomy, one remedying the inadequacies of the other. They may be seen as parallel to each other or as hostile to each other, but more normally as a hierarchy, one of them superior to the other, for as Escobar (1995: 39) reminds us, labels tend to create hierarchies.
4.   It has been argued (for example Jellema & Archer 1997) that this polarisation of formal and non-formal education prevents each from influencing the other. Despite the fact that one aim of the discourse is to use one to reform the other, contrasting NFE against formal education makes it hard to build bridges even when both are being handled within the same Ministry of Education (usually however in different Divisions/Departments) and even more so when the state handles formal schooling and NGOs provide most of NFE. Hopper (2000a) suggests that most NFE programmes and providers are not interested in influencing formal education.
5.   Behind most approaches to NFE today is a belief that it is the role of government to include NFE in its remit. "Education is one of the key responsibilities of the State" (ADEA 1999a: 1). Governments have become interested in co-ordinating NFE in order to co-opt and direct it to the state's agenda; and many NGO providers have joined with the state in trying to mainstream NFE. "Some nations restrict local groups in their sponsorship of nonformal education programs unless the programs serve to maintain or enhance the state's goals" (LaBelle & Ward 1994: 4142; see Wright 2001). It is this move which is giving NFE a higher profile and legitimisation in some countries.
6.   But there is no comparability when governments and other agencies use the term 'Non-formal Education'. For some, it means all non-governmental programmes; for others, those government-sponsored educational programmes provided by other Ministries (Ministry of Agriculture or Health activities, or Ministry of Labour or Ministry of Defence youth training programmes etc.); for yet others, all those Ministry of Education programmes not handled by the Department(s) in charge of primary and secondary schools. It is this wide range of interpretations that causes the main problem with the language of NFE today.

Formal is normal: Whatever the view taken, NFE is not 'the norm'. All discourses of NFE start with formal education; NFE is a divergent form of education, usually inferior. "The dominant discourse in education is formal schooling, which assumes that most (if not all) educational provision should be provided at the start of life" (ADEA 1999a: 6). "As a second chance, it [NFE] can supplement formal schooling, for example for such target groups as teenagers and adults who have never been to school, drop-outs and child workers, but even then it should have a clearly defined connection to the formal education system to enable transition and the opportunity to take recognised examinations ... [In Burkina Faso], parents rejected a well thought-out curriculum concept because they considered this model of basic education a dead-end street. There was no link to the formal system, no transition and no equivalency of school-leaving qualifications. For the parents, the relevance of the learning content alone was insufficient"; they saw the formal system as more relevant to their needs (Bergmann 2002: 84). Such attitudes are not of course universal but they are widespread.

One result of this is that, in an attempt to overcome such hostility, and despite the talk of non-formalising the formal system, in practice much NFE is getting to look more and more like formal schooling. "The term 'non-formal education' is somewhat imprecise, since many of its activities and programmes are 'formalized' to the extent that participants are registered, instruction times are defined, textbooks and materials are provided etc." (Wilson 1997: 88). The NFE discourse almost always privileges, even when it seeks to reform, formal education.

We have already noticed a tendency towards seeing education as a single entity, bringing formal and non-formal education closer together in a single educational system under the general control of the government. The ACCESS programme openly advocates this; it talks about NFE being inside the formal system without clarifying what 'formal' and 'non-formal' mean. UNESCO talks about helping countries to build a unitary educational system, getting away from the "child education/adult education" divide (UNESCO 2001b: 12). Today, the stress is placed on the unity of all educational activities rather than on the differences between the various educational programmes on offer .

It is then very difficult to reconceptualise NFE today. Indeed, it may be impossible to do so – for two reasons. First, a dualistic model can no longer adequately describe educational provision today. And secondly, NFE imposes common characteristics on different kinds of education. In other words, many would argue that it no longer fits as a tool of analysis and it no longer works as a tool of planning.

NFE as a tool of analysis

The concept of formal and non-formal in education no longer fits reality. Education cannot be cleanly divided into two pigeon-holes. There have been, as we have noticed above, some who have said this for a long time, but it has become particularly apparent today.

Formal is now highly diverse: For one thing, formal schooling is no longer clearly defined. When NFE is described as "the learning which is not effected as part of a country's regular formal school system" (Lynch et al. 1997: xi), it is assumed that this regular formal system can be recognised. NFE constructs formal education as single and simple and uncontested. But the formal system of education is becoming highly diversified as new approaches to teaching and learning are opening up, so that what is to be included in formal education and what excluded are now harder to determine. Are the increasing number of private/voucher/charter schools and colleges which often teach to the state curriculum and use the state textbooks for state examinations part of the formal system or not? Are NGO- and religious-provided schools taking state examinations formal? Are the increasing numbers of state specialist and community schools teaching different curricula still formal? Can learning on the world-wide web undertaken through school or as part of homework or in leisure time all be classified as the same; and are these formal or non-formal? And what about the additional schooling which many teachers give to pupils outside of school hours?

This ambiguity concerning the boundary of the formal system of education is not just confined to Western societies. Different kinds of secondary schools such as technical colleges, religious or secular schools, the expansion of mobile and part-time schooling, state, NGO, church, community, private charity and private commercial, refugee, for-profit schools and colleges are all jostling side by side, with schools offering different curricula in different languages. The state monopoly rarely exists. In Lesotho, "although government control over the formal systems [sic] has steadily increased ... Lesotho's educational system [sic] is still mainly managed by three major church denominations" (Morolong 2000: 83); all but 20 of that country's 1200 primary schools and 13 out of the 206 secondary schools[2] are run by the various church denominations – so that the formal system clearly includes voluntary schools. In Mali, community schools almost outnumber state schools (for Lesotho, see Sekoati & Sloper 1997). In Cambodia, 60% of schools are community schools, in Tanzania 43%, in Togo 19% are 'clandestine' schools, in Malawi 20% of schools are 'unassisted', and in Zambia some 200 new community schools have been established since the late 1980s (see Bray 1999). In Senegal, ACAPES schools for drop-outs, using volunteer teachers, pursue their own path ("un autre regard", ACAPES). Throughout the world there are "parallel tracks to educational outcomes" (Serpell 1999: 130-131).In this situation, where do the boundaries of formal education stand? We see the problem most clearly when we read that indigenous education can be called formal education because it "takes place in organized groups in fixed and secluded places under the guidance of acceptable instructors" (in which case many NFE programmes are formal), or when bush schools and even secret societies are called "formal learning situations with a course of study to be followed systematically over a period of time", but when on the other hand 'Training of Trainers for Rural Areas' can be called NFE (Bockarie 1997: 104-105, 109).

And beyond school, the diversity of educational programmes, vocational, continuing, adult, distance education, makes a definition of formal which is confined to schooling no longer acceptable. Many national adult education programmes appear to be within national systems of education. The Indian National Literacy Mission with its Community Education Centres, the South African Adult Basic Education and

---

[2] Latest figures available.

Training Programme with its highly trained and certificated instructors have all the appearance of being formal education. There are increasing numbers of continuing professional development programmes inside or outside of educational institutions (Bond 1998: 213-223). "What about evening classes ... held in schools and taught regularly and leading to a certificate – are they formal or non-formal?" (Lauglo pers comm.). Are distance/open and other learning programmes offered by the increasing number of Open Universities formal or non-formal (Hoppers 2000b; Garrido 1992; Lynch et al. 1997: xi)? When we see churches and museums and other bodies now providing what would appear to be formal education, when for example, in the UK, the Victoria and Albert Museum runs a degree in design and Kew Gardens mounts a degree in horticulture, when companies and health services run 'universities', when a state-sponsored University for Industry is created, the difficulty of identifying any educational activity as 'formal' or 'non-formal' must be acknowledged. This is more than simply recognising that "Some educational activities may straddle formal and non-formal modes of delivery" (Lynch et al. 1997: xi). Rather the 'mainstream' (to use a different discourse) is changing into multiple forms.

So that existing definitions of 'formal' can no longer be applied universally. For example, when the World Bank says that "Formal education consists of primary and secondary schools that focus on basic general skills, which are language, science and mathematics, and communications ... and ... the development of attitudes for the work-place" (World Bank 1995: xi cited in Carr-Hill et al. 2001: 341), such a definition will apply to many local community (non-formal) schools. Thus, Non-formal Education cannot any longer be identified with any certainty. 'Outside of formal' no longer works as the sole reason for distinguishing one group of highly divergent educational programmes from another. "To define NFE as a residual category relative to whatever in a particular country fits into the mainstream institutionalized system ... is not a sustainable definition of anything that is to have international currency" (Lauglo pers comm..). When Carron and Carr-Hill (1991: 20) describe NFE as "a wide variety of activities which at one extreme differ very little from what is going on in the traditional school system and which at the other extreme are close to informal learning practices", we are forced to ask what there is which binds this wide variety of activities together, what it is that enables all of them to be labelled 'non-formal'. Why construct them as a unity when they differ so markedly from each other? What really is there in common between a BRAC or Mali community primary school and a pre-natal clinic-based course on parenting and nutrition? or between a distance learning course leading to a degree and an agricultural extension Farmers' Training Day? Just as formal education can no longer be easily identified, so too NFE is not and never has been a unity. The case studies show this clearly.

In addition, the language used tends to universalise both categories. It hides the fact that both sectors are now contextualised and contingent as well as being contested. The NFE discourse helps its users to feel that NFE and formal schooling represent two standardised and relatively unchanging educational sectors. It hides the fact that both sectors are not only culturally different in different contexts; they are not fixed entities but always changing, especially under the pressures of globalisation and the post-welfare society.

NFE as a tool of planning

Imposed characteristics: And, it is often argued, the discourse no longer 'works' as a tool for planning new educational interventions. For inevitably the terms 'formal' and 'non-formal' impose characteristics on both sectors. The "meaning of words is related to, and even dependent on, the meaning of other words, and the ways in which they are used" (Williams 1993: 345). The word 'formal' carries with it many implied features. A formal ceremony (e.g. the opening of a conference or seminar), formal dress, formal introductions, formal letters etc. are all characterised by the imposition of a set of more or less impersonal rules, established, customary or traditional conventions, by a sense of control lying outside of the immediate situation, by a loss of equality between the participants, a need to conform to someone else's decisions about what is said and who should say it, how to speak or write, what to wear. Such meanings are highly context-dependent, they are not universal. In other contexts, the word 'formal' will bring with it different characteristics in different contexts – but it will certainly bring *some* implied characteristics. And the use of the term 'non-formal' rather than 'informal' (which is its normal English antonym) also creates expectations, imposes a set of context-dependent characteristics. 'Non-formal' tends to imply that it is 'not-formal'. It takes away, it does not add; it does not imply the positive values of informality but rather the absence of formality, the opposite of formality, however that is described in different cultural contexts. So that when planning NFE programmes, we feel obliged to build into them some 'absence-of-formality' elements, the removal of formal features.

The argument then is that the NFE discourse does not describe reality adequately. Like other simplistic language, it over-simplifies "highly complicated social relations ... [which] conceal inequalities" (Cooke & Kothari 2001: 152). It creates a non-existent dichotomy in education; it artificially unifies disparate kinds of educational provision and hides the changes within each sector; it privileges one form of education over the other; and it imposes constraints onto the kind of programmes being developed.

All this raises the question of why the language of NFE persists and even indeed shows signs of increasing in the last few years. It has already been shown to be inadequate, so that it was largely abandoned in the mid-1980s. Can it now be finally left to one side and another discourse be used instead? Would we lose much if we abandoned the formal-NFE construction?

OTHER POSSIBLE CONSTRUCTS

As we have already noticed, many bodies have largely abandoned it, as their reports show. The use of terms such as non-formal learning (e.g. Bjornavold 2000: 29 – "learning that takes place outside formal education and training institutions") or 'non-formal institutions' or 'learning in non-formal organisations and non-formal settings' reveals discontent with non-formal *education*, or at least a sense of disassociation from the earlier discussion, even when it maintains the dichotomy: "Nonformal Learning is often defined by activities outside the formal learning setting, characterized by voluntary as opposed to mandatory participation" (Crane et al. 1994; see Heimlich et al. 1996). Equally 'informal education' is on occasion used deliberately to avoid the term 'non-formal' (Jeffs & Smith 1990; Richardson & Wolfe 2001).

The first question of course is whether it is possible to construct the world in different terms from that of formal and non-formal education. There are and always have been alternative ways of constructing society and education. The world abounds with discourses relating to education in society. The field of education, like development, is incrementalist; new paradigms and discourses are added but old ones are rarely completely abandoned. It is not my intention here to analyse all of these alternative discourses but simply to point out that we can construct education in other ways if we so wish. Discourse is always a matter of choice.

Education, non-education and learning

Discourses, as we have seen, construct the world and give us a handle by which to change that world. There is a common agreement that the world can be constructed in such a way that an activity called 'education' can be separated out from all the other social activities which people engage in. But this will of course depend on how the word 'education' is defined. When ADEA proposes that "Education is no longer the exclusive preserve of the state. ... although the state still has to take political responsibility for it" (ADEA Publ.), what does the word 'education' mean here – a process, a set of activities and programmes, a system or what?

It would seem that a construct of a discrete set of activities labelled 'education' is not helpful in some societies. They have learning processes and even some learning programmes (initiations; apprenticeship-like relationships; religious instruction programmes etc.) but do not see these as 'education' (Bockarie 1997; Aikman 1999). We can only define such activities as education if we construct 'education' as *process* – that is, as any activity *designed* to assist and direct learning. And as has been pointed out, this may be too wide for some people, for it will extend 'education' into the field of youth work, community work, social work and probation, addiction treatment, crime prevention, health and safety promotion, the media and even advertising – all of which can be seen to seek to promote learning. At what point do we cut 'education' off from other planned and intentional learning activities? It is this difficulty which has caused many recent writers to abandon the term 'education' completely in favour of 'learning'.

But as we have already seen (pp.73-74), there is a distinction to be drawn between the natural processes of learning in which we all engage all the time and those planned and purposeful processes which society puts in place to help people to learn and which can usefully be called 'education' (Wilson 1979). Such processes and the structures in which they are framed will of course vary from society to society; nevertheless, however we answer the question, 'education' can be distinguished at one end from unassisted learning and at the other end from other forms of activity such as social work, community action, sports activities and other similar activities, even though these contain much learning in them. Education consists of "planned processes of learning undertaken by intent", activities where the primary focus is learning and the criteria of achievement will be learning (Rogers 2003).

Dividing up the cake: different kinds of education

But once identified in any particular cultural setting, we are faced with the issue of how to divide up that set of activities which may be called 'education'? Is the distinction between formal and non-formal the best way of distinguishing between the various kinds of planned processes of learning which exist in different societies?

Writers and planners everywhere have found it useful and indeed at times necessary to identify different types of education, using different terms and different categories for such distinctions. We can think of adult education, experiential education, popular education, community education, continuing education, distance education, recurrent education as some of the terms used. All of these are constructs, practices which we categorise in order to manage the world which we inhabit. They are distinctions which people use to separate certain kinds of educational activities from others. It is significant that these do not in general have the same polarity which formal and non-formal education possesses. We don't for instance speak of non-distance education, non-adult education, non-popular education, non-community education etc., but at the same time we recognise that not all education is distance education, adult education, popular education or community education. Indeed, the very label is devised to separate one kind of education from another.

Four main kinds of such distinctions within 'education' can be identified.

a) Some people see education in terms of **dichotomies**, fixed and exclusive categories such as child-adult, andragogy versus pedagogy etc. (Knowles 1970). Such dichotomies are comprehensive, exclusive and often unequal in value. Education is either domesticating or it is liberating, reproductive or transformative, argued Freire (1972) – it cannot be both and it cannot be anything else. There is education which is aimed at individual growth as against education which is aimed at collective/social goals, education which is based on the wants of the participants (the felt needs) set against education based on needs as identified by others. There is the dichotomy of state education and NGO education (Lynch et al. 1997). There is vocational or non-vocational education, practical or theoretical education. There is voluntary or compulsory education. There is certificated and non-certificated education, education and training, education which widens choice and education which narrows choice. There is education which is top-down and education that is bottom-up in terms of whose agenda predominates. There is education which is based on a constructivist 'creation of knowledge' approach as opposed to education which is based on a 'transfer of knowledge' approach. There is education with pre-set objectives contrasted with open-ended education with unpredicted outcomes. There is basic and post-basic education, graded and multi-grade education. All these and other dichotomous constructs have been used when discussing those activities we call 'education'.

b) On the other hand, several of the above have been interpreted not in terms of exclusive categories, but as **polarities**, opposite ends of a continuum. A planned learning opportunity may not be either reproductive *or* transformative, but it may possess elements of both, so that it can be classified as being *more* reproductive or *more* transformative. Each educational encounter may contain elements of both ends in different proportions. Education then can lie along a continuum between two poles. The individual and collective (whether social collective or organisational collective) goals of education can be seen as polarities; so too can the socialisation and individuation approaches to education (whether education is *primarily* for individual free growth or for socialisation into a common culture), or the transfer of knowledge versus the development of critical thinking, or the dependency versus independence outcomes of education. Education can be constructed in terms of provider or participant control as lying somewhere along that continuum rather than being an either-or. It can lie somewhere between being hierarchical or democratic. These are not exclusive categories but the way they are combined constitutes the uniqueness of each teaching-learning situation.

c) Some writers have combined more than one set of polarities into **matrices**. We have noticed above (p.126) one instance of this (expanded into a three-dimensional matrix) in relation to formal and non-formal education. There are others: for example, provider-control and participant-control along one dimension, and domesticating and liberating along another dimension. There are many such possible combinations. To give one such example: Wilber sees education as aimed primarily at individual growth *or* primarily at collective/community development along one dimension, and as being primarily 'internal' (personal) *or* primarily 'external' (interrelational) along the other dimension (Wilber 1996).

d) These three analyses rely on dualism of some sort. But others resort to Aristotle's principle of **multiple categories** rather than Newton's law of opposites, dualism. Thus education can be divided into stages – pre-primary (with various names such as early childhood education and development), primary, secondary, tertiary and adult, for example. Some divide education on the basis of its content into basic, vocational and academic, or basic, work-related and continuing; some into child, adolescent and adult. In curriculum terms, education has been seen to consist of either a schooling model (academic in content and approach), a 'credentialist' model (mainly vocational leading to qualifications), an 'access' model (individualised de-institutionalised programmes), or a 'connective' model which combines different elements (Young 1998).

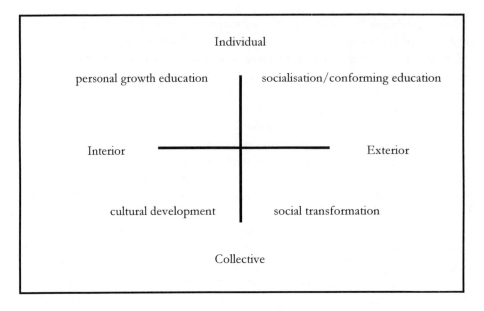

This is not intended to be a full discussion of a large and complicated area of study. All I wish to do is to demonstrate that there are alternative discourses which can achieve the same ends as the formal and non-formal education discourse. I do not assert the validity of any of these constructs, nor the primacy of any one over the others. I simply suggest that there are other ways of dividing the cake than simply formal and non-formal. The NFE discourse is not essential – which reinforces the question as to why the language of formal and non-formal which has so many disadvantages persists and shows signs of growing again. It is clear from our case studies that the construct cannot reflect the diversity of educational provision. There are competing discourses and changed meanings. The changed world of the first decade of the twenty-first century seems to call for different language. The concepts of non-formal education and the language in which the concept has been clothed came from a world of certainty and inclusiveness; everything was either inside or outside of formal education. Today, there is much less certainty; dichotomies and dualism are no longer acceptable to many educationalists.

Diversity in education

Many people feel that a discourse reflecting diversity rather than dichotomy appears to fit reality better. For them, the most striking feature of education today is the increasing number of forms which it takes (see IIEP 1989).

Diversity in education is of course not a new phenomenon. Edmund Husserl, the German philosopher, contrasting his own education with that received by many of his contemporaries, wrote: "I received the education of a German, not that of a Chinaman. But my education was also that of the inhabitant of a small town, with a home background, attending a school for children of the lower middle class, not that of a country landowner's son educated at a military college" (Bourdieu 1971: 182).[3] We have already noticed signs of increasing diversity within schooling – diversity of providers, diversity of curricula, and the beginnings of diversity of qualifications.

In part, this is the consequence of the growing "radical alterity", seeking alternatives to formal schooling (Paulston 1996) but couching the search in a very different discourse from that of NFE. For example, in Lima, Peru, a group of teachers dissatisfied with the state system set up their own schools; these taught to the formal school qualification (Wilson 1989: 9-10). In part, however, it is the result of the commodification of education, including the increased control of some participants who use their purchasing power to influence educational provision. The growing commercialisation of formal schooling in Western societies is well known. But the same increase in diversity for much the same reasons is true of those countries frequently categorised as 'developing'. In some parts of the developing world, government schools are closing because of the growth of the private sector (e.g. English medium schools in Rajasthan). Commercial, NGO and community schools are now in the process of making their own provision. "In Nepal, 18 percent of the secondary schools existing in 1991 were operated by communities with little or no support from the government ... in 1995 Bhutan had 102 lower primary community schools compared with 143 government full primary schools and just 19 government junior high schools" (Bray 1999: 185). "There are two main types of secondary schools in Cameroon, government and private. Private secondary schools are further categorised into mission schools, which are government-aided, and lay private schools which receive no financial assistance from the government" (Tembon 1999: 212). In Uganda, different NGOs provide different forms of schooling, so that PLAN International schools are different from Action Aid schools, sometimes leading to different forms of certification. In Mali, as we have seen, Save the Children (US) community schools were originally set up in opposition to state schools, while World Education community schools were closely linked to government schools. There is a recognition that "just as many businesses are having to deal with the fact that standardised mass production is becoming uncompetitive and needs to be replaced ..., [so] educational planners will need to move the education system from uniformity to diversity and from standardised treatment to flexible responses to a variety of learning needs" (Verspoor 1992: 233-244). Equally, employers, governments and higher education establishments are having to come to terms with an increasing number of different forms of qualifications

The discourse of difference thus seems to fit the situation today better. A discourse of diversity cannot see education as divided between only two sectors, formal and non-formal. Rather, it recognises a multitude of varieties of education, a plurality of educations, multiple forms of assessment – not just equivalency but alternatives. Such a discourse will seek to understand their differences rather than their unities (see Crossley & Watson 2003 for a similar argument in the context of

---

[3] I owe this reference to Professor John Morgan of Nottingham University.

comparative education). It is interesting that the ADEA NFE Working Group tried to have both diversity and NFE discourses at the same time; as we have seen, its workshop in 1999 was entitled 'Diversifying Education Delivery Systems: reviving discourse on the Formal/Non-formal Interface'; and much of the report and background papers was devoted to issues of diversity rather than the formal/non-formal divide.

Governments are not sure whether to encourage diversity or discourage and try to limit it. "While it would be very expensive to have education subsystems that provide relevant education for different categories of people, [such diversity] may prevent parents and communities from withdrawing their children from formal schooling when they think the school is alienating the children from their culture as occurs among some pastoral communities in Kenya" (Nyamu 1999: 311). In the planning of educational activities, the issue of whether one seeks to impose uniformity or seeks to develop different educations for different situations is now being faced on a regular basis. There are however societies where increasing diversity is not encouraged, where monolithic or dualistic systems still continue to be built, where common curricula are imposed on all participants, where 'Education for All' means 'the Same Education for All'. It is perhaps in these societies that the discourse of NFE is most strongly kept alive.

THE VALUE OF THE NFE DISCOURSE

Replacing the discourse of NFE with one of diversity would mark the major shift of viewpoint and programmes which has taken place. But if we abandon the language of NFE for one of diversity, we need to ask whether anything of value would be lost. Some people see value still in the term 'non-formal' and try to retain it even when reflecting on the diversity of educational provision: thus in Argentina (Gallart 1989; see Carr-Hill et al. 2001: 343), NFE (taken as adult education without qualifications) is distinguished from 'para-formal' education (adult education leading to qualifications), and in Haiti, "a training programme to prepare professional artisans is considered vocational and technical, while an income generating project in which rural people learn a craft is considered NFE" (USAID 1987: 111 cited in Carr-Hill 2001: 343).

The language of NFE is thus still considered helpful and is being retained. What then are the key values seen to reside in the NFE discourse?

NFE challenges the educational world in two main respects. It is of course not alone in this – but its combination of challenges is unique.

First, the NFE discourse, like the lifelong education discourse, points to educational opportunities "outside of the educational silo" (Lit. Africa 2001: 13). And that is important, for the general move of international aid from programmes to sector assistance (King & Buchert 1999: 21-23) could lead once again to such activities being marginalised in the eyes of governments and donors as Ministries of Education and their staff at various levels, central, regional and local, are given greater prominence. The concept of NFE quite specifically reminds us that there is more to education than the programmes which Ministries of Education mount (livelihoods is a good example of this, for it is often omitted from definitions of education but is included in NFE; on the other hand, HIV/AIDS is now regularly included in education programmes). What the term NFE has to offer is to direct attention to a whole sector of educational activities which lie outside of the educational sector as defined by government and their donors; whereas the diversity discourse on the whole tends to concentrate on the diversity *within* that defined educational sector.

But the more important loss would seem to be the 'non-formality' concept, flexibility. Flexibility has been at the heart of NFE from the start of the debate. Coombs (Coombs et al. 1973) pointed to the flexibility which he suggested gave NFE the ability to make swift responses to new needs (an Ideological stance, for there are few signs that NFE has in fact made such swift responses). Hamadache (1994: 4132-4134) repeats that NFE is "creative, innovative, able to respond quickly to new and changing needs". UNICEF along with many others has characterised NFE as "an approach to education ... leading to greater flexibility in organisation and management of educational programmes with a decentralized structure and less authoritarian management style" – again an Ideological construct (UNICEF 1993a: 1, 12-13). Hoppers more recently asserts that flexibility is one of the key features of NFE: "formal education remains largely the responsibility of the state ... [NFE consists of] spaces ... left for communities, however defined, and local authorities to develop their own visions about basic education and negotiate adjustments to mainstream provisions or push for modalities for learning that take cognisance of specific circumstances and needs" (Hoppers 1999: 22; see Hoppers 2000a: 11-12; see also Visser 2001: 447). The loss of the NFE discourse may lead to the loss of any sense of the need for innovative and flexible modes of education – the ability to employ non-professional or para-professional teachers alongside the existing formal teaching profession; the need to adapt the curriculum or to develop new curricula to meet local needs (Morphet 1986; Kishan 1998); the need to adopt different assessment processes in certain situations; the need to adopt locally determined timetables rather than a national uniform programme. In this sense, the prescriptive elements in the discourse of NFE encourage new developments in the way the diversity discourses do not.

It is this reforming agenda which the NFE discourse keeps alive and which would be lost if the NFE discourse were to be abandoned, for the diversity discourses (especially lifelong learning) by definition have no agenda, they lack any general principles upon which diversity can be built, they describe more than they prescribe. As Hoppers suggests, a revised NFE "could identify an agenda for a degree of deformalisation of schooling or, within our new systems perspective, a degree of 'loosening up the straitjacket'" (Hoppers 2000b: 19).

FLEXIBLE SCHOOLING

If then NFE programmes were to become formal, absorbed into the 'educational mainstream', as has been suggested by ADEA, ACCESS and others, they would lose a large measure of their flexibility; they would become more standardised, controlled from the centre. On the other hand, if formal educational programmes were to become non-formalised, they would be characterised by increased flexibility and some measure of local control. The difference between the formal and the non-formal in education today is seen as being between standardised and the non-standardised schooling. There is of course some hesitation and even fear of flexible schooling as leading to lower standards, but on the whole many, perhaps most, 'developing' countries have found the need to introduce forms of flexible schooling.

This flexibility may be seen in positive terms – as 'better' than the 'real' thing or at least more appropriate to a particular group or groups (rural populations, girls, the very young, pastoralists etc.). Or it can be seen more negatively – as temporary, or as an adjustment to formal schooling, a regrettable necessity caused by factors which will eventually disappear. It would seem that this view is more usual than the former, for attitudes towards formal schooling have changed significantly since the hostility of the 1970s. Even adult literacy is sometimes regarded as an unfortunate stopgap to meet a need which future generations may not require as primary education becomes more fully effective. Nevertheless flexible NFE is seen as a valuable tool in the armoury of educational providers in many countries.

There has certainly been a remarkable spread of flexible forms of schooling. The reason for this seems to be two-fold. On the one hand, there is a downward pressure. Governments and international aid agencies are seeking decentralisation of education under the force of Structural Adjustment procedures. The desire to co-opt local communities into sharing the costs and responsibilities of school provision is leading to increased recognition of the necessity for some limited local variation in patterns of schooling. On the other hand, there is upward pressure, a demand for more localised schooling adapted to the needs of particular groups of students. Such flexible schooling is frequently called Non-formal Education.

We can thus see that much of NFE today consists of 'non-formal schooling'.[4] For most educational planners today, the term means *alternative and more flexible forms of schools*, the increasing kinds of programmes that the state and other bodies create in their search for an expanded provision of educational/learning opportunities. The reason why the language of NFE persists and is growing is that there is no other term which adequately represents this flexibility element in so much of education today.

---

[4] This term is beginning to appear in the literature; see e.g. a planning document by CIDA 2001. 'Non-formal schools' is much more common. Some see the term as oxymoronic.

Flexible schooling and participatory education

Many educational programmes which call themselves NFE, especially the non-formal primary education movement, suggest that the flexibility which they show is due to the fact that they are 'participatory'. The participants or their parents (they allege) control the local schooling; management is decentralised. Village Education Committees are set up which frequently determine a range of matters relating to the non-formal school programme. This is an issue which was raised early in the debate (e.g. see Pigozzi 1982 for references). Evans put it most clearly when he asked of any educational programme whether "the primary locus of initiative, problem definition, solution generation, and administrative control is at the center in a government ministry or a national organization. Or is the locus primarily with the users in the village, with the learning group, with a league of *campesino* leaders, or other local organization?" (Evans 1976: 306-307; but see Evans 1981a which argues strongly for central planning, taking into account local views).

PARTICIPATION IN EDUCATION

Here we need to examine briefly the concept of participation in education. Participation in education is seen to be a 'good thing': "It is now coming to be widely accepted that the best and most secure learning occurs when students are centrally involved in controlling, directing and monitoring their own learning progress" (Aspin et al. 2001: 21; see Campbell & Burnaby 2001).

The discussion of participation in education must take place within a context of participation for development. Three main approaches may be distinguished.

a) The first is *participation as presence*. In developmental terms, this means persuading different groups to 'take up' the inputs offered to them (health or farming or income generation etc.). In educational terms, studies of 'participation' almost always concentrate on access to education by specific groups such as girl children, street children and other child workers, women (or sometimes men) in adult literacy programmes, tribal groups, nomads and other sections of national populations. Such 'target groups' need to be motivated to attend classes; 'how to motivate the learners', how to ensure their participation (attendance), how to stop their 'drop-out' are among the key elements in the training of development change agents within this construct. Participation will be achieved through persuasion. This has sometimes been called 'participation for incorporation' (Cooke & Kothari 2001: 182).

b) A second approach speaks of *participation as activity*. In development contexts, PAR (participatory action research), PRA (participatory rural/rapid appraisal) and their variants mean persuading the local community to join in the already determined activities of the project – for example, to supply answers to questions which outsiders have posed, such as health or agricultural practices and the like. Consultation is the keyword. But as Youngman reminded us, such "participation in practice meant either information-giving or non-binding consultation. The state [and other development agencies] thus gave the impression of seeking popular involvement while pursuing an essentially top-down and paternalistic approach to development and democracy. Forms of participation were therefore implemented to extend the legitimacy of the state and its policies, while leaving the power in the hands of the dominant classes and social groups". Botswana is not the only country where "consultation is a means whereby [the] political elite aggressively manipulates public thinking" (Youngman 2000: 227, 228, 231). The purpose behind this approach to participation is of course altruistic but at the same time coercive. Such "programmes ostensibly sought to mobilise African participation in local decision-making and development projects, but their fundamental purpose was to contain popular dissatisfaction and reinforce the legitimacy of colonial rule" (Youngman 2000: 216). But asking the local participants to help by "providing ... input in the form of information during a survey ... [and by] carrying out orders in implementing an activity" has been likened to "the bullocks' participation in ploughing" (BOBP 1987; see also Fernandes 1980: xxix; Cooke & Kothari 2001).

In educational terms, such participation means encouraging (persuading) those present in the classroom to become active learners, to join in the pre-set activities of the class. Rather than being passive recipients of knowledge imparted by the teacher/facilitator, participation in interactive learner-centred methods such as play, ice-breakers, simulation, discussion, group work, and other forms of activities chosen by the teacher or provider will, it is urged, lead to more effective learning. This is what Evans calls the *dialogic* approach to education rather than the *didactic* approach (Evans 1976: 307). But it is in fact 'directive participation'. The teacher/agency invites the participants to participate in learning activities which others have already devised, even when the participants do not wish to do so. This approach legitimises the control of the teaching-learning agency while preserving a facade of popular participation.

c) The third approach is *participation as control*, encouraging (not just 'allowing') the participants to take control, to take responsibility: it is the way "governance structures ... are made more transparent, open and inclusive" (Tight 2003: 86). The participants share in the decision-making and implementation and evaluation, so that the programme no longer reflects the concerns and wisdom of the providers alone but reflects the concerns and wisdom of all its stakeholders. The argument here is that any development activity will be unsustainable unless the people own it for themselves; it is *their* programme with aid agency support rather than an outsider's programme in which local communities have been invited to participate. Ownership of the programme does not belong to the state or outside development agency; it does not belong to the field workers; it is fully and equally shared between the local groups and other development agencies (Moleko & Betz 1995). Thus participation no longer means local groups or communities joining in someone else's development pro-gramme, or in someone else's activities, even someone else's revolution; rather it is a matter of the outside development workers joining in the people's programmes, implementing their decisions, however contradictory those decisions may seem on a larger stage.

This is participation for self-determination. For it is argued that development cannot lead in the end to the *goal* of self-reliance, independence, to empowerment, unless self-reliance, independence, empowerment are encouraged *within* the process of development. Full participation means enabling the participants to have control of the process as well as the goals, to be the decision-makers, to be self-implementing and self-evaluating.

Perhaps the most important outcome of this approach is that there can be no universal solutions, no universal approaches to development. Each group will decide, not only the goals but also the processes of achieving those goals for themselves. There will then be highly specific, localised development activities, often apparently contradictory. Aikman (1995) points out in her study of tribal groups in the Peruvian Amazon basin how two neighbouring and culturally similar villages chose opposite approaches to education in their own contexts, one using their indigenous language for primary education, the other using the standardised national language. Such decisions, she argued, made sense in terms of these local communities, for they were brought about by the different experiences of these two groups of people. One-answer development (or education) cannot fit the diversity of the world.

Fully participatory education then is not simply access, encouraging young people or adults to join in set programmes of education by adapting these programmes to local conditions. Nor is it simply learner-centred approaches, asking the student-learners to join in activities which the teacher has already chosen. Rather it is helping individuals and groups to learn *what* they want to learn, *when* they want to learn it, and *for as long* as they want to learn it. It is helping them to meet their individualised learning needs to fulfil their own life tasks as defined by themselves within their own particular context.

Participatory education and non-formal education:

The example drawn from Peru reminds us however that participatory education is not always the same as 'non-formal' education. For experience in the field suggests that some participants (parents or adult participants), when asked to decide the form of education they wish to participate in, will choose formal approaches rather than non-formal approaches. Many feel that they have missed out on formal schooling and that a second chance should as closely as possible approximate to such formal schooling.[5]

---

[5] This has not been tested so far as I know in empirical and documented research, but all field workers I have spoken with and my own observations suggest that many adult learners feel this. Experience also suggests however that after a time such groups of adults find themselves challenging the very formality they desired; they test that which they are being taught against their own experience; and they soon come to feel that their personal experience needs to be

Really participatory education can be formal as well as non-formal. Participatory education is not necessarily the same as non-formal education.

These three approaches to participation correlate in some way with the three major paradigms we saw above, the deficit paradigm (participation as presence), the disadvantage paradigm (participation as consultation) and the diversity paradigm (participation as control).

Limited participation in NFE: On this analysis of participation in education, it is clear that in most forms of non-formal flexible schooling, we are not dealing with fully participatory education. Flexibility in almost every case is severely limited, and the areas and levels of local control are determined by the providers, not the participants. The local community may be asked to choose the *location* of the school or learning programme; indeed, they may be called upon to build the school or community learning centre. The school *calendar* (especially the holidays) and the school *hours* are often determined locally – although both of these often result in a timetable closely akin to those in the formal sector, they show remarkable similarity throughout the region where the non-formal school programme is operating. The local community may be involved in the recruitment and selection of the para-professional *teacher* within the criteria established by the agency, and sometimes the local community pays the teachers, although more often they are paid by the agency.

But local control does not extend to *educational* matters: "Efforts to adapt the ... teaching-learning strategies ... appear to take their cues from the circumstances of the learners [rather] than from their specific learning needs. Thus they tend to deal more with organisational arrangements than pedagogical content and styles" (Hoppers 1999: 21). It does include the curriculum – this is determined by the agency. And although the agency programme may use an adapted form of the national formal school curriculum or one specially written for the non-formal schooling programme, it is rarely adjusted to different local communities. In Mali, in Bangladesh, in Pakistan, in Egypt, as elsewhere, one non-formal school's teaching programme looks remarkably similar to those of other non-formal schools in the same programme. The same subjects, the same textbooks are used, the same time is spent on each subject area, irrespective of any demands of the local community. Local content and/or materials may be added to the core content and materials, but the core remains the same. The length of time of the educational programme (the number of hours, months or years) is not within the control of the participants. The timing and the modes of evaluation too are not subject to local decision-making. Participation in NFE schools is carefully restricted by the providers to logistical matters; these programmes can be described as 'participatory' in only very limited terms.

The result is that, with this limited measure of local determination, it is noticeable how similar each of these community schools are to each other. All BRAC NFPE schools look alike. Proshika non-formal primary schools in Bangladesh, the

---

taken seriously as part of the learning process. This is a complicated field which needs much more research.

ACCESS schools in a number of African and Asian countries, the Save the Children (US) Mali community schools, and the Philippine accreditation and equivalency programme all have as much internal congruity as do their respective state primary schools. To give but one example, in each of the non-formal school programmes examined, the Village Education Committee or its equivalent is formed on the basis of a constitution and a set pattern of membership which is centrally, not locally, determined, whatever local conditions may apply. In the BRAC schools, for instance, every VEC must have seven members with some ex officio members, irrespective of local culture. It is odd that there is more real flexibility (local individualism) in the Lok Jumbish programme in India which is a programme for non-formalising formal schools than there is in the BRAC-type schools. What we are dealing with here is really an alternative school system with different criteria for the teachers, a different but uniform management system involving the local community, a slightly different curriculum which however is used universally in all of the schools in that programme, more informal premises, and in a few cases some adaptation of forms of assessment (again universally applied to all schools within the particular programme concerned) – but there is very little real local control. Large scale national programmes such as those of Thailand and the Philippines and other countries continue to use the designation 'non-formal' for what amounts to a 'one-size-fits-all' programme. NFE in these cases means a different variety of uniform schooling.

It would seem then that we have three main approaches to education – formal schooling in which the participants have very little say on any matters, flexible schooling in which the participants have a limited range of decision-making, and participatory education in which the participants determine the contents and time scale of the learning programme as well as the logistics. And it would seem that the term NFE has moved from being most closely related to participatory education to referring to flexible schooling (limited participatory education). These are not of course separate categories of education. Rather they lie along a continuum from extreme formality to extreme participation with flexible schooling forming a hybridity.

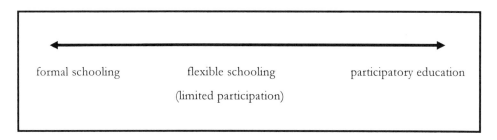

formal schooling   flexible schooling   participatory education
                          (limited participation)

USING ORGANISATIONAL THEORY/GROUP DYNAMICS

In attempting to describe this continuum, I have found the language used in organisational theory and group dynamics helpful.

Although springing from different disciplinary backgrounds, the one from sociology and the other from social psychology, both organisational theory and group dynamics point to the wide variety of social entities which exist and refer to organisations and groups in terms of being 'formal' and 'informal' (Argyris & Schon 1996; Handy 1985; Clark 2000; Forsyth 1999; Brown 2000). At one extreme, some organisations are seen as 'formal' in that they do not change or change very little when individuals join them. Such organisations are not influenced or are influenced very little by the numbers and nature of those who participate in them. The army, the police and most bureaucracies are examples of formality in this respect; they continue to function in their own autonomous ways irrespective of whether any particular individual is a member or not; different units have a high degree of universality. The participant is expected to adapt him/herself to the needs of that organisation. Such a formal organisation/group is characterised by the fixed roles of its members.

At the other extreme lie 'informal' groups – groups which are substantially altered by the individual participants (Tajfel 1981; Jaques 1991; Imel 1996). A drama society is an example of this kind of group. The plays which such a group can produce depend to a large extent on the persons it recruits, and the departure of a single member can make major changes to the activities of the group essential. Sports teams and voluntary committees are examples of organisations or groups which display varying degrees of informality; they are influenced to a greater or lesser degree and in different ways by the persons who enrol in them (Blumberg & Golembiewski 1976; Levine & Moreland 1990; Smith 1980; Cartwright & Zander 1968; Miller et al. 1994; Zander 1994).

One of the key elements in this is the roles which participants are expected to play, the identities they adopt for this purpose (Cragan & Wright 1991; Rogers 2003: 49-63). In some, the roles are fixed, in others they change. Formal organisations tend to consist of those in which the roles open to the participants are limited and firmly set; in informal groups, on the other hand, roles and identities change according to the kind of activities their members are engaged in.

Most groups of course lie between these two extremes, hybrids of formality and informality. It is a matter of degree – how much adaptation *and in what areas* such adaptation is allowed or encouraged to meet the special contributions of its members. And indeed, group dynamics suggest that most groups are not static in this respect. Some informal groups adopt for a time a good deal of formality in order to achieve their goals; roles become fixed for a time and as such are accepted by all members of the group. Similarly, a formal organisation may contain or adopt from time to time more informal structures and processes in order to achieve specific tasks. Roles will change temporarily – but always within limits which are normally known to all its members. Groups and organisations are formed by rules and roles.

Such a model can be applied to educational activities and groups. Formal and non-formal education can be seen in this light. Educational groups can be seen as either more formal in the sense that they do not change when different participants engage in the activity. A university course in chemistry is unlikely to change according to the number and nature of the students who join it; its contents and processes will be decontextualised. Such formal groups can of course still be flexible, changed *by the providers* in order to ensure greater access of particular kinds of participants or to encourage individual and more effective learning activities. But control of both the extent and the nature of such changes still lies with the providers. Or educational groups can be seen as "more discrete and specific" (Grandstaff 1976: 303), more highly personalised, the learning programme being contextualised to meet the special needs of each group and even of each individual participant. An adult local history class is likely in large part to follow the particular interests of the individual members of that group rather than a pre-set course of study, and a women's assertiveness programme will clearly need to focus on the particular concerns of the participants, different in each group (for examples of such individualised learning activities, see Walters & Manicom 1996; Campbell & Burnaby 2001).

Most educational groups will lie somewhere between these two extremes. **Contextualisation** then seems to me to be the key to any future understanding of the terms formal and non-formal in education. Programmes can be identified as being either more towards the decontextualised end of the continuum or more towards the contextualised end of the continuum. Between these will lie programmes which are context sensitive (slightly adapted to the participants) and context adjusted (rather more fully adapted to the participants) rather than fully contextualised.[6]

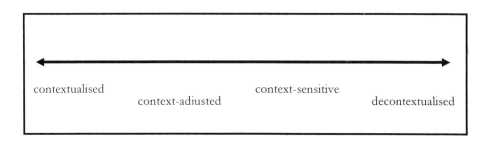

This is not of course a new concept. Paul Goodman in 1971 spoke about schools which teach 'alienated knowledge', knowledge which is divorced from both its origins and its applications (Goodman 1971). Among the many criticisms of formal schooling was the feeling that it "treats all pupils and geographic areas uniformly, on the fallacious assumption that their learning needs and general circumstances are basically similar" (Coombs 1976: 287-288). 'Localizing the school' would be to move it more towards the contextualised end of the spectrum (Schramm 1973: 259ff). And such a model has been related to NFE. LaBelle (1982: 159) suggested that any programme which is more closely adapted to a specific socio-economic, sex or ethno-religious

---

[6] Harvard (Harvard 1997), in a study of literacy programmes, suggested that the continuum might be marked by milestones such as highly contextualised, contextualised, context-adjusted, decontextualised and highly decontextualised.

group has more right to the title 'non-formal' than a standardised and generalised learning programme applied to all groups irrespective of their nature.

A POSSIBLE NEW CONSTRUCT

In contextualisation, we have then a possible paradigm which we can use as a tool for analysis and as a tool of planning educational encounters. It will draw upon the insights of the formal and non-formal discourses but is no longer bound by these discourses.

This paradigm would seem to be characterised by a continuum along which there lie at least three main points. All educational programmes can be constructed as being somewhere along this continuum marked by

- **formal education (de-contextualised education)** [7] – that is, schooling which is characterised by a high degree of standardisation, like formal groups. It is not adapted to the needs of the participants but the participants are called upon to adapt to it. The same learning programme is provided for all the members of the group
- **flexible schooling** – that is, standardised educational programmes adapted in limited ways to meet local needs. These are programmes which can be either context-sensitive or context-adjusted, altered to meet local conditions but still recognisably standardised
- **participatory education (contextualised)** – that is, programmes which are highly participatory, adapted to the needs of the particular set of participants in every respect – curriculum, teaching-learning materials, length of the programme, the timing and methods of evaluation etc.. In these programmes, the participants learn what they want to learn, when they want to learn it, where they want to learn and in their own mode, and for as long as they want to learn it (Campbell & Burnaby 2001). The immediate participants help to construct the learning programme so that it meets their specific needs, desires, aspirations and intentions (Rogers 1992: 146-158), and the programme will change as those needs, desires, aspirations and intentions change. In fully participatory education, the final evaluation is made by the participants at a time which suits the participants and is framed in terms of the achievements of the participants in fulfilling their own intentions rather than fulfilling the standards set by the providing agency.

These are not three separate categories, of course. All programmes will lie somewhere along this continuum; and most programmes will change their position along the continuum as they progress. There will be times when even the most highly contextualised programme will become more formalised, requiring the participants to adapt to the discipline which most learning programmes call for. Equally, most forms of formal schooling will at times become flexible, calling upon the participants to work on their own projects, bring about their own learning. But the primary focus of

---

[7] As we have noticed, the term 'formal education' has an independent life apart from the NFE discourse, e.g. Husen 1979.

each programme will remain; most programmes will find themselves more closely towards the formal group (decontextualised) end or in the middle (flexible schooling, context-adjusted) or towards the non-formal, participatory end of the continuum, contextualised to a greater or lesser degree.

Non-formal education, flexible schooling and participatory education

At the moment, rather uncomfortably, the term 'non-formal education' covers *both* flexible schooling *and* fully participatory education.

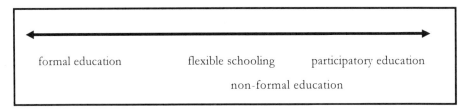

Our case studies have shown that some see NFE as diverse, contextualised, small-scale educational activities, centred on local specific problems determined by the participants rather than on a pre-set curriculum – in short, "aimed at different groups with different needs and requiring different approaches", very distinct from the decontextualised formal education which "is intended to meet the common needs of all children to acquire accredited basic skills" (Moulton 2000: 2). But it is also clear from our case studies that many programmes "intended to meet the *common* needs of all [the participants] to acquire accredited skills" are today being called NFE – such as the Mali community schools, the Philippines A and E Programme, the Thailand vocational training programme, the South African ABET programme and others.

In part decontextualisation is related to scaling up. TOSTAN and some of the case studies in Latin America started out very contextualised, specific to the local communities in which they commenced. But when they were 'scaled up', the extent of contextualisation declined; they became somewhat more 'formal' (de-contextualised). Most forms of flexible schooling such as BRAC and the Mali schools could be called 'context-adjusted'. Although different from the formal state schools, they are nevertheless still standardised programmes with limited logistical adaptation to local circumstances rather than being fully contextualised in the educational components. We do not find one BRAC school teaching a different course from that of another BRAC school in order to meet the needs of the local participants.

Such a wide variation under the one heading of NFE contrasted with formal education seems no longer acceptable: "It would be impossible, indeed pointless, to give this concept a single, universal definition, as what distinguishes NFE is the variety of forms it can take on in response to the different demands and needs of different individuals or groups" (Hamadache 1993: 113). Some distinction clearly needs to be drawn between those NFE programmes which are highly contextualised, small-scale and fully participatory, and those which take the form of flexible schooling. I argue that group dynamics provides us with a basis for making some distinctions within the whole field of education, not just within NFE.

Non-formal and informal education: Here we need to remind ourselves of the early use of the term 'informal education'; this can perhaps be more appropriately applied to those small-scale individualised learning programmes which are highly contextualised.

There is much to be said in favour of this. In the past, as we have seen, 'informal education' has been used to cover what most people today would call informal learning, that is the unstructured, incidental learning we all do when engaged in various tasks. This is what I have called elsewhere 'task-conscious learning' (Rogers 2003: 20-21) as distinct from 'learning-conscious learning'. But since as we have seen all education is "a set of guided experiences", pre-planned, "organized, systematic educational activity" (LaBelle 1986: 3-6), it is clear that 'informal learning' is not the same as 'informal education'. "On the whole, there has been no disagreement that it is appropriate to distinguish between informal learning and ... educational activities by the fact of organisation ... It makes sense to exclude casual learning which accompanies some other activity" (Carr-Hill et al. 2001: 332-333). I would suggest that we use the term 'informal learning' to cover this incidental learning; and that we use the term 'informal education' to cover all the many individualised contextualised learning programmes on a small scale which are created in a fully participatory way with different groups of learners.

Such a use of the term 'informal' for educational activities rings true with the group dynamics approach to formal and informal groups. Educational programmes which do not adapt themselves in any significant way to those who join (i.e. decontextualised) may be called 'formal'; those which do adapt themselves fully to those who join (i.e. contextualised) may be called 'informal'; hybrid programmes which adapt themselves in some respects but do not adapt themselves in other respects may be called 'non-formal'.

decontextualised	context-adjusted	contextualised
←		→
formal	non-formal	informal

Once again it is important to remember that these are not hard and fast categories – any particular educational encounter will involve movement along the continuum.

And movement *in both directions*. For both ends of the continuum will be valued, unlike the older discourse of NFE. Although NFE will retain its radical reform dimension urging formal education to become more non-formal, formal education too will be valued. Both are important. One programme in South Africa has identified the need for this approach: "We envisage a dual approach to education and training ... On the one hand, a range of context-specific courses offered to meet the needs prioritised by the [learners] ... On the other hand, an initiative to ensure access to more formal, decontextualised education for those who want it" (Breier et al. 1996: 232). However, rather than two separate kinds of provision as suggested here, perhaps all educational activities should aspire to have elements of both. Both decontextualised and contextualised education have their value; both are needed to ensure effective learning. The starting point, whether at the formal end or the participatory end of the continuum, can vary according to the needs of the participants and/or the providing agency, so long as there is movement towards the opposite end.

I therefore wish to suggest the following definitions:

- **formal education:** that education which is highly decontextualised, not adapted to the individual student participants
- **non-formal education:** that education which is partially de-contextualised and partially contextualised (flexible schooling)
- **informal education:** that education which is highly contextualised, individualised and small-scale (participatory education)

Such language, I suggest, provides us with a useful *tool of analysis* when regarding educational activities called formal or non-formal education. In analysing any educational programme, we can ask to what extent and *in what areas* (logistics or educational) the participants are able to influence the construction and implementation of the programme.

And it also provides us with a useful *tool of planning*. It enables us to devise and implement learning programmes which have different levels and different kinds of local or centralised control and which have built in mechanisms which encourage more and more participant participation as the programme progresses. Educational planners can draw up programmes which make it plain how far *and again in what areas* they are willing to agree that the participants can control the programme, both at the start and subsequently as the educational activity develops.

NON-FORMAL EDUCATION AND THE FUTURE

Books like this do not create discourses; discourses are created, adopted and used because it is in our interest to use them. So that it remains to be seen what the future holds for the term Non-formal Education. But some comments can be made.

It would seem that the *discourse* of NFE is dead. The term continues to be used within other discourses (especially lifelong learning/education) rather than as a discourse on its own. It still carries with it some of its earlier values – a sense of dualism in education, a sense of reform, a sense of greater flexibility; but it is no longer a discourse on its own. Its meaning has become obscure.

It seems to me that there are three possible futures. On the one hand, the term NFE may be abandoned altogether. In its place, the search for increasing clarity may lead to terms like 'flexible schooling' and 'participatory education' used to distinguish between the more fully contextualised learning programme and the context-adjusted schooling programmes, both of which will continue to grow. However, I do not think this is likely, for as we have seen the term NFE is valuable and valued.

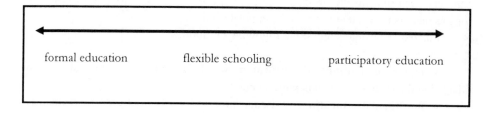

A second possibility is that the term NFE comes to be focused on the participatory end of the continuum and that many programmes currently labelled Non-formal will be seen for what they are, 'flexible schooling', partly but not fully non-formal. Again I think this is unlikely to happen, for the term NFE is too deeply rooted in the flexible schooling approach.

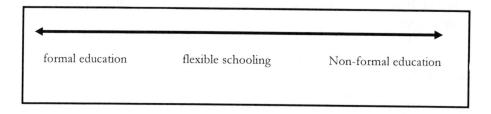

More likely is the possibility that the term will become restricted to the flexible schooling model which is where its main focus is today; and the term 'informal education' will be revived to cover the more individualised contextualised learning programmes.

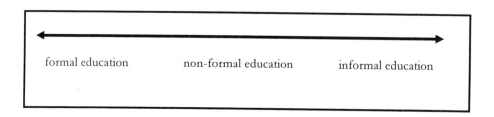

This at least will clear up the current confusion which the term NFE – which no-one understands – generates. We will then have three terms: **formal education** for educational programmes which do not adapt themselves to the different groups of students who join them; **non-formal education** for those programmes which are modified to meet local situations but still retain standardised elements – a hybrid form of education; and **informal education** for those highly contextualised and fully participatory educational activities created by and for individual learning groups, learning programmes which will change as different people join. Once again these are not categories but points along a continuum.

In this model, NFE can become the focal point for all educational programmes, combining as it does both some formal structures and decontextualised material and some elements of contextualisation and individualisation. Learning programmes need to move in both directions along the continuum, constantly seeking to draw upon general principles and decontextualised content and yet to engage each of the learners in applying the new learning within their own specific lifeworlds. Just as formal schooling needs some elements of participatory education, so participatory education will at times need some elements of formal schooling.

But current NFE is not necessarily an ideal for other forms of education to aim at. It too needs to change; for its participatory and contextualised elements normally remain confined to logistical matters rather than to content and processes. To allow participation in some educational areas but not others is to manipulate participation, to use it to achieve externally inspired goals. Current NFE needs to move towards the participatory end of the continuum, to become more individualised to the needs of different groups of learners in content, teaching-learning materials, methodologies and assessment as well as in timing and location.

For the underlying fact is that what the discourse of non-formal education does is to challenge all education in terms of power – who controls the process as well as the format? This, it seems to me, is the radical element which NFE offers to both formal education and informal education.

12

Conclusion

We have seen *the debate about formal and non-formal education* emerge and die away. Arising from a development context in an era when the lifeworld was seen in terms of dichotomies, formal and non-formal education were defined in terms of opposites. Even the pragmatists who argued that every educational activity contained elements of both formal and non-formal were dualistic; they saw these as two (and only two) contrasting forms of or approaches to education.

We have seen *the contemporary practice of non-formal education* which no longer fits that construct. The emergence of many diverse forms of educational provision, especially flexible schooling, labelled as non-formal education, has resulted in the terms 'formal' and 'non-formal' becoming almost meaningless. The NFE discourse no longer serves as a useful tool of analysis or of planning. But the language of NFE remains embedded within other discourses, often without any clear meaning.

I have suggested an alternative analysis which draws upon this heritage and makes sense of the formal and non-formal distinction in today's world of increasing diversity. This uses group dynamics and organisational development theory. Its main element is the **contextualisation construct.** *Formal education* is that education which is highly decontextualised, which does not change with changes of participants. I suggest that highly contextualised education, where the framing, the subject matter and the processes change with each new group which is enrolled, might be called *informal education*. These are not different categories, for other hybridities are possible; rather they are points on a continuum. So that between these two lie programmes combining elements of both.

Looked at in this way, we can see that most of the educational programmes which are today labelled as NFE are in fact of a hybrid type. They are partially contextualised, often in not the most important educational elements, and partially decontextualised. They are flexible schooling which may properly be called *non-formal education*.

It is then possible to analyse any lifelong education programme not just in terms of how far but just as importantly *in what respects* it is contextualised or decontextualised. In particular, we can ask of every programme labelled as NFE how far it is flexible schooling or participatory education. Such an approach continues to make sense of the formal and non-formal divide and extends it to informal education along a continuum. And since education is a dynamic encounter, each individual learning group will not occupy a static position on the continuum but will constantly move along the continuum in either direction. For unlike the old discourse of NFE which saw one partner as good and the other as evil, this new approach will value both. To be fully effective, all education will need to have both contextualised and decontextualised material and approaches.

Such an approach may also serve as a tool of planning; for it introduces the possibilities of several hybrid forms of education (e.g. context-sensitive, context-adjusted) along that continuum. It will encourage those programmes of NFE that at present only allow participation in areas of logistics to extend it to more central educational matters such as curriculum, teaching-learning materials and evaluation.

The way that the terms formal, non-formal and informal education will be used in future remains obscure. Whether NFE will be confined to those flexible educational programmes which combine elements of both formal and participatory education or whether it will remain in vogue to cover *both* flexible schooling *and* fully participatory education will become apparent as time passes. The former would appear to be the most satisfactory way in which we can retain the language of NFE with its implied reform agenda which many countries show signs of wishing to do, while at the same making sense of the rapidly increasing diversity of programmes.

Bibliography

Note: throughout this bibliography, the abbreviation NFE has normally been used for Non-formal Education, whether the abbreviation appears in the title or not.

Abadzi Helen (1994): NFE for Women in Latin America and the Caribbean: solving the mystery of the unreported trainees, paper for World Bank.

Abed F H: personal communication.

ACAPES report on the ACAPES School Project, NOVIB Senegal; see website www.coe.int/T/E/North-South-Centre/Resources-Center.

ACCESS (2000): papers on the ACCESS Programme produced by Anne Jellema and David Archer and others for Action Aid, London (covering Gambia, Ghana, Kenya, Pakistan Tanzania, Uganda).

ActionAid (1997a): Critical reflections on strategies for including the marginalised in quality education, unpublished paper, London: Action Aid.

ActionAid (1997b): From Providing to Enabling: report of international Action Aid workshop in children's education strategies, unpublished paper London: Action Aid.

ADB (1989): Publicity leaflet issued by Asia Development Bank about NFE Project in the Philippines

ADB (1996): Asia Development Bank Philippines NFE Project: implementation manual, Bureau of NFE, Manila 1996.

ADEA (Association for the Development of Education in Africa): working papers; reports on seminars.

ADEA (1997): *Capacity 2000 Plus: competency-based community skills development*, report of ADEA WG-NFE Workshop Namibia 1997.

ADEA (1999a): *Diversifying Education Delivery Systems: reviving discourse on the formal/nonformal interface, report of a workshop in Botswana*, published by Commonwealth Secretariat.

ADEA (1999b): Diversifying Education Delivery Systems: reviving discourse on the formal/nonformal interface, unpublished papers from a workshop in Botswana (as presented) available from Commonwealth Secretariat.

ADEA (2000a): *Dynamics of NFE: report of a symposium*, Johannesburg December 1999 published by Commonwealth Secretariat.

ADEA (2000b): *Dynamics of NFE: papers from a symposium*, Johannesburg December 1999 published by Commonwealth Secretariat.

ADEA Newsl: Newsletter of Association for the Development of Education in Africa.

ADEA Publ: ADEA NFE-Working Group publicity leaflet.

ADEA WG: Newsletters of ADEA NFE-Working Group.

Adegbija M V (2000): Improving effectiveness of NFE through the use of instructional media, *Indian Journal of Adult Education* 61.1: 10-23.

Adiseshiah M S (1975): *Towards a Functional Learning Society*, Tamil Nadu Board of Continuing Education, Madras.

Adiseshiah M S (1985): Trends and prospects in education, in UNESCO 1985.

AET/Africa Educational Trust (2001): Annual Review.

Afrik T (1995): *Basic Adult Non-Formal Education Curricula: a scenario in Sub-Saharan Africa*, Dakar: UNESCO.

Ahmed M (1975): *Economics of Nonformal Education: resources, costs and benefits*, New York Praeger.

Ahmed M (1982): Putting into practice the perspective of lifelong recurrent education, *International Review of Education*, 28.2: 133-142.

Ahmed M (1983): Critical educational issues and NFE, *Prospects*, 13.1: 35-44.

Ahmed M (1985): NFE, Economics of, in Husen T & Postlethwaite T N (eds.) *The International encyclopedia of education: research and studies*, Oxford: Pergamon Press: 3543-3546.

Ahmed M (1994): NFE Economics of, in Husen T & Postlethwaite T N (eds.) *The International encyclopedia of education* (2nd edition), Oxford: Pergamon Press: 4136-4141.

Ahmed M (1996): Economics of NFE, in Tuijnman A C (ed.) *International encyclopedia of adult education and training*, (2nd edition) Oxford; Tarrytown, N.Y.: Pergamon: 131-135.

Ahmed M (1997): Economics of NFE *Adult Education and Development*, 49: 199-208.

Ahmed M (1999): Literacy and NFE: overlap and divergence, in Wagner D A, Venezky R L & Street B V (eds.): *Literacy, an International Handbook*, Boulder, Colorado: Westview Press.

Ahmed M & Coombs P H (1975): *Education for Rural Development: case studies for planners*, New York: Praeger.

Ahmed M & Torres R M (1993): Reaching the unreached: non-formal approaches and universal primary education, paper prepared for UNICEF consultation.

Ahmed M, Ming K C, Jalaluddin A K & Ramachandran K (1991): *Basic Education and National Development*, Paris: UNESCO.

Ahmed S (1995): *Forms and Formats of NFE for Monitoring and Evaluation of the project: NFPE and Bunyad Literacy Community Council*, Lahore: BLCC.

Ahmed Zebun (1997): Mapping Rural Women's Perspectives on NFE Experiences: a case study in a Bangladeshi village, unpublished PhD thesis University of Pittsburgh.

Aikman S (1999): *Intercultural Education and Literacy*, Amsterdam: Benjamin.

Aikman S (1995): Language, literacy and bilingual education: an Amazon people's strategies for cultural maintenance, *International Journal of Educational Development*, 15.4: 411-422.

Akbar M (1997): Do communities own non-formal schools? *NGO News*, Asia Foundation, Islamabad.

Alam M & Rob M Abdur (1991): *Basic education and life skills at non-formal primary level in Bangladesh*, Dhaka: BIDS.

Alexander David (1990): Evaluating NFE in Thailand: the significance of more qualitative approaches, in Corner 1990.

ALICE (2000): http://alice.eaea.org/what/index.html accessed March 2000.

Allemano E (1981): *NFE, RAMS Project Report* Rural Assessment Manpower Surveys, USAID, Washington.

Alpha 10 (1985): *Le formel et le non-formel dans l'education de masse*, Agence de cooperation culturelle et technique, Paris.

Altbach P G, Arnove R F & Kelly G P (eds.) (1982): *Comparative Education*, London: Macmillan.

Altbach P G & Kelly G P (eds.) (1986): *New Approaches to Comparative Education*, Chicago: University of Chicago Press.

Amaratunga C M (1977): Field studies in Ghana and Sri Lanka: indigenous non-formal adult learning in two rural communities, *Convergence*, 10.2: 41-52.

Amin S (1975): What education for what development? *Prospects*, 5.1: 48-52.

Anderson John E (1974): The formalization of non-formal education: village polytechnics and pre-vocational youth training in Kenya, *World Yearbook of Education*, 1974: 283-301.

ANTEP: Papers of Association for Non-Traditional Education in the Philippines.

Anyanwu C N (1984): NFE and training for citizenship participation in rural development programmes, in Anyanwu C N 1984, *Adult Education in Nigeria*, Ibadan: Moba Press.

Apeid (1986): *Formal and Nonformal Education: co-ordination and complementarity*, Bangkok: UNESCO PROAP.

Apple M W (1988): Facing the complexity of power: for a parallelist position in critical education studies, in Cole M (ed.) *Bowles and Gintis Revisited*, London: Falmer: 112-130.

Apter D E (1987): *Rethinking Development: modernization, dependency and postmodern politics*, London: Sage.

Apthorpe R (ed.) (1970): *People, Planning and Development Studies*, London: Frank Cass.

Apthorpe R & Gasper D (1996): *Arguing Development Policy: frames and discourses*, London: Frank Cass.

Apthorpe R & Krahl A (eds.) (1986): *Development Studies: critique and renewal*, Leiden: Brill.

Argyris C & Schon D A (1976): *Organizational Learning: theory, method and practice*, Reading, MA: Addison-Wesley.

Armengol M A de (1990): *Alternative and non-formal approaches to provide primary level education for out of school children: a synthesis of six case studies*, Hamburg: UNESCO Institute of Education.

Armstrong G (1984): Implementing educational policy: decentralization of NFE in Thailand, *Comparative Education Review*, 28.3: 454-466.

Aronowitz S & Giroux H (1991): *Policy and Policy-Making in Education*, London: Routledge.

ASECA (1998): A Secondary Education Curriculum for Adults (ASECA) Programme, paper presented to trustees May.

Asia SE (1977): Recommendations for action in SE Asia: regional conference on NFE, *Convergence*, 10.3: 65-66.

Aspin D, Chapman J, Hatton M & Sawano Y (eds.) (2001): *International Handbook of Lifelong Learning*, London: Kluwer.

Assefa K (1997): *Managing Non-formal Adult Education by NGOs in Ethiopia*, Addis Ababa: IIZ/DVV.

Atchoarena D & Hiti S (2001): Lifelong learning policies in low development contexts: an African perspective, in Aspin Aspin D, Chapman J, Hatton M & Sawano Y (eds.): *International Handbook of Lifelong Learning*, London: Kluwer: 201-228.

Avenstrup R & Swarts P (2000): Towards equitable diversity in education: move towards a paradigm shift, in ADEA 2000b: 1-14.

Ayers R C (1983): *Banking on the Poor*, Cambridge MA: MIT.

Ayres R (ed.) (1995): *Development Studies: an introduction through selected readings*, Dartford, Kent: Greenwich University Press.

BACE (1989): Non-formal Universal Primary Education Project (report) Dhaka: Bangladesh Association for Community Education.

Bacquelaine M & Raymaekers R (1991): NFE in developing countries, *International Journal of Educational Management*, 5.5: 15-24 (a reprint of International Bureau of Education 1987).

Bagnall R (2001): Locating lifelong learning and education in contemporary currents of thought and culture, in Aspin D, Chapman J, Hatton M & Sawano Y (eds.): *International Handbook of Lifelong Learning*, London: Kluwer: 35-52.

Bainer D L, Cantrell D & Barron P (2000): Professional development of nonformal environmental educators through school-based partnerships, *Journal of Environmental Education*, 32.1: 36-45.

Barber E G (1981): General education versus special education for rural development, *Comparative Education Review*, 25: 216-231.

Barnett T (1988): *Sociology and Development*, London: Routledge.

Barrow R (1978): *Radical Education: a critique of free-schooling and de-schooling*, London: Martin Robertson.

Barton David (1994): *Literacy: the ecology of written language*, Oxford: Blackwells.

Beevers R (1972): NFE: the role of the churches, in Ward Marian (ed.) *Change and Development in Rural Melanesia*, Canberra: ANU.

BELOISYA (2001): *Basic Education and Livelihood Opportunities for Illiterate and Semiliterate Young Adults*, Washington DC: World Bank.

ETH-BEN (2000): papers of Basic Education Network, Ethiopia.

Benhabib S (1996): *Democracy and Difference: contesting the boundaries of the political* Princeton: Princeton University Press.

Benseman John (2000): *Thriving and surviving on the fringe: adult education in Aotearoa/New Zealand and the New Right*, unpublished paper.

Benseman John, Findsen B & Scott M (eds.) (1996): *The Fourth Sector: adult and community education in Aotearoa/New Zealand*, Palmerston North, NZ: Dunmore Press.

Berg I (1970): *Education and Jobs*, New York: Praeger.

Bergmann H (2002): What works and what doesn't work, in *Adult Education and Development*, 59: 79-90.

Berstecher D B (ed.) (1985): *Education and Rural Development: issues for planning and research*, Paris: UNESCO IIEP.

Betts J (2001): *Marching onwards: the social practices of literacy in Usultan, El Salvador*, unpublished PhD thesis, University of Oxford.

Bhabha H (1990): The other question: difference, discrimination and the discourse of colonialism, in Ferguson R (ed.): *Out There: marginalization and contemporary cultures* Cambridge, MA: MIT Press: 71-89.

Bhabha H (1994): *The Location of Culture*, London: Routledge.

Bhola H S (1979): *Curriculum Development for Formal and Non-formal Education Programs*, Bonn: DSE.

Bhola H S (1983): NFE in perspective, *Prospects*, 13.1: 45-53.

Bhola H S (1984): *Campaigning for Literacy: a critical analysis of some selected literacy campaigns of the 20th century*, Paris: UNESCO.

Bishop D (1989): *Alternative Strategies for Education*, New York: Martins Press.

Bjornavold J (1997): Assessment of non-formal learning: the quality and limitations of methodologies, *Vocational Training*, CEDEFOP 12: 68-74.

Bjornavold J (2000): *Making Learning Visible: identification, assessment and recognition of non-formal learning in Europe*, Thessaloniki: CEDEFOP.

Blake N, Smeyers P, Smith R & Standish P (eds.) (1998): *Thinking Again: education after post-modernism*, Westport, CT: Bergin and Garvey.

Blaug M (1973): *Education and the Employment Problem in Developing Countries*, Geneva: ILO.

Blumberg A & Golembiewski R (1976): *Learning and Change in Groups*, Harmondsworth: Penguin.

Blunt A (1988): Education, learning and development: evolving concepts, *Convergence*, 21.1: 37-54.

Bobillier C W (2000): Possible Collaboration between Thailand and Bangladesh in the field of NFE, report, Dhaka: DNFE.

BOBP (1987): Bay of Bengal Programme Newsletter, Madras: FAO.

Bock J C (1976): Institutionalization of NFE: a response to conflicting needs, *Comparative Education Review*, 20.3: 346-367.

Bock J C & Bock C M (1985): NFE policy in developing countries, in Husen T & Postlethwaite T N (eds.), *The International encyclopedia of education: research and studies*, Oxford: Pergamon Press: 3551-3556.

Bock J C & Papagiannis G J (1976): *The Demystification of NFE*, Amherst MA: CIE.

Bock J C & Papagiannis G J (1983a): *NFE and National Development: a critical assessment of policy, research and practice*, New York: Praeger.

Bock J C & Papagiannis G J (1983b): *Issues in NFE*, Amherst MA: CIE.

Bockarie S A (1997): School-community integration: a microcosm of the processes of NFE, in Lynch James, Modgil Celia & Modgil Sohan (eds.): *Non-Formal and Non-Governmental Approaches*, vol 4 of *Education and Development: tradition and innovation*, London: Cassells: 102-116.

Boeren A J J M & Epskamp K P (eds.) (1990): *Education, Culture and Productive Life*, The Hague: CESO.

Boli J, Ramirez F O & Meyer John W (1985): Explaining the origins and expansion of mass education, *Comparative Education Review*, 29.2: 145-152.

Bond D (1998): How can university work-based courses contribute to lifelong learning, in Holford J, Jarvis P & Griffin C (eds.), *International perspectives on lifelong learning*, London: Kogan Page: 213-223.

Botswana (1992): *Pulling Together To Do Better*, Third Report of DNFE 1989-1991, Gaborone: Ministry of Education.

Botswana (1994): *Revised National Policy on Education*, Gaborone: Ministry of Education.

Botswana (1997): Report of International Workshop in Affordable Communication Technologies for Non-formal Distance Education and Development Communication Gaborone: Ministry of Education.

Boudon R (1974): *Education, Opportunity and Social Inequality: changing prospects in Western societies*, New York: Wiley.

Boukary H (1998): Village schools of Save the Children (USA) in Mali: a case study of NGOs, communities and the state's emerging roles in the provision of basic education in the Sahel, unpublished paper based on author's PhD thesis Indiana University, Bloomington, USA.

Bourdieu P (1971): Systems of education and systems of thought, in Hopper Hopper E (ed.): *Readings in the Theory of Educational Systems*, London: Hutchinson: 159-183.

Bowers J & Fisher E A (1972): Search for a terminology of adult education and for better statistics: explorations in a semiotic jungle, *Convergence*, 5.4: 44-49.

Bowles S & Gintis H (1976): *Schooling in Capitalist America*, New York: Basic Books.

BRAC (1995a): *News*, Dhaka: BRAC.

BRAC (1995b): NFPE Supplement to ACCESS Newsletter, Dhaka: BRAC.

BRAC (1996): *NFPE Phase One Report 1993-1996*, Dhaka: BRAC.

BRAC (1997): *Annual Report*, Dhaka: BRAC.

Bray M (1984): Obstacles to NFE development: the case of Papua New Guinea, *Convergence*, 17.2: 43-50.

Bray M (1999): Community financing of education: cultural variations and policy dilemmas in less developed countries, in F E Leach & A W Little (eds.), *Education, cultures, and economics: dilemmas for development*, New York: Falmer Press: 183-202.

Breier M, Taetsane M & Sait L (1996): Taking literacy for a ride: reading and writing in the taxi industry, in Prinsloo M & Breier M (eds.), *The Social uses of literacy : theory and practice in contemporary South Africa*, South Africa: Sached Books; Philadelphia: John Benjamins: 213-223.

Brembeck C (1971): *Strategic Uses of Formal and NFE*, Bangkok: SEAMEO.

Brembeck C (1974): *Economics of NFE*, East Lansing, MI: Michigan State University.

Brembeck C (1979): Linkages Between Formal and Non-Formal Education, *Bulletin*, Paris: International Bureau of Education.

Brembeck C S & Grandstaff M (1974): *NFE as an alternative to schooling*, East Lansing, MI: Michigan State University Institute for International Studies in Education.

Brembeck C S & Thompson T J (eds.) (1973): *New Strategies for Educational Development: the cross-cultural search for nonformal alternatives,* Lexington: D C Heath.

Brennan B (1997): Reconceptualizing nonformal education, *International Journal of Lifelong Education,* 16.3: 185-200.

British Council (1994): *Literacy Practice in Non-formal Education,* report on a seminar, British Council Karachi.

Brockington D & White R (1983): UK: NFE in a context of youth unemployment, *Prospects,* 13.1.

Brock-Utne B & Nagel T (1996): *Role of Education in the Development of Education for All,* Oslo: Oslo University Press.

Brokenshaw D W, Warren D M & Werner O (1980): *Indigenous Knowledge Systems and Development,* Lanham: University Press of America.

Brown R (2000): *Group Processes: dynamics within and between groups,* Oxford: Blackwells.

Buchert L (ed.) (1992): *Education and Training in the Third World,* The Hague: CESO.

Buchert L (1995): *Recent Trends in Education Aid: towards a classification of policies,* Paris: UNESCO IIEP.

Buchholz J (1987): *Promotion of Regional Rural Development through Formal and NFE,* Eschborn: Tz-Verlagsgesellschaft.

Burke R C (1987): Getting the mixture right: NFE through community radio in the Bolivian Altiplano, *Convergence,* 20.2: 69-80.

Burkey S (1993): *People First: a guide to self-reliant participatory rural development,* London: Zed Books.

Burnett N (1996): Priorities and strategies for education: a World Bank review, *International Journal of Educational Development,* 16.3: 215-220.

Callaway A (1972): Training young people within indigenous small-scale enterprises: the Nigerian example, in IIEP 1972.

Callaway A (1973): Frontiers of out of school education, in Brembeck C S & Thompson T J (eds.), *New strategies for educational development: the cross-cultural search for non-formal alternatives,* Lexington, Mass.: Lexington Books: 13-24.

Cameron D (1994): Language and Gender in Socio-linguistic Perspective, in *Language and Gender in Development Symposium Report,* Manchester: British Council: 5-10.

Campbell P & Burnaby B (eds.) (2001): *Participatory Practices in Adult Education,* London: Erlbaum.

CAMPE (1995): *Mapping of NGOs and Non-formal Education Programmes in Bangladesh,* Dhaka: CAMPE.

CAMPE (1996): *Formal and Nonformal Primary Education Systems in Bangladesh: an exploratory study,* Dhaka: CAMPE.

Cape Town (2001): Characteristic Elements of a Lifelong Learning Higher Education Institution, http://www.uwc.ac.za/dll.

CARE Nepal (1996): Evaluation of CARE Nepal's Literacy Program, report Kathmandu: CARE Nepal.

Carew-Reid J et al. (1994): *Strategies for National Sustainable Development,* London: Earthscan.

Carley M & Christie I (1992): *Managing Sustainable Development*, London: Earthscan.

Carnoy M (1974): *Education as Cultural Imperialism*, London: Longman.

Carnoy M (1982): Education for Alternative Development, *Comparative Education Review*, 26.2: 160-177.

Carnoy M (1989): Education, state and culture in American Society, in Giroux H A & McLaren P L (eds.), *Critical pedagogy, the state, and cultural struggle*, Albany, N.Y.: State University of New York Press.

Carr W & Kemmis S (eds.) (1986): *Becoming Critical: Education, Knowledge and Action Research*, Victoria, Australia: Deakin University.

Carr-Hill R A (1988): *Information Base for the planning of the diversified educational field*, Paris: UNESCO IIEP Report 68.

Carr-Hill R A & Lintott J (1985): *Comparative Adult Education Statistics for 84 countries*, Paris: UNESCO.

Carr-Hill R A, Carron G & Peart E (2001): Classifying out of school education, in Watson K (ed.), *Doing Comparative Education Research: issues and problems*, Oxford: Symposium.

Carron G & Carr-Hill R A (1991): *NFE – information and planning issues*, Paris: UNESCO IIEP Research Report 90.

Carron G C & Chau T N (eds.) (1980): *Regional Disparities in Educational Development: a controversial issue*, Paris: UNESCO IIEP.

Carson A Scott (1984): Education and schooling, *International Review of Education*, 30.1: 41-53; and rejoinder by John Wilson: 54-56.

Cartwright D & Zander A (eds.) (1968): *Group Dynamics: research and theory*, London: Tavistock.

Case H L & Niehoff R O (1976): *Educational Alternatives in National Development: suggestions for policymakers*, East Lansing, MI: Michigan State University.

Cassara B B (ed.) (1995): *Adult Education through World Collaboration*, Malabar: Kreiger.

CER (1976): special issue of *Comparative Education Review* on NFE.

CER (1989): special issue of *Comparative Education Review* on World Bank Education Policies.

CERID (1994): Courses on Non-Formal Education, University of Tribhuvan, Nepal.

Chambers R (1983): *Rural Development: putting the last first*, Harlow: Longman.

Chambers R (1997): *Whose Reality Counts? putting the first last*, London: ITDG.

Chauncey H (1962): *Talks on American Education*, New York: Teachers College, Columbia University.

Chowdhury A M R, Ziegah L, Haque N, Shrestha G L & Ahmed Z (1994): Assessing Basic Competencies: a practical methodology, *International Review of Education*, 40: 437-454.

Chu S K (1994): Adult and NFE: statistics, in Husen T & Postlethwaite T N (eds.) *The International encyclopedia of education* (2nd edition), Oxford: Pergamon Press: 94-100.

Chu S K (1996): Statistics of adult and non-formal education, in Tuijnman A C (ed.) *International encyclopedia of adult education and training*, (2nd edition) Oxford; Tarrytown, N.Y.: Pergamon: 878-883.

CIDA (2001): CIDA's Draft Action Plan on Basic Education http://www.acdi-cida/gc.ca.

Clark H F & Sloan H S (1958): *Classrooms in the Factories*, Rutherford New Jersey: Institute of Research Farleigh Dickenson University.

Clark M (1978): Meeting the needs of the adult learner: using NFE for social action, *Convergence*, 11.3-4: 44-52.

Clark P A (2000): *Organisations in Action: competition between contexts*, London: Routledge.

Closson Rosemary, Capasci Chris & Mavima Paul (1997): Synthesis of ADEA Research in NFE in Eastern and Southern Africa, report Tallahassee Florida: Center for Policy Studies in Education.

Clover D E (2000): Educating for a change: reconceptualizing formal and/or nonformal environmental education, *Comparative Education Review*, 44.2: 213-219.

Coben D (1998): *Radical Heroes: Gramsci, Freire and the politics of adult education*, New York: Garland.

Coffield F (ed.) (2000): *The Necessity of Informal Learning*, Bristol: Policy Press.

COL (2000): *Connections*, Newsletter of Commonwealth of Learning 5.3.

Colbert V (1999): Escuela Nueva, Improving the access and quality of education for the rural poor, the case of the new school in Colombia, unpublished paper presented to seminar in London.

Colclough C & Manor J (eds.) (1991): *States and Markets: neo-liberalism and the development policy debate*, Oxford: Clarendon.

Colletta N J (1971): *Bibliographies in NFE*, (3 volumes) East Lansing, MI: Michigan State University.

Colletta N J (1976): Participatory research or participation put-down? reflection on an Indonesian experiment in NFE, *Convergence*, 9.3: 32-44.

Colletta N J (1996): Formal, nonformal and informal education, in Tuijnman A C (ed.) *International encyclopedia of adult education and training*, (2nd edition) Oxford; Tarrytown, N.Y.: Pergamon: 22-27.

Colletta N J & Kidd R (1980): *Indigenous Structures, Folk Media and NFE for Development*, Berlin: DSE.

Colletta N J & Radcliffe D J (1980): NFE: an educological approach, *Canadian and International Education*, 9.2: 1-27.

Colletta N J & Todd T A (1983): The limits of NFE and village development: lessons from the Sarvodaya Shramadana movement, in Bock & Papagiannis: 205-218.

Colletta N J, Ewing R T & Todd T A (1982): Cultural Revitalization, Participatory NFE and Village Development in Sri Lanka: the Sarvodaya Shramadana Movement, *Comparative Education Review*, 26.2: 271-285.

ComSec (1979): *NFE for Development: mobilizing human resources*, London: Commonwealth Secretariat.

ComSec (1986): *Alternative Forms of Post-Primary Education and Training in Africa*, report, London: Commonwealth Secretariat.

Cooke B & Kothari U (2001): *Participation: the new tyranny?* London: Zed Books.

Coombs P H (1968): *World Educational Crisis: a systems approach*, New York: Oxford University Press.

Coombs P H (1976): NFE: myths, realities and opportunities, *Comparative Education Review*, 20.3: 281-293.

Coombs P H (1985a): *The World Crisis in Education: the view from the eighties*, New York: Oxford University Press.

Coombs P H (1985b): NFE: Comparative Studies, in Husen T & Postlethwaite T N (eds.) *The International encyclopedia of education: research and studies*, Oxford: Pergamon Press: 3540-3543.

Coombs P H (1988): Comparative studies in NFE, in Postlethwaite T N (ed.), *The Encyclopedia of comparative education and national systems of education*, Oxford: Pergamon Press: 72-75.

Coombs P H (1989): Formal and NFE: future strategies, in Titmus C J (ed.), *Lifelong education for adults: an international handbook*, Oxford: Pergamon: 57-60.

Coombs P H & Ahmed M (1974): *Attacking Rural Poverty: how NFE can help*, Baltimore: John Hopkins University Press.

Coombs P H & Hallak J (1972): *Managing Educational Costs*, New York: Oxford University Press.

Coombs P H, Prosser R C & Ahmed M (1973): *New Paths to Learning for Rural Children and Youth*, New York: ICED.

Corbridge S (1995): *Development Studies: a reader*, London: Edward Arnold.

Corner T (ed.) (1990): *Learning Opportunities for Adults*, London: Routledge.

Coun Eur (1999): Council of Europe Report Doc 8595, *Non-Formal Education*, December 1999.

Courtney Wyn & Kutsch G (1978): *Planning and management of the integrated development of formal and non-formal education: a review of the possibilities and difficulties*, Paris: UNESCO.

Cragan J F & Wright D W (1998): *Communication in Small Groups: theory, process and skills*, Belmont, CA: Wadsworth.

Crane V, Nicholson H, Chem M & Bitgood S (1994): *Informal Science Learning: what the research says about TV, Science Museums and Community-Based Projects*, Dedham, MA: Research Communications.

Creative Associates (1981): *The Non-formal Education Assessment/Analysis Model*, Washington DC: Creative Associates.

Creative Associates (1982): *Non-formal Education in Botswana: an assessment*, Washington DC: Creative Associates.

Creative Associates (1983): *Non-formal Education in the Cameroons: an assessment*, Washington DC: Creative Associates.

Crossley M (1984): Planning the SSCEP Core project, unpublished, University of Papua New Guinea.

Crossley M, Sukwianomb J & Weeks S (eds.) (1987): *Pacific Perspectives on NFE*, Waigani Papua New Guinea: University of Papua New Guinea.

Crossley M & Vulliamy G (eds.) (1997): *Qualitative Research in Developing Countries: current perspectives*, New York: Garland.

Crossley M & Watson K (2003): *Comparative and International Research in Education: globalisation, context and difference*, London: RoutledgeFalmer.

Crush J (ed.) (1995): *Development as Power*, London: Routledge.

Cruz A Y (2000): *Functional Literacy: heart of empowerment*, Mumbai: ASPBAdult Education 'Beyond Literacy' series.

Curle A (1973): *Education for Liberation*, London: Tavistock.

Dakar (2000): The Dakar Framework for Action, Education for All – meeting our collective commitments, Paris: UNESCO.

Dani A J (1995): NFE, population problems and rural development in the Sudan, *Journal of Practice in Education for Development*, 1.2: 39-42.

Darder A, Baltdaro M & Torres R D (eds.) (2003): *The Critical Pedagogy Reader*, London: RoutledgeFalmer.

Dave R H (1976): *Foundations of Lifelong Education*, Oxford: Pergamon.

Dave R H, Ranaweera A M & Sutton P J (1990): *Educacion no formal*, Hamburg: UNESCO Institute of Education.

Davies L (2003): *Education and Conflict: complexity and chaos*, London: RoutledgeFalmer.

De Beer A S (ed.) (1993): *Mass Media for the 90s*, Pretoria: van Schaik.

Dejene A (1980): *NFE as a Strategy in Development: comparative analysis of rural development projects*, Lanham, Maryland: University Press of America.

Deleon Asher (1978): Adult education as a corrective to the failure of formal education, *Prospects*, 8.2: 169-176.

Delors Jacques et al. (1996): *Learning: the Treasure Within*, Paris: UNESCO.

Derryck V L (1979): *Comparative Functionality for Formal and NFE for Women*, Washington: USAID.

Deyo Lisa (personal communication).

DFID (1994): *Using Literacy: a new approach to post-literacy materials*, Research Report 10, London: DFID.

DFID (1997): *Eliminating World Poverty: a challenge for the twenty-first century*, London: DFID.

Dhaka Ahsania Mission undated (2003): *Training Manual on NFE for Poverty Alleviation* (three volumes).

Dilts Russ & Associate (1982): The Indonesian NFE project *International Review of Education* 28.2: 270-272.

Dodds T (1996): *Non-Formal and Adult Basic Education through Open and Distance Learning in Africa: developments in the nineties towards Education for All*, Cambridge: International Extension College.

Dore R (1976): *The Diploma Disease*, London: Allen and Unwin.

Dore R (1980): *The Diploma Disease Revisited*, London: Routledge.

Dovey K (1993): Sport as a site for transformative NFE: a South African action research project, *International Journal of Educational Development*, 13.4: 359-371.

Dovey K (1994): Nonformal educational strategies as a means of effecting positive change in institutions of formal education in South Africa, *Journal of Practice in Education for Development*, 1.1: 15-20.

Dovey K (1995): Making up the deficit: a South African NFE project for industrial personnel, *International Journal of Lifelong Education*, 14.1: 39.

Draper J A (1986): Universities and non-formal Adult Education, *Convergence*, 19.3: 70-75.

Duke C (2001): Lifelong learning and tertiary education: the learning university revisited, in Aspin D, Chapman J, Hatton M & Sawano Y (eds.), *International Handbook of Lifelong Learning*, London: Kluwer: 501-528.

Duke C & Varapipatana K (1982): *NFE in Asia and the Pacific*, Bangkok: UNESCO PROAP.

Durston S (1996): *Increasing EFA: community schools in Zambia*, Lusaka: UNICEF.

Dyer C (2000): *Operation Blackboard: policy implementation in Indian elementary education*, Wallingford: Symposium.

Easton P A (1997): *Sharpening our tools: improving evaluation in adult and nonformal education*, Hamburg: UNESCO Institute of Education.

EC (2000): European Communities notice on NFE dimension of sporting activities in the European Community youth programmes, *European Communities Information and Notices Journal*, 43.8: 5.

Economic Commission for Africa (1994): *Literacy and NFE: perspectives and responses to changing development environments*, Durban SA: ECA.

Ecuador (1975): NFE in Ecuador 1971-1975, papers, CIE, UMass Amherst.

Edwards P (2000): Formal and nonformal education, in *Aquaculture, Poverty Impacts and Livelihoods*, Natural Resource Perspectives, June 2000 London: ODI.

Eisemon T, Crawford M & Marble K (1999): Investing in Adult Literacy: lessons and implications, in Wagner D A, Venezky R L & Street B V (eds.): *Literacy, an International Handbook*, Boulder, Colorado: Westview Press: 360-366.

Elias M J (1994): Non-Formal Adult Education for Maritime Fisherfolk in *CARITAS* 1 (Jan 1994), Madras.

Elimu (2000): Report of international meeting Brazil 2000, London: ActionAid.

Elimu (2001): Dakar Plus One report (website www.elimu.org, update 2000).

Ellis J (1999): The Learning Nation, paper presented to ADEA NFE Working Group Workshop, ADEA 1999b.

Ellis P (1995): NFE and empowerment of women: insights from the Caribbean, *Convergence*, 28.3: 86-94.

Eraut M (2000a): Non-formal learning, implicit learning and tacit knowledge in professional work, in Coffield F (ed.), *The Necessity of Informal Learning*, Bristol: Policy Press: 12-31.

Eraut M (2000b): Non-formal learning and tacit knowledge in professional work, *British Journal of Educational Psychology*, 71: 113-136.

Escobar A (1995): *Encountering Development: the making and unmaking of the Third World*, Princeton, NJ: Princeton University Press.

ETH Focus 1-12: *Focus on Adult and Non-Formal Education in Ethiopia*, Newsletters of IIZ/DVV project 1-12.

Ethiopia (2000): *Alternate Routes to Basic Primary Education*, Addis Ababa: Ministry of Education unpublished paper.

Ethiopia, Directory (1997): *Directory of Adult and NFE in Ethiopia*, Addis Ababa: IIZ/DVV.

EU Comm (2001): *Communication on Making a European Area of Lifelong Learning a Reality*, COM: 678.

EU Memo (2000): Memorandum on Lifelong Learning, Commission Staff Working Paper.

Evans D R (1976): Technology in NFE: a critical appraisal, *Comparative Education Review*, 20.3: 305-327.

Evans D R (1981a): *The Planning of NFE*, Paris: UNESCO IIEP.

Evans D R (1981b): Ghana and Indonesia: reforms in NFE at the community level, *Prospects*, 11: 225-241.

Evans D R (1981c): The educational policy dilemma for rural areas, *Comparative Education Review*, 25: 232-243.

Evans D R (1983): Participation in nonformal education at the local level: Ghana and Indonesia, in Bock & Papagiannis 1983.

Evans D R & Smith W (eds.) (1973): NFE in a World Context, manuscript, Amherst, MA: CIE.

Evans D R & Smith W (1971): *Non-formal Alternatives to Schooling: a glossary of educational methods*, Amherst, MA: CIE.

Evans D R & Smith William (1972): *Non-formal Education*, Amherst, MA: CIE.

Ezeomah C (1985): *Land tenure constraints associated with some recent experiments to bring formal education to nomadic Fulani in Nigeria*, London: ODI.

Fagerlind I & Saha L J (1989): *Education for National Development: a comparative perspective* (2nd edition), Oxford: Pergamon.

Faure E et al. (1972): *Learning to Be: the world of education today and tomorrow*, Paris: UNESCO.

Ferguson R (ed.) (1990): *Out There: marginalization and contemporary cultures*, Cambridge, MA: MIT Press.

Fernandes W (ed.) (1980): *People's Participation in Development: approaches to NFE*, New Delhi: Indian Social Institute.

Filson G (ed.) (1991): *Political Economy of Adult Education in Nigeria*, Ibadan: Ibadan University Press.

Fitzgerald P (1997): *Managing Sustainable Development in Africa*, Cape Town: Oxford University Press.

Fluitman F (ed.) (1989): *Training for Work in the Informal Sector*, Geneva: ILO.

Foley G (1999): *Learning in Social Action: a contribution to understanding informal education*, London: Zed Books.

Fordham P (1979): *The interaction between formal and non-formal education*, Report on New Delhi Conference, London: Commonwealth Secretariat.

Fordham P (1980): *Participation, Learning and Change: Commonwealth approaches to non-formal education*, London: Commonwealth Secretariat.

Fordham P (1990): Commonwealth experience in using distance teaching for the non-formal education of adults, paper of INCED University of Warwick, Coventry.

Fordham P (1993): Informal, Nonformal and Formal Education Programmes, paper, INCED University of Warwick, Coventry.

Fordham P, Poulton G & Randle L (1979): *Learning Networks in Adult Education: NFE on a new housing estate*, London: RKP.

Fordham P, Poulton G & Randle L (1983): Non-formal work: a new kind of provision, in Tight M (ed.), *Opportunities for Adult Education*, London: Croom Helm.

Forsyth D R (1999): *Group Dynamics*, Belmont CA: Brooks Cole.

Foster P & Sheffield J R (eds.) (1974): *Education and Rural Development: the World Yearbook in Education*, London: Evans.

Foubert C (1983): A journey through development theories, *Convergence*, 16.3: 65-72.

Foucault M (1972): *The Archaeology of Knowledge and the Discourse on Language*, New York: Tavistock.

Fountain S (1999): *Peace Education in UNICEF*, New York: UNICEF.

Fox Christine (1996): Listening to the Other: mapping inter-cultural communication on post-colonial educational consultancies, in Paulston R G (ed.), *Social Cartography: mapping ways of seeing social and educational change*, New York: Garland: 291-306.

Frank A G (1969): *Capitalism and Under-Development in Latin America* (2nd edition), New York: Monthly Review Press.

FREDP (1979): *A Pilot Research Project on Nonformal Education: a micro-study*, Dhaka: Foundation for Research on Educational Planning and Development.

Freire Paolo (1972): *Pedagogy of the Oppressed*, Harmondsworth: Penguin.

Freire Paolo (1975): *Cultural Action for Freedom*, Harmondsworth: Penguin.

Frith M & Reed H B (1982): *Lifelong Learning Manual*, Amherst, MA: University of Massachusetts.

Fry G N (1981): Evaluating NFE Programmes: the need for appropriate technology in evaluation methods and procedures, Bangkok: DNFE Ministry of Education.

Fry G W & Thurber C E (1989): *International Education of Development Consultants: communicating with peasants and princes*, Oxford: Pergamon.

FSCE (2000): Report on Non-formal Basic Education as an alternative approach to address education needs of working children, Addis Ababa: Forum of Street Children-Ethiopia.

Gachanja B N (2000): *Non-Formal Education in Kenya*, unpublished paper presented at Seminar in Ethiopia November.

Gajaido M (1983): Chile: an experiment in NFE in rural areas, *Prospects*, 13.1.

Gallart M A (1989): *The Diversification of the Educational Field in Argentina*, Paris: UNESCO IIEP Research Report 73.

Galtung J (1971): A structured theory of imperialism, *Journal of Peace Research*, 8.2: 81-117.

Garrido J L G (1992): Open and Nonformal Education: new paths for education in a new Europe, *Comparative Education*, 28.1: 83-89.

Gathu K (1998): Communication media and technology: the role of radio in NFE programmes revisited, *Adult Education and Development*, 51: 177-188.

Gee J P (1992): *The Social Mind: language, ideology and social practice*, New York: Bergin and Garvey.

Gee J P (1996): *Social Linguistics and Literacies: ideology in discourses* (2nd edition), London: Taylor and Francis.

Gee J P (1999): *An Introduction to Discourse Analysis, Theory and Method*, London: Routledge.

Geertz C (1993): *The Interpretation of Cultures*, London: Fontana.

Gillette Arthur (1974): The Ecuador NFE Project, *Prospects*, 4.

Gillette Arthur (1977): *Beyond the non-formal fashion: towards educational revolution in Tanzania*, Amherst, MA: CIE.

Ginsburg M B & Arias-Godinez B (1984): NFE and Social Reproduction/Transformation: educational radio in Mexico, *Comparative Education Review*, 28.1: 116-127.

Giroux H A (1983): *Theory and Resistance in Education: a pedagogy for the opposition*, S Hadley, MA: Bergin and Garvey.

Giroux H & McLaren P (eds.) (1989): *Critical Pedagogy, the State and Cultural Struggle*, Albany, New York: SUNY Press.

Global Campaign for Education (2000): www.campaignforeducation.org.

GMR (2002): Global Monitoring Report, *Education for All: is the world on track?* Paris: UNESCO.

Gonzales C T & Pijano C V (1997): NFE in the Philippines: a fundamental step towards a system of lifelong learning, in Hatton M J (ed.), *Lifelong Learning: policies, practices and programs*, Toronto: Humber College School of Media Studies.

Goodale G (1989): Training for women in the informal sector, in Fluitman F (ed.), *Training for Work in the Informal Sector*, Geneva: ILO.

Goodman Paul (1971): *Compulsory Miseducation* (2nd edition), Harmondsworth: Penguin.

Goody J (1977): *The Domestication of the Savage Mind*, Cambridge: Cambridge University Press.

Gordon D (1987): Autonomy is more than just the absence of external constraints, in Sabar et al.: 29-36.

Gordon H L A (1985): *Adult and NFE in the Third World: a Jamaican perspective*, Vancouver: University of British Columbia.

Gordon Peter & Lawton Denis (1987): *Curriculum Change in the Nineteenth and Twentieth Centuries*, London: Hodder and Stoughton.

Goulet D & Hudson M (1971): *The Myth of Aid*, New York: Orbis.

Govinda R (ed.) (2002): *India Education Report*, New Delhi: Oxford University Press.

Graham-Brown Sarah (1991): *Education in the Developing World*, London: Longman.

Grandstaff M (1973a): Are formal schools the best place to educate?, in Brembeck C S & Thompson T J (eds.), *New Strategies for Educational Development: the cross-cultural search for nonformal alternatives*, Lexington: D C Heath: 41-52.

Grandstaff M (1973b): *NFE and an expanded conception of development*, East Lansing, MI: Michigan State University.

Grandstaff M (ed.) (1974a): *Economics and NFE*, East Lansing, MI: Michigan State University.

Grandstaff M (1974b): *Alternatives in education: a summary view of research and analysis on the concept of NFE*, East Lansing, MI: Michigan State University.

Grandstaff M (1976): NFE: some indications for use, *Comparative Education Review*, 20.3: 294-304.

Grandstaff M (1978): NFE as a concept, *Prospects*, 8.2: 177-182.

Green A (1990): *Education and State Formation*, London: Macmillan.

Green R H (1979): Organisation and finances of NFE, *Convergence*, 12.3: 42-54.

Griffin W N et al. (eds.) (1977): *Education and Lifelong Learning*, Washington, DC: American Association of Colleges for Teacher Education.

Grillo R & Stirrat R L (eds.) (1997): *Discourses of Development: anthropological perspectives*, Oxford: Berg.

Grillo R D (1998): *Pluralism and the Politics of Difference: state, culture and ethnicity in comparative perspective*, Oxford: Clarendon.

Grillo R D (ed.) (1989): *Social Anthropology and the Politics of Language*, London: Routledge.

Gunn C (1996): Learning in the Community: non-formal and informal education, in Benseman John, Findsen B & Scott M (eds.), *The Fourth Sector: adult and community education in Aotearoa/New Zealand*, Palmerston North, NZ: Dunmore Press.

Gunter J F (1975): *NFE-TV: television for NFE*, Amherst, MA: CIE.

Guttman Cynthia (1995a): *Breaking Through: TOSTAN's non-formal Basic Education programme in national languages in Senegal*, Paris: UNESCO.

Guttman Cynthia (1995b): *Voices across the hills: Thailand's hill areas education project*, Paris: UNESCO.

Guttman Cynthia (1995c): *Within Reach: the story of PROPEL, a non-formal project for rural children in India*, Paris: UNESCO.

Guzman R J (2001): Non-formal education accreditation and equivalency system, in *Asia/ Pacific Programme for Education for All Final Report*, Tokyo: ACCU.

Guzman R J (2002): An alternative learning system for disadvantaged communities in the Philippines, in Singh Madhu (ed.) 2002 *Institutionalizing Lifelong Learning: creating conducive environments for adult learning in the Asian context*, Hamburg: UNESCO Institute of Education.

Hall A (1986): Education, schooling and participation, in Midgeley J, *Community Participation, Social Development and the State*, London: Methuen.

Hall B L (1986): Role of NGOs in the field of adult education, *Convergence*, 19.4: 1-20.

Hall Bud (1993): Rich and vibrant colors: 25 years in NFE, *Convergence*, 25.1: 4-13.

Hall J W & Shiffman P H (1996): Evolving to the campus of the future, in *New Horizons in Adult Education*, vol. 10.1.

Hall K (1999): Understanding educational processes in an era of globalization, in Lageman E C & Shulma L S (eds.), *Issues in Educational Research: problems and possibilities*, San Francisco: Jossey Bass.

Hallak Jaques (1990): Beyond the School Systems: priorities in managing NFE programmes, in *Investing in the Future: setting educational priorities in the developing world*, Paris: UNESCO IIEP.

Halsey A W, Floud J & Anderson C A (eds.) (1961): *Education, Economy and Society*, New York: Free Press of Glencoe.

Hamadache A (1991): NFE: a definition of the concept and some examples, *Prospects*, 21.1: 111-124.

Hamadache A (1994): Nonformal and alternative approaches to basic education: comparative studies, in Husen T & Postlethwaite T N (eds.), *The International encyclopedia of education* (2nd edition), Oxford: Pergamon Press: 4132-4136.

Handy C (1985): *Understanding Organisations* (3rd edition), Harmondsworth: Penguin.

Hans Gurmeet (1985): *NFE for Rural Women*, Bombay: NSS Tata Institute of Social Science.

Haq M N (1989): Non-formal and alternative approach to primary level education (Swanirvar, Bangladesh) paper, UNESCO Institute of Education Hamburg.

Harbison F H (1965): Development of Human Resources: an analytical outline, in Jackson E E & Blackwell Basil (eds.), *Economic Development in Africa*, London: Collins.

Harbison F H (1973a): Human resources and NFE, in Brembeck C S & Thompson T J (eds.), *New Strategies for Educational Development: the cross-cultural search for nonformal alternatives*, Lexington: D C Heath: 5-12.

Harbison F H (1973b): *Human Resources as the Wealth of Nations*, New York: Oxford University Press.

Harbison F H & Seltzer D (1970): unpublished paper, in Krueger C & Moulton J (1981): *DS/ED Nonformal Education 1970-1980: a retrospective study*, Washington: USAID paper: 6.

Harman D (1974): *Community Fundamental Education: a nonformal educational strategy for development*, Lexington, MA: D C Heath.

Harvard (1997): website http://hugse1.harvard.edu/~ncsall (Focus on Basics) accessed 1999.

Harvard (2002): Course Papers on Nonformal Education in Developing Areas (N P Stromquist).

Hausmann Christine (1995): *NFE for Women in Zimbabwe: empowerment strategies and status improvement*, Frankfurt: Peter Lang.

Heimlich J E (1993): *Non-formal Environmental Education: towards a working definition*, Columbus, Ohio: ERIC.

Heimlich J E, Diem J & Farrell E (1996): *Adult Learning in Non-formal Institutions*, Columbus, Ohio: ERIC Digest 173.

Held D (1980): *Introduction to Critical Theory: Horkheimer to Habermas*, Berkeley: University of California Press.

Heredero J M (1977): *Rural Development and Social Change: an experiment in NFE*, New Delhi: Manohar Press.

Hettne B (1995): *Development Theory and the Three Worlds* (2nd edition), Harlow: Longman.

Heward C & Bunwaree S (eds.) (1999): *Gender, Education and Development: beyond access to empowerment*, London: Zed Books.

Hiehoff Richard O (1977): *NFE and the rural poor*, East Lansing, MI: Michigan State University.

Hilliard J F (1971): NFE: Key Problem Area No 2, USAID paper.

Hilliard J F (1973): Elements of an action program, in Brembeck C S & Thompson T J (eds.), *New Strategies for Educational Development: the cross-cultural search for nonformal alternatives*, Lexington: D C Heath: 137-146.

Hinzen H & Hunsdorfer V H (1979): *Education for Liberation and Development: the Tanzanian Experience*, Hamburg: UNESCO Institute of Education.

Hochleitner D (1991): in report of Fundacion Santillana Madrid 1991 cited in Garrido 1992: 88.

Hofstede G (1991): *Cultures and Organisations: software of the mind*, London: McGraw Hill.

Holford J, Jarvis P & Griffin C (1998): *International Perspectives on Lifelong Learning*, London: Kogan Page.

Hopper E (1971): *Readings in the Theory of Educational Systems*, London: Hutchinson.

Hoppers Wim (1985): *From School to Work: Youth, Nonformal Training and Employment in Lusaka*, The Hague: CESO.

Hoppers Wim (1999): A systems approach to the problems of Jomtien, paper presented to ADEA Workshop, Botswana, ADEA 1999b.

Hoppers Wim (2000a): Nonformal Education, Distance Education and the restructuring of schooling: challenges for a new basic education policy, *International Review of Education*, 46.1-2: 5-30.

Hoppers Wim (2000b): Towards a policy agenda for diversified delivery in formal basic education: the contribution of non-formal education, in ADEA 2000b.

Horkheimer M (1972): *Critical Theory*, New York: Seabury Press.

Horton M & Freire P (1990): *We Make the Road by Walking*, Philadelphia: Temple University Press.

Hossain M K & Rahman M H (1995): Nonformal Education in Bangladesh: an analysis of costs, *Educational Research Digest*, 2: 17-34 Dhaka: CAMPE.

Houle C O (1963): *The Inquiring Mind*, Madison: University of Wisconsin (1988 edition).

Hoxeng James (1973): *Let Jorge Do It: an approach to rural NFE*, Amherst, MA: CIE.

Hunt D (1989): *Economic Theories of Development: an analysis of competing paradigms*, New York: Simon and Schuster.

Hunter J M, Borus M E & Mannan A (1974): *Economics of NFE*, East Lansing, MI: Michigan State University.

Husen T (ed.) (1979): *The Future of Formal Education*, Stockholm: Almqvist and Wiksell.

Husen T (1974): *The Learning Society*, London: Methuen.

Husen T & Postlethwaite T N (eds.) (1985): *The International Encyclopedia of Education: research and studies*, Oxford: Pergamon Press.

Husen T & Postlethwaite T N (eds.) (1994): *The International Encyclopedia of Education* (2nd edition), Oxford: Pergamon Press.

IBE (1975): *The UNESCO-International Bureau of Education Education Thesaurus*, Geneva: International Bureau of Education.

IBE (1987): *NFE in Developing Countries*, Information File, Geneva: International Bureau of Education (see Bacquelaine & Raymaekers 1991).

IBE (1996): *Educational Innovations 86*, Geneva: International Bureau of Education.

IBE (1998): Innodata: Databank on Educational Innovations, Geneva: International Bureau of Education (see Innodata 1998).

IDRC (1991): *Perspectives on Education for All*, Ottawa: IDRC.

IEC (1996a): Course 6 Reader, Cambridge: International Extension College.

IEC (1996b): Course 7 Non-formal and Adult Basic Education at a distance: study guide and reader Cambridge: International Extension College.

IIEP (1972): *Planning out of school education for development*, Paris: UNESCO IIEP.

IIEP (1981): *The Organisation of Education in Remote Rural Areas*, Lyons R F, Paris: UNESCO IIEP.

IIEP (1985): *Educational Planning in the Context of Current Development Problems*, vol 2: 141-270 Paris: UNESCO IIEP (Colombia survey).

IIEP (1989): *Diversification of the Educational Field*, (papers dated 1983 and 1985; published 1989).

IIEP (1995a): *Education and Aid: policies and practice*, Paris: UNESCO IIEP, IWGE.

IIEP (1995b): *Developments after Jomtien: EFA in SE Asia and the Pacific Region*, de Grauwe A and Bernard D, Paris: UNESCO IIEP.

IIEP 1999: *Non-formal vocational training programmes for disadvantaged youths and their insertion into the world of work: towards a framework for analysis and evaluation*, Ana Christina Leonardos, Paris: UNESCO IIEP.

Illich I (1973): *De-Schooling Society*, Harmondworth: Penguin.

ILO (1971a): *Employment Incomes and Equality*, Geneva: ILO.

ILO (1971b): *Matching Employment Opportunities and Expectations*, Geneva: ILO.

Imel S (ed.) (1996): *Learning in Groups: exploring fundamental principles, new uses and emer-ging opportunities*, San Francisco: Jossey Bass.

Imhabekhai C I (1998): Towards effective planning of adult and NFE programmes in developing countries, *Indian Journal of Adult Education*, 59.1: 5-9.

Indabawa S A (1999): The Case of Nonformal Education provisions in Namibia, paper presented to ADEA NFE Working Group Workshop, ADEA 1999b.

India DNFE nd: Ministry of Education and Social Welfare (1970s) NFE leaflet published by Directorate of Non-formal (Adult) Education.

India MHRD (1995): Mid-term Review of EFA, New Delhi: MRHD.

India MHRD (1996): National Policy on Education, New Delhi: MRHD.

India MHRD (1997): *Adult Education and Development*, New Delhi: MRHD.

Indonesia (1982): *Indonesia: implementation of a large scale NFE project*, Amherst, MA: CIE.

INFEP (1994): *Combating Illiteracy: an introduction to the Integrated Non-formal Education Programme*, Dhaka: PMED, Ministry of Education.

Ingadayehu R (1985): *Continuing Professional Development in Ethiopia*, unpublished PhD thesis, University of Ulster.

Ingle H T (1974): *Communication Media and Technology: a look at their role in NFE Programs*, Washington DC: Academy for Educational Development.

Inkeles A & Holsinger D B (1974): *Education and Individualism: Modernity in Developing Countries*, Leiden: Brill.

Inkeles A & Smith D (1974): *Becoming Modern: individual change in six developing countries*, London: Heinemann.

Innodata (1998): *Databank on educational innovation*, Paris: UNESCO IIEP (see International Bureau of Education 1998).

Iredale Roger (1978): NFE in India: dilemmas and initiatives, *Comparative Education*, 14: 267-275.

ISCED (1975, 1976, 1985): *International Standard Classification of Education*, Paris: UNESCO.

Israeli E (1986): Fiji's nonformal education for youth and adults, the next phase of development, *International Journal of Lifelong Education*, 5.2: 123-132.

Istance D, Schuetze H G & Schuller T (eds.) (2002): *International Perspectives on Lifelong Learning*, Milton Keynes: Open University and SRHE.

IUACE 1971 *Continuing Education and Universities,* Report of Conference, published by Indian University Association for Continuing Education, and University of Madras, Madras.

Jackson E E & Blackwell Basil (eds.) (1965): *Economic Development in Africa,* London: Collins.

Jacques D (1991): *Learning in Groups* (2nd edition), London: Kogan Page.

Jamil Baela (1995): Teachers Empowerment Fund, addressing quality and people – the non-formal Basic Education revolution, unpublished paper, Lahore: BUNYAD.

Jarvis P (1996): Sociology of Adult Education, in Tuijnman A C (ed.), *International Encyclopedia of Adult Education and Training* (2nd edition), Oxford: Pergamon: 158-163.

Jarvis P (2001a): *Age of Learning,* London: Kogan Page.

Jarvis P (2001b): *Learning in Later Life,* London: Kogan Page.

Jayaweera S (1979): Programmes of NFE for women, *Convergence,* 12.3: 21-31.

Jeffs T & Smith M (eds.) (1990): *Using Informal Education,* Milton Keynes: Open University Press.

Jellema A & Archer D (1997): *Critical reflection on strategies for including the marginalised in quality education,* unpublished paper, London: Action Aid.

Jencks C J & Smith M et al. (1973): *Inequality: a reassessment of the effect of family and schooling in America,* London: Allen Unwin.

Jerudasa R & Koshy T (eds.) (1976): *NFE for rural women,* New Delhi: Allied Publications.

Jilani A A (1998): Labouring among conflicts: challenges of NFE on a Tamil tea-plantation in Sri Lanka, *Convergence,* 31.3: 50-58.

Jimma (2000): Proceedings of Workshop on Assessment of Academic Performance of Department of Adult and NFE July 2000, issued by Jimma Training College, Ethiopia.

Johnson D A (1976): *NFE and Rural Youth,* Paris: OECD/CERI.

Jones A M E (1997): Training for empowerment? a comparative study of NFE for women in small island states, *Compare,* 27.3: 277-286.

Jones A & Ellis P (1995): A Caribbean-South Pacific perspective on NFE and women's empowerment, *Convergence,* 28.2: 17ff.

Jones P W (1992): *World Bank Financing of Education: lending, learning and development,* London: Routledge.

Jung I & King L (eds.) (1999): *Gender, Innovation and Education in Latin America,* Hamburg: UNESCO Institute of Education.

Kapoor A (2000): Bridging non-formal education with formal education: some impediments, *Indian Journal of Adult Education,* 61.1: 5-9.

Kassam Y (1979): Towards the integration of formal and NFE, in Hinzen H & Hunsdorfer V H (eds.): *Education for Liberation and Development: the Tanzanian Experience,* Hamburg: UNESCO Institute of Education.

Kassam Y (1982): Formal, non-formal and informal modes of learning: a glimpse of the Tanzanian experience, *International Review of Education,* 28.2: 263-264.

Kebede S (1993): *Rural Development in Ethiopia with emphasis on education,* Addis Adaba.

Keil F C (1989): *Concepts, Kinds and Cognitive Development,* Cambridge MA: MIT.

Kenya (1998): *Policy Guidelines on NFE*, Nairobi: Ministry of Education and Human Resource Development.

Kenya (1999): Non-Formal Education in Kenya, a country paper (Government of Kenya) presented to ADEA Workshop.

Kenya nd: Non-formal Education Course Outline, Nairobi: University of Nairobi.

Khan Abdul (1977): All India Radio's non-formal education broadcasts for rural development, in International Extension College 1996b: 71-85.

Khaqwaqja S & Brennan B (1990): *NFE: myth or panacea for Pakistan*, Islamabad: M R Books.

Khare S & Grewal (1997): A comparative study of academic achievement and creative abilities of the students in formal schools and NFE centres, *Asian Journal of Psychology and Education*, 30.5-6: 23-26.

Kidd Ross (1982): *Performing Arts, NFE and Social Change in the Third World*, The Hague: CESO.

Kidd Ross (1984): Popular theatre and NFE in the Third World: five strands of experience, *International Review of Education*, 30.3: 65-288.

Kilpatrick S, Morgan H & Falk I (1998): Change, visions and values and NFE, *Australian Journal of Adult and Community Education*, 38.1: 3-8.

Kindervatten S (1979): *NFE as an empowering process*, Amherst, MA: CIE.

King Edmund (ed.) (1979): *Learning for Uncertainty*, London: Sage.

King Jane (1967): *Planning NFE in Tanzania*, Paris: UNESCO IIEP.

King K (1975): *The African Artisan: a study of training, technology and the informal sector in Kenya*, Edinburgh: Edinburgh University Press.

King K (ed.) (1976): *Education and Community in Africa*, Edinburgh: Edinburgh University Press.

King K (1982): Formal, Nonformal and Informal Learning: some North-South contrasts, *International Review of Education*, 28.2: 177-187.

King K (1991): *Aid and Education in the Developing World*, London: Longman.

King K & Buchert L (1999): *Changing International Aid to Education: global patterns and national contexts*, Paris: UNESCO.

Kinsey D & Bing J W (1987): NFE in Ghana, Project Report, Amherst MA: CIE.

Kinsey D C (1978): *Evaluation in NFE*, Amherst MA: CIE.

Kishan N R (1998): Curriculum designing for NFE and adult education, *Progress of Education*, 73.5: 100-102.

Kitching G (1989): *Development and Under-Development in Historical Perspective*, London: Routledge.

Klees S & Wells S (1978): *Cost-benefit analysis of Non-formal Educational Techniques for Agricultural Development: a case study of the basic village education project in Guatemala*, Washington DC: Academy for Educational Development.

Kleis R (1974): *Case studies in NFE*, East Lansing, MI: Michigan State University.

Kleis R J (1973): *NFE: the definitional problem*, East Lansing, MI: Michigan State University.

Knowles M (1970): *The Modern Practice of Adult Education: pedagogy versus andragogy*, New York: Association Press.

Kotze Astrid von (1991): Training grassroots educators: provision of NF Adult Education in the Durban region, *Convergence*, 24.4: 16-23.

Krueger C & Moulton J (1981): *DS/ED Nonformal Education 1970-1980: a retrospective study*, Washington: USAID paper.

Kulatunga J A K (1997): *Nonformal Education Strategies in Sri Lanka*, Maharagama, Sri Lanka: National Institute of Education Press.

Kumar S (1998): Components of anti-tobacco NFE program for India, *Journal of Clinical Epidemiology*, 51 (supplement): 365.

LaBelle T J (ed.) (1975): *Educational Alternatives in Latin America: social change and social stratification*, Los Angeles: University of California Los Angeles.

LaBelle T J (1976a): *NFE and Social Change in Latin America*, Los Angeles: University of California Los Angeles.

LaBelle T J (1976b): Introduction, *Comparative Education Review*, 20.3: 278-280.

LaBelle T J (1976c): Goals and strategies of NFE in Latin America, *Comparative Education Review*, 20.3: 328-345.

LaBelle T J (1981): Introduction to the nonformal education of children and youth, *Comparative Education Review*, 25.3: 313-329.

LaBelle T J (1982): Formal, nonformal and informal education: a holistic perspective on life-long learning, *International Review of Education*, 28.2: 159-175.

LaBelle T J (1986): *NFE and the Poor in Latin America and the Caribbean: stability, reform or revolution*, New York: Praeger.

LaBelle T J (1987): From consciousness-raising to popular education in Latin America and the Caribbean, *Comparative Education Review*, 31.2: 201-217.

LaBelle T J (2000): The changing nature of non-formal education in Latin America, *Comparative Education*, 36.1: 21-36.

LaBelle T J & Sylvester J J (1990): Delivery systems, formal, non-formal and informal, in Thomas R M (ed.): *International Comparative Education: practices, issues and prospects*, Oxford: Pergamon: 141-160.

LaBelle T J & Verhine R (1975): NFE and occupational stratification: implications for Latin America, *Harvard Educational Review*, 45: 160-190.

LaBelle T J & Ward C R (1994): *NFE policy in developing countries*, in Husen T & Postlethwaite T N (eds.) *The International encyclopedia of education* (2nd edition), Oxford: Pergamon Press: 4141-4145.

LaBelle T J & Ward C R (1996): *Development through NFE*, in Tuijnman A C (ed.), *International Encyclopedia of Adult Education and Training* (2nd edition), Oxford: Pergamon: 228-233.

Laclau E & Mouffe C (1985): *Hegemony and Socialist Strategy: towards a radical democratic politics*, London: Verso.

Laclau E & Mouffe C (1990): Post-Marxism without apologies, in Laclau E (ed.), *New Reflections on the Revolution of Our Time* London: Verso: 97-132.

Laclau E (ed.) (1990): *New Reflections on the Revolution of Our Time*, London: Verso.

Lageman E C & Shulma L S (eds.) (1999): *Issues in Educational Research: problems and possibilities*, San Francisco: Jossey Bass.

Lamichane S & Kapoor D (1992): NFE and rural evolution: multiple perspectives, *Convergence*, 25.3: 44-49.

Landazuri H & Piaggesi D (1998): Satellite-based non-formal environmental education: a case in Guyana, *European Space Agency*, 412: 131-145.

LaTowsky R J (1997): *Egypt's NGO Sector: a briefing paper*, Occasional Paper, Reading: Education for Development.

Lauglo J (1995): Banking on education and the uses of research: a critique of World Bank priorities and strategies for education, *International Journal of Educational Development*, 16.3: 221-233.

Lauglo J (2000): *Engaging with Adults: the case for increased support to adult basic education in sub-Saharan Africa*, Washington D C: World Bank.

Lauglo Jon (2003): *Education, Training and Contexts: studies and essays*, Frankfurt: Peter Lang.

Leach F (1998a): Gender, education and training: an international perspective, in Sweetman C (ed.), *Gender, Education and Training*, Oxford: Oxfam: 9-18.

Leach F (1998b): Gender on the aid agenda: men, women and educational opportunity, in Drake P & Owen P (eds.), *Gender and Management Issues in Education: an international perspective*, Stoke on Trent: Trentham Books: 49-66.

Leach F (2000): Gender implications of development agency policies on education and training, *International Journal of Educational Development*, 20.4: 333-347.

Leach F & Little A (eds.) (1999): *Education, Cultures and Economics: dilemmas for development*, London: Falmer.

Lengrand P (1982): Structures de l'apprentissage dans les pays de l'Europe Occidentale, *International Review of Education*, 28.2: 189-207.

Lerner D (1958): *The Passing of Traditional Society*, Glencoe, NY: Free Press.

Levine J M & Moreland R L (1990): *Progress in Small Group Research*, special issue of *Annual Review of Psychology*, 41.

Lewin K (1987): *Education in Austerity: options for planners*, Paris: UNESCO IIEP.

Lister I (ed.) (1975): *DeSchooling*, Cambridge: Cambridge University Press.

Lit Africa (2001): *Literacy in Africa*, paper prepared for meeting of African Ministers of Education 2002 Paris: UNESCO.

Lok Jumbish (1999): papers of Lok Jumbish project 1999.

Long N & Long A (eds.) (1992): *Battlefields of Knowledge: the interlocking of theory and practice in social research and development*, London: Routledge.

Lovell C & Fatema K (1989): *The BRAC NFPE Program in Bangladesh*, New York: UNICEF.

Loveridge A J (1978): *British colonial experience in educational development: a survey of non-formal for rural and agricultural development*, Cardiff: University College Press.

Lowe J (1985): Non-formal post-secondary education, in Husen T & Postlethwaite T N (eds.) *The International encyclopedia of education: research and studies*, Oxford: Pergamon Press: 3556-3559.

Lowe J, Grant N & Williams T D (1971): *Education and Nation Building in the Third World* Edinburgh: Scottish Academic Press.

Lucas A M (1983): Scientific literacy and informal learning, *Studies in Science Education*, 10: 1-36.

Lynch James, Modgil Celia & Modgil Sohan (eds.) (1997): Non-Formal and Non-Governmental Approaches, vol 4 of *Education and Development: tradition and innovation*, London: Cassells.

Maarschalk J (1988): Scientific literacy and informal science teaching, *Journal of Research in Science Teaching*, 25.2: 135-146.

Macfarlane A (1978): *The Origin of English Individualism*, Oxford: Blackwell.

Macharia D, Mbunda D & Buberwa A K (1990): Report on the evolution of literacy and NFE in Namibia, Windhoek: Ministry of Education, Government of Namibia.

MacIntyre A (1987): The idea of an educated public, in Haydon G (ed.) *Education for a pluralist society*, London: Institute of Education, University of London.

Maclure R (1994): NFE and Strategies of Intervention: a case study in Burkina Faso, *Africana*, 1994: 269-291.

Maclure R (1995): NGOs and the education of children in Africa: a preliminary investigation in Senegal, cited in Boukary 1998.

Mahroof M M M (1993): Nonformal and Informal Education among Muslims of Sri Lanka 1890-1990, *Muslim Education Quarterly*, 10.4: 46ff.

Manna M A (1975): *Economic Aspects of NFE (Bibliography)*, East Lansing, MI: Michigan State University.

Marchand M H & Parpart J L (eds.) (1995): *Feminism, Post-Modernism and Development*, London: Routledge.

Marja T (1993): Role of voluntary organisations and NFAdult Education in the struggle for freedom and democracy, *Convergence*, 26.1: 59-65.

Maruatona T (1999): Issues in Policy and Provision in Non-Formal Basic Education in East and Southern Africa, in ADEA 1999b.

Matheson D J (1991): Non-vocational non-formal further education in the highland region in Scotland and the canton of Valais in Switzerland, *Comparative Education*, 27.2: 153-164.

Mayo P (1999): *Gramsci, Freire and Adult Education*, London: Zed Books.

McCall S (1970): *NFE: a definition*, Washington DC: USAID paper.

McClelland D (1961): *The Achieving Society*, New York: Free Press.

McClelland D (1969): *Latin America: under-development or revolution?*, New York: Monthly Review Press.

McGrath S (2001): Research in a cold climate: towards a political economy of British international and comparative education, *International Journal of Educational Development*, 21: 391-400.

Mead Margaret (1943): Our educational emphasis in primitive perspective, *American Journal of Sociology*, 48: 633-639.

Mehta A C (1996): Development and utilisation of database for non-formal literacy programmes and networking of computers, *Indian Journal of Adult Education*, 57.2: 35-45.

Meredith J E, Fortner R W & Mullins G W (1997): Model of affective learning for nonformal science education facilities, *Journal of Research in Science Teaching*, 34. 8: 805-818.

Merriam S B & Cafarella R S (1999): *Learning in Adulthood* (2nd edition), San Francisco: Jossey Bass.

Meyer John (1992): World expansion of mass education, *Sociology of Education*, 65: 128-149.

Mfum-Mensah (2003): Fostering educational participation in pastoral communities through non-formal education: the Ghanaian perspective, *International Journal of Educational Development*, 23.6: 661-677.

Mickelwaite D R, Sweet C F & Elliott R M (1979): *New Directions in Development*, Boulder, Colorado: Westview Press.

Midgeley J (1986): *Community Participation, Social Development and the State*, London: Methuen.

MIDS (1987a): Papers of National Seminar on Development-Oriented Non-formal Education Research, Madras: Madras Institute of Development Studies.

MIDS (1987b): *Role of university in NFE Research*, seminar paper, Balasubramanian P S, Madras: Madras Institute of Development Studies.

Miles M B (ed.) (1964): *Innovation in Education*, New York: Teachers College, Columbia University.

Millar C (1991): *Adult education: delineating the field*, unpublished paper, Pretoria, S Africa: NEPI.

Miller J E, Trimbur J & Wilkes J M (1994): Group dynamics: understanding group success and failure in collaborative learning, in Bosworth K, Hamilton S J (eds.) *Collaborative Learning: underlying processes and effective techniques*, San Francisco: Jossey Bass.

Mitchell T (1991): America's Egypt: discourse of the development industry, *Middle East Report*, March-April: 18-36.

Mocker D W & Spear G E (1982): *Lifelong Learning: formal, nonformal, informal and self-directed*, Columbus, Ohio: ERIC.

Mohanty B B (1999): Role of distance education in promoting literacy, adult education and nonformal basic education for rural and social development, *Indian Journal of Adult Education*, 60.4: 9-21.

Mohanty C, Russo A & Torres L (eds.) (1991): *Third World Women and the Politics of Feminisim*, Bloomington: Indiana UP.

Mohanty J (1993): *Adult and Nonformal Education*, New Delhi: Deep and Deep.

Mohsin S (2000): Impact of technology on women: strategies for NFE, *Indian Journal of Gender Studies*, 7.1: 101-124.

Moleko P & Betz R (1995): *Training Manual for Non-Formal and Adult Trainers*, Maseru, Lesotho: Lesotho Distance Teaching Center.

Moore W E (1964): *Social Change*, New Jersey: Prentice Hall.

Morales F X Swett (1983): Aspects of financing NFE, *Prospects*, 13.1: 55-60.

Moro'oka K (1985): NFE in Japan, in Husen T & Postlethwaite T N (eds.) *The International encyclopedia of education: research and studies*, Oxford: Pergamon Press: 3546-3548.

Morolong P M (2000): *Nonformal education and income generation in self-managed rural groups in Lesotho*, unpublished thesis University of Johannesburg.

Morphet A R (1986): Curriculum issues in NFE: a case study and interpretation, *International Journal of Lifelong Education*, 5.2: 133-152.

Mosley P, Harrigan J & Toye J (1995): *Aid and Power: the World Bank and policy-based lending*, London: Routledge.

Moulton J (2000): Thinking strategically about non-formal education, in ADEA 2000b.

Moulton Jeanne (1997): *Formal and Nonformal Education and Empowered Behavior: a review of the research literature*, Washington: USAID.

Michigan State University (1973a): *NFE and the structure of culture*, East Lansing, MI: Michigan State University.

Michigan State University (1973b): *NFE - the definitional problem*, East Lansing, MI: Michigan State University Discussion Papers 2.

Michigan State University (1980): *Non-formal approaches to primary education in Asia*, East Lansing, MI: Michigan State University.

Michigan State University (1981): *Annotated Bibliography of NFE and health*, East Lansing, MI: Michigan State University.

Michigan State University (1982a): *Annotated Bibliography of NFE and Agriculture*, East Lansing, MI: Michigan State University.

Michigan State University (1982b): *Annotated Bibliography of NFE and the handicapped*, East Lansing, MI: Michigan State University.

Michigan State University (1983a): *Annotated Bibliography of Evaluation in NFE*, East Lansing, MI: Michigan State University.

Michigan State University (1983b): *Annotated Bibliography of NFE and the use and management of water*, East Lansing, MI: Michigan State University.

Michigan State University (1983c): *Annotated Bibliography: Financial Resources for NFE*, East Lansing, MI: Michigan State University.

Mucunguzi P (1995): Review of nonformal environmental education in Uganda, *Environmental Education Research*, 1.3: 337ff.

Mudimbe V Y (1988): *The Invention of Africa*, Bloomington, IN: Indiana University Press.

Mueller J (1997): Literacy and non-formal (basic) education: still a donor's priority?, *Adult Education and Development*, 48: 37-60.

Mukherjee T (1997): Non-formal Education: a deceptive prop for EFA, *Indian Journal of Adult Education*, Apr-Jun: 5-20.

Mumba E C (1999): *Diversification of Adult Education Provision in Zambia*, paper presented to ADEA NFE Working Group Workshop 1999.

Mumba E C (1994): Delivery system and organization of NFE in Zambia, *International Journal of University Adult Education*, 33.3: 45-54.

Musa O (2001): *Non-formal Education in Post-Conflict Sierra Leone*, unpublished paper prepared for Education for Development AGM September.

Muskin J A (1999): Including local priorities to assess school qualities: the case of Save the Children Community Schools in Mali, *Comparative Education Review*, 43.1: 36-63.

Muyeed A (1982): Some reflections on education for rural development, *International Review of Education*, 28.2: 227-238.

Myrdal G (1971): *Challenge of World Poverty*, Harmondsworth: Penguin.

Naik C (1989): *Non-formal Education for out of school children, a case study*, Indian Institute of Education, Pune.

Naik Chitra (1983): India: extending primary education through non-formal approaches, *Prospects*, 13.1: 61-72.

Naik Chitra (1985): *Developing Non-formal Primary Education: a rewarding experience*, Pune: Indian Institute of Education.

Naik J P nd *Some Perspectives on NFE*, Pune: Indian Institute of Education.

Naik J P (1978): *Education for Our People*, Pune: Indian Institute of Education.

Namibia (1991): NFE and literacy programmes in Namibia: the host country, *Convergence*, 24.1-2: 8-18.

Namibia (1997): *NF Adult Education: the way forward in Namibia*, Washington DC: World Education.

Narang R H (1992): Social justice and political education through nonformal training, *International Review of Education*, 38.5: 542-546.

Naswa S (1997): NFE in rural India, *Kurukshetra*, 45.12: 24.

Nath S R (1999): Level, pattern and socio-economic determinants of enrolment in formal schools of the graduates of BRAC's Non-formal schools, *Perspectives in Education*, 15.3: 179-189.

Nath S R (2000): *Basic Competencies of the graduates of BRAC's non-formal schools: levels and trends from 1995 to 1999*, Dhaka: BRAC.

Nath S R, Sylva K & Grimes J (1999): Raising basic education levels in rural Bangladesh: the impact of a non-formal education programme, *International Review of Education* 45.1: 5-26.

Nath S R & Chowdhury A M R (1998): *Levels of basic competences of BRAC school graduates of 1995 and 1997*, Dhaka: BRAC.

NCC (1971): National Council of Churches, First World Symposium on Innovation and Policy in NFE, East Lansing MI: Kellogg Center.

NEPI (1992): *New Education Policy Initiative, South Africa*, Pretoria: Government of South Africa.

New Zealand (1985): *Lifelong Learning, Non-formal and Community Education*, Wellington: Report of Working Group on Non-Formal and Community Education.

New Zealand (1989): Report of Working Group on Non-Formal and Community Education, Ministry of Education.

NFE Exchange, journal of Michigan State University, East Lansing, MI 1976-1982.

NFL (2001): Exploring potentials of non-formal learning, review of recent research, www.b. shuttle.de/wifo/lll/ln.htm accessed July 2001.

Niehoff R (1977): *NFE and the Rural Poor*, East Lansing, MI: Michigan State University.

Niehoff R O & Wilder B (1974): *NFE in Ethiopia*, East Lansing, MI: Michigan State University.

NOVIB (2000): *Network*, publication of NOVIB, The Netherlands.

Nyamu F K (1999): Cultural perceptions of the role of mathematics and mathematics education in economic development: examples from Kenya, in Leach F & Little A (eds.), *Education, Cultures and Economics: dilemmas for development*, London: Falmer: 301-326.

Nyirenda J E (1995): Radio broadcasting for adult nonformal environmental education in Bots-wana, *Convergence*, 28.4: 61-70.

O'Hanlon R & Washbrook D (1992): After orientalism: culture, criticism and the politics of the Third World, *Comparative Studies in Society and History*, 34.1: 141-167.

Oakley P & Marsden D (1984): *Approaches to Participation in Rural Development*, Geneva: ILO.

Ocitti J P (1988): Indigenous African pedagogy, *Adult Education and Development*, 30: 347-358.

Ocitti J P (1994): *An Introduction to Indigenous Education in East Africa*, Bonn: DVV.

ODA (1975): *Changing Emphasis in British Aid Policies: more help for the poorest*, London: ODA.

ODA (1976): *Guidelines for UK Aid to Education in Developing Countries*, London ODA.

ODA (1984): *British Aid to Education in Developing Countries*, London: ODA.

ODA (1986): *Educational priorities and Aid Responses in Sub-Saharan Africa*, edited by Hawes H & Coombe T, London: ODA.

Odora Catherine A (1992): Decentralization and the re-validation of the indigenous learning systems, in Buchert L (ed.), *Education and Training in the Third World*, The Hague: CESO.

OECD (1996): Making Lifelong Learning a Reality for All, statement of meeting of education committee at ministerial level.

Ofcansky T P & Berry LaVerle (1993): *Ethiopia, a country study*, Washington DC: Library of Congress.

Omolewa M (1998): *NFE in Nigeria*, unpublished paper, Ibadan: University of Ibadan.

Ong W J (1982): *Orality and Literacy: the technologizing of the word*, London: Methuen.

Ordonez (1990): speech in UIE 1990.

Overwien Bernd (1997): Employment-oriented non-formal training for young people in the informal sector in Latin America, *Education*, 55-56: 146-157.

Oxenham J (1975): *Non-formal approaches to teaching literacy*, East Lansing, MI: Michigan State University.

Oxenham J (2002): *Skills and Literacy Training for Better Livelihoods*, Washington D C: World Bank.

OXFAM nd: Aid and Education: the squandered opportunity, Oxford: OXFAM paper.

Paik H K (1973): NFE in Korea: programs and prospects, in Brembeck C S & Thompson T J (eds.), *New Strategies for Educational Development: the cross-cultural search for non-formal alternatives,* Lexington: D C Heath: 175-184.

Pakistan (2000): Challenges in the 21st Century: Nonformal Education and Literacy in Pakistan, paper prepared by T Shinji & M Shahid for Pakistan Literacy Commission, Islamabad, September.

Pakistan CARE (1997): Evaluation report on Home School Project.

Pakistan undated: WEPA programme, Lahore: Bunyad.

Paolucci B et al. (1976): *Women, Families and Non-formal Learning Programs*, East Lansing, MI: Michigan State University.

Papagiannis G (1977): *NFE and national development*, PhD dissertation, Stanford University.

Parpart J L (1995a): Post-modernism, gender and development, in Crush J (ed.) (1995): *Development as Power*, London: Routledge: 253-265.

Parpart J L (1995b): Deconstructing the development 'expert': gender, development and the 'vulnerable groups', in Marchand M H & Parpart J L (eds.), *Feminism, Post-Modernism and Development*, London: Routledge: 221-243.

Paul M C (1999): Dimensions of NFE in Bengal during the Bengal Renaissance, *Indian Journal of Adult Education*, 60.4: 9-21. (also in *Indian Journal of University Adult and Continuing Education*, 1997, 36.2: 36-47).

Paul S & Gupta V (1999): Expenditure of primary education through non-formal channels or centres, *Progress of Education*, 60.3: 39-49.

Paulston R G (1970): NFE in Peru, *Comparative and International Education Society Newsletter*, June.

Paulston R G (1971): *Society, Schools and Progress in Peru*, Oxford: Pergamon.

Paulston R G (1972): *Non-formal Education: an annotated international bibliography of the non-school sector*, New York: Praeger.

Paulston R G (1973): Nonformal education alternatives, in Brembeck & Thompson (eds.), *New strategies for educational development: the cross-cultural search for nonformal alternatives*, Lexington, Mass.: Lexington Books: 65-85.

Paulston R G (1980): Education as anti-structure: non-formal education in social and ethnic movements, *Comparative Education*, 16.1: 55-66.

Paulston R G (ed.) (1996): *Social Cartography: mapping ways of seeing social and educational change*, New York: Garland.

Paulston R G & LeRoy G (1982): NFE and change from below, in Altbach P G, Arnove R F & Kelly G P (eds.), *Comparative Education*, London: Mac-millan: 336-362.

Pennells J & Ezeomah C (2000): Basic education for refugees and nomads, in Yates C & Bradley O (eds.), *Basic Education at a Distance*, London: RoutledgeFalmer & Commonwealth of Learning: 173-191.

Percy C (1997): On formal, nonformal and informal lifelong learning: reconceptualising the boundaries for research, theory and practice, *Proceedings of SCUTREA 27th Conference*, University of Warwick.

Percy Keith (1983): *Post-initial Education in the North-West of England: a survey of provision*, Leicester: ACACE.

Perraton H (ed.) (1982): *Alternative Routes to Formal Education: distance teaching for school equivalency*, Baltimore: John Hopkins University.

Philippines (1999): Accreditation and Equivalency, Papers from BNFE.

Philipps H M (1975a): *Basic Education: a world challenge*, New York: Wiley.

Philipps H M (1975b): *What is Meant by Basic Education?* Paris: UNESCO IIEP.

Pigozzi M J (1982): Participation in NFE projects: some possible negative outcomes, *Convergence*, 15.3: 6-18.

Pigozzi M J (1999): *Education in Emergencies and for Reconstruction: a developmental approach*, New York: UNICEF.

Pilar A & Retamal G (1998): *Education in Complex Emergencies*, Hamburg: UNESCO Institute of Education.

Pillai P G (1998): NFE through Nehru Yuvak Kendras, *Kurukshetra* (New Delhi) 47.1: 21-22.

Piquero M B (1998): Continuing nonformal adult education for the grassroots community in the Philippines, *Adult Education and Development*, 50: 117-128.

Poizat D (2003): *L-education nonformelle* published by L'Harmattan, collection Education compare.

Postlethwaite T N (ed.) (1988): *Encyclopedia of Comparative Education and National Systems of Education*, Oxford: Pergamon.

Postman N & Weingartner C (1971): *Teaching as a Subversive Activity*, Harmondsworth: Penguin.

Poston S (1976): *NFE in Latin America*, Berkeley: University of California.

PPA (1997): Pusat Pengembangan Agribisnis, *Impact Evaluation of NFE Program in Batch I and II*, Jakarta: Ministry of Education and Culture.

Prather C J & Ahmed M (eds.) (1993): *Primary Education for All: learning from the BRAC experience, a case study*, Washington DC: ABEL.

Prinsloo M & Breier M (eds.) (1996): *Social Uses of Literacy*, Amsterdam: Benjamin and Pretoria: SACHED.

PROPEL nd (1997): *The Propel Story: promoting primary and elementary education*, Pune: Indian Institute of Education.

Proshika (1994): *UEP: Report on Universal Education Programme 1993-4*, Dhaka: Proshika.

Proshika (1995): *Five Year Universal Education Programme Plan 1994-1999*, Dhaka: Proshika.

Prosser R (1967): *Adult Education for Developing Countries*, Nairobi: East Africa Publishing House.

PROTEC nd: Vocational education in the non-formal sector: the case of PROTEC, unpublished briefing paper prepared by Link Africa undated but c 1997.

Puchner L (2003): Women and literacy in rural Mali: a study of the socio-economic impact of participating in literacy programs in four villages, *International Journal of Educational Development*, 23.4: 439-458.

Qayyum A (1981): *Non-formal approaches to revitalize basic education: some stray experiences of Pakistan*, Paris: UNESCO/UNICEF.

Rabinowitz J (2000b): ASECA, in ADEA 2000b.

Radcliffe D J & Colletta N J (1985): Nonformal Education, in Husen T & Postlethwaite T N (eds.) *The International encyclopedia of education: research and studies*, Oxford: Pergamon Press: 3536-3540.

Rahman A N S Habibur (1994): *Non-formal Primary Education: curriculum*, Dhaka: Proshika.

Rahman A N S Habibur (1996): *Non-formal Primary Education – Proshika Approach*, unpublished briefing paper, Dhaka: Proshika.

Rahman Md Anisur (1993): *People's Self-Development: perspectives on participatory action research*, London: Zed Books.

Rahman R H (1992): *Cost Determination of Government Primary Schools and BRAC's Non-Formal Primary Schools*, 2 vols, Washington DC: Academy for Educational Development.

Rahman S Attiqur (2000): *Taking Control: women emerge from poverty*, Mumbai: ASPBAdult Education 'Beyond Literacy' series.

Rahnema M (1991): Global Poverty, a pauperizing myth, *Interculture*, 24.2: 4-51.

Rajan J V (1999): Forum for fostering rural initiatives in nonformal education, science and technology for development, *Chemical Business Journal*, Bombay 13.3: 53-54.

Ramachandran Vimala (ed.) (2003): *Getting Children Back to School: case studies in primary education*, Delhi: Sage.

Ranaweera A M (ed.) (1989): *Non-conventional Approaches to Education at the Primary Level*, Hamburg: UNESCO Institute of Education.

Ranaweera A M (1990): Innovative approaches to achieving Universal Primary Education and its democratization: a synopsis; paper at Round Table on complementarity of formal and non-formal approaches at the primary education level, Hamburg: UNESCO Institute of Education.

Re'em M (2001): Young minds in motion: interactive pedagogy in non-formal settings, *Teaching and Teacher Education*, 17.3: 291-305.

Reed H (1984): NFE, in Reed H & Loughran E L (eds.), *Beyond Schools: education for economic, social and personal development*, Amherst, MA: University of Massachusetts: 51-72.

Reed H & Loughran E L (eds.) (1984): *Beyond Schools: education for economic, social and personal development*, Amherst, MA: University of Massachusetts.

Reed H B (1987): Conflicting Images of NFE, *Lifelong Learning*, 10.6: 23-25.

Reimer E (1971): *School is Dead: an essay on alternatives to school*, Harmondsworth: Penguin.

REP (1998): *Rapid Educational Response in Complex Emergencies: a discussion document*, by P Anguilar & G Retamal, Geneva: International Bureau of Education.

Retamal G & Aedo-Richmond R (eds.) (1998): *Education as a Humanitarian Response*, Geneva: International Bureau of Education; London: Cassell.

Rheinhold A J (1993): *Working With Rural Communities in Nepal: some principles of Non-formal Education Intervention*, Paris: UNESCO.

Richardson L E & Wolfe M (ed.) (2001): *Principles and Practice of Informal Education*, London: Routledge.

Robertson C C (1984): Formal or NFE: entrepreneurial women in Ghana, *Comparative Education Review*, 28: 639-658.

Robinson B (1995): Mongolia in transition: a role for distance education?, *Open Learning*, November: 3-14.

Robinson B (1999): Open and distance learning in the Gobi desert: NFE for nomadic women, *Distance Education*, 20.2: 181-204.

Robinson B (2001): *Open Learning in the Gobi Desert: Non-formal Education for Nomadic Women*, unpublished paper prepared for UNESCO 2001.

Robinson Pant A (2001): Development as discourse: what relevance to education?, *Compare*, 31.3: 311-328.

Robinson-Pant A (2000): *Discourses of development*, paper prepared for Uppingham Seminar www/uppinghamseminars.org.

Rockhill K (1993): Gender, language and the politics of literacy, in Street B V (ed.) *Cross-Cultural Approaches to Literacy*, Cambridge: Cambridge University Press: 156-175.

Rodney W (1972): *How Europe Underdeveloped Africa*, London: Bogle-L'Ouverture Publications.

Rogers A (1992): *Adults Learning for Development*, London: Cassell.

Rogers A (1994): *Women, Literacy, Income-generation*, Reading: Education for Development.

Rogers A (2000): Cultural transfer in adult education: the case of the Folk Development Colleges in Tanzania, *International Review of Education*, 46.1-2: 67-92.

Rogers A (2002): *Re-Thinking Adult Literacy and Post-Literacy from an International Perspective*, The Roby Kidd Memorial Lecture, Uppingham: Uppingham Press.

Rogers A (2003): *What is the Difference? a new critique of adult learning and teaching*, Leicester: NIACE.

Rogers Carl (1983): *Freedom to Learn for the 80s*, Columbus, Ohio: Merrill.

Rogers E & Danzieger S (1975): NFE and Communication Technology: the second dimension of development and the little media, in LaBelle T J (ed.), *Educational Alternatives in Latin America: social change and social stratification*, Los Angeles: University of California Los Angeles.

Rogers E M (1976): Communication and Development: the passing of the dominant paradigm, *Communication Research*, 3: 121-148.

Rogers E M, Colletta N J & Mbindyo J (1981): Social and cultural influences on human development, in World Bank, *Implementing Programs of Human Development*, Washington DC: World Bank.

Romi S (2000): Distance learning and NFE: existing trends and new possibilities of distance learning experiences, *Educational Media International*, 37.1: 39-44.

Rostow W W (1960): *Stages of Economic Growth: a non-communist manifesto*, Cambridge: Cambridge University Press.

Russell C S & Nicholson N K (1981): *Public Choice and Rural Development*, Washington DC: Resources for the Future.

Rydstrom (1995): Sweden: adult education for democracy, in Cassara B B (ed.), *Adult Education through World Collaboration*, Malabar: Kreiger.

Sachs Wolfgang (ed.) (1992): *Development Dictionary* London: Zed Books.

Saeed (2000): Background paper on Action Aid NFE program in Haripur, Pakistan, prepared for workshop in Addis Ababa, November.

Saghir A R (1987): Case study of selected non-formal population education in Pakistan, *Pakistan Journal of Distance Education*, IV.2: 45-57; V.1: 51-62.

Sampson E (1993): *Celebrating the Other*, Hemel Hempstead: Harvester Wheatsheaf.

Santillana (1991): *La educacion no-formal, una prioridad de futuro: documentos de un debate*, Fundacion Santillana Madrid.

SARA (1998): Support for Analysis and Research in Africa, Formal and Nonformal Education and Empowered Behavior: a review of the research literature (www.id21/eldis).

Schiele B (1995): The non-formal communication of scientific knowledge, *Prospects*, 25.1: 87ff.

Schramm W (1973): *Big Media - Little Media*, Washington DC: Academy for Educational Development.

Schultz T W (1977): Investment in Human Capital, in Karabel J & Halsey A H (eds.), *Power and Ideology in Education*, New York: Oxford University Press: 313-324.

Schumpeter J A (1961): *Theory of Economic Development*, Oxford: Oxford University Press.

Schuurman F J (1993): *Beyond the Impasse: new directions in development theory*, London: Zed Books.

SEAMEO (1975): *Beyond School Walls: a study of non-formal education in the SEAMEO region 1973-4*, Bangkok: SEAMEO.

Sedere M U (1998): *Financing NFE in the context of Bangladesh Education Sector*, Dhaka: SDC.

Seers D (1969): Meaning of development, *International Development Review*, 1.4: 2-6.

Sekoati M & Sloper D (1997): Expanding the delivery of distance education in Lesotho, in Lynch James, Modgil Celia & Modgil Sohan (eds.), Non-Formal and Non-Governmental Approaches, vol 4 of *Education and Development: tradition and innovation*, London: Cassells: 131-152.

Sen A (1999): *Development as Freedom*, Oxford: Oxford University Press.

Sen G & Grown C (1987): *Development, Crises and Alternative Visions*, New York: Monthly Review Press.

Senegal nd (after 1992): Final Evaluation Report, NFE for Development, unpublished paper.

Serpell R (1999): Local Accountability to Rural Communities: a challenge for educational planning in Africa, in Leach F & Little A (eds.), *Education, Cultures and Economics: dilemmas for development*, London: Falmer: 111-139.

Shaeffer Sheldon F (1992): *Collaboration for Educational Change in Non-formal Basic Education*, Paris: UNESCO IIEP.

Sharafuddin A M (1995): The information age and the learning society, *Educational Research Digest*, 2: 1-16.

Shavelson R J, Jiyono M B & Obemeata J O (1985): *Evaluation of NFE Programmes: the applicability and utility of criterion sampling approach*, Hamburg: UNESCO Institute of Education.

Sheffield J R & Diejomaoh V P (1972): *Non-formal Education in African Development*, New York: African-American Institute.

Shepherd Andrew (1998): *Sustainable Rural Development*, London: Macmillan.

Shirur Rajani R (1995): *NFE for Development*, New Delhi: APH Publishing.

Shorey L L (1983): Training for formal and non-formal education: a Caribbean perspective, *Convergence*, 16.4: 57-64.

Siaciwena R & O'Rourke J (2000): Basic education curriculum: contexts and contents, in Yates C & Bradley J (eds.), *Basic Education at a Distance*, London: RoutledgeFalmer.

Siaciwena R (ed.) (in press): *Case Studies of NFE by Distance and Open Learning in Africa*, Vancouver: Commonwealth of Learning.

Siegel J (1997): Formal versus non-formal education: the educational reform in Papua New Guinea, *Journal of Multilingual and Multicultural Development*, 18.3: 206-222.

Simkins T (1977): *Non-formal Education and Development*, Manchester: Manchester University Press.

Simmons J (ed.) (1980): The *Education Dilemma: policy issues for developing countries in the 1980s*, Oxford: Pergamon.

Simmons J (1975): *How Effective is Schooling in promoting learning?*, Washington DC: World Bank Paper 200.

Sinclair M (2002): *Planning Education in and after Emergencies*, Paris: UNESCO IIEP.

Sinclair Margaret (1990): Education and training for out of school youth and adults in Pakistan, *Convergence*, 23.3: 49-58.

Sine B (1979): *NFE and Education Policy in Ghana and Senegal*, Paris: UNESCO.

Singh R P & Shukla Neerja (1979): *NFE: an alternative to the formal system*, Chandigarh: Bahri Press.

Singleton J (1974): Schools and rural development: an anthropological approach, in Foster P & Sheffield J R (eds.), *Education and Rural Development: the World Yearbook in Education*, London: Evans: 117-136.

Smith P (1980): *Group Processes and Personal Change*, London: Harper and Row.

South Commission (1990): *The Challenge of the South*, Oxford: Oxford University Press.

Southampton (1978): Report on Non-formal Adult Education Seminar, University of Southampton.

Spivak G C (1987): *In Other Worlds: essays in cultural politics*, London: Methuen.

Spivak G C (1990): *The Post-Colonial Critic*, London: Routledge.

Srinivasan Lyra (1977): *Perspectives on Nonformal Adult Learning – functional education for individual, community and national development*, New York: World Education.

Srinivasan Lyra (1985): NFE: Instruction, in Husen T & Postlethwaite T N (eds.) *The International encyclopedia of education: research and studies*, Oxford: Pergamon Press: 3548-3550.

Stavenhager R (1986): Ethnodevelopment: a neglected dimension in development thinking, in Apthorpe R & Krahl A (eds.), *Development Studies: critique and renewal*, Leiden: Brill: 71-94.

Stone H S (1983): Nonformal Adult Education: case studies from India, *International Journal of Lifelong Education*, 2.3: 297-304.

Street B V (1984): *Literacy in Theory and Practice*, Cambridge: Cambridge University Press.

Street B V (ed.) (1995): *Cross Cultural Approaches to Literacy*, Cambridge: Cambridge University Press.

Street B V (ed.) (2001): *Literacy and Development*, London: Routledge.

Stromquist N (1986): Empowering women through education: lessons from international co-operation, *Convergence*, 19.4: 5-22.

Stromquist N (1988): Women's education in development: from welfare to empowerment, *Convergence*, 21.4: 5-17.

Surrey (2001): Report of Research Project on Education and Training for Governance and active Citizenship in Europe: analysis of adult learning design of formal, non-formal and informal educational intervention strategies, Guildford: University of Surrey.

Svetina M & Jelenc Z (eds.) (1993): *Rethinking Adult Education for Development*, Ljubljana: Slovene Adult Education Centre.

Swaziland nd, *Non-formal and Adult Education in Swaziland*, unpublished paper from Ministry of Education.

Sweetser A T (1999): Lessons from the BRAC Non-Formal Primary Education Program, report published by USAID.

Tajfel H (1981): *Human Groups and Social Categories: studies in social psychology*, Cambridge: Cambridge University Press.

Tawil S (ed.) (1997): *Educational Destruction and Reconstruction in Disrupted Societies*, Geneva: International Bureau of Education.

Taylor P V (1993): *The Texts of Paolo Freire*, Buckingham: Open University Press.

Tedesco J C (1990): State reform and educational policies in Latin America, in *Planning and Management of Educational Development*, Mexico: UNESCO.

Tembon M (1999): Educational financing strategies in developing counties: the case of Cameroon and Uganda, in Leach F & Little A (eds.) (1999): *Education, Cultures and Economics: dilemmas for deve-lopment*, London: Falmer: 203-224.

Thailand (1988): NFE in Thailand, Bangkok: Department of Nonformal Education.

Thailand DNFE (1993): publicity leaflet of work of Department of Nonformal Education.

Thailand DNFE (1996): Policy Framework and Main Emphasis of NFE (version in English provided).

Thailand DNFE (1998a): Master Plan for NFE to address problems created by the economic crisis 1998-2001 (summary version in English provided).

Thailand DNFE (1998b): Summary of Results of DNFE's Income-generating Project (summary version in English provided).

Thailand DNFE (2000): statistics issued by Department of Nonformal Education, Ministry of Education.

Thomas C Y (1974): *Dependence and Transformation*, New York: Monthly Review.

Thomas M (1980): *Formal and NFE options: some suggestions for creating and commu-nicating*, New York: UNESCO/UNICEF.

Thomas Pam (1995): *Teaching for development: an international review of Australian formal and NFE for Asia and the Pacific*, Australian Development Studies Network.

Thomas R M (ed.) (1990): *International Comparative Education: practices, issues and prospects*, Oxford: Pergamon.

Thompson J (1983): Adult education and the disadvantaged, *Convergence*, 16.2: 42-47.

Thompson J D (1995): *Curriculum Development in NFE*, Nairobi: AALAE.

Tight M (ed.) (2003): *Access and Exclusion*, Oxford: Elsevier.

Titmus C J (1989): *Lifelong Education for Adults: an international handbook*, Oxford: Perga-mon.

Tobias R (1992): Defining non-formal and community education, *New Zealand Journal of Adult Learning*, 20.1: 77-92.

Tobias R (1996): What do adult and community educators share in common?, in Benseman John, Findsen B & Scott M (eds.), *The Fourth Sector: adult and community education in Aotearoa/New Zealand*, Palmerston North, NZ: Dunmore Press: 56-64.

Tomlinson S (2001): *Education in a Post-welfare Society*, Buckingham: Open University Press.

Torres C A (1990): *The Politics of NFE in Latin America*, New York: Praeger.

Torres C A (1991): The State, NFE and Socialism in Cuba, Nicaragua and Grenada, *Com-parative Education Review*, 35.2: 110-130.

Torres C A & Schugurensky D (1994): The politics of adult education in comparative perspective, *Comparative Education*, 30.2: 131-152.

Torres Rosa Maria (1993): *Reaching the Unreached: nonformal approaches and universal primary education*, New York: UNICEF.

Torres Rosa-Maria (2001): What Works in Education? facing the new century, report for International Youth Foundation.

Touwen A (1996): *Gender and Development in Zambia: empowerment of women through local NGOs*, The Hague: Eburon Press.

Townsend Coles E K (1982a): *Maverick of the Education family: two essays in NFE*, Oxford: Pergamon.

Townsend Coles E K (1982b): Détente between formal and nonformal: the experience of Botswana, *International Review of Education*, 28.2: 259-262.

Trainer T (1989): *Developed to Death*, London: Green Print.

Trompenaars F (1993): *Riding the Waves of Culture*, London: Brearley.

Tuijnman Albert C (ed.) (1996): *International Encyclopedia of Adult Education and Training* (2nd edition), Oxford: Pergamon.

Tussing A D (1978): *Irish Educational Expenditure, past, present and future*, Dublin: Economic and Social Institute.

Twining J (1987): *Vocational Education: world yearbook of education*, London: Kogan Page.

UIE (1988): Exploratory study of curricula and instructional methods for non-formal and alternative approaches for education at the primary level in the framework of lifelong education, report, Hamburg: UNESCO Institute of Education.

UIE (1990): Report of Round Table on Complementarity of formal and non-formal approaches at the primary level, Hamburg: UNESCO Institute of Education.

UIE (1997): CONFINTEA V, Agenda and Hamburg Declaration, Hamburg: UNESCO Institute of Education.

UIE (2001): UNESCO Institute of Education, Hamburg, Annual Report 2000-2001.

UNDP (1990): *Human Development Report*, New York: Oxford University Press.

UNESCO (1980): *Formal and NFE in Rural Development: sample survey in Karnataka, India*, Paris: UNESCO.

UNESCO (1982): *Regional Planning in Education*, Paris: UNESCO.

UNESCO (1983): NFE Resources, *Prospects*, 13.1.

UNESCO (1984): *L'articulation de l'education scolaire et de la formation extra-scolaire: problemes relatif au developpement coordonne de l'education scolaire et non scolaire*, Furter P, Paris: UNESCO.

UNESCO (1985): *Reflections on the Future Development of Education*, Paris: UNESCO.

UNESCO (1987): Report of International Symposium on Co-ordinated Planning of Development of Formal and Non-Formal Education, Paris: UNESCO.

UNESCO (1991): EFA: an expanded vision, Paris: UNESCO.

UNESCO (1992): Manual for Statistics on NFE, Paris: UNESCO.

UNESCO (1993): EFA: status and trends, Paris: UNESCO.

UNESCO (1997a): *Impact of Non-formal Adult Education*, Paris: UNESCO.

UNESCO (1997b): Final Report on CONFINTEA V, Hamburg: UNESCO Institute of Education.

UNESCO (1999a): *Education to Fight Exclusion*, Paris: UNESCO.

UNESCO (1999b): *Education: global patterns and national contexts*, Paris: UNESCO.

UNESCO (2001a): UN Literacy Decade Project Discussion Paper http://www.unesco.org/education/litdecade.

UNESCO (2001b): *Literacy and Nonformal Education in the E-9 Countries*, Paris: UNESCO.

UNESCO nd (2001): EFA Guidelines: Country Guidelines on the preparation of national EFA plans of action, Paris: UNESCO.

UNESCO PROAP (1979a): *Universalizing education: linking formal and non-formal programmes: final report of meeting*, Bangkok: UNESCO.

UNESCO PROAP (1979b): *Asian Programme of Educational Innovations for Development; linking formal and nonformal programmes*, Bangkok: UNESCO.

UNESCO PROAP (1982): see Duke and Varapipatana 1982.

UNESCO PROAP (1996): see Apeid 1986.

UNESCO PROAP (1997): *Impact of Non-Formal Adult Education in the Asia-Pacific Region*, Bangkok: UNESCO.

UNICEF (1980): Education and community self-reliance, innovative formal and non-formal approaches, *Assignment Children*, Geneva: UNICEF 51-52, Autumn 1980.

UNICEF (1993a): *Reaching the Unreached: nonformal approaches and universal primary education*, Ahmed M & Torres R M, New York: UNICEF.

UNICEF (1993b): *Popular Participation, mobilisation and decentralisation for EFA*, New York: UNICEF.

UNICEF (1997): *State of the World's Children: NFE: a bridge for working children*, New York: UNICEF: 50-55.

UNICEF (1999a): *Education in Emergencies and for Reconstruction: a developmental approach*, New York: UNICEF.

UNICEF (1999b): *Peace Education in UNICEF*, New York: UNICEF.

USAID (1970): NFE Action program and Work Plan, paper.

USAID (1971): NFE Bibliography.

USAID (1971): NFE: Key Problem Area No 2, working paper, Hilliard J F Washington: USAID.

USAID (1975): NFE Bibliography.

USAID (1981): Draft of USAID Congressional Presentation for 1982, cited in Krueger C & Moulton J (1981): *DS/ED Nonformal Education 1970-1980: a retrospective study*, Washington: USAID paper: 45.

USAID (1992): Education Sector Review, Destefano J & Wilder B, Washington DC: USAID.

USAID (2001): Basic Education in sub-Saharan Africa, Technical Paper 106 (February 2001).

USAID ABEL: papers on Advancing Basic Education and Literacy.

Usher R & Edwards R (1994): *Postmodernism and Education*, London: Routledge.

Vaizey John & Debeauvais M (1961): Economic aspects of educational development, in Halsey A W, Floud J & Anderson C A (eds.), *Education, Economy and Society*, New York: Free Press of Glencoe.

van der Westen M (1990): *Women, literacy and NFE: a reader*, Leiden: Brill.

van Riezen K (1996): NFE and Community Development: improving the quality, *Convergence*, 29.1.

Vargas Adam E & Bastian S (1983): *NFE in Lesotho*, Washington: World Education.

Velandia W et al. (1975): La educacion no-formal en Colombia: hacia un diagnostico de su realidad, Bogota, as cited in IEC 1996b: 28.

Verhine R E (1993): *Educational Alternatives and the Determination of Earnings in Brazilian Industry*, Frankfurt: Peter Lang.

Verhine R E & Lehmann R H (1982): NFE and occupational obtainment: a study of job seekers in NE Brazil, *Comparative Education Review*, 26.3: 374-390.

Verspoor A (1991): *Lending for Learning: 20 years of World Bank support for basic education*, Washington DC: World Bank.

Verspoor A (1992): Planning of education: where do we go?, *International Journal of Educational Development*, 12.3: 233-244.

Visocchi A M (1978): *NFE for Rural Development in Western Uganda*, Manchester: Manchester University Press.

Visser J (2001): Integrity, completeness and comprehensiveness of the learning environment: meeting basic learning needs of all throughout life, in Aspin D, Chapman J, Hatton M & Sawano Y (eds.), *International Handbook of Lifelong Learning*, London: Kluwer: 447-472.

von Hahmann Gail (1978): *Collaborative programming in NFE*, Amherst, MA: CIE.

Wagner D A (1999): Indigenous education and literacy learning, in Wagner D A, Venezky R L & Street B V (eds.): *Literacy, an International Handbook*, Boulder, Colorado: Westview Press: 283-287.

Wagner D A, Venezky R L & Street B V (eds.) (1999): *Literacy, an International Handbook*, Boulder, Colorado: Westview Press.

Wain K A (1996): Lifelong Education and the philosophy of education, *International Journal of Lifelong Education*, 4.2: 107-117.

Wallace Ian (1990): Across the interface: non-formal agricultural education and innovation at the formal/nonformal interface, *AERDD Bulletin*, Reading 29: 7-16.

Wallman S (ed.) (1979): *Social Anthropology at Work*, London: Academic Press.

Walter S & Manicom L (eds.) (1996): *Gender in Popular Education: methods for empowerment*, London: Zed Books.

Wangoola P (1995): The Political Economy of NGOs, in Cassara B B (ed.), *Adult Education through World Collaboration*, Malabar: Kreiger: 59-69.

Waqanivalu M & Jones AME (1997): Changing structures: generating rural employment through NFE for young Fijian women, *Adult Education and Development*, 48: 255-270.

Ward Marion W (ed.) (1972): *Change and development in rural Melanesia*, Canberra: Research School of Pacific Studies, Australian National University.

Ward T (1973): *The Why and How of Evaluation in NFE*, East Lansing, MI: Michigan State University.

Ward T & Herzog W (1974): *Effective Learning in NFE*, East Lansing, MI: Michigan State University.

Wari P, Kairey A & Tawaiole P (1995): NFE: Pacific 2010 Workshop report, *Pacific Economic Bulletin*, 10.1.

Wass P (1976): Community learning systems: some thoughts for African educators, in King K (ed.), *Education and Community in Africa*, Edinburgh: Edinburgh University Press.

Webster A (1990): *Introduction to the Sociology of Development* (2nd edition), London: Macmillan.

Webster A (1995): Modernisation Theory, in Ayres R (ed.), *Development Studies: an introduction through selected readings*, Dartford, Kent: Greenwich University Press.

Wedemayer C A (1981): *Learning at the back door: reflections on non-traditional learning in the lifespan*, Madison: University of Wisconsin Press.

Weidner E W (1962): *The World Role of Universities*, New York: McGraw Hill.

Wijetunga W M K (1979): What can NFE do about income generation?, *Convergence*, 12.1-2: 120-121.

Wilber K (1996): *A Brief History of Everything*, London: Shambhala.

Wilder B (1974): *Nonformal Education*, East Lansing, MI: Michigan State University.

Wilder B D (1977): Evaluation of NFE, in Griffin W N et al. (eds.), *Education and Lifelong Learning*, Washington, DC: American Association of Colleges for Teacher Education.

Williams R T (1997): *Curriculum development in Non-formal and Formal Education in South Africa 1992-1997*, unpublished paper.

Williams RPC (1991): *EFA: a view from the nineties*, BATROE Conference Report 1991.

Williams T C (1993): *Kant's Philosophy of Language: Chomskyan linguistic and its Kantian roots*, Lewiston NY: Mellen Press.

Wilson D N (1997): NFE: policies and financing in the poorest nations, in Lynch James, Modgil Celia & Modgil Sohan (eds.) (1997): Non-Formal and Non-Governmental Approaches, vol 4 of *Education and Development: tradition and innovation*, London: Cassells: 85-101.

Wilson J (1977): *Philosophical and Practical Education*, London: Routledge Kegan Paul.

Wilson J (1979): *Preface to the Philosophy of Education*, London: Routledge Kegan Paul.

Wilson J (2001): Lifelong learning, the individual and community self-help, in Aspin D, Chapman J, Hatton M & Sawano Y (eds.), *International Handbook of Lifelong Learning*, London: Kluwer: 733-754.

Wilson John (1984): see Carson 1984.

Wilson R (1989): New hope in Villa El Salvador, *Development and Co-operation*, 4: 9-10.

Wodak R (1996): *Disorders of Discourse*, London: Longman.

Wood A W (1974): *Informal Education and Development in Africa*, The Hague: Mouton.

Wood F (Save the Children US) personal communication.

World Bank (1972): *NFE for Rural Development*, 2 vols Washington: World Bank.

World Bank (1974): Education Sector Paper, Washington D C: World Bank.

World Bank (1975): *The Assault on World Poverty: problems of rural development, education and health*, (reprint of World Bank 1974 by John Hopkins University).

World Bank (1979): *Issues in Nonformal Education and Training for Rural Development*, Washington DC: World Bank.

World Bank (1981): *Implementing Programs of Human Development*, Washington DC: World Bank.

World Bank (1986): *Financing Education in Developing Countries: an exploration of policy options*, Washington DC: World Bank.

World Bank (1987): *Review of World Bank Operations in NFE and Training*, Romain Ralph I and Armstrong Lenor, World Bank Education and Training Series Discussion Paper 63, Washington DC: World Bank.

World Bank (1990): *Policy Paper on Primary Education*, Washington D C: World Bank.

World Bank (1991): *Vocational and Technical Education and Training: Policy Paper*, A Verspoor, Washington DC: World Bank.

World Bank (1995): *Priorities and Strategies for Education: a World Bank review*, Washington DC: Oxford University Press.

World Bank (1998): *Recent Developments in NFE: implications for Cote d'Ivoire*, Michael Wilson, unpublished paper, Washington DC: World Bank.

World Bank (2001): *Report of Distance Learning Seminar: Use of Outsourcing in the Implementation of Literacy and Non-Formal Basic Education Programs*, May-July, World Bank paper.

World Bank (2003): Rethinking World Bank policy and practice in support of adult and non-formal education, draft working paper prepared by Peter Easton, Maman Sidikou, Aya Aoki and Luis Crouch, May 2003 World Bank paper.

World Bank Tanzania (2001): proposal for assistance to Tanzania with the development of NFE, World Bank Office, Dar es Salaam.

World Education Report (2000): Paris: UNESCO.

Wright C & Govinda R (1994): *Three Years After Jomtien: EFA in the eastern and southern Africa region*, Paris: UNESCO IIEP.

Wright Cream (ed.) (2000): *Issues in Education and Technology*, London: Commonwealth Secretariat.

Wright Cream (2001): Learning how to mainstream: experiential knowledge and grounded theory, paper prepared for ADEA meeting, Tanzania October.

Wright pers comm: interview with Dr Cream Wright 2000.

Young M F D (1998): *The Curriculum of the Future*, London: Falmer.

Youngman F (2000): *The Political Economy of Adult Education*, London: Zed Books.

Zander A (1994): *Making Groups Effective* (2nd edition), San Francisco: Jossey Bass.

Index